Into Russian Nature

Into Russian Nature

Tourism, Environmental Protection, and National Parks in the Twentieth Century

ALAN D. ROE

UNIVERSITY PRESS

OXFORD
UNIVERSITY PRESS

Oxford University Press is a department of the University of Oxford. It furthers the University's objective of excellence in research, scholarship, and education by publishing worldwide. Oxford is a registered trade mark of Oxford University Press in the UK and certain other countries.

Published in the United States of America by Oxford University Press
198 Madison Avenue, New York, NY 10016, United States of America.

Library of Congress Cataloging-in-Publication Data
Names: Roe, Alan (Alan Daniel), author.
Title: Into Russian nature : tourism, environmental protection, and national parks in the twentieth century / Alan D. Roe.
Description: New York : Oxford University Press, 2020. |
Includes bibliographical references and index.
Identifiers: LCCN 2019044705 (print) | LCCN 2019044706 (ebook) |
ISBN 9780190914554 (hardback) | ISBN 9780190914578 (epub) | ISBN 9780190914585 (online)
Subjects: LCSH: National parks and reserves—Russia (Federation)—History—20th century.
Classification: LCC SB484.R9 R64 2020 (print) | LCC SB484.R9 (ebook) |
DDC 363.6/80947—dc23
LC record available at https://lccn.loc.gov/2019044705
LC ebook record available at https://lccn.loc.gov/2019044706

1 3 5 7 9 8 6 4 2

Printed by Sheridan Books, Inc., United States of America

In a civilization which requires most lives to be passed amid inordinate dissonance, pressure and intrusion, the chance of retiring now and then to the quietude and privacy of sylvan haunts becomes for some people a psychic necessity.

Robert Marshall, United States (1935)

People need the beauty and majesty of nature: its harmonious sounds; for instance the splashing of waves, the humming of the stream, the singing of birds, and also the fragrant odors of the forest, the fields, the sea. . . . The spiritual resources of nature lift the soul of humans, positively act on one's mental state, give energy, joy, and strengthen *creative* powers.

David Armand, USSR (1964)

But there is a grand sense of freedom preserved in feeling the preciousness of space, in feeling the uniqueness of each blade of grass on which the dew gleams like tiny eyes of the earth. Precisely because we die with rapture before the wide-open lap of the Grand Canyon, and before Baikal, which seethes in anger and caressingly licks its shores in moments of tenderness, we are in this instant neither Russian nor American, but heirs of the indivisible treasure of all humankind: nature.

Evgeny Evtushenko, Russian Federation (1992)

CONTENTS

PART III THE CRISIS OF RUSSIA'S NATIONAL PARKS

ACKNOWLEDGMENTS

On June 18, 2007, I was increasingly concerned as my flight from Moscow to Barnaul, located in the heart of Siberia, continued to get delayed. I was already nervous enough, knowing that I would be the only foreign guide working for a Russian company leading backpacking trips in the Altai Mountains. By the time I arrived in Barnaul three hours late, the other guides in training—none of whom I knew—had left for Tiungur, where the main base was located. After I rode in a cab for about two hundred kilometers to catch up to them, my future fellow guides and friends were standing around the vans with somewhat impatient looks. We shared a rather awkward greeting. The initial tensions caused by my late arrival and some of my challenges with the Russian language gradually dissipated as the scenery became more strikingly beautiful with each passing hour of our drive.

Three days later on our training trip, we decided to set up camp late in the afternoon. That evening, a few of us hiked up to a rock precipice from which we had a spectacular view on Belukha—the highest point in the Russian Altai. I was somewhat lost in the conversation. After we had been sitting for a few minutes, Natasha, Sergei, and Aleksey started singing. One song was followed by another. To my amazement, everyone except me knew all the lyrics. These were songs about traveling, hiking, mountains, campfires, and group camaraderie on the trail. I later learned that these were part of a tradition of tourist songs, which became popular in the Soviet Union's last few decades. Over the next week and throughout that summer—one of the most memorable of my life—I learned more about the distinctive culture of Russian tourism, and as I researched and wrote this book, I continued to travel in different parts of the Russia both as a guide and as a participant on multi-day trips.

When I started this journey, I sought to see Russia on its own terms and, insofar as I could, avoid chauvinistic judgments. Luckily for me, over the years I acquired dozens of tutors. I am incredibly fortunate to have made so many dear friends who have opened the world of Russian tourism to me. While the following pages tell

Training trip in the Altai Mountains (*author in the center in the back*).

a story in which their fellow citizens have become increasingly disillusioned with their government's weak commitment to environmental protection, the friends that I have made in the Russian backcountry, like so many Russians, have a love for the spectacular nature of their country. The love for Russian nature that I share with them has driven me to immerse myself as deeply as possible in this subject.

Although I started thinking about this project during my first summer in the Altai, this book, like most, has deeper origins. Had it not been for Sally McMillen's encouragement at Davidson College in 2000, I never would have pursued graduate work in history. Between my bachelor's and master's programs, I hiked the Appalachian Trail. This experience inspired me to write a history of the Continental Divide Trail for my master's thesis at the University of Montana. There, Dan Flores not only introduced me to environmental history and made me a much better writer but also showed me through his example the importance of deep personal engagement with one's subject.

When I was planning to move to St. Petersburg in 2006 to work on my Russian before starting my PhD at Georgetown University, I learned that a former high school classmate, Mark Pettus, was living there as he was doing a doctorate in Russian literature. Mark met me at the Pulkovo Airport, introduced me to St. Petersburg, and made suggestions for studying Russian and cultural immersion that had a profound influence. At Derzhavin Institute, where I studied Russian for nearly a year after arriving in St. Petersburg, I had outstanding teachers whose patient and flexible approach allowed me to start becoming comfortable with the language. After a few months of studying there, I connected with people in the outdoor recreation community in St. Petersburg, which led me to the Altai. For inviting me to the office to interview for a guide position, I will never be able to adequately thank Maria Alfianova. By taking a chance in hiring me, Anatoly Minichkin and Galina Lebedeva shaped my future path in ways that I could never have predicted at the time. I am thankful for my friendships with fellow guides Aleksandr Andreev, Ekaterina Gribova, Timofey Minichkin, Anna Minichkina, Vasilii Nikiforenko, Anna Pendiuk, and Natalia Shelankova. These women and men opened my eyes to a side of Russian life that I never imagined I would experience firsthand.

The friends that I made on tourist trails, on rivers, and around the campfire not only in Altai but in Karelia, the Komi Republic, the Samara Bend, and the Sayan Mountains and on the Kamchatka Peninsula have influenced my research in indirect and direct ways. I would especially like to thank Aleksey Kazakov, Denis Semenov, Elena Aleksandrova, Boris Efremov, Aleksey Popov, Pavel Kudriatsev, Aleksey Kalashnikov, Natalia Kalashnikova, Dmitri Khromov, Andrei Konstantinov, Konstantin Langburd, and Dmitri Novozhenin (notwithstanding him telling me that it is fine to eat an uncooked boletus mushroom; its not!). Since I met them in 2007, Aleksey Kazakov and Maria Alfianova have warmly welcomed me to their home in St. Petersburg more times than I can possibly count. Konstantin Langburd broadened my perspective on Russian outdoor recreation by letting me work for him as a backpacking and fishing guide on the Kamchatka Peninsula in the summer of 2014.

I could not have hoped for a more supportive institution for my graduate work than Georgetown University. My work benefited from the input and friendships of fellow graduate students. I would especially like to thank Clark Alejandrino, John Corcoran, Meredith Denning, Chris England, Chad Frazier, Isabella Kaplan, Erin Stewart Mauldin, Erina Megowan, Robynne Mellor, and Daniel Scarborough. Patrick Dixon and Andrey Gornostaev each deserve special mention. Patrick edited this work when it was in dissertation form, and his always probing questions about the project, whether over a beer, at a basketball game, or on a hiking trail, have been both helpful and enjoyable to discuss. Andrey dedicated a significant amount of time to helping me get my transliterations right. I would also like to give special thanks to Maria Snyder, who helped me successfully navigate the application process for both Mellon-IIE Dissertation and a Fulbright-Hays DDRA Fellowships. Additionally, the Georgetown Environmental Initiative and the Department of History provided me with grants that gave me time to write my dissertation. This book would not have been possible without all of this generous support.

I was fortunate to have such supportive professors and mentors at Georgetown. Memories of the intensity and joy that the late Richard Stites brought to Russian history continue to inspire me. Catherine Evtuhov was unfailingly generous with her time, knowledge, and perspective. Always encouraging me to follow my passion, she suggested that outdoor recreation might be a good dissertation topic, which gave me much needed affirmation. After coming to Georgetown in 2011, Michael David-Fox was always supportive, and his broad knowledge of Soviet history was invaluable in helping me better contextualize my research. David Goldfrank's feedback on chapters and his kind and encouraging words helped immensely as I moved through the dissertation process.

John McNeill has been everything and more that I could ever hope for in a mentor. John believed in me and my idea before I knew a word of Russian. After I moved to Russia, we communicated over the next two years by email until I matriculated in 2008. During my time at Georgetown, he pushed me to think more broadly, to write more clearly, and to always set high standards. He is kind and generous with his time. While his productivity and accomplishments as a historian are remarkable and inspiring, he understands that historical research and writing are only part of life and that his mentees are much more than just historians. My words will never be able to convey adequately John's positive influence on me as a historian and as a person.

I am grateful to the Environmental Science and Policy program at the College of William and Mary for awarding me a Mellon Postdoctoral Fellowship, which allowed me to teach and work on this project for another two years. For giving me this opportunity and for their support while I was there, I would like to thank Andy Fisher and Brent Kaup. I am also grateful to Frederick Corney for warmly welcoming me to the Department of History and the Russian and Post-Soviet Studies program. I would like to thank Kate Staples and Joseph Hodge for giving me an academic home in West Virginia University's History Department while I finished this project.

This book has benefited immensely from the comments and questions of scholars far beyond the academic communities with which I have been affiliated. In addition to providing feedback on two chapters, David Moon organized a series of three conferences in Russia that brought together many scholars of Russian environmental history. This book benefitted much from this experience. Nicholas Breyfogle and Ryan Jones read the entire manuscript, and both provided invaluable suggestions. Douglas Weiner not only pointed me in several new directions but also helped me avoid many errors through his reservoir of knowledge on the history of Russian nature protection. Moreover, his pathbreaking works on Russian conservation have inspired me deeply. The suggestions from an anonymous reviewer for Oxford University Press also helped immensely. Recognizing all of those who have in one way or another influenced this book though probing questions and insightful comments in conversation or at conference panels, is more than I can do here, but I would like to recognize those who have read and provided feedback on parts of it, whether in the form of a conference paper or a scholarly article. They include Melanie Arndt, Andy Bruno, Laurent Coumel, Bathsheba Demuth, Marc Elie, Ilya Gerasimov, Laura Henry, Mikhail Kovalev, Julia Lajus, Daniel Pratt, Kate Pride-Brown, Mark Sokolsky, Christopher Ward, and Donald Worster.

Over the course of my research, I visited nearly twenty Russian state archives and was fortunate to work with so many patient, helpful, and often enthusiastic archivists. I want to give special thanks to Irina Tarakanova at the Russian Academy of Sciences Archive and Vladimir Volodin, who gave me a warm welcome to the Komi Scientific Center. I also talked to numerous Russian tourists or individuals who were deeply involved in Russia's national parks in different ways. They helped me better understand different aspects of Soviet tourism, challenges faced by park supporters, and the role and challenges of national parks in the Russian Federation today. They include Vladimir Antipin, Adolf Bratsev, Oleg Cherviakov, Julius Dobroshin, Valerii Erofeev, Aleksandr Gubernatorov, Alla Gudym, Konstantin Langburd, Iurii Machkin, Vladimir Riabtsev, Iurii Roshchevskii, Boris Samoilov, Iurii Vedenin, Irina Vorozheikina, and Natalia Zabelina. Several others with whom I have talked about Soviet tourism and Russian national parks have passed away: Stanislav Drozdov, Leonid Levitan, Vitalii Men'shikov, Iurii Pustovalov, and Radomir Savastyonov.

I will forever be grateful to my editor Susan Ferber at Oxford University Press, who took interest in this project. Her professionalism, patience, and warmth make her an absolute pleasure to work with. Her attention to detail and her ability to transform the feel of a sentence by changing one or two words are nothing short of amazing. And it means a lot to me that every time I see her in person, the first thing that she asks about is my son. Thank you, Susan.

Finally, I would like to thank my family. My father (John H. Roe, Jr.), brother (John H. Roe III), sister (Lillian Gilmer), and their spouses (Jane Roe, Alicia Brinton, and Nate Gilmer) have shown their love and support in a variety of ways over the years. To my nieces and nephew (Amelia, Emi, Hannah, Lila, and Tasman), if you choose to read it one day, this book will be the best way for you to learn a little more about what Uncle Alan was doing all those years in Russia.

Not long before completing this project in its dissertation form, I reconnected with an amazing woman who also happened to be the first person to teach me a few words of Russian as I was preparing to start this journey. There will always be something deeply poetic about this to us. Tatiana Busu-Roe has taught me that falling in love and starting a family are the most meaningful things in life. She is a constant source of support and inspires me to be a better person every day. Elena, Georghe, and Sergei, thank you for letting me take Tania's hand in marriage and for all of your love and support. In late 2018, Tania and I welcomed our son, Matthew Henry, into the world. The love we share as a family fills my every day with joy and a sense of purpose. I love you more than my words can ever express.

This book is dedicated to the memory of my mother—Emily Hunt Roe (1948–2002). During the five years that she battled ovarian cancer and in the years after her death, I sought peace more frequently than ever before or since in remote backcountry, away from the stresses, pressures, and what frequently seemed to me the artificiality of civilization. She never enjoyed sleeping in the woods, and she was not broadly interested in things outside of her family or community. She was a cautious person, and my spending extended periods in the woods made her very nervous. In all likelihood, she would have tried to talk me out of moving to Russia had she been here to do so. But the love that she gave me during her life remained with me every step of the way on this journey, and my memories of her ability to always maintain a positive outlook even when facing her own mortality have helped me keep my gaze directed forward on the brightest and darkest of days.

Into Russian Nature

Introduction

When Joseph Stalin called for the end of the New Economic Policy (NEP) and the transformation of Soviet society under the rubric of the "Great Break" in 1929, Vasilii Nikolaevich Skalon was on one of his many research trips into a little-explored area of Siberia. Over the next decade, Stalin collectivized Soviet agriculture, led a crash industrialization program based on five-year plans, and ramped up policies of political repression that included the creation of a system of forced labor camps, known as the Gulag, and the killing of hundreds of thousands of "enemies of the people." Skalon likely felt these changes less intensely than most Soviet citizens. During these years, he spent most of his time on expeditions traveling by foot, boat, horse, and reindeer sled through thousands of kilometers of Siberia's dense forests, mountains, and steppe.[1]

After serving in Mongolia in the Great Patriotic War (1941–1945) and then working in Ulaanbaaatar for two years, Skalon moved the Siberian city of Irkutsk, located less than seventy kilometers from Lake Baikal.[2] As he explored the lake and its environs widely in the late 1940s and early 1950s, Soviet citizens were traveling more frequently and further from home as living standards rose and domestic transportation improved. However, the Central Trade Union Council, which was responsible for tourism, realized that facilities were woefully underdeveloped and that a dearth of guidebooks for some of the USSR's most scenic and remote places discouraged many Soviet citizens from traveling to them. The council asked Skalon to write its first book on tourism in Siberia. Published in 1953, *Through Siberia* (*Po Sibiri*) celebrated traveling on Siberia's rivers, climbing its mountains, and meeting with its people. Skalon rhapsodically described Siberia's landscapes, including the "Sacred Sea," as Lake Baikal was frequently called.

From the time of the publication of *Through Siberia* until Skalon left Irkutsk in 1962, the number of Soviet tourists who came to Baikal and the mountains and rivers around it increased significantly. More tourists coming to the region seemed, on balance, a good thing to most environmentalists and tourism supporters. Compared to stationary recreation at spa resorts (*otdykh*),

Into Russian Nature. Alan D. Roe, Oxford University Press (2020) © Oxford University Press.
DOI: 10.1093/oso/9780190914554.001.0001

tourism (*turizm*; travel requiring self-locomotion, often in the backcountry), though still less popular, did much more to instill a love for their motherland by allowing Soviet citizens to see some of the country's most dramatic and unique landscapes. When Skalon returned to Irkutsk in 1968, however, Baikal's surrounding landscapes, like many other areas in the USSR, were showing increasing scars from the tourism boom in the USSR. Around Baikal, tourists littered, "mercilessly" chopped down trees, trampled vegetation, and carelessly caused large forest fires. Their actions had led to the disappearance of animals in some places. Worse yet, these impacts often were visible in the protected nature reserves (*zapovedniki*), which had long been the pride of Russian biologists and geographers.[3]

Skalon believed that the USSR's failure to organize tourism carefully might soon result in irreversible degradation of Baikal's shoreline and the adjacent forests. To address this problem, he, along with a few of his students from the Irkutsk Agricultural Institute, conducted a study on protecting Baikal from the deluge of tourists while at the same time ensuring that they would continue to enjoy this wonder of Russian nature. Although the USSR had no national parks at the time, Skalon's report recommended the Soviet government establish a single national park protecting the lake's entire shoreline.

Skalon's plan was indicative of the lofty—sometimes wildly unrealistic—expectations for national parks in the Baikal region and throughout the USSR from the 1960s through the 1980s. Calling the shoreline a "natural phenomenon of planetary significance,"[4] he stated that it must be protected from all resource extraction and industrial development. In this "park of wild nature," tourists, whose numbers park administrators would carefully regulate, would only be allowed to travel by footpath (roads would be banned) so that they could experience the "lifestyle of the subarctic forest."[5] Spending time in "wild" nature, he argued, would help them rejuvenate physically and spiritually. By viewing some of the USSR's most spectacular scenery, Soviet citizens, Skalon believed, would develop a stronger environmental ethic and learn about the "Baikal type of nature use," which he hoped to be a model for other regions.[6] Skalon's plan thus reflected the general Soviet belief that tourism should help develop the character and shape the worldview of the tourist.[7] However, in saying almost nothing about inculcating a Marxist-Leninist worldview, Skalon's plan, like those for most other Russian national parks conceived in this era, illustrated the weakening of the state's official ideology in the USSR's final decades.[8]

While some other Soviet republics had established national parks during the 1970s, the Communist Party had informed Russian park supporters that the Russian Soviet Federated Socialist Republic (RSFSR) would not have national parks until Soviet law gave them federal status.[9] Five years after the USSR Council of Ministers passed the "Model Regulation on State Nature

National Parks" (henceforth Model Regulation) in 1981, the RSFSR Council of Ministers established Pribaikal'skii National and Zabaikal'skii National Parks on parts of the western and eastern shoreline respectively. Although no place had inspired higher hopes among Soviet environmentalists for Russia's national parks than Baikal, local populations did not understand the parks' purpose or respect their regulations, and the government was too overwhelmed by an economic crisis to pay much attention to their development. Exasperated, Peter Abramenok, Pribaikal'skii National Park's director, said in 1996, five years after the collapse of the Soviet Union: "It is shameful that in our country until this time it is still not clearly understood what is meant by the term national park."[10] The situation has improved little for Russian national parks since Abramenok uttered these words. While Skalon did not live to see national parks established on Baikal's shoreline, he undoubtedly would have been disappointed by how far Baikal's national parks fell short of his vision for them. Indeed, no idea has inspired loftier hopes and caused greater disappointment among Russian environmentalists than national parks.

* * *

Into Russian Nature recounts the previously untold history of Russia's national parks. Spanning the late nineteenth century into the twenty-first century, it is a history of grandiose plans that were in most cases never actualized but that illuminate important aspects of late Soviet history, Russian environmental history, and global environmental history. It considers the interaction of actors at many levels—local, regional, republic, USSR-wide, and international. It examines internal developments within Russian/Soviet society that made parks appealing, the evolving discourses and goals of global environmental protection organizations and networks, and the strengthening connections of Russian environmentalists with foreign counterparts, whose ideas and influence carried considerable and progressively more weight among Russian environmentalists. While this book looks at the first Soviet parks in the Baltics, Kyrgyz SSR, and Armenian SSR during the 1970s, it focuses primarily on Russia.

The story begins in the nineteenth century, when strengthening nationalist sentiments led Russians and Americans to tie specific landscapes to their respective ideas about national identity. In creating the first national park, the United States established a model for the protection of its scenic wonders that other countries would enthusiastically embrace. Several members of the Imperial Russian Geographical Society called for a system of parks in the Russian Empire, which they believed would be the most spectacular in the world. However, following the Great October Revolution of 1917, Russian conservationists and game management professionals instead pushed the state to establish *zapovedniki* dedicated to scientific research as well as some that served as game preserves.[11] During the 1920s, the Soviet government established *zapovedniki* in large numbers. But as the state became increasingly suspicious of "science for science's sake" in the 1930s, many argued that promoting tourism in them was more desirable than other uses deemed "productive" by Communist Party and government officials. By the late 1930s, tens of thousands of tourists entered the *zapovedniki* every year. Even as Stalin's repressive policies were creating a climate of fear and xenophobia, some tourism promoters used the example of US national parks in arguing that Soviet *zapovedniki* should accommodate far more tourists.

The national park movement in the USSR began during the late 1950s—the time of Nikita Khrushchev's liberalizing reforms known as the "thaw era." As the policy of "peaceful coexistence" encouraged greater participation of Soviet scientists with foreign colleagues, Soviet scientists started attending conferences of the International Union of the Conservation of Nature (IUCN) in the late 1950s where they became more familiar with national parks. Moreover, the less repressive cultural environment emboldened many concerned environmentalists to make bold suggestions on how the state could improve its environmental protection practices. Although the hostility of the state towards *zapovedniki* convinced many environmentalists that government and Communist Party officials were not particularly interested in nature protection, some high-ranking officials, including Khrushchev, publicly stated that accessible tourism for all in the world's "most beautiful" nation was one of the advantages of living in the USSR.[12] In turn, environmentalists argued that national parks could help the USSR meet the growing demand for tourism in a way that minimized its environmental impact and promoted economic development.[13] A growing number of Russian environmentalists became more convinced of this position, and they increasingly invoked the success of national parks in other countries, especially the United States, even as the Communist Party took more reactionary positions in some areas following Khrushchev's ouster.

Although Russian park supporters became frustrated during the 1970s by the USSR Council of Minister's failure to pass a law giving national parks official recognition at the highest level, the attention that the Soviet government gave to environmental protection encouraged them to conceive ambitious visions for park projects.[14] Not long after the RSFSR started establishing parks in the mid-1980s, environmental issues became mainstream in the Soviet Union as Gorbachev's reforms encouraged Soviet citizens to discuss a variety of problems more openly. In turn, national parks often became focal points in demonstrations against regional environmental threats, and their founders increasingly touted their potential to transform the economy of entire regions and the lifestyles of their inhabitants. While the state could not provide the funds for parks to carry out their most basic functions, park supporters placed hopes in attracting foreign tourists and new opportunities to collaborate with international organizations.

Russian environmentalists and park supporters knew that state support for park development would be difficult in the wake of the USSR's collapse, but they initially believed that Yeltsin and the new government would become still more responsive to environmental concerns.[15] Moreover, they now felt more connected than ever before to Western colleagues and hoped that support from international NGOs and organizations might help develop parks until the state was able to undertake this independently. However, by the end of the decade, Russian park supporters realized that international support was no panacea and were increasingly convinced that their government had little genuine interest in national parks or environmental protection. Vladimir Putin has further limited the possibilities for international support for environmental protection initiatives in the Russian Federation, and Russian national parks remain infrastructurally undeveloped, mired in land use conflicts, frequently littered, and unknown to many Russians.

Today, Russia has fifty-five national parks, many of which undoubtedly provide stronger protection for their territories than if no park existed. From this perspective, individual Russian parks and the larger Russian national park movement has been a limited success on the part of scientific institutes, civic organizations, and private citizens to push the state to make meaningful changes in environmental protection practices. However, most of these parks are shells of what their founders envisioned. The gap between the visions of park founders and the realities of Russia's national parks has left their supporters disappointed and disillusioned.

Into Russian Nature tells a Russian environmental history from a bottom-up perspective of scientists, environmental activists, and tourism boosters. It draws on the personal document collections of five individuals associated with national parks, interviews with veterans of the ill-starred movement, Soviet tourism literature, local and regional journalism about parks, and documents of different levels of government and the Communist Party as well as scientific and civic organizations. To demonstrate the interconnections of these different actors and the individual national park stories over a vast territory, I visited nearly twenty Russian state archives from St. Petersburg to Kamchatka, archives of the former Baltic Republics, the UNESCO archives in Paris, and the National Archives in College Park, Maryland.

National parks fit into a long history of Russian Western-oriented reform efforts. Particularly since the reforms of Peter the Great in the early eighteenth century, Russian reformers have borrowed from the West in efforts to modernize the state.[16] During the nineteenth century Westernizers argued that Russia needed to embrace Western ideas to overcome "backwardness," while the Slavophiles asserted that Russia had a distinctive course of development grounded in traditions of Orthodox Christianity and autocratic rule.[17] Throughout Soviet history, "overcoming backwardness" was central to the modernization narratives of the state.[18] "Backwardness" may be in the eye of the beholder, but perceptions of it have indisputably influenced the motivations and hence choices of educated Russians, including many involved in the environmental movement. Russian scientists who backed stronger conservation measures, even before the Revolution, have looked to the West as an "ever-present measuring stick."[19] Meanwhile, in the second half of the twentieth century, international organizations such as the IUCN frequently held up national parks as exemplars of effective environmental protection and suggested that their absence was a sign of a country's "backwardness."[20]

This discourse about national parks was and is problematic.[21] However, it was commonplace among environmentalists throughout the world and compelling to many in countries that did not have parks. The longstanding mindset in the Russian intelligentsia predisposed Russian environmentalists to internalize this narrative. As they continued to become more integrated in global environmental protection networks, Russia's lack of national parks and then its failure to develop them effectively became a ready-made example to environmentalists of their state's "backwardness." By deploying this rhetoric against a government sensitive to such characterizations, they hoped to gain greater state support, only to almost always be disappointed.

National parks have long attracted much attention from environmental historians.[22] Many have celebrated their American origins while holding them as the world's gold standard in environmental protection.[23] Others have argued that they reflect a neocolonial agenda and have shown that parks have in many cases either forcibly removed indigenous groups or stripped them of their traditional use of the land.[24] Although proposed Russian national parks did in some cases create tensions with indigenous groups, forcible removal was never part of park making, and the conflicts between these groups and park administrations were largely the same as conflicts with others living within park territory. By banning some land uses that had long taken place within awkwardly drawn park boundaries, many of Russia's national parks have had highly acrimonious relationships with local populations.

Many recent works have taken a global perspective on national park history and provide a more nuanced view of the diffusion of the concept throughout the world.[25] But strikingly, the Russian story is completely missing.[26] Scholarly works that trace the expansion of international environmental networks in the late twentieth century have given little mention to the USSR before the Chernobyl disaster.[27] As part of a larger story in environmental diplomacy, the

Russian national park story illustrates the significant influence that the Western-dominated environmental organizations exerted on the ideas, priorities, and expectations of Russian environmentalists during the Cold War and beyond.

Russian and Soviet environmental history is a rapidly growing and vibrant field, but historians in this field have only started to scratch the surface of the international dimensions of Russian nature protection.[28] Moreover, existing scholarship on Russian conservation has also not thoroughly addressed environmentalists' ideas for alternatives to industry-intensive and environmentally destructive forms of economic development. National parks were perhaps the strongest attempts made by Russian environmentalists to encourage broad regional economic transformations.

The Russian national park story sheds fresh light on broader aspects of late-Soviet and post-Soviet history. It does not fit neatly into traditional chronologies that delineate eras by change in political leadership. The Russian park movement emerged far from the heights of state or party power and spanned the final three decades of Soviet history, thereby illustrating the continuity of reform efforts between the Khrushchev and Gorbachev eras. Thus, this story adds to the recent works that have presented dynamic aspects of Soviet society during the Brezhnev era, which was long misunderstood as a period of stagnation.[29] During this era, the reduced role that official ideology played in daily life allowed individuals to pursue a wide range of interests and express beliefs that were not necessarily broadly shared, as long as they downplayed their political implications.[30] Moreover, some individuals and groups were even envisioning ways to transform Soviet society without approval by the state. The Communist Party's stated commitment to environmental protection gave environmentalists the needed justification to conceive transformative park projects. Their champions proposed park projects, which went against the status quo of central economic ministries and entrenched extractive industries, as modernization projects that advanced stated Communist Party goals. However, lacking strong input from planning organizations, park plans were often unmoored from Soviet realities.

Into Russian Nature focuses significantly more attention on the links between Soviet tourism and environmentalism than any previous English- or Russian-language work.[31] Moreover, it examines the efforts made by geographers to mitigate tourism's increasingly destructive impact as well as how these same geographers along with economists and architects sought to transform regional economies through tourism. The plans for national parks often took both into account.

Into Russian Nature is divided into three parts. Part I (chapters 1–4) chronologically narrates the establishment of the first Russian *zapovedniki,* the international history of the national park movement, and the Soviet park movement until the USSR's fall. These four chapters provide case studies of proposed and established parks, as well as tourism in the *zapovedniki*. Part II focuses on individual national parks in the RSFSR from the years before their conception to the years after they were established, specifically those on the shore of Baikal, on the Samara Bend—a peninsular formation across from Kuibyshev on the Volga—in the Circumpolar Urals of the Komi Republic, and in the Karelian taiga. The final part looks at the Russian Federation's expansion of its park system, its enticement and then discouragement of foreign support to develop it, its failure to allocate resources for parks and other protected territories, and the profound disillusionment that this has caused for park administrators and proponents, as well as the larger Russian environmental protection community.

* * *

Not long after the Central Committee of the Communist Party eliminated a large number of *zapovedniki* in 1951, the Presidium of the Soviet Academy of Sciences created the Commission on Zapovedniki to work for their reestablishment. Writing to the commission in 1954, a decade and a half before he began planning a national park on Baikal's shoreline, Vasilii Skalon stated:

> Is it really decent for the Soviet people, stewards of the world's best natural landscapes, to forget about fundamental nature protection in their own country, the development of the *zapovedniki*? We must make the *zapovedniki* the pride of the people as much as the beauty of the Kremlin Cathedrals and the jewels of the Hermitage.[32]

Had Skalon been writing several years later when the commission changed its name to the Commission on Nature Protection and was looking to foreign examples as it sought to establish national parks in the Soviet Union, he would have mentioned national parks in addition to or perhaps instead of *zapovedniki*.

Today, many Russians unquestionably take pride in their country's spectacular landscapes, and Russia has significantly more remote territory without the visual reminders of civilization than any other country. There, many citizens with the means and opportunity to do so can find a reprieve from whatever stresses they face in their daily lives in civilization. However, unlike citizens in many countries, Russians generally do not associate their most celebrated landscapes or these wild places with the specific institutions established for their protection. While the transformative visions for parks undoubtedly increased support for them and helped them to be established, few supporters of national parks are proud of the Russian government's efforts to protect or bring them increased attention through developing them in a way that is both economically profitable and environmentally sustainable. The following pages will examine the long history of the park idea, the transformative visions that it inspired among Russian environmentalists, the sort of parks that were created, and, ultimately, the deep disappointment caused when parks fell far short of their founders' and supporters' hopes.

PART I

THE RUSSIAN/SOVIET NATIONAL PARK MOVEMENT

Before the Great October Revolution of 1917, many members of the Imperial Geographical Society called for the establishment of a set of national parks throughout the Russian Empire. In its first years, however, the USSR instead established a system of nature reserves (*zapovedniki*) dedicated primarily to scientific research. At first, the system's staunchest supporters argued that tourists should not enter the *zapovedniki*. However, between the 1930s and the 1960s, they increasingly accommodated limited tourism in the *zapovedniki,* arguing that this would help them gain stronger support from government officials.

In the decades after World War II, Soviet scientists became more familiar with national parks as they expanded their interactions with environmentalists from the West. In turn, they pushed for an extensive system of national parks that would expand tourism opportunities for Soviet citizens, reconcile economic development and environmental protection, and bring greater international recognition to Soviet environmental protection efforts. By the late 1960s, growing damage caused by tourists in the *zapovedniki* increased the sense of urgency for the Soviet Union to establish national parks and again direct tourist traffic away from the *zapovedniki*.

While several Soviet republics established national parks in the 1970s, Russia only established its first in 1983. By the time of the Soviet Union's collapse, Russia had seventeen national parks. The grandiose plans for Russia's national parks were facing the reality of a state unable to support or develop them.

1

For Science or Tourism?

Protected Territories before World War II

During the summer of 1928, the Russian botanist and prominent conservationist Daniil Kashkarov took a trip to the United States. In an account of his trip published the following year in the journal *Scientific Word* (*Nauchnoe slovo*), Kashkarov emphasized, as his censors would have strongly suggested if not demanded, how the principle of private property had caused many environmental problems in the United States. However, he also praised his American counterparts. "Much of what I saw deserves imitation, and it must be said that it should serve as an example to us for more energetic work in the area of nature protection," he wrote.[1]

Kashkarov saved his most effusive compliments for America's national parks. He recounted his talks with informed national park rangers and described the strong organization of tourism. He reported on the spectacular beauty of Old Faithful, Mount Rainier, Yellowstone Falls, and California's sequoia trees. While Kashkarov was critical of the limited attention national parks paid to scientific research, he applauded them for being accessible to "all" US citizens, at least "to the extent that this is possible" in a capitalist state.[2] In the article's conclusion, he wrote that national parks were for "the use, enjoyment, and inspiration of the people," without mentioning that these words came directly from the mission statement of the United States National Park Service (NPS).[3] This mission of the NPS stood in stark contrast to the Soviet *zapovedniki*, which many scientists believed should exist exclusively for scientific research.

Kashkarov took this trip at a time when the young Soviet state was designating a large number of lands for *zapovedniki* and increasingly investing resources in them. Many Soviet scientists expressed confidence that their initial hopes for the Great October Revolution had been justified, and some believed that their research in protected territories was at the vanguard of biological sciences throughout the world. And yet Kashkarov's admiration for US national parks

Into Russian Nature. Alan D. Roe, Oxford University Press (2020) © Oxford University Press.
DOI: 10.1093/oso/9780190914554.001.0001

exemplified a deep ambivalence among Russian scientists about restricting access to protected territories to nonscientists.

Throughout the world, many conservationists had come to view national parks as the best way to both preserve landscapes and meet the growing demands of increasingly mobile populations for tourism opportunities. Although many Russian geographers and biologists had proposed national parks in the years leading up to and following the Revolution, Russia still did not have national parks, or any other protected territories designed specifically for tourism. Even as the Soviet Union became more isolated, its conservation community became more aware of the practical benefits offered by national parks in the years after Kashkarov's trip. As more Soviet citizens traveled throughout the USSR and Stalin's "Great Break" forced the conservation community to focus on projects deemed "useful" by the state, many of the staunchest supporters of the *zapovedniki* suggested expanding tourism in them to make them more like national parks.

This chapter examines the parallel and intertwined histories of the national parks around the world and Russian *zapovedniki* from the late nineteenth century to the eve of World War II. In this period of expanding global networks, educated citizens increasingly compared, when politically possible, the advantages and shortcomings of the country in which they lived to those of other countries, including their respective tourism systems and nature protection practices. Long before, both Russian and America educated elites were asking if their natural landscapes measured up to what could be found in Europe.

Expanding Visions of a National Landscape

Despite having dramatically different political systems, the United States and the Russian Empire had much in common in the early nineteenth century. Both nations had huge territorial expanses, much of which had not been thoroughly mapped. Political leaders, patriots, and foreign intellectuals remarked that both countries were destined to exert tremendous influence on global affairs, with Alexis de Tocqueville predicting that they would one day compete for world dominance.[4] However, both countries expressed a sense of inferiority vis-à-vis Western Europe in their respective education levels, scientific accomplishments, cultural achievements, and even natural landscapes.

In the late eighteenth and early nineteenth centuries, Russian ideas about scenic beauty, as the historian Christopher Ely has argued, derived from European standards.[5] By the early nineteenth century, European Romantic poets and artists particularly emphasized the sublime beauty of rugged mountain landscapes.[6] In their frequent travels to Western Europe, Russian elites noted that the scenery—particularly the Alps—was far superior to their country's own, and Russian artists were more inspired to paint the landscapes of Western Europe. By mid-century, many Russian writers emphasized that Russia's lack of scenic landscapes reflected the depth and lack of pretension of the national character.[7] Such endorsements remained unconvincing to many Russians, who did not want to forego the scenic marvels of Europe to venture through a Russian countryside with atrocious roads and few accommodations for tourists.

At the beginning of the nineteenth century, much of the United States' landscape remained "undiscovered" by non-indigenous Americans, even as many among the educated elite felt compelled to prove that their country had nature that matched Europe's. Thomas Jefferson's praise of the beauty of the Shenandoah Mountains vis-à-vis the Alps demonstrated just how awkward these comparisons could be.[8] In subsequent decades, transcendentalist writers such as Ralph Waldo Emerson and Henry David Thoreau and landscape artists of the Hudson River School showcased the unaltered landscapes of the Eastern United States. However, writers from Washington Irving to James Fenimore Cooper still conceded that Europe had more "noble" scenery than the eastern United States.[9]

By mid-century, more easterners were traveling to the West to see the region's spectacular landscapes firsthand. Above all, the Yosemite Valley captured the eastern imagination. In his guidebook to the Yosemite Valley, James Mason Hutchings, a miner turned journalist, wrote, "When we come to Yosemite Falls proper, we behold an object which has no parallel in the Alps."[10] Writing in the *Boston Evening Transcript* in 1861, Thomas Starr King crowed that Yosemite's scenery was unparalleled in any place in the Alps or the Andes. Only the Himalayas, he said, could perhaps compare.[11] When Abraham Lincoln signed the Yosemite Park Act on June 30, 1864, he made the state of California responsible for the management of fifty-six square miles in the Yosemite Valley and gave the federal government final jurisdiction over the territory. The federal government put Yosemite under its direct management and renamed it a national park in 1894. For a nation whose founders believed that private property was the foundation of liberty, the idea that the federal government could reserve land for the "public good" was revolutionary.[12]

With Yosemite serving as the model, Yellowstone National Park was designated the first national park in 1872 and immediately put under the management of the federal government.[13] The two parks quickly gained attention globally. Other countries soon started establishing national parks of their own. Royal National Park in New South Wales, Australia, became the world's second national park in 1879. Civic organizations from different regions agitated for national parks, and the Australian government established another in 1894. William Fox, the premier of New Zealand, would visit Yosemite in 1873, and soon after he called for a national park in his country's thermal district. In 1887 that district became Tongariro National Park, whose boosters said of it that "Switzerland had nothing to compare."[14] In Canada, where managers of the recently completed Canadian Pacific Railway promoted its territory as "fifty Switzerlands in one," Banff National Park was established in 1885.[15] Indeed, it was not just the United States and Russia comparing their landscapes to those of Europe.

The growing popularity among easterners for traveling west on transcontinental railways to enjoy the wonders of Yellowstone and Yosemite demonstrated the viability of the national park idea.[16] The US government established Sequoia, Mount Rainier, and Crater Lake Parks in 1890, 1899, and 1902, respectively. While many writers extolled US national parks as possessing scenery superior to anywhere else, even to Switzerland, no writer did more than John Muir to make national parks icons of American nature and emphasize their importance in broader, universalistic terms.[17] In an 1898 *Atlantic Monthly* article, Muir wrote, "Thousands of tired, nerve-shaken, over-civilized people are beginning to find out that going to the mountains is going home; that wildness is a necessity; and that mountain parks and reservations are useful not only as fountains of timber and irrigating rivers, but as fountains of life."[18] Some Russians were thinking along similar lines.

Russian Landscape

The Russian Empire was changing dramatically by the end of the century. Over the previous three decades, the emancipation of serfs had propelled a dramatic growth of cities, especially St. Petersburg/Petrograd and Moscow, which had 2.5 and 2 million inhabitants, respectively, in 1917.[19] While Russia had started industrializing later than Western Europe and the United States, numerous industrial factories were operating in large cities by the late nineteenth century. The middle class, while still relatively small, was growing.[20] Finance Minister Sergei Witte secured foreign investments to expand the state's railway network, which he believed was essential for exploiting the empire's vast natural resources and facilitating the mobility of its population.[21] This railway network, especially the Trans-Siberian Railway, also made many of the empire's remote scenic landscapes more accessible to both foreign and domestic tourists.

Russians could choose among various types of domestic tourism in nature. Cruises along the Volga River had become popular by the end of the century, and writers sometimes compared its beauty favorably to what one might see in Europe.[22] With the formation of Alpine clubs, more Russians traveled to the mountains of Crimea and the Caucasus.[23] Black Sea resorts, especially those in

Odessa and on Crimea, became increasingly popular in the final three decades of the nineteenth century; however, more Russians visited European spas than domestic ones by the turn of the century.[24] By emphasizing various services available to tourists—drugstores, hotels, and transportation services, tourist guidebooks showed that Russian tourists could enjoy the same comforts on their travels abroad as they did at home.[25] Formed in 1903, the joint-stock company Turist promoted destinations in the European and Asiatic parts of the empire.[26] The first Russian tourism journal, *Russian Tourist* (*Russkii turist*), was published from 1899 to 1903.[27] Two others, *Traveler* (*Puteshestvennik*) and *The Beautiful Afar* (*Prekrasnoe daleko*), began publication in 1905 and 1912, respectively.[28] While fewer than two hundred guidebooks to Russian tourism destinations were published in the nineteenth century, 208 guidebooks, which focused on both European and Asiatic parts of the empire, were published between 1900 and 1917.[29] While many Russians still believed their landscapes compared unfavorably to Europe, Russian tourists were in greater numbers seeing the wonders of Baikal, the Caucasus, the Altai, and many other faraway natural wonders firsthand by the early twentieth century.[30] These remote places did not, however, have comparable promoters, to John Muir, who helped weave them into the fabric of American national identity.

Foreign visitors were also attracted to traveling throughout the empire. John Muir was one of a growing number of foreigners using Russia's railway network to marvel at the empire's spectacular natural scenery.[31] In the summer of 1903, only a few weeks after finishing his celebrated Yosemite camping trip with US president Theodore Roosevelt, Muir left for over a month of travel in Russia.[32] After several days in St. Petersburg, he was eager to leave the "semi-dismal old town" to discover the "real Russia" of the north. Muir was assigned a young forester as a guide before leaving for Lake Ladoga. After spending a couple of days at the lake, Muir and the guide went to Finland to observe the latest practices in Russian forestry. Muir briefly returned to St. Petersburg and then went to the Caucasus, which he described as "Yosemite-like" and as beautiful as any mountains that he had ever seen.[33] Muir traveled back to Moscow before setting off for Siberia on the Trans-Siberian Railway, which surprised him by being "far more comfortable" than German trains.[34] He waxed ecstatic about Baikal's "pure water," its deep inlets, its rugged, craggy shoreline, and its surrounding forests.[35] But Muir was most moved by Siberia's large rivers: "None of the features of vast Siberia more excites the imagination than the great rivers pouring their mighty flood from thousands of dark forested mountains and broad flowery plains, and sweeping on over the level tundra to the Arctic Ocean."[36]

Unfortunately, Muir's journal entries from his time in Russia and personal letters to Russian scientists prior to his trip do not mention specific conversations or even the names of his traveling companions. But it is almost inconceivable that Muir did not talk about American national parks with the young forester. He might have mentioned the idea to one of the well-traveled and internationally recognized scientists who was informed about his trip beforehand. These included climatologist Alexander Ivanovich Voeikov, paleontologist Vladimir Prokhorovich Amalitskii, and geologist Sergei Nikolaievich Nikitin.[37]

Even if Muir's trip did not influence Russia's first supporters of parks, it illuminated the increasing importance of scientific exchange in the industrialized and industrializing world. Such exchanges facilitated the broad diffusion of conservation ideas. While Western science had been significantly influencing Russia at least since the rule of Peter the Great, its authority became stronger in the mid to late nineteenth century.[38] During the 1830s, German-trained Russian foresters began proposing public ownership of the forests in *Forest Journal* (*Lesnoi zhurnal*), which frequently included translated articles by American and German foresters.[39] As the historian Ekaterina Pravilova has convincingly argued, foresters initially pushed for preservation not out of objective necessity but because they wanted to borrow from Western science in order to help modernize the Russian Empire.[40] Similarly, in the early 1860s, Westernizers at the Moscow Agricultural Institute aggressively embraced the cause of conservation.[41] Toward the end of the century, foresters and Western-oriented, conservation-minded Russian citizens were preoccupied with the urgent issue of the wide destruction of forests.[42]

While Alexander III's government opposed Western ideas about political liberalization, conservation was the sort of pragmatic, nonideological reform agenda that the reactionary tsar tended to view with less suspicion. His government passed a Forest Conservation Law that created the Forestry Department in 1888. Resting on the Western legal concept of the "public good," which Russian liberal society increasingly embraced, the law allowed the Forest Department to expropriate forests when private owners failed to conserve forest holdings.[43] However, Russian forest protection efforts came up short compared to those in Western Europe. European Russia lost more than 2.5 percent of its forest from the introduction of the 1888 law and the outbreak of World War I in 1914.[44] During this same period, Germany's forested territory had expanded despite its breakneck pace of industrialization, as forestry experts and Russian scientists who received doctorates abroad were undoubtedly aware.

While new railway lines had allowed for increased domestic tourism and more efficient exploitation of forests, they also enabled concerned scientists to observe this destruction firsthand. Aware of the increasing calls for the protection of landscapes in different countries throughout the world, the Russian conservation community realized that the vast unexploited territory of the Russian Empire presented an incredible opportunity.

Ideas about Protected Areas in the Russian Empire and the RSFSR

It is difficult to pinpoint the first conversations about national parks within Russia's liberal-minded conservation community, but the first proposals for protected territories in the Russian Empire are well documented.[45] The proposals' philosophical basis was profoundly different from those underlying the establishment of national parks throughout the world. Elsewhere and in pre-Revolutionary Russia, aesthetic and utilitarian approaches had great appeal but the scientific approach would provide the basis for the first proposals for landscape protection in the Russian Empire.

Russian scientific conservation emerged from the field of phytosociology—the study of vegetation communities—which developed out of the traditions of agronomy, forestry, and meadow management.[46] Russian phytosociologists stressed that it was necessary to study pristine natural communities to establish "baselines" that would help scientists better understand agriculture's impact on the land and thereby organize it by scientific methods. In their formulation, protected territories of "virgin" nature would serve as a "model" (*etalon*).[47] While Nikolai Ivanovich Kuznetsov was the first to publish this idea in 1890, Vasilii Dokuchaev, the progenitor of Russian soil sciences and perhaps the most internationally renowned Russian scientist of his day, used it as the basis for establishing protected territories.[48]

Following a severe drought in 1891 and 1892, which resulted in a famine throughout the Russian steppe, Dokuchaev closely examined the damage that the expansion of agriculture and primitive agricultural techniques had caused to the steppe.[49] Soil depletion had led to decreased productivity, and agriculture's expansion threatened much of the native plant and animal life. Dokuchaev believed that in order to make well-grounded conclusions, there needed to be "models of nature," where agriculture's impact would not be felt. He proposed three reserves on the Luganskaia Steppe, which the Samarskaia Gubernia created in 1892.[50] These territories had little appeal for tourists, nor did Dokuchaev want tourists visiting them.

While the discussion of the establishment of future reserves continued over the next decade and a half within the Russian scientific community, it remained largely out of print until the reforms following the Revolution of 1905 that forced Tsar Nicholas II to form a Duma. Many in the scientific community had long been critical of autocracy and fervently hoped that political reform would lead to improvement in the empire's conservation of nature. Having pushed for putting more land under state control in service of the "public good," liberals hoped that modernizing reforms would provide fertile ground for the establishment of a system of protected territories.

A wide range of opinions existed about what form the protected territories should take. Some favored Dokuchaev's ideas. Others preferred American-style national parks. Most seemed, in the early years of discussion, to want the best of both, without fully articulating what exactly this would look like.

Geographers and biologists were at the forefront of this discussion. Andrei Semenov-Tian-Shanskii, a member of the Imperial Russian Geographical Society and son of a famous internationally minded, multilingual Central Asian explorer, expressed what was perhaps the first call for national parks in the Russian Empire.[51] In his 1908 book, *Our Urgent Tasks in the Far East* (*Nasha blizhaishaia zadacha na Dal'nem Vostoke*), he wrote, "The significant, pristine forest territory must be protected in a way similar to what North America has done with national parks, in which the taiga is preserved in an 'inviolable' form in perpetuity."[52] "Inviolability" would come to mean inaccessibility to tourists. However, his later writings imply that the analogy to American national parks was a stronger indication of his vision than his calling for the "inviolability" of the territories. For many in the Russian conservation community, the concept of inviolability was more flexible than it would be for Dokuchaev and zoologist Grigorii Kozhevnikov.

Born in Tambov Province, Grigorii Kozhevnikov presented more defined ideas about protected territories. In the first decade of the twentieth century, he became increasingly worried that the advance of civilization was leading to the extinction of animal life.[53] After visiting London and Boston, Kozhevnikov gave the keynote address at the jubilee held on the fiftieth anniversary of the Imperial Russian Society for the Acclimatization of Animals and Plants. He declared that the Russian Empire needed a system of protected territories oriented to preserving complete "inviolability." These territories, he believed, should be entered only for "strictly scientific goals."[54] Many conservation-minded scientists, such as I. P. Borodin and Andrei Semenov-Tian-Shanskii immediately embraced the idea of a system of protected territories, albeit with more flexible positions on their possible uses.

While Kozhevnikov focused exclusively on scientific research, utilitarian, aesthetic, and ethical arguments for the preservation of landscapes were as or more common in the years before the revolution. The utilitarian approach was exemplified by the creation of the Barguzin Zapovednik to the east of Lake Baikal in 1916 for preserving the declining sable population.[55] Perhaps nothing better illustrates the appeal of aesthetic arguments for protecting landscapes than their embrace by the ever-pragmatic forestry community. Inspired by the establishment of national parks in many countries throughout the world, a Special Congress of Forest Owners and Foresters in 1911 identified public parks and forests as being of "aesthetic value" and needing protection.[56] Foresters, who were sharing conservation ideas with scientists of many specializations, increasingly argued that the state should have full ownership of the forests of the empire.[57] The conviction—prevalent among conservationists—that the state should have control of resources and the appeal to preserving the natural beauty of the motherland for the enjoyment of tourists fueled a movement for the establishment of national parks.

The liberalization of censorship laws following the 1905 Revolution led to a more widespread discussion of many socially important issues, including nature protection. Liberal publications, such as the journal *New Era* (*Novoe vremia*), dedicated considerable attention to it, and smaller journals, such as *Our Hunting* (*Nasha okhota*), discussed the establishment of protected territories analogous to American national parks.[58] While the term *zapovednik* would become widely understood as the model first called for by Dokuchaev, this term was often used as a synonym for national park until the mid-1920s. Preserving the principle of inviolability, providing opportunities for tourists, and the protection of valuable game animals were all discussed as functions that could be carried out by individual protected territories. The strongest calls for the formation of national parks, or "*zapovedniki* of the type of an American national park," came from Ivan Borodin and the Tian-Shanskii brothers, Veniamin and Andrei.

At the Twelfth Conference of Russian Naturalists and Physicians in 1910, Ivan Borodin, a botanist who taught at the St. Petersburg Forestry Institute, delivered a presentation entitled "Preserving Areas of Botanical and Geographical Interest" in which he gave particular attention to protecting different areas of Bessarabia and Siberia.[59] Three years later, together with Kozhevnikov, Borodin attended the First International Conference for the Protection of Nature in Berne, Switzerland. By that time, Sweden and Canada had already established federal bureaucracies to manage their growing number of parks.[60] At the conference, Paul Sarasin's efforts to establish a Swiss national park led to discussions among participants representing eighteen countries about forming a global network of protected territories and the formation of a Permanent Commission on International Nature Protection.[61]

Borodin recognized the shortcomings of nature protection in the Russian Empire but projected his hopes for the future in his address to the conference participants:

> Having heard many interesting reports by representatives of different states, I consider it my obligation to say a few words about the country of which I am a delegate. I gladly promise to present a full report on the question of nature protection in Russia; moreover, in three years, I am confident that I will be able to report not only hopes and projects but real results.[62]

He then asserted that Russia's extensive territories provided it with the opportunity to establish "grandiose" national parks comparable to those of the United States. He concluded by expressing his "firm conviction that Russia, occupying one-sixth of the earth's surface, is fully cognizant of its obligations to humanity to protect nature."[63]

The following year, in the proceedings of the Imperial Russian Geographical Society's Nature Protection Commission, Borodin called for establishing a vast system of national parks in the Russian Empire. He noted repeatedly that Russia's conservation record compared unfavorably to European countries and even less well to the United States, and he asserted that nature protection was an essential task of "civilized countries."[64] Borodin and other conservationists probably knew that Nicholas II and the imperial government would not embrace their cause. But they hoped that employing words like "modern" and "civilized" might resonate with a government that, while sclerotic and complacent, was increasingly sensitive to perceptions of its backwardness.[65] He added that nature protection was "a moral duty, before the motherland, humanity, and science" and that a failure to preserve some of the empire's most important natural monuments would be a "crime" against Russia's descendants.[66]

While recent scholarship has demonstrated that the United States was also learning from other countries' experiences in park making and administration, Borodin explicitly described Americans as "the leaders" in this endeavor.[67] He praised them for their successes in protecting Yosemite, Yellowstone, Sequoia, Mount Rainier, Crater Lake, Sullys Hill, Mesa Verde, and Glacier National Parks. After also expressing admiration for the efforts of Swedish, Swiss, and German nature protection movements, Borodin asserted that Western Europe's high population density made preserving expansive tracts of pristine nature impossible there. Like the western United States, the Russian Empire's vast geographical expanses and tremendous natural variety presented the opportunity for the establishment of national parks of a similar scale to those in the United States.[68] Borodin made proposals for the establishment of a park in the Caucasus and one in Poland's Belovezhskaia Pushcha, a densely forested area on the border with Belorussia.

Borodin worried that the "low cultural level" and lack of education among most of the Russian Empire's inhabitants was hindering conservation efforts.[69] This characterization highlights another strong difference between the nature protection efforts in Russia and those in Western Europe and the United States. There, numerous civic organizations were pushing for more proactive measures by the government to protect existing parks and establish new ones.[70] The Russian conservation community undoubtedly believed that broad public support would help their cause. While Russian scientists frequently pushed for sensible reforms in their areas of expertise, mobilizing Russian subjects behind these efforts was incredibly difficult in a society with weak civic traditions and low levels of literacy.[71]

"Scenic Patriotism" in War and Revolution

During World War I, nature protection and domestic tourism were not priorities for most Russians. During this time, however, the United States government, recognizing that its citizens could not readily vacation in Europe, actively promoted "scenic patriotism" by dedicating more resources to national parks. Railroads led the "See America First" campaign, which encouraged Americans to travel to the national parks.[72] Parks could legitimately claim that their scenic attributes made parks assets to the national economy.[73] Against this backdrop, President Woodrow Wilson signed a law creating the National Park Service on August 25, 1916.[74]

While the scope of Russia's involvement in World War I and the imperial government's increasing fragility made a similar government investment in domestic tourism unthinkable, the war also led to increased travel in the Russian Empire. In 1916, the Russian Society for Tourism and Study of the Native Land, established six years earlier, argued that seeing the motherland's scenic wonders was a necessary palliative to the stresses of urban life. One of its publications asserted:

> Our spacious fatherland includes in its territory many places that, with respect to natural beauty and historical, cultural, and economic importance not only do not stand second to Western Europe's but often surpass the various regions of Western Europe celebrated by the whole world.[75]

To be sure, such endorsements of native nature were rarer in Russia than in the United States, because domestic tourism was poorly developed by comparison. Nonetheless, the conservation community believed that Russians needed an institutional framework to protect the beautiful and diverse landscapes that more of the empire's inhabitants would travel to in the years to come.

Less than one month before the Bolsheviks came to power, Veniamin Semenov-Tian-Shanskii proposed the first comprehensive plan for a system of national parks at a meeting of the Imperial Russian Geographical Society's Nature Protection Commission. His proposal perhaps marked the height of the "aesthetic-ethical" approach to nature protection in early Russian conservation efforts. Like Borodin, he emphasized the traditional Russian love of the natural world. He invoked the words of the nineteenth-century poet Fyodor

Tiutchev: "In Nature, there is the soul; there is freedom; there is love; there is language," and of the popular novelist Alexei Tolstoy: "I worship before Nature, my master."[76] The love for native nature should, according to Tian-Shanskii, provide adequate justification for its protection, which had, he stated, occurred in societies from "time immemorial." However, to address this issue, Russia needed to look to contemporary international models, especially that of the United States.[77]

Semenov-Tian-Shanskii stated that the Russian Empire was blessed with landscapes that equaled or surpassed the geothermal wonders of Yellowstone, the towering sequoias of California, and the spectacular cliffs and waterfalls of the Yosemite Valley. He called for national parks in the taiga of the far north and the Khibiny Mountains of the Kola Peninsula, in the Altai and Sayan Mountains, in the Pamir Mountains and Fergana Valley of Turkestan, around Lake Baikal, in the Zhiguli Mountains of the Samara Bend, on the Crimean Peninsula, in the Caucasus Mountains, on the Black Sea coast, along the Amur and Syr Daria in Central Asia, and in many other parts of the empire—nearly fifty in all—with awe-inspiring landscapes. He added a map of the Northern Hemisphere that included proposed locations for the future parks and existing parks in the United States. When the "vast storm of the war's destruction" had subsided, he wrote, people would need to return to such places of unspoiled nature for "inspiration, relaxation, and invigoration."[78] Without legal protection and rational organization, these places that "ennobled humanity" would, he feared, be despoiled. "With tender solicitude," he said, "we must relate to these surviving remnants and guard them as sacred places after the hushed storm."[79] Fortunately, according to Semenov-Tian-Shanskii, the transitional historical moment of revolution presented conservationists with an unprecedented opportunity. Highlighting the scientific advances made under the Directory in the French Revolution, he asserted that the elevation of science in the country's future government made the establishment of his proposed parks a real possibility.[80]

In the months that followed, Semenov-Tian-Shanskii's comparison of Russia's revolutionary crisis to the French Revolution and his optimism about "national parks" would prove ironic in ways that neither he nor other conservationists could have anticipated. The French Revolution had enshrined the concept of the "public domain" in service of the greater good for society.[81] The concept provided the legal foundation for national parks in the United States, where private property was held as a pillar of democracy. Part of what was so revolutionary about the national park idea was the notion that some scenic territories should serve a greater "public good" or "national" interest and must therefore remain protected from individual property ownership. Less than two weeks after Semenov-Tian-Shanskii's proposal, the Bolsheviks came to power and two months later passed a decree "On the Land" in January

Figure 1.1 Veniamin Tian Shanskii's plan for national parks. Courtesy of Russian Geographical Society Archive.

1918, which nationalized all forests, waters, and subsoil minerals.[82] If state owned all of the land, the question naturally followed: What would constitute a "national park?" By abolishing private ownership, had the Bolsheviks not turned all of Russia into one large national park? Such legal fine points did not deter the conservation community from identifying territories as locations of future national parks in the years after the Great October Revolution.

Many conservationists were guardedly optimistic about how the new regime would deal with issues related to conservation.[83] The passage of new forest conservation laws and hunting restrictions seemed to justify conservationists' hopes, as did the establishment of several *zapovedniki,* which the Council of People's Commissars placed under the People's Commissariat of Education (Narkompros). Andrei Lunacharskii, the commissariat's director, was particularly sympathetic to the cause of nature protection.[84] As the fledgling regime precariously clung to power in the ensuing years of civil war, the Russian Geographical Society continued to discuss a plan for the creation of large nature reserves.

While the future organization and management of protected territories remained unclear, neither the conservation community nor the new regime had fully sorted out the complications of the term "national park" and in turn continued to use it, often as a synonym for *zapovednik.* Some conservationists, such as D. K. Solov'ev, suggested that some national parks / *zapovedniki* should focus on scientific research, and others could be modeled on meeting the "aesthetic demands" of the masses, as had been done in the national parks of the United States.[85] Andrei Semenov-Tian-Shanskii showed a clear preference for the American model in his article entitled "Free Nature" in the journal *Nature* (*Priroda*).[86] As Lenin, Trotsky, and other Party leaders had expressed their anxieties about the "backwardness" of Russian society and industry and a begrudging admiration for American technological advancements, Semenov-Tian-Shanskii conveyed similar civilizational anxieties in discussing the idea of protected territories.[87] He argued that nature protection was a task of "enlightened intellects" and "civilized countries," asserted that it was "important to all of humanity," and he opined that it was "necessary for enlightenment and intellectual development" of the people of the RSFSR.[88]

Well aware of the developing American narrative about the importance of national parks, Andrei Semenov-Tian-Shanskii argued that through the establishment of parks the United States had "redeemed the sins and errors that had been committed from the beginning" of settlement in North America.[89] He complimented the nature protection efforts of Sweden, Germany, Switzerland, and Belgium while showering praise on popularizers of nature protection, such as Ernest Thomas Seton, Paul Sarasin, and Hugo Conwentz. Although Russian folk lyrics and songs conveyed a deep love for native nature, Russians, he lamented, had always had a "merciless relationship" to it.[90] He wrote, "To the shame of our country, always having had and still having the largest amount of uncultivated land, Russia is always near the last place in protecting nature."[91]

The establishment of national parks, according to Semenov-Tian-Shanskii, would help avert the destruction to landscapes threatened by Russia's rapid industrial progress. Semenov-Tian-Shanskii believed that these parks should serve the pedagogical function of educating Soviet citizens about nature and its protection, provide scientists with an area to conduct studies of natural processes, and, like American national parks, give tourists the opportunity to enjoy spectacular scenery. Unlike Solov'ev, Semenov-Tian-Shanskii did not suggest that any of these territories should be dedicated exclusively to scientific research. In fact, Feliks Shtil'mark, a champion and historian of the *zapovedniki*, has written that Semenov-Tian-Shanskii's vision was much more analogous to American national parks than the future *zapovedniki* established in the USSR.[92] Stating that humanity had a great moral debt to nature, like a "filial duty before one's mother," Semenov-Tian-Shanskii concluded the article by proclaiming the "right of existence of everything living on earth."[93] While it is not clear if the elder Semenov-Tian-Shanskii ever met John Muir, his sentiments were undoubtedly similar to those of America's champion of wild places.[94] Indeed, the aesthetic-ethical case for nature protection was becoming increasingly global.

Semenov-Tian-Shanskii's mix of aesthetic, moral, scientific, and utilitarian motives for establishing reserves demonstrated the flourishing of different justifications for the protection of landscapes. However, all these proposals seemed almost quixotic with the country engaged in a bloody civil war that decimated industry, substantially damaged agricultural production, and made forest cutting nearly impossible to regulate, despite state ownership of the land.[95]

The fledgling Bolshevik-controlled government would need to find more stable footing before a system of protected territories could become a national priority.

Competing "Models of Nature"

The tenets of the New Economy Policy (NEP) allowed for considerably greater freedom than what preceded or followed. Instituted in March 1921 to appease a population devastated by war, NEP introduced market-based incentives to both industrialists and the predominantly rural population and gave citizens greater freedom of expression.[96] Within this new cultural climate, the conservation movement flourished in both the RSFSR and the new Union of Soviet Socialist Republics (USSR), which fused much of the shattered Russian Empire in 1922.

Just months after the Communist Party announced NEP, the government sent the conservation community another promising signal by passing the law On the Protection of Monuments of Nature, Gardens, and Parks. Signed on September 21, 1921, this law referred to national parks, *zapovedniki*, natural monuments (*pamiatniki prirody*), and gardens without enumerating the specific purposes and functions of each.[97] Because conservationists had used the terms national park and *zapovednik* interchangeably during the previous decade, this law created understandable confusion. Moreover, in both the years leading up to and after the passage of the decree, Russia had established *zapovedniki* but no national parks. The law did not make clear what a Russian, then Soviet, national park would be. On top of that, even *zapovedniki* had different purposes. While the *zapovedniki* under the People's Commissariat of Agriculture served strictly as game reserves, a vibrant discussion about the organization of scientific reserves would take place in the People's Commissariat of Education in the years that followed.

In the early 1920s, some conservationists continued to believe that *zapovedniki* should have some functions similar to national parks in the United States. Even though the Il'men Zapovednik was the first state reserve dedicated to science, visitors, including tourists, were allowed to visit the "most scenic parts of the *zapovednik*."[98] The Austrian-born Frants Shillinger, who had done much exploration around Lake Baikal and made proposals for several reserves in the area before the establishment of the Barguzin Zapovednik in 1916, asserted that the *zapovedniki* should have guided tours, publish literature and photos to promote themselves, and construct hotels to accommodate large numbers of tourists.[99] Yellowstone, he believed, had done this without harming nature. Arguing that conservation was inherently an "international endeavor," he thought it advisable to invite foreigners to manage the "national parks" in the RSFSR.[100]

Shillinger's emphasis on conservation being an "international endeavor" reflected the longstanding conviction within the Russian conservation community that its members belonged to an international scientific community unified in its pursuit of objective truth. However, to zoologist Grigorii Kozhevnikov, Shillinger and Smirnov's ideas seemed to undermine the potential of protected territories as places for scientific research. Like Kozhevnikov, many in the Russian conservation community strongly believed that developing an original, scientifically oriented vision for protected territories would appeal to the materialist ideological positions of a government founded on "scientific principles."[101] They also probably thought that this might position the Soviets as leaders in global conservation efforts—a strong appeal, no doubt, to a scientific community that had long felt the contempt of foreigners.[102] Moreover, because of the importance it placed on restorative rest (*otdykh*) for restoring labor productivity, the young Soviet government invested more in spa resorts than in tourism requiring self-locomotion (*turizm*) near urban areas or in more remote locations.[103] While Shillinger would continue to push for using the *zapovedniki* to promote tourism and in turn nature protection ideas among the masses throughout the decade, Kozhevnikov and much of the conservation community preferred reserves that would be inaccessible to all but the scientific community.[104]

At the time of the passage of the 1921 law, it was still not clear if "national park" or *zapovednik* would become the preferred name for protected territories. The environmental historian Patrick Kupper has argued that countries throughout the world have been either enthusiastic or reluctant to embrace national parks based on a country's view of North America, especially the United States.[105] Many Soviet citizens admired the United States as a "land of opportunity," and Soviet leaders sometimes praised American technology and management techniques during the NEP years.[106] The official view, however, held the United States as the apex of capitalist values antithetical to communism.[107] Many older intellectuals, including those in the conservation community, maintained connections with the West, and many Russians continued to receive higher education abroad. However, they were also always vulnerable to accusations of spreading dangerous, Western-influenced ideas among Soviet youth.[108]

No documents have been uncovered that record exactly why the Soviet government did not establish national parks during the years of NEP. However, in addition to the official view of the United States, it is worth considering some other the reasons that the Communist Party might have decided that they were undesirable. Members of the Imperial Russian Geographical Society (renamed the State Geographical Society in 1926), an organization that had traditionally embraced a strong vision of Russian nationalism, strongly backed the idea.[109] Perhaps more importantly, the term national park likely raised questions of how the institution would be perceived in the multinational state, given that the term national referred to nationality rather than state in the Russian language. During the 1920s, the USSR enacted an affirmative action policy in different republics based on "nationality." While the Soviet Constitution had declared the principle of "self-determination," member republics understood that exercising this "right" would likely lead Moscow to respond militarily.[110] Thus, even as the Soviet government sought to promote national consciousness as part of the social evolution leading to Communism, "national parks," government officials perhaps feared, had the potential to tie this consciousness to the land of the republic in ways that might have undermined Soviet federalism.

With no national parks, the *zapovedniki* under the management of the People's Commissariat of Education became the pride of the Russian conservation community. *Kraevedenie* (local history) organizations, the All-Russian Society for the Protection of Nature (VOOP), and other quasi-independent organizations actively supported them. Throughout the 1920s, Kozhevnikov's developing ideas about the function, purposes, and broader social value of these reserves won zealous adherents, many of whom understood "inviolability" in increasingly absolute terms. Kozhevnikov emphasized that the RSFSR's vast undeveloped expanses presented an unprecedented opportunity for studying natural processes.

Many Soviet scientists, especially biologists, pushed for the establishment of *zapovedniki* that conformed to territories that they conceived as discrete ecological units, which Kozhevnikov argued comprised a "closed system." He believed "inviolable" reserves with biologically determined boundaries could demonstrate "such momentous laws governing the course of organic life as natural selection, the struggle for existence, mutation, and heredity."[111] The *zapovedniki*, but only in a completely "inviolable" form, would, in short, facilitate understanding of the life of nature correctly. Such an understanding, he stated, was "one of the most important duties of civilized humanity" and would promote the "material well-being of individuals and humanity as a whole."[112] While Borodin and the Tian-Shanskii brothers looked at the Russian Empire's nature protection record with a sense of shame during the previous decade, Kozhenvikov was developing a conception that he and other conservationists hoped would put the Soviet Union at the vanguard of "civilized" humanity.

As the decade progressed, the conservation community grew increasingly optimistic that its initial hopes following the revolution were justified. Although the Soviet government initially underfunded the *zapovedniki* and natural monuments, the State Interagency Committee for Conservation, established in late 1925, increased funding for the *zapovedniki* dramatically in the second half of the 1920s.[113] *Zapovedniki* were administered both by the central government and at the regional level. Scientific staffs expanded. Research stations were built. Scientific associates established the practice of keeping "nature logs" (*letopis' prirody*). While nine state *zapovedniki* covered 984,000 hectares in 1925, sixty-one *zapovedniki* with a territory of nearly four million hectares—many of them were located in the territories of the parks proposed by Veniamin Semenov-Tian-Shanskii—existed in the RSFSR by 1929. The number of local *zapovedniki* increased from fifteen to forty-six, covering territory about half the size of the state *zapovedniki*.[114]

While the scientific community increasingly held the idea of inviolability as an ideal, it never actually realized this conception in the way that Kozhevnikov and others intended. Historian Douglas Weiner has demonstrated that the idea of inviolability rested on an unproven idea about the existence of "closed systems" within territorial units.[115] As many species of migrating mammals demonstrate, ecosystems do not have closed borders. Moreover, one could argue that scientists conducting research compromised this ideal. Even though the state invested far more in spas than in tourism infrastructure, more tourists did travel independently as living standards improved during the 1920, and growing numbers of them entered the *zapovedniki*.[116] The remoteness and seeming inaccessibility, in fact, appealed to the belief of many tourist activists that tourism in its most authentic form demanded that tourists deviate from well-traveled routes and be self-sufficient.[117] Over 1,500 tourists visited Aksana Nova, a *zapovednik* in Ukraine SSR, in 1926.[118] *Pravda* advertised tourism in the Crimea Zapovednik.[119] The director of a Caucasus Zapovednik allowed for the construction of cabins, the development of a packhorse trail, and the establishment of rest camps and other facilities.[120] Reflecting the general conflation of Russian and US system of protected territories, a *Pravda* article reported that the Caucasus Zapovednik "competes with any of the best *zapovedniki* in the United States of America."[121] The very title of one article, "En Route to the Soviet Yellowstone," in the VOOP journal, *Protection of Nature* (*Okhrana prirody*), suggested that "inviolability" was far from absolute.[122]

Inviolability Reconsidered: Rethinking Nature Reserves under Stalin

Upon consolidating control over the Communist Party following years of deft and opportunistic political maneuvering, Joseph Stalin declared the end of the New Economic Policy under the rubric of the "Great Break" in 1929. Stalin was announcing the "revolution from above" that had already begun to transform Soviet society profoundly. His "revolution" sought to reshape agrarian life through the policy of collectivization, spur a breakneck pace of industrialization with "five-year plans," eliminate all dissent, and subvert the lingering forms of social hierarchy carried over from tsarist Russia.[123] Institutions and values deemed "bourgeois" came under vociferous assault. Scientists, in turn, felt compelled to justify their research and activities before a state that expected their complete obedience and unquestioned participation in the task of "socialist construction."[124] This new political reality made the People's Commissariat of Agriculture's longstanding criticism that *zapovedniki* under the People's Commissariat of Education were engaging in "science for science's sake" much more dangerous.

As Stalin was instituting vast changes to the Soviet economy, the First All-Russian Conservation Congress convened in 1929. Participants included numerous scientific, government, and nature protection organizations. No doubt a generational rift emerged among them, but some of the conflicts displayed longstanding disagreements about Russian environmental protection that had persisted since Kozhevnikov, Borodin, and the Semenov-Tian-Shanskii brothers presented their different visions of protected territories.[125] While the inviolability principle formed the predominant rationale, and for some a "sacred prescription,"[126] for protecting landscapes, Frants Shillinger and Daniil Kashkarov demonstrated that aesthetic arguments never died completely. To the former stalwart defenders of the inviolability principle, attracting tourists through the aesthetic appeal of the *zapovedniki* seemed much less dangerous than the prospect of using the reserves for species' acclimatization, as some had recommended. Moreover, many in the nature protection community expressed their belief that this elitist orientation had isolated conservationists from government officials and society and consequently prevented them from attracting broad public support for the cause of conservation.[127]

Having seen the many benefits that national parks brought to citizens of the United States, Daniil Kashkarov argued for the "democratization of leisure" in the *zapovedniki* more passionately than any other participant. The public, he claimed, poorly understood the scientific functions of the *zapovedniki*. Conservation, he argued, needed to "appeal to the self-interest of the masses in readily understandable terms."[128] To serve multiple functions, he called for the *zapovedniki* to be divided into four zones: the first oriented around scientific research, the second dedicated to preserving the principle of inviolability, the third focusing on education, and the last one dedicated to providing recreation opportunities.[129] Such calls for a broad redefinition of the purposes of the *zapovedniki* would have gained little support in previous years when the scientific community could maintain the purist line of Kozhevnikov. But times had changed.

Perhaps the most persuasive case for compromising the principle of inviolability came from the entomologist S. I. Malyshev, who stated that "the propaganda of the idea of protecting nature among the surrounding population must be tied to the existence of the *zapovednik*."[130] The resolution of the congress could not have been more explicit about tourism's role in the *zapovedniki* going forward. It stated:

> For attracting the masses to the *zapovedniki*, it is necessary to have the most extensive development and popularization and propagandistic work. Without this, developing the system *zapovedniki* is unthinkable.[131]

It was clear to many that expanding visitation to the *zapovedniki* would help raise the "cultural level" of the masses, the low level of which, conservationists had long maintained, was an obstacle to nature protection.

The People's Commissariat of Education had already entered into the tourism business two years earlier with the creation of a joint-stock company, Sovetskii Turist, dedicated to providing "rational rest" for workers. "Cultural revolution" strengthened the impetus to make tourism a "mass movement" as part of the broader efforts of "socialist construction." Tourism's promoters argued that, unlike in capitalist countries, Soviet tourism would be available to all. It would encourage dedication to collectivist ideals, a Marxist-Leninist worldview, independence (*samodeiatel'nost'*), respect and admiration for the feats of socialist construction, and a love for native landscapes.[132]

With many of Sovetskii Turist's excursions explicitly focused on showing Soviet citizens some of the country's most scenic landscapes, it is hardly surprising that the People's Commissariat of Education looked to the tourism potential of *zapovedniki*.[133] A 1929 decree of the commissariat, passed not long after the Nature Protection Congress, asserted that *zapovedniki* should carry out seminars, organize excursions, hold public lectures, and otherwise promote ideas about nature protection and knowledge of natural history.[134] Meanwhile, the Society for Proletarian Tourists (OPTE) formed in 1927 with the specific purposes of making tourism accessible to the Soviet masses. The OPTE would quickly establish branches in the Far East, the northern Caucasus, and Azerbaijan. Largely dependent on volunteer activism, the OPTE boasted fifty thousand members by the end of 1929.[135] Dedicated to "travel, adventures, local history study, tourism, science fiction, invention, and discovery," *On Land and on Sea* (*Na sushe i na more*), the organization's journal, began publication later that year.[136] The journal strongly emphasized that the vast size of the Soviet Union presented Soviet citizens with greater opportunities for exploration than those of any other state. While Switzerland had served as the gold standard for beautiful scenery for many throughout the world since the early nineteenth century, the journal insisted that the USSR's spectacular natural variety made it a much more exciting country for curious tourists.[137]

The OPTE promoted tourism more widely and made it more accessible to citizens than any other Soviet state or independent organization. The number of tourists traveling throughout the country increased from 300,000 in 1930 to 800,000 by 1932.[138] The OPTE sold *putevki* (permits) for trips to areas of cultural interest, sites of large industrial projects, and spas on the Black Sea coast. With the goal to make independent tourism (*samodeiiatel'nyi*) the foundation of mass tourism in the USSR, *On Land and on Sea* provided instructions to tourists on how to construct kayaks, backpacks, tents, and other equipment necessary for long-distance, backcountry travel.[139] Tourists found their way to the *zapovedniki*, and the OPTE successfully managed to convince directors of several *zapovedniki* to establish tour bases within their territory in the years that followed.[140]

As tourist traffic increased in the *zapovedniki*, the nature protection community was feeling the pressures of meeting the demand of "socialist construction" more strongly. Ecological doctrines that focused on limits to exploitation, as Douglas Weiner has argued convincingly, became suspect.[141] In 1929, Nikolai Kashchenko, the director of the Kiev acclimatization garden, had written, "All living nature will live, thrive, and die at none other than the will of humans and according to their designs. These are the grandiose perspectives that open up before us."[142] Maxim Gorky's Promethean dictum that "in transforming nature man transforms himself" probably best exemplified the new philosophy.[143] Along with xenophobia, Stalinism's anti-ecological ethos made the conservation community vulnerable in the context of the broader attacks on university professors, scientific laboratories, cultural institutions, and bourgeois cultural influences.[144] The Interagency State Committee for Nature Protection was eliminated in 1931.[145] The Party savaged the journal *Protection of Nature* for its criticisms of state collectivization efforts.[146] With the Party equating them with anarchism and national separatism, independent organizations were under attack throughout the USSR.[147]

The conservation community largely acquiesced. Worried that the Party would label its members "wreckers" of socialist construction, the VOOP adopted the new name Society for Nature Protection and Assistance of the Development of Natural Riches and renamed its publication *Protection of Nature* to *Nature and the Socialist Economy* (*Priroda i sotsialisticheskoe khoziastvo*).[148] Similar to foresters, who managed to bring large new tracts of forests under protection for the stated practical purpose of watershed protection, the defenders of the *zapovedniki* defended their position on increasingly pragmatic grounds.[149] V. N. Makarov, the head of the VOOP, asserted that the nature protection community must "rid itself of the old attitudes, which had somehow crept in, to protect nature for its sake."[150] He and many others were concerned that the government would transfer the *zapovedniki* to the economic commissariats. Accordingly, many participants at the First All-Union Conference for the Protection of Nature, which convened on January 25, 1933, were bent on proving the practical uses of the *zapovedniki* and in turn dismissed "inviolability" as a relic of the past. Makarov called this once-cherished scientific principle a "fetish" and a "bourgeois theory."[151]

Workers of the *zapovedniki* and even the most fervent previous defenders of "inviolability" acknowledged the importance of tourism in the *zapovedniki* at the 1933 Conference. Many *zapovedniki* directors boasted of the growth of tourism in recent years and spoke in ebullient terms about its prospects. The director of the Kungurskii Ice Cave Zapovednik reported that his reserve hosted as many as 1,600 tourists at one time. He proposed the construction of roads directly to the cave, digging tunnels in places with small openings, building bridges over underwater stream flows, erecting fences around dangerous points, establishing a recreation base, and even setting up electric lights throughout it. Calling for a state investment of 13,500 rubles, he claimed that tourism revenue would quickly compensate for the cost of infrastructural development.[152] The director of the Karelia Zapovednik spoke about the development of roads, museum exhibitions, and collaboration with the OPTE at his *zapovednik.*[153] He called for publicity to bring the public's attention to the *zapovedniki* and informed the participants that his *zapovednik* would begin hosting foreign visitors with the help of Intourist the following year.[154] After saying that the Krasnoyarsk Zapovednik was important "not only to the workers of Krasnoyarsk but of all of Siberia," the manager of that *zapovednik* called for an expansion of the budgets of *zapovedniki* to develop tourism.[155]

Even Kozhevnikov acknowledged that tourism had a valuable place in the *zapovedniki.* While he stated that *zapovednik* administrations should control the numbers of tourists, Kozhevnikov compromised by saying that tourists traveling in *zapovedniki* should undertake useful scientific-research tasks, as had been done in the Krasnaia Poliana area of the Caucasus Zapovednik.[156] Tourism might not only inform the broader public about the reserves but could serve as a school for teaching about natural processes and a "materialistic worldview."[157]

The Resolution on the *Zapovedniki* passed at the conference called for the development of excursion bases in the *zapovedniki* with the goal of "the development of mass Soviet and foreign tourism."[158] Comparisons to American parks undoubtedly influenced this paradigm shift. One participant had stated, "In America, every schoolchild knows the national parks of his or her country, but no professors in our country can name the main *zapovedniki,* which have not only Union but world significance."[159] It was astonishing that during a time of increasing xenophobia and political repression, Soviet environmentalists still held up the American example in discussions about how their *zapovedniki* could better serve the tasks of "socialist construction."

By enshrining the "right to rest" in the 1936 Soviet constitution, the Communist Party signaled a greater commitment to developing all forms of domestic leisure.[160] In 1937, the newly created Tourism Excursion

Administration (TEA) of the Central Trade Union Council took over most of the responsibilities of the disbanded OPTE. It increased funding for tourism, and travel increased dramatically in the USSR, including in the *zapovedniki. On Land and on Sea* and even *Pravda* more aggressively promoted tourism in the *zapovedniki.*[161] Funding for the *zapovedniki* increased sevenfold from 1935 to 1938 (from 1.6 million rubles to 11.5 million rubles), and a significant portion of the funds went to the development of tourism infrastructure.[162] By 1939, tourist numbers had reached a point that the defenders of inviolability would have never thought possible during the mid-1920s. That year, over five thousand tourists visited the Il'men Zapovednik in the Urals; ten thousand tourists visited the Crimea Zapovednik; and the Krasnoyarsk Pillars (Stolby) had thirty thousand registered visitors. Long the most popular *zapovedniki* among tourists, the Caucasus and Teberda Zapovedniki hosted forty thousand tourists each. While these numbers came nowhere close to the nearly sixteen million tourists visiting US national parks each year, some *zapovedniki* had indeed become more similar to US national parks than they were in the late 1920s, albeit with far less infrastructural and road development and minimal services.[163] The following year, in a book *Zapovedniki SSSR* (Zapovedniki of the USSR), Vasilii Makarov, the head of the VOOP, described *zapovedniki* as "the best place for recreation for working people" and proclaimed that "there is not a more universal university than nature."[164]

Meanwhile, as Soviet conservationists were becoming more isolated from Western colleagues under increasingly repressive political conditions, parks were established in Europe, Latin America, Asia, and colonial territories in Africa.[165] At the London Conference of 1933, participants declared the need to use national parks to protect African flora and fauna in the Africa Convention.[166] Park promoters spoke of them in transformational terms, emphasized that they were measures of a "civilized" country, and frequently asserted the growing resonance of the term national park.[167] In 1940, as the clouds of war loomed, Arno Cammerer, the head of the US National Park Service, stated, "The nature reservations and historic shrines of all countries can be united, not only by international peace parks but by the international language of the park idea."[168]

Despite the 1921 decree that specifically mentioned "national parks," in the USSR, the term must have been seen by many as more dangerous than previously even as some of the *zapovedniki* effectively came to resemble national parks more closely. Many *zapovedniki* were accused of harboring anti-Soviet elements and were frequently accused of embracing "alien values."[169] Numerous prominent conservationists, including Frants Shillinger, who had invoked the success of US national parks as frequently as anyone in the USSR, fell victim to the Great Terror.[170] Minority nationalities, at the same time, often found themselves targeted.[171] Undoubtedly concerned about the Communist Party's perception of a minority nationality embracing such "alien values," the L'vov Republican Library took a book about national parks by the famous Polish conservationist Władisław Shafer out of circulation because of the political risk, according to Ukrainian historian Vladimir Boreiko.[172] Nonetheless, comparisons of Russian *zapovedniki* to US national parks did not completely end. In one article written in 1940, a journalist commented that Yellowstone had 2.5 million visitors in 1935 alone. He then argued that the USSR should provide tourist services comparable to national parks in the United States while educating a broader public about the location of the *zapovedniki*.[173] Such matters would concern few Russians in the years that followed as the Soviet Union fought for its survival against Nazi Germany.

Conclusion

The emergence of nature protection movements in different countries and the spread of conservation ideas between them were perhaps a natural development given the scope of change that industrial civilization was wreaking on the natural world and improvements in communication and transportation technologies. However, the specific shape that nature protection institutions took was far from inevitable. US national parks and Russian *zapovedniki* were designed with significantly different purposes in mind. Russia's international isolation following the Great October Revolution and the formation of the Soviet Union ensured that its "models of nature" would not be widely emulated throughout the world. The efforts of writers, artists, and photographers, national parks, on the other hand, had already gained wide renown before the Revolution. In the two decades that followed, even though not all countries used the US model as a blueprint for their national parks, this institution was most thoroughly associated with the United States, and the discourse surrounding national parks would become increasingly infused with American idealism. Taking a political risk at the height of Stalinist repression, some in the USSR continued to express admiration for them. National parks were indeed widely regarded, including by many Soviet citizens, as the institution through which other countries addressed their demands to improve tourism infrastructure—an area in which the USSR was still lacking considerably. Even more dramatic increases in domestic tourism and the entrance of Russian/Soviet geographers and biologists into international conversation would spur future debates about the USSR's protected territories.

2

Taking the "Best" from the West?

The Beginnings of the Soviet National Park Movement

Nikita Khrushchev was characteristically garrulous when he sat down with a journalist from the Italian magazine *Tempo* in the spring of 1958.[1] The First Secretary had much to be happy about. Over the course of the previous years, he had assumed the position of uncontested leader of the USSR by routing his rivals. He had overseen the Soviet space program's launch of the world's first satellite, Sputnik, into orbit, and Soviet scientists were working hard on a rocket to reach the moon. He had scored a huge win in cultural diplomacy when more than twenty thousand young people from around the world had flooded into Moscow for the 6th World Festival of Youth and Students. With the construction of many private apartments and increasing numbers of consumer products, standards of living were rising considerably in the USSR.[2]

The First Secretary's tendency to brag about Soviet achievements to the Western press was well known. However, neither the USSR's growing economic strength nor rapid technological advancement was the subject of Khrushchev's boasts to his Italian interviewer. On that day, he showed his greatest pride for the Soviet Union's spectacular nature.

Khrushchev's boasts about Soviet natural beauty came in response to a question about why only three thousand Soviet tourists visited Italy each year. Seemingly put off, Khrushchev answered that tourism was just becoming a mass movement in the USSR. More than that, however, he took exception to the suggestion that Soviet citizens were missing out. He said, "You have to keep in mind that there are places in the Soviet Union as beautiful as those in Italy."[3] After asking the interviewer if he had been to Crimea or the Caucasus, Khrushchev continued:

> You see, we are reproached for tourists going few places, but you have only been to Moscow! Do you know that people who have been in

Into Russian Nature. Alan D. Roe, Oxford University Press (2020) © Oxford University Press.
DOI: 10.1093/oso/9780190914554.001.0001

> Italy and Crimea or Sochi say that we have as beautiful places as you have. . . . I have never been, but they say that the Altai Mountains have an entrancing beauty. And take the Kyrgyz SSR, the Uzbek SSR, and the Kazakh SSR, and other Central Asian Republics and cities. I have been to Frunze, Alma-Ata, Tashkent, and Stalinabad. These are places with indescribable beauty. See how many opportunities a Soviet person has to spend his free time.[4]

He continued: "Or take the Black Sea coast, the Republic of Georgia, the areas of Batumi, Gagra, Sukhumi, and others. These are charming places, well landscaped and with exceptional nature. I have not been to Italy, but it seems that these places can compete with the nature of Italy with respect to their beauty. And I have said nothing about the Far East. And what about our North? They also have many charms. A human life is not enough time to become familiar with all of the beauty of the Soviet Union."[5]

While Khrushchev was no friend to the nature protection community, his interview helps explain why Soviet environmentalists were becoming increasingly enthused about the prospect of national parks and why the movement gained broad support from different groups in Soviet society. The Soviet Union was transitioning from a producer to a consumer society. With increased standards of living allowing Soviet citizens to travel more frequently and further from home, Soviet political leaders touted tourism, along with more material comforts, as part of the Soviet good life.[6] The state was starting to devote significantly more resources to developing a domestic tourism system that would help Soviet citizens enjoy the country's spectacular natural variety. Khrushchev's policy of "peaceful coexistence," which made him more accessible to Western journalists, allowed the Commission on Nature Protection under the Academy of Sciences in 1956 to join the International Union for the Conservation of Nature (IUCN), which was aggressively promoting the establishment of national parks throughout the world. Soviet political leaders, meanwhile, showed increasing disdain for the *zapovedniki*.[7] Forced as never before to consider how they might gain the support of high-ranking government officials, the Commission on Nature Protection and other advocates for protected territories redoubled their efforts to show that these areas could serve the needs of domestic tourism.

The conservation community developed a two-pronged strategy in the late 1950s. First, they promoted increased tourism in the *zapovedniki* to make them seem more relevant to high-ranking officials and the public. Secondly, these same environmentalists argued passionately that national parks would help reconcile tourism and environmental protection, bring revenue to the state, and expand the territory protected from industrial development and resource extraction. Increased tourism in the *zapovedniki*, however, resulted in significant environmental damage to them, prompting many leading environmentalists to argue that *zapovedniki* must once again be dedicated exclusively to science. This position strengthened the impetus for establishing national parks. With the ideological concerns about embracing the national park idea fading as Soviet elites came to see the USSR as a "country among others,"[8] the Soviet nature protection community argued forcefully for a system of national parks to meet the needs of Soviet tourists.

This chapter will focus on the increasingly organized international movement for the establishment of national parks in the two and a half decades following the end of World War II and the beginnings of the Soviet national park movement. While it ends with Soviet environmentalists feeling more connected to their international colleagues than they ever had previously, it begins at the peak of their isolation, in the years following World War II.

Nature Protection after the War

While Soviet citizens had hoped that their wartime sacrifices might be rewarded with new freedoms at home, Stalin actively sought to block Western influences on Soviet life until his death in 1953.[9] The United States and countries in Western Europe, alarmed by the Soviet Union's presence in Eastern Europe, shared a growing sense that their fates were inextricably linked. The United States worked to rebuild economies of Western European countries through Marshall Plan aid and thereby make them less vulnerable to socialist influence. With internationalism being seen by many as a way to reduce the possibility of future conflict, the United States and Western European countries also sought to establish institutional structures that would strengthen transnational cooperation on matters that reflected shared concerns and values of "all of humanity." The economic and military strength of the United States, however, gave it disproportionate influence even as it sought to create the appearance of equal partnership.[10]

Cooperation in the preservation of historical and cultural monuments and environmental protection was one important area of postwar internationalism. On November 6, 1945, forty-four nations agreed to the formation of the United Nations Educational, Scientific, and Cultural Organization (UNESCO) with the purpose of preserving monuments of cultural heritage and the conviction, as expressed by Franklin Roosevelt before his death, that "civilization is not national—it is international."[11] Before the end of the war, Gifford Pinchot had encouraged Franklin Roosevelt to spearhead an international conference on conservation.[12] Although this conference did not happen, in the immediate postwar years, a growing number of conservationists from Western Europe and the United States began discussing the best ways to work together. With this goal in mind, in late 1948, eighteen governments, seven international societies, and 107 nature conservation organizations in different countries signed an act forming the International Union of the Protection of Nature (IUPN) under the auspices of UNESCO in Fontainebleau, France. It announced its first meeting would be held at Lake Success, New York in 1949.[13]

The Lake Success conference reflected the growing tensions between the socialist bloc and the West, although this friction was downplayed by participants. The Soviet foreign minister, Sergei Molotov, had rebuffed three invitations for the USSR to join UNESCO in the years after the war, so it is hardly surprising that no Soviet representatives came to Lake Success, something about which one conference participant expressed particular regret.[14] A single report sent from Poland was the only information shared from an Eastern bloc country.[15] While dominated by representatives from Western Europe and the United States, the conference did include representatives from Central and South America, India, Southeast Asia, and Africa.[16] In his opening remarks to the conference, Fairfield Osborn, the president of the Conservation Foundation of New York, stated that it was necessary to protect "global heritage," to overcome the hubris that "we are masters of the universe," and to remember humanity's "oneness with the natural world."[17] He called for a "reawakening" and an acknowledgment that humans were not "exempt" from natural laws.[18]

Despite disproportionate representation by the United States and Western Europe, many participants suggested the possibility of establishing a "world convention" on nature protection.[19] Portending the edge that the West would have in establishing environmental protection as a stage for Cold War cultural diplomacy, Western democracies at this meeting framed the tone and agenda for the global movement they would lead. They made efforts to use "value neutral, internationalist language," which, as historian Steven Macekura has convincingly argued, would come to characterize the discourse used by the international community when talking about conservation in the postwar decades.[20]

Throughout the meeting, participants emphasized the interdependence of civilization and nature and of societies with one another, the need to achieve harmony and stability with the natural world, and the conservation of natural resources. Of the many topics discussed, national parks received perhaps the most attention. Participants praised the role of national parks in preserving landscapes, protecting threatened species, and promoting international tourism, which had the potential to strengthen the relationships among citizens of different countries. Most importantly, national parks provided a place for people to satisfy aesthetic needs deeply ingrained in human nature. Iolo Williams, the director of the Kew Gardens in Surrey, England, expressed this sentiment best:

> They [national parks] serve, moreover, on the philosophical plane, to remind the world that man's immediate material needs are not necessarily and in every case the controlling factor in the general good—even of man himself.[21]

Because these needs transcended culture, language, and nationality, nations throughout the world, participants frequently noted, were coming to understand the importance of establishing national parks.[22]

The "extraordinary work" by Russian ecologists, as a representative of the Pan-American Union at Lake Success characterized it, was increasingly under attack by the Soviet state.[23] Orchestrated by Andrei Zhdanov, who was seen as a possible successor to Stalin, official state cultural policy called for the annihilation of Western influences and shielding Soviet society from them, which made scientific collaboration with the West impossible.[24] At the same time, the state was conceiving plans for a vast transformation of the natural world. Under the rubric of the Great Stalin Plan for the Transformation of Nature, Stalin's propagandists called for turning north-flowing rivers to the south, the creation of new species, the transformation of regional climates, and the construction of industrial projects that would dramatically transform landscapes.[25] Government agents scrutinized and maligned *zapovednik* workers as politically unreliable.[26]

Whereas their counterparts at Lake Success never ascribed nature protection to a particular political system, political pressures forced the Russian nature protection community to assert that nature protection could only be done effectively under socialism.[27] To stave off the possible liquidation of the *zapovedniki,* the head of the All-Russian Society for the Protection of Nature (VOOP), Vasilii Makarov, somewhat nonsensically asserted that "inviolability" (*zapovednost'*) and the transformation of nature were inextricably linked.[28] Their ideational contortions were in vain. On August 29, 1951, the USSR Supreme Soviet passed a decree eliminating 88 of 126 *zapovedniki,* which reduced the system's territory by 90 percent.[29] Soviet environmentalists now faced the destruction of this system and possibly professional irrelevance within a state that increasingly viewed nature through the monolithic paradigm of resource exploitation.

Tourism in the *Zapovedniki*

The *zapovedniki* were liquidated as the Soviet government worked to restore and expand tourism infrastructure.[30] The state increasingly focused on improving the standard of living of Soviet citizens, especially the middle class, by expanding availability of consumer items and developing numerous new cultural establishments during the late 1940s and early 1950s.[31] However, tourism infrastructure initially remained in disrepair (119 of 165 tourist bases were destroyed during the war), and tourists had difficulty finding guidebooks and equipment.[32] By its own admission, the Tourism Excursion Administration (TEA) had failed to treat tourism as a mass movement and created the false impression that Crimea and the Caucasus were the only areas worth visiting.[33] In the words of one participant at a June 1948 meeting of the TEA, Soviet citizens were "afraid of the Urals, afraid of Altai, and afraid to learn about the opportunities in their region."[34]

Despite the ideological conformity that it demanded, the Soviet government was allowing significantly greater freedom for citizens to express critical viewpoints in certain spheres during the postwar years, and tourism was one area in which in which citizens were publicly making their demands known.[35] In 1950, P. Vershigora, a member of the TEA, criticized the Trade Union Council and the Committee of Physical Culture and Sport for "complete indifference" to tourism in a *Literary Gazette* article.[36] In failing to promote domestic tourism effectively, a letter published as part of this article asserted, publishing houses and Soviet writers were missing an invaluable opportunity to instill patriotism in fellow citizens:

> We still use the terms "Russian Switzerland," "Russian Riviera," and so forth. However, by the banks of Baikal, the Lena, and the Yenisei there are views to which all the beauty in Europe cannot compare. While writers have described Europe to us, they have not adequately done this with their own country.[37]

In subsequent years, articles in the central newspapers, *Pravda, Izvestiia,* and *Literary Gazette* pressed the Trade Union Council and the Committee of Physical Culture and Sport to more aggressively develop the infrastructure that would accommodate the anticipated tourism explosion.[38]

While spa resorts continued to receive more funding than tourism facilities, the Soviet government responded to popular demand by investing more in tourism with each passing year. The Central Trade Union Council's investment in tourism infrastructure increased from six hundred thousand rubles per year in 1952 to 3.4 million in 1960.[39] The number of tourist bases increased from seventy-one in 1952 to 220 in 1960.[40] While the TEA served 1.2 million tourists in 1952, it was serving 5.6 million by the end of the decade. It also set up rules for awarding the "Tourist of the USSR" badge, which required tourists to undertake rugged, multi-day trips in the remote backcountry.[41] It also created a system of sporting tourism with ranks (*razriady*) based on the difficulty of backcountry treks. This classification system would form the basis of tourism competitions that continue in Russia to this day. Additionally, Komsomol worked extensively to promote tourism among Soviet youth.[42] Tourist clubs established by citizens' initiative also flourished. In 1950, the Moscow Club of Tourists was the only club of its kind in the USSR. By 1960, the Soviet Union had fifty active tourist clubs. There, tourists met on weeknights to hone their backcountry skills, listen to guest lectures, check out tourism literature, and dream about and plan extended trips, sometimes of several weeks' duration, in many of the remote, scenically spectacular regions of the USSR.[43]

Because tourism literature remained limited, tourist groups described their travels in meticulous detail in tourist reports (*otchety*) for future visitors to these areas.[44] The Trade Union Publishing House (Profizdat), Physical Culture and Sport Publishing House (Fizkul'tura i sport), and Young Guard (Molodaia gvardiia) began publishing travel narratives and guidebooks. Oriented primarily toward long-distance hiking or boating trips that would not require the use of state-supported tourism facilities, these books frequently described native landscapes as the most beautiful in the world while providing tourists with essential information for their treks.[45] They emphasized the character-building aspects of tourism, including learning valuable skills, developing comradery within the group, and expanding the tourist's worldview. Their authors often suggested that the USSR was large enough and endowed with enough natural variety to satisfy a lifetime of travel.

Almost always asserting that patriotism came from "knowing one's country" through seeing it, these books struck quite a different chord than the attendee of the 1948 TEA meeting who expressed frustration at the lack of travel opportunities in the USSR.[46] In the introduction to *In the Mountains of Crimea, the Caucasus and Central Asia* (*Po goram Kryma, Kavkaza i Srednei Azii*, 1954), for instance, the author, Dmitrii Scherbatov emphasized the country's nearly unlimited travel opportunities. He wrote, "Our motherland stretches from the Arctic to the Pamir, from the Baltic Sea to the Pacific Ocean, and there is not another country in the world that is more beautiful or more expansive."[47] The prolific travel writer Iurii Promptov celebrated the travel opportunities offered under socialism, about which he could "only dream" in pre-Revolutionary times. In *In the Mountains and Valleys* (*V gorakh i dolinakh*, 1954), he wrote, "With my eyes, I saw what I had previously only heard, that we have primeval forests, clear lakes, magnificent mountains, and blue seas; moreover, they are ours—native, accessible, and can be seen in real life."[48] Promptov's words would have resonated even more with his readers two years after the book's publication when the Soviet Union introduced a twin-engine jet, TU-104, into commercial service, making once seemingly remote locations increasingly accessible.[49]

There remained considerable ambiguity about whether the landscapes found in the *zapovedniki* were among those accessible to the Soviet public. But from the Valley of Geysers in Kamchatka to the stark tundra landscape of the Nether-Polar Urals, the *zapovedniki* undoubtedly contained some of Russia's most beautiful landscapes. They also contained useful natural resources, which years before the liquidation of these lands the state had started using more extensively.[50] The liquidations had made the "inviolability" principle even more untenable. The newly created Main Zapovednik Administration under the USSR Ministry of Agriculture insisted on more intensively using the remaining *zapovedniki* for economic purposes during the early 1950s.[51] Compared to the exploitation of *zapovedniki* for natural resources, tourism seemed, once again, a more practical and potentially profitable use of the reserves.[52]

Tourism in the *zapovedniki* found stronger and more wide-ranging support than ever before during the 1950s. The educational staff in *zapovedniki* began to read more lectures and led more excursions.[53] Established in 1952, the Commission on the Zapovedniki in the Academy of Sciences, which focused on reestablishing the liquidated reserves and expanding the system, embraced the opportunity for tourism to raise the system's appeal. At a 1954 conference, the Geographical Society of the USSR (renamed from the State Geographical Society in 1936) took the official position that tourism in the *zapovedniki* was important for promoting the "ideas of nature protection and geographical knowledge of our motherland."[54] Toward the end of 1954, D. L. Armand, a geographer whose book *For Us and Our Grandchildren* (*Nam i vnukam*, 1964) would be the most widely read book about nature protection for a general audience, wrote to the commission as it was expanding its mandate and in the process of renaming itself the Commission on Nature Protection. He encouraged the printing of guidebooks and tourist maps of the *zapovedniki* with the "proper" propagandistic message. Tourist travel in the *zapovedniki,* he argued, would help engender "aesthetic and moral feelings that would instill a patriotic love for the beautiful nature of the motherland" as had been done in the national parks of other countries.[55] The director of the Caucasus Zapovednik wrote to the commission that publicizing ideas about nature protection through mass tourism should become the foundational task of the *zapovednik.*[56] Tourism's importance and the untenability of "inviolability" were mentioned frequently at a 1954 conference that included participants from the VOOP, the Moscow Society of Naturalists (MOIP), the Moscow Branch of the Geographical Society of the USSR, and the Commission on the Zapovedniki.[57]

Others, including Vasilii Nikolaevich Skalon, further pushed the commission. After pointing to the importance of national parks for tourism in other countries and the potential profits that tourism in *zapovedniki* could bring to the USSR, Skalon asserted that the "state's dignity is at stake." He wrote:

> It is necessary to understand, and not to justify the sad memory of the project for extirpating the *zapovedniki* in the USSR. They said that the *zapovedniki* occupied too much land. What naiveté! They said

> that *zapovedniki* cost too much. What niggling! But the opportunity of tourism pays for all of these costs. All countries of the world have dedicated land for nature reserves, and several continue to establish new ones, not pitying lost land, even in overpopulated France. In all countries of the world, hundreds of books on the protection of nature are published. Hundreds of thousands of tourists and thousands of scientists travel to the *zapovedniki*. Is it really decent for the Soviet people, stewards of the world's best natural landscapes, to forget about the fundamental nature protection of their country, the development of the *zapovedniki*? We must make the *zapovedniki* the pride of the people as much as the beauty of the Kremlin Cathedrals and the jewels of the Hermitage.[58]

They could not become the "pride of the people" if entrance was limited to the scientific community. While Skalon's letter seemed to equate Soviet *zapovedniki* with national parks in other countries, the growing familiarity of Soviet environmentalists with the latter helped them to more carefully distinguish the two in the years that followed.

Changing Political Winds and an Expanding Network

Even before the Twentieth Party Congress in 1956, during which Nikita Khrushchev denounced the crimes of Stalinism, Soviet society had started to change considerably under Khrushchev's leadership. Each year, large numbers were leaving the Gulag.[59] Ilya Ehrenburg's novel *The Thaw*, which leant its name to the Khrushchev era, created optimism that there would be greater openness and loosening censorship.[60] A sign of that relaxation was the press's willingness to start printing articles about sensitive environmental issues in 1954, a trend that would intensify through the decade.[61]

Statements by leaders in the Academy of Sciences, many of whom worked assiduously to develop the USSR's international scientific connections, echoed Khrushchev's desire for "peaceful coexistence" and normal relations and businesslike cooperation between all countries. At the end of 1954, the academy's president, Aleksandr Nesmeianov, wrote in *Izvestiia*:

> We feel that mutual understanding and active scientific ties, the exchange of the experience and results of work among scientists of various countries, can and must develop independently of the social systems of these countries and independently of the political convictions and philosophic and religious views of scientists.[62]

In the second half of the 1950s, thousands of Soviet scientists traveled to the West for conferences and hosted their counterparts from the capitalist world.[63] The Commission on Nature Protection had made international cooperation a priority from the moment of its formation out of the Commission on the Zapovedniki. In the summer of 1955, the commission hosted Roger Heim, president of the International Union for the Conservation of Nature (IUCN), in the Soviet Union as part of a French delegation of academics.[64] The following year, after the Commission on Nature Protection officially joined the IUCN, Lev Konstantinovich Shaposhnikov, the commission's secretary, represented the commission at the IUCN's Fifth General Assembly in Edinburgh, Scotland. There, delegates called for a series of regional meetings on national parks and equivalent reserves and information exchanges between the parks and reserves of different countries.[65]

The Commission on Nature Protection's participation at its first IUCN Conference took place amid an unprecedented flood of self-criticism in Soviet society following the Twentieth Party Congress. This pervasive mood, no doubt, predisposed Shaposhnikov and other members of the commission to reflect on the aspects of environmental protection in the USSR that compared unfavorably to the West. In an internal report written almost immediately after the conference, he concluded that the Soviet Union "needs serious improvement in the area of nature protection."[66] He called for regional conferences on *zapovedniki* between 1958 and 1961. At the end of the report, he wrote, "Taking into consideration that the reserve system of the USSR must be a model [*obrazets*] for other countries, the commission is preparing a proposal for the organization of a rational set of *zapovedniki* in our country."[67]

Shaposhnikov worked on many fronts to help the Soviet nature protection community learn more about environmental protection efforts of other countries, especially those of the United States and Western Europe. Just as Soviet citizens had begun exchanging letters with people abroad, Shaposhnikov began regularly corresponding with environmental leaders from many countries and amassing a significant library of literature on subjects related to environmental protection.[68] By the end of the decade, the commission had established literature exchanges with environmental organizations from twenty different countries, obtained over one thousand books related to environmental protection, and was sending its bulletin, *Protection of Nature and the Reserves of the Soviet Union* (*Okhrana prirody i zapovednoe delo* v *SSSR*), to eighty addresses in thirty countries.[69] Shaposhnikov was self-conscious, and perhaps a bit embarrassed, by the USSR's relatively few publications on environmental protection. He wrote:

> Whereas in other countries a large amount of literature on nature protection is published (for example in New York and Washington there

> are around ten journals and in London five), in the USSR there is only one bulletin of the Commission on Nature Protection of the AN USSR, *Protection of Nature and the Reserves of the Soviet Union.*[70]

If the Soviet Union wanted to be a leader in this area, he and others knew that they had a lot of work to do.

Greater exposure to the West in business, culture, and politics created a more liberalized environment for reconsidering long-held philosophical positions.[71] Soviet philosophers became less inclined to emphasize the exceptional aspects of their society. They argued that cultural products from the capitalist world could have "all-human" (*obshchechelovecheskaia*) value, while asserting that values from the socialist and capitalist worlds were establishing the foundation for a common "world culture."[72] By emphasizing the "common humanity" of people in the USSR with the West, these philosophers legitimated strengthening connections and cultural borrowing.[73]

The developing set of defined priorities among environmentalists throughout the world and enshrined by international organizations was part of the shared world culture that Soviet philosophers believed was emerging in the late 1950s. Shaposhnikov expressed such sentiments following the Edinburgh Conference. Nature protection was "not only a problem of individual states but an international problem" that deeply concerned the "economic interests of humanity."[74] In the IUCN, the UN, and UNESCO, this sentiment was strongly expressed in discussions of national parks. The UN's Scientific Technical Council adopted a resolution that referred to national parks as important to "the welfare of mankind" and recommended that UNESCO and the Food and Agricultural Organization (FAO) compile a list of national parks and equivalent reserves.[75] Established at the IUCN's Sixth General Assembly in 1958, the Commission on National Parks called for international cooperation in scientific research in national parks and the publication of a book, *The Last Refuges,* which would feature national parks and equivalent reserves throughout the world.[76] The IUCN asked Shaposhnikov to make a list of Russian reserves for the book. Assembling this list likely created a sense of urgency for the Committee of Nature Protection to reestablish the *zapovedniki,* and also to expand its conception of protected territories. The committee had succeeded in restoring many of the liquidated *zapovedniki,* despite the efforts of high-level officials to transform some of them into hunting reserves.[77] While only forty *zapovedniki* and 1.46 million hectares of reserve territory remained in 1955, within four years, this had increased to eighty-two reserves covering 5.3 million hectares.[78]

Just as Soviet books, movies, and other cultural products were not well known to Western audiences, *zapovedniki* were considerably less known throughout the world in comparison with national parks.[79] And while a country's establishment of national parks garnered praise from many in the Western environmental community, the absence of parks often invited scorn. As international organizations such as UNESCO worked to facilitate the creation of national parks in Africa, the evolutionary biologist and first director general of UNESCO Julian Huxley asserted that "in the modern world a country without a national park can hardly be considered civilized."[80] The developing international discourse thoroughly emphasized that, in the words of the historian Roderick Nash, "a civilized country protected its treasures."[81] The Commission on Nature Protection hardly wanted the international environmental community to include the USSR in the "uncivilized" part of the world.

In late 1959, Shaposhnikov appealed to different branches of the Academy of Sciences in Union Republics, newly-created Regional Economic Soviets (*sovnarkhozy*), the Central Trade Union Council, the RSFSR Main Administration for Hunting and Zapovedniki, and several other parties for recommendations on the establishment of national parks. The Commission on Nature Protection presented its conclusions to the State Planning Committee (Gosplan) in January 1960 as part of its general recommendations for the development of the economy. The commission was reluctant to adopt the term "national park" on ideological grounds and instead proposed using "people's parks." It advised establishing parks in the Southern Urals, the Altai Mountains, around Baikal, throughout Central Asia, and in the Carpathians. Additionally, it proposed establishing parks near big cities—Kiev, Sverdlovsk, Leningrad, and Moscow—to meet the recreational needs of the USSR's rapidly increasing urban population. The commission expressed particular concern about tourism's adverse environmental impact and saw the need for parks to counter this. Shaposhnikov wrote:

> Landscapes are being disfigured or destroyed in a large number of well-known spa resorts and places of mass tourism. In the USSR, many natural landscapes are still not organized for tourism, but they could become places of mass recreation and tourism for working people. Fifty-million people visit US national parks every year, and a government program has the stated goal of increasing this number to eighty million people a year. The demand of our people for such protected and well-designed natural landscapes ("parks") is steadily growing. The number of people taking part in tourism attests to this fact.[82]

Such glowing praise for US national parks was not heard a decade earlier when Zhdanov's anti-Western campaign was shaping much of Soviet cultural policy.

In June of that year, a Soviet delegation of sixteen prominent conservationists visited the Seventh General Assembly of the IUCN in Warsaw, where, again, national parks were a central focus. At the conference, which included an excursion to Tatra National Park on the Czechoslovak-Polish border, the host country boasted of its plans to establish several new national parks. The secretary general called for the compilation of a list of national parks and equivalent reserves, stating that it would be "the most important task the Union has ever undertaken."[83] He wanted the list to be ready for the First World Conference on National Parks scheduled for Seattle in 1962, the theme of which was to be "that national parks are of international significance for all UN member countries."[84]

The IUCN's promotion of the national park idea reflected the growing universalist positions common to intellectuals in the USSR at the time. As the conference neared, the IUCN publicized the park idea more widely. In 1961, it passed the Arusha Declaration, which asserted that the first priority for Africa was the creation of national parks that would serve not just African nations but the "whole of humanity."[85] The universal value of parks notwithstanding, park promotion often reflected Cold War geopolitics. With tensions between the USSR and the West ratcheting up in the early 1960s and the United States and Soviet Union engaging in a competition for influence in the Third World, the IUCN and World Wildlife Fund (WWF) increasingly touted the economic benefits of national parks in developing countries as something that would make them less susceptible Soviet influence.[86]

Despite the absence of Soviet delegates, the First World Conference on National Parks in Seattle displayed the attempts of the West's leading conservationists to present the establishment of parks as a goal that transcended political systems. Participants repeatedly emphasized that land, water, and air are indifferent to political boundaries.[87] John F. Kennedy's letter to the conference emphasized the sustaining influence of wild nature for those living in the industrialized world. This point was repeated in the keynote address given by US Secretary of the Interior Stewart Udall and reiterated throughout the conference. Udall asserted that the opportunity to preserve wild corners of pristine nature would be lost in the next fifty years. These places were, in Udall's words, the "earth's temples" and an "indispensable part of modern civilization."[88] Ensuring that they remained in pristine form was the responsibility of nations throughout the world acting in close collaboration with one another. In addition to saving these precious places, national parks provided opportunities to develop the "inexhaustible economic asset" of tourism.[89]

Participants frequently referred to conservation as a "world doctrine." Yet speakers from the host country carefully emphasized the distinctive American origins of the national park idea. As the director of the US National Park Service, Conrad Wirth, asserted, "National parks symbolize democracy in action."[90] By taking participants to Mount Rainier and Olympic National Parks before the conference and Yellowstone and Grand Tetons National Parks afterward, the host country also attempted to show how this distinctively American idea preserved some of the country's most spectacular natural beauty.[91] It was also announced at the conference that the Second World Conference on National Parks would take place in Yellowstone in 1972 to commemorate the centennial of the world's first national park. The USSR still did not have national parks, which was, no doubt, part of the reason why it did not send delegates. However, tensions over the Berlin crisis, the U-2 incident, and the Bay of Pigs invasion coupled with the anticipation that the US participants would infuse this nationalistic narrative into the international efforts to promote parks, likely also played a strong role in the decision.

Khrushchev's Challenge to the *Zapovedniki*

The Commission on Nature Protection had strengthened its efforts to establish national parks in the two years leading up to the conference in Seattle. The commission's advocacy appeared especially prescient when the *zapovedniki* came under attack again. On December 31, 1960, the USSR Council of Ministers passed a resolution that called on Gosplan, the USSR Ministry of Agriculture, the Ministry of Finance, the Academy of Sciences, and the council of ministers of union republics to submit a report within a month on "eliminating excess" *zapovedniki*.[92] At a plenary meeting of the Central Committee less than three weeks later, Khrushchev explained the decision with the sort of rambling tirade that high-ranking Party members knew well by that time. After disparaging environmentalists as oddballs (*chudaki*), the general secretary used a particular film that showed a squirrel eating an acorn in the Altai Zapovednik to illustrate the questionable value of scientific study in *zapovedniki*. Above all, Khrushchev resented that *zapovedniki* were locking up valuable natural resources:

> What is this thing called a *zapovednik*? It is the nation's wealth, which we must preserve. But in our country, we have frequently organized *zapovedniki* in places that do not represent anything of serious value. We must impose order on this business. *Zapovedniki* should be located where it is essential to preserve valuable corners of nature and to conduct authentically scientific observations. Indeed, our country has these kinds of *zapovedniki* already. But a significant proportion of the *zapovedniki* currently in existence represent a contrived operation.[93]

He concluded by stating, "It is necessary, of course, to protect nature and care for it. But not by organizing *zapovedniki* everywhere with large staffs."[94]

The commission emphasized the appeal of *zapovedniki* beyond the scientific community and their importance to the USSR's international prestige. In a letter to the USSR Council of Ministers in the days following the plenary session, the commission wrote:

> A large number of people use the *zapovedniki* of the RSFSR, and of these Caucasus, Teberda, Voronezh, Central Black Earth, and Astrakhan have achieved international fame. They attract the attention of domestic and international scientists. In 1959 alone, over 252,000 tourists and excursionists, including three thousand foreigners, visited the *zapovedniki*. Two thousand students from twenty-five to thirty universities visit them. The development of the *zapovedniki* in the USSR has enormous international significance. The Soviet Union is a member of the International Union of the Conservation of Nature. Accordingly, it carries corresponding international obligations for protecting natural monuments, territory, and landscapes for the protection of rare and disappearing types of plants and animals in the country.[95]

The commission would continue to defend the *zapovedniki*, even as Khrushchev eliminated thirty-two of them. However, many in the nature protection community viewed national parks as offering a potentially more viable and flexible form of protection that would resonate more widely in Soviet society and perhaps more deeply among government officials.[96]

On the day after Khrushchev's tirade, the commission passed a resolution that stated:

> The economic use of natural resources must mix with the foundational elements of the *zapovedniki* as has been done in 'people's' [national] parks in other countries. It is worth using the experience of other countries and establish in our country a more diverse system of reserves.[97]

The resolution proposed transforming some *zapovedniki* that exceeded one hundred thousand hectares into national parks. Less than two weeks later, the commission specifically called for turning the Altai, Zhiguli, Teberda, Krasnoyarsk Pillars (Stol'by), and Marii Zapovednik into national (people's) parks under the management of the USSR Central Council of Trade Unions.[98] While the administrations of the individual *zapovedniki* and several interested scientific institutes rejected this proposal, they did acknowledge that tourism needed to take on an enlarged role in the activities of these *zapovedniki*.[99]

The Environmental Footprint of Tourism in the 1960s

The Communist Party under the leadership of Leonid Brezhnev, who became the dominant figure in Soviet politics after Khrushchev was ousted in 1964, tightened some of the restraints that the Party had loosened under Khrushchev. However, with regard to the development of domestic tourism and the discussion of environmental issues, the change meant little for either. The state continued to devote more resources to domestic tourism and to bringing more attention to the importance of a clean environment as citizens spoke even more expansively about environmental problems.

The USSR Council of Ministers' passing of the law On the Further Development of Tourism in the USSR in 1962—two years before Khrushchev's ouster—marked the country's most significant step toward expanding tourism throughout the country. The decree abolished the much-maligned Tourism Excursion Administration (TEA) and established the Central Council on Tourism under the Central Trade Union Council. The Central Council established branches in each of the union republics and every oblast and autonomous republic in the RSFSR. This new administrative organ provided for the extensive development of tourism infrastructure and the expansion of tourism personnel, eventually bringing the funding of tourism facilities much closer to the level of spa resorts. Soviet economists resoundingly supported this; they crowed about tourism's profitability, especially after the passage of the Kosygin reforms in 1965, which emphasized profit incentives as an important principle in the operation of enterprises.[100] Because the state tourism budget was funded 80 percent by the sale of *putevki* (passes/tickets to tourism/spa facilities) in 1965, the development of tourism facilities seemed to many of them like a propitious way to implement the principles made possible by these reforms.[101]

The growth in the numbers of Soviet tourists traveling domestically and tourism's expanding economic footprint in the USSR closely reflected global trends. In both the USSR and the West, an economic boom of unprecedented strength and duration made the development of mass tourism possible. The money spent by tourists traveling internationally increased threefold, and the number of tourists traveling outside of their home country increased from 55 million to 250 million between 1958 and 1970.[102] Because few Soviet citizens could go abroad, the state invested in tourism infrastructure in order to assure Soviet citizens that life was better under socialism. While only six thousand full-time tourism professionals worked in the USSR in 1962, there were twenty-one thousand by 1970.[103] The number of tourism bases increased from 2,400 to 5,000.[104] In 1962, Soviet citizens could rent tourism equipment from under a thousand locations, but by 1970 there were twelve thousand such points.[105]

Profits accrued from tourism in trade union establishments increased from three million to forty-five million rubles a year between 1962 and 1970.[106]

Tourism was promoted widely in books and on television programs. Between 1965 and 1970, Physical Culture and Sport (*Fizkul'tura i Sport's*) series Through Native Expanses (Po rodnym prostoram) published seventeen books.[107] The tourism magazine *Turist* was published for the first time in 1965, and the yearly tourist almanac *The Winds of Wanderlust* (*Veter stransvii*) was published the following year.[108] Those with televisions, which included most Soviet families by this time, could watch popular programs such as *The Far Roads Call* (*Zovut dorogi dal'nie*), *Tourist Trails* (*Turistskie tropy*), *Soviet Landscape* (*Sovetskii landshaft*), *Paths of Youth* (*Puti iunosti*), and the very popular *Club of Film Travelers* (*Klub kinoputeshestvennikov*), which took viewers to the far corners of the USSR beginning in 1965, and in full color by decade's end.[109]

General Secretary Leonid Brezhnev publicly recognized the importance spending time in nature and the need to protect it during the era of "developed socialism." In 1967, at a meeting of the Central Committee dedicated to the fiftieth anniversary of the Great October Revolution, he stated:

> The rapid growth of science and technology has made the problem of the relationship of humans with nature especially important. Even the first socialists considered that an important aspect of the society of the future was the closeness of humans with nature. Since that time, a century has passed. Having constructed a new society, we brought into life much of what our predecessors of scientific socialism could only dream of. However, nature has not lost its enormous value for us as the first source of material benefits and as an inexhaustible source of health, joy, love of life, and spiritual richness of every person.[110]

Brezhnev's sentiments were reflected in the tourism boom. The number of tourists traveling throughout the USSR increased tenfold throughout the decade, and by 1970 trade union establishments under the Central Council on Tourism served over thirty-seven million tourists each year.[111] The number of tourists traveling independently, for which there are no reliable statistics, likely exceeded this number.

Supporters of environmental protection had mixed feelings about tourism's growth. On the one hand, tourism was seen as a means to engender love for the motherland and to help with the "spiritual renewal" of the Soviet citizens, especially those living in increasingly crowded cities. This sentiment was clearly articulated in the geographer David Armand's *For Us and Our Grandchildren*, a book that brought popular attention to environmental problems in the USSR. He wrote:

> It is said that the most powerful means of engendering love for nature among children and adults is tourism. . . . Tourism opens the eyes to such abundance of varied natural landscapes. A person finds it difficult not to love nature after having undertaken a tourist trek.[112]

On the other hand, Armand and many influential Soviet environmentalists drew attention to tourism's negative environmental impact, closely resembling concomitant concerns about the adverse environmental impact caused by both the backpacking boom and increased visitation to national parks in the United States.[113] Armand also conveyed these concerns in *For Us and Our Grandchildren*:

> But if these millions of people passing through the country cause harm and deprive nature of its beauty and health qualities and do not become patriots and guardians of their beautiful motherland, is it worth rejoicing about the fact that millions are spending time in nature?[114]

Problems caused by weekend sojourners damaging nature in and around large cities were causing numerous headaches. In 1964, tourists cut down an estimated four hundred thousand cubic meters of forest in Moscow's protected green belt surrounding the city.[115] After weekend visitors left, empty tin cans lay scattered across the landscape.[116] A 1970 *Izvestiia* article described such images in the lands adjacent to the Krasnoyarsk Sea. The author then asserted:

> We must be patriots of nature. It has long been known that the most genuine, mature patriotism starts with a careful relationship to the very part of the motherland where you live, that you answer for today. That starts most of all with taking care of the place where you set up camp.[117]

Popular tourist destinations in more remote areas were also significantly affected. Journalists in the central and regional press described an array of problems caused by visitors, including forest fires, litter, the breaking of stalactites in caves, fishing in spawning grounds, and graffiti in areas such as Lake Baikal, Lake Seliger, the Valley of Geysers, caves in the Caucasus, and the Zhiguli Mountains.[118] The increased environmental damage to the *zapovedniki*, however, most concerned the nature protection community.

Throughout the 1960s, tourism in the *zapovedniki* gained strong support from the RSFSR Council of Ministers.[119] Many laws of nature protection passed in union republics gave a stronger mandate for the development of tourism in them. The USSR Main Administration for Nature Protection, Zapovedniki, and Hunting affirmed tourism's importance several times.[120] The Krasnoyarsk Pillars, Kivach Zapovednik in Karelia, the Pechoro-Ilychskii

Zapovednik in Komi, the Barguzin Zapovednik near Baikal, and many others produced guidebooks and pamphlets that invited Soviet tourists to revel in their natural wonders but sometimes failed to inform them fully of the specific regulations for traveling in the *zapovednik*.[121] Central newspapers frequently published articles featuring tourism in the USSR's most scenic *zapovedniki*.[122] In 1959, the commission had asserted that the current annual level of 250,000 tourist visits would not be sustainable over the long term. Less than a decade later, eight hundred thousand tourists were visiting the *zapovedniki* annually.[123]

The Teberda Zapovednik in the Caucasus and Kamchatka's Kronotskii Zapovednik, home to the world-famous Valley of Geysers, arguably suffered more damage from tourism than any other reserves. Because of the widespread popularity of mountain climbing, tourists traveled to the Teberda Zapovednik in large numbers in comparison to other *zapovedniki* as early as the 1930s.[124] Until the 1960s, however, the majority of those tourists came independently. Fearing that they could lose a research base, scientific organizations agreed that the *zapovednik* could cater to tourists in their efforts to prevent its transformation into a national park. The Stavropol Regional Council on Tourism under the Tourism Excursion Administration, therefore, had significant leverage in negotiating the development of tourism facilities. Beginning in 1961, the council sought to build hotels and tourist bases in Teberda Zapovednik so that it would become, as an *Izvestiia* article reported, a "genuine tourist *zapovednik*."[125]

As the construction progressed and more tourists came to the *zapovednik*, the VOOP grew alarmed. The Scientific-Technical Council of the Central Section of the VOOP passed a resolution in the spring of 1964 that called for banning the transformation of *zapovedniki* into places for long-term stay by constructing hotels and other accommodations in their territory. "All development," the resolution asserted, "must be carried out in a way that assures the preservation of the landscape."[126] When this action elicited no response from the RSFSR Council of Ministers, the VOOP's Scientific-Technical Council expressed its concerns again the following spring. At the council's meeting on April 12, 1965, Iurii Efremov asserted:

> Now I would like to talk about protecting nature from tourists. Tourists can be a frightening thing. Tourist groups are carrying out destructive rituals. They loudly sing their tourist songs as they bang on drums, which drives away the animals. We need to approach tourist organizations and take measures to end this noise in the *zapovednik*.[127]

The resolution passed at the end of the session petitioned the Central Trade Union Council to carry out specific projects that would "elevate the culture of tourism" and called for local history (*kraevedcheskii*) museums to take a more active role in using the *zapovedniki* for educational tourism.[128]

The *zapovednik*, however, faced more serious problems, ones that threatened the *zapovednik's* ecosystem, as the Scientific-Technical Council of the Teberda Zapovednik characterized the situation. Because they were not receiving proper information about restrictions from the tourist bases in the Arkhyz Valley, campers frequently ventured into protected zones to gather firewood. With the hotel in the Dombai Valley and a tour base in Arkhyz expanding and the Trade Union Council planning to build a new sanitarium as well as sporting fields, some members of the VOOP began calling for the removal of all tourism infrastructure.[129] Referring to these plans at a meeting of the presidium of the VOOP in the spring of 1967, one participant asked, "How can an ecological *zapovednik* allow such violations?"[130] It seemed that the Teberda Zapovednik could not, in the eyes of many environmentalists, simultaneously be a "genuine tourist" *zapovednik* and maintain the "purity" expected of a *zapovednik*.

The Valley of Geysers

An even more contentious conflict emerged in Kamchatka's famed Valley of Geysers between the Kamchatka branch of the Central Council on Tourism and the Kronotskii Zapovednik. At the time of its establishment in 1934, much of Kronotskii Zapovednik's one million hectares remained unmapped. In the spring of 1941, Tat'iana Ustinova, a twenty-eight-year-old geologist who had recently arrived to work at the *zapovednik*, led a geological expedition by dog-sled up the Shumnaia River Valley. She stumbled upon the fourth known geyser field in the world, and the only one on the Eurasian landmass.[131] Immediately after the war, a *Pravda* article touted Kamchatka's potential as a future spa region, and in 1949 two popular films, *Valley of Geysers* and *In the Country of Fire Breathing Mountains* (*V Krayu Ognedyshashchikh Gor*), brought attention to the area.[132] During the 1950s, books, films, and newspapers popularized the world's largest geyser field.[133] While geologists and volcanologists carried out extensive research in this location, tourists began to journey to the Valley of Geysers.[134]

By the time of the Kronotskii Zapovednik's liquidation in 1961, over one thousand tourists traveled through it annually. Without protected status, its landscape suffered from the onslaught of both scientists and tourists. In late 1961, a geological expedition cut down significant swathes of a larch forest around Kronotskii Lake. The following year, the Bogachevskii Geological Expedition carried out a systematic hunt that killed sixty-four brown bears, damaged several geysers, and harvested large numbers of salmon for just their eggs.[135] Tourists regularly broke off pieces of geyserite for souvenirs, trampled rare geothermal vegetation, left trash heaps at temporary campsites, and dug fire pits that scarred areas with fragile vegetation.

Several participants at the Second All-Union Conference of Volcanologists (1963) wrote an open letter proposing the formation of a national park in place of the former Kronotskii Zapovednik. They called the valley superior to Yellowstone.[136] A national park, they argued, would regulate tourism and protect the environment better than the Oblast Council on Tourism, which that same year had developed a trail leading directly to the valley. Three years later, the council established the Valley of Geysers Tour Base in Zhupanovo, located a few days' hike from the *zapovednik.*

When the RSFSR Council of Ministers reestablished the Kronotskii Zapovednik on January 17, 1967, nearly two thousand people were visiting the Valley of Geysers every year. It faced a considerably more challenging situation with tourists than when it was closed. With the regional and central press publishing articles touting the area's beauty, the *zapovednik*'s ban on *dikari* (tourists without permission from the Council on Tourism) had little effect in stemming the tide.[137] The Novosibirsk-based Institute of the Economy and Organization of Industrial Production, which was a leader in innovative economic thinking, argued that the Valley of Geysers should be the centerpiece of the tourism industry on the Kamchatka Peninsula. It calculated that this territory was ten times more valuable than the peninsula's gold.[138] However, the press and television shows began asserting that tourism in the Valley of Geysers was not sustainable. In early 1967, the popular tourist show *The Far Roads Call* lamented the "mutilation" of rare geological formations in the valley.[139] Writing in the visitor's

Figure 2.1 Valley of Geysers and Kamchatka.

log of the Kronotskii Zapovednik in 1967, Tat'iana Ustinova, who had discovered the valley twenty-six years earlier, stated:

> I think that under the pressure of increasing tourist appetites, some sort of measures, even if halfhearted, must be taken. In any case, thousands of people walking through the valley is unacceptable! The area's uniqueness and vulnerability require proper protection.[140]

Vladimir Geptner, who frequently wrote about tourism's environmental impact, and the well-known Kamchatka journalist and musician Valerii Kravchenko raised grave concerns about the damage wrought by the "low culture" of tourism in the popular science magazine *Knowledge is Strength* (*Znanie-Sila*).[141] As tourists trampled fragile geothermal vegetation and left trash heaps in their wake, bears had habituated to the valley's human visitors, leading to incidents such as the 1973 shooting of a female who repeatedly tried to enter campers' tents.[142]

Workers at the Kronotskii Zapovednik concluded that the Council on Tourism had failed to "train" tourists to be responsible guests of the *zapovednik*. The press continued to side with the *zapovednik*. In a *Kamchatskaia pravda* article

Figure 2.2 Tourists in Kronotskii Zapovednik, early 1970s. Photo Courtesy of Konstantin Langburd.

from February 3, 1974, one journalist wrote, "Tourism as an active form of nature use should be banned in *zapovedniki*. And in the places *zapovedniki* cannot be saved as models of nature, we should reorganize them as national parks."[143] After unsuccessful attempts by the Trade Union Council and the Kronotskii Zapovednik to negotiate a compromise, the Kronotskii Zapovednik banned tourism until the Valley of Geysers Tour Base could more effectively mitigate the environmental impact of tourists.[144] The Council on Tourism lacked the funds to equip the *zapovednik* to do so. As a result, the Valley of Geysers would remain officially closed to tourists for the next fifteen years.

Plans for National Parks

As concern over tourism in the *zapovedniki* grew, national parks were gaining more support.[145] Kazakh SSR and Turkmen SSR gave legal status to nature parks with the passage of nature protection laws in 1962 and 1963, respectively.[146] National parks received much attention at All-Union Conferences for the Protection of Nature in Dushanbe (1960), Novosibirsk (1961), Chisinau (1962), and Minsk (1965).[147] Participants frequently emphasized the need to learn from the Western, especially US, example.[148]

Formed out of the Commission on Nature Protection, which was moved to Gosplan in 1961 and then disbanded in 1963, the Central Laboratory of Nature Protection in the USSR Ministry of Agriculture sent out requests for park proposals to different organizations.[149] These included oblast executive committees, the council of ministers of union republics, universities, commissions on environmental protection of union republics, and other government and civic organizations. By 1965, it had received over two hundred from almost every geographic region in the Soviet Union.[150] *Pravda, Izvestiia,* and *Literary Gazette* published articles that publicized ideas for national parks along Baikal's shoreline and by the Oka River.[151]

There was little coordination between the Central Laboratory and efforts to establish individual national parks during the 1960s. Without Soviet precedents, an official international definition of the term, or knowledge of which governmental agencies would design and manage national parks, the philosophical basis for Soviet parks was not uniform. Nonetheless, plans for different parks shared critical features. The planners wanted parks to have well-developed recreational infrastructures to accommodate a large number of tourists while preserving the natural environment within the park's territory. The parks would seek to imbue visitors with not only a love for Soviet landscapes but also an environmental sensibility that would encourage them to become "defenders of nature." Influenced by the Kosygin economic reforms of 1965, which incentivized enterprises to increase revenue, park proponents argued that national parks would be self-sustaining enterprises that generated significant earnings for the state. Finally, they often emphasized the international significance of their respective projects and the prestige parks would bring to the USSR.[152] The proposals for Russian Forest National Park on the north bank of the Oka River, a park on the shoreline of Lake Seliger, and a national park in a mostly uncut portion of forest in the northwest part of Moscow shared all these features.

Russian Forest National Park

Perhaps no Russian landscape has been considered more formative in the development of national character than the forest.[153] The nineteenth-century historian V. O. Kliuchevskii believed that life in forested conditions made the Russian eternally "unsociable, introspective, and lost in his mind."[154] In his novel *The Russian Forest* (*Russkii les*, 1954), Leonid Leonov wrote, "The forest greeted the Russian at his birth and attended to him in all stages of his life."[155] Given the extent of Russia's forested area and its deep cultural significance, it is hardly surprising that the first serious efforts to establish a national park focused on this landscape.

Foresters from the Institute of the Forest in the Soviet Academy of Sciences began discussing where they could create a national park near Moscow just a few months after the Twentieth Party Congress in 1956, timing that was likely not a coincidence. They wanted this park to not only preserve but "improve the species composition" of a well-preserved tract of Russian forest, provide recreational opportunities, promote ideas about nature protection, and display innovations in Soviet forestry practices.[156] After surveying the forests in sixteen oblasts, krais, and republics west of the Urals during the late 1950s, the Institute of the Forest decided to design the national park on the northern bank of the Oka River. In 1960, the Main Forestry Administration under the RSFSR Council of Ministers commissioned its research department to develop the general plan for Russian Forest National Park.[157]

The designers conceived of a park that blurred the lines between the natural and the artificial as well as the authentic and the ideal. They wanted a highly managed yet "representative" landscape that through species introduction and landscape architecture would demonstrate an "ideally managed" forest. The park's largest section, which would be characteristic of a "typical" Russian forest, would have open fields, lakes, outstanding trails, dense mushroom and berry growth, birch groves, oaks, and pine stands. The second part of the park, referred to as a "museum under an open sky," would include species of trees and shrubbery imported from different regions of the Soviet Union. The last area would be a

Figure 2.3 Foresters from the Institute of the Forest planning Russian Forest National Park in the early 1960s. From *Literary Gazette*, May 21, 1963.

territory where people could plant trees to commemorate weddings, the birth of a child, and graduations.[158] Consistent with the founders' emphasis on the park's international significance, this section would also include a space where foreign delegations could plant trees from their home countries. These three sections of the park would be able to accommodate up to fifty thousand people in a single day. There would be daycare centers, pioneer camps, campsites, hotels, motels, and tourist bases.[159]

The Moscow Administration for Forest Economy and the Protection of the Forest reviewed and approved the foresters' general plan for the new park on August 16, 1962.[160] The institute subsequently appealed to the VOOP for its help with the project in early 1963. The Scientific-Technical Committee of the VOOP particularly emphasized landscaping the park in a way that would display the "typical" species of the Russian forest, especially spruce, pine, birch, and poplar.[161] Maintaining the proper ecological balance would require close monitoring and potentially thinning the elk population in the park's territory. While foresters would carry out selective and experimental cuts for preserving the health of the forest, the council called for the designation of *pamiatniki prirody* (natural monuments) for specific groves. The council agreed that the park should open on the fifty-year anniversary of the Great October Revolution.[162]

Though specialist circles continued to talk about the project, the park disappeared from the press in 1965 and 1966. In early 1967, a mechanic from Moscow asked *Pravda*'s editorial board about its progress. He wrote, "A few years ago in print, there was a story about the establishment of a national park in the Moscow area. I ask that the newspaper address whether the park will be established and when?"[163] By that point, the Main Forestry Administration had outlined nine tourist trails, which would cover 150 kilometers, and 158 kilometers of new roads around the territory of the park. With its opening now planned to coincide with the inauguration of a park in Crimea for Vladimir Lenin's hundredth birthday on April 22, 1970, the designers projected the park's cost at 2.5 million rubles and predicted that revenues from tourism and selective cuts within the territory of the park would recover the costs of development within five years, after which it would be profitable.[164] Most importantly, the park would help instill a love for Russian nature.

Ten days after the *Pravda* article, the primetime television program *The Far Road Calls* featured the proposed park. The program ended with picturesque images of Russian forest landscapes as the narrator recited the following poem:

A new day has dawned for the Russian Forest
The pride of Russia lies therein
It is celebrated in song
Its power is inexorable
It reaches toward the blue skies
Now enlightened,
I whisper the revelation
All that is in you is good
Thank you, Russian forest![165]

When it became clear that the Soviet government was not going to allow the RSFSR to establish national parks before the USSR Council of Ministers passed a law recognizing national parks, the Department of Forestry ruled against the creation of the park later that year and created an experimental forestry station.[166] Despite its failure, the proposal for Russian Forest National Park, the first proposed park covered by the central press, helped bring the national park idea to the Soviet public.

The Forest in the Megapolis

No park did more to galvanize Moscow civic organizations around the park idea than the proposal for Elk Island (Losinyi Ostrov) National Park, a large area of forest in the northwest part of the city. Home to many animals, including elk, wild boar, and fox, this area had been protected as a hunting reserve since the sixteenth century and was the site of the first experimental forestry work in the Russian Empire. By the early twentieth century, Russian conservationists had started paying considerable attention to it.

At the 1908 Congress for the Acclimatization of Plants, Grigorii Kozhevnikov, the champion of the *zapovedniki,* contrasted how poorly this area was being protected with areas in Western Europe and the United States, such as Blue Hills Park in Boston.[167]

He voiced alarm that Muscovites were turning this unique urban ecosystem into a "summer resort" (*dachnaia mestnost'*) and were no longer following the hunting restrictions in the area.[168] The territory continued to receive considerable attention from the conservation community and was proposed as a location for a national park in 1924 and again in 1934.[169]

During the Great Patriotic War, Moscow conservationists expressed alarm over the felling of nearly twenty square kilometers of the forest's territory. At their behest, the city designated it as a temporary reserve (*zakaznik*) in 1944, but it rescinded this status after the war because it would limit the expansion of urban infrastructure needed for a growing population. Alarmed, well-known conservationists Aleksandr Formozov and Vladimir Geptner called for the area's protection in 1948 and again in 1958.[170] The Twenty-First Congress of the Communist Party in 1959 placed particular emphasis on creating an improved urban environment, and the State Committee on Construction made preserving green spaces and providing recreation opportunities central to this goal.[171]

While the Commission on Environmental Protection had placed particular emphasis on establishing parks with large tracts of protected green space near industrial centers, the plans of architectural institutes for expanding recreation amenities often seemed to be at cross purposes with the vision of the environmental protection community[172] On August 18, 1960, the Presidium of the RSFSR Supreme Soviet passed a decree that gave the General Plan of Moscow (Genplan) responsibility for the extensive development of recreational zones in the Soviet Union's capital.[173] Commonly referred to as the "Big Moscow" project, the proposal called for the expansion of recreation facilities and infrastructure throughout the capital, including the construction of dance halls, movie theaters, parking lots, hotels, reservoirs with yacht clubs, and a three-kilometer canal for sporting competitions in the northern part of the city.[174] The designers envisioned developing infrastructure that would allow Elk Island to accommodate over one hundred thousand people simultaneously. Despite the claims of some members of the Moscow City Council of People's Deputies, who asserted that Moscow should be the "greenest and most beautiful city in the world," many members of the Academy of Sciences saw these plans as a serious environmental threat.[175]

One month after the publication of the Big Moscow plan, the head of the Academy of Sciences, Aleksandr Nesmeianov, wrote to the Moscow Communist Party Committee to assert that the city must preserve large expanses of forests in a "pristine" (*pervozdannyi*) state.[176] The central press would reiterate these arguments.[177] The following spring, Lev Shaposhnikov also wrote to the Moscow Communist Party, echoing this concern while emphasizing that the USSR must "learn from the examples" of industrially developed countries, which had successfully protected green areas with the goals of mitigating urban pollution and expanding recreation opportunities.[178] He stated, "The capital and its surroundings must be an example, a showcase of world significance with respect to the rational use of the natural complex and the formation of the optimal landscape for man."[179]

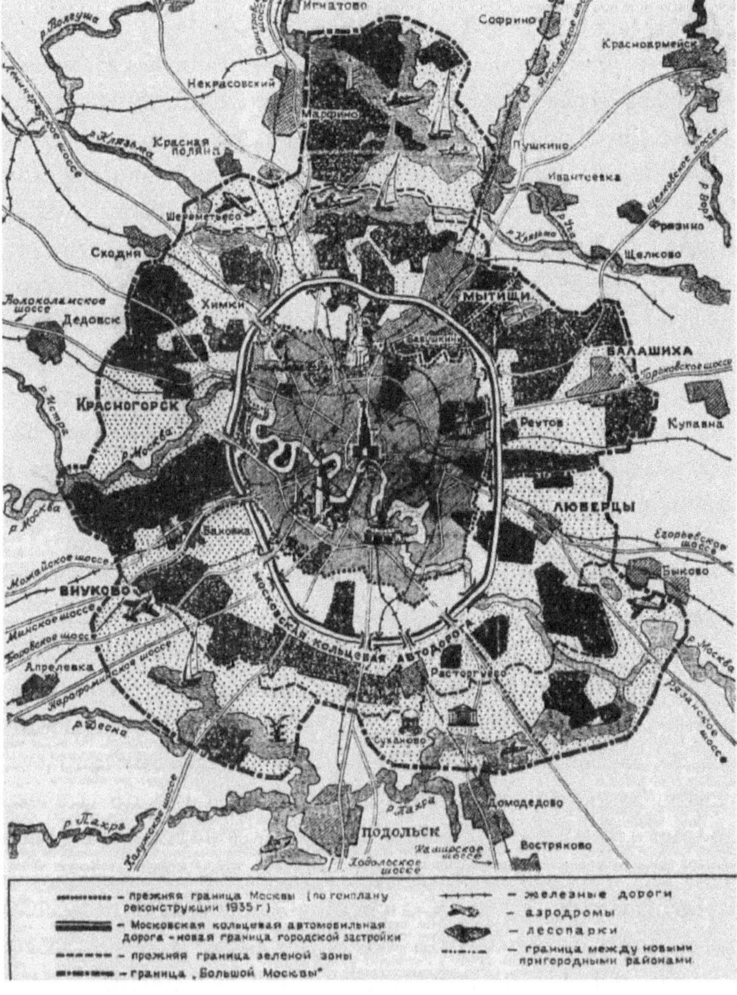

Figure 2.4 The "Big Moscow" Project, 1960. From *Pravda*, August 19, 1960.

The environmental impact of both expanding infrastructure and weekend sojourners deeply concerned the nature protection community in Moscow. Protecting these areas for and from tourists was the subject of the 1964 VOOP conference "Landscaping and Protecting Zones of Mass Recreation." Participants noted many examples of tourists wreaking havoc on the city's forests. In a typical comment, one participant asserted, "If we continue further down this path, if we do not take measure, not much of our magnificent forests will remain."[180] Participants recognized that preserving green spaces should be a matter of great concern for Communist Party organizations. While one participant suggested that national parks offered a rational solution to these problems, another emphasized that learning from the United States would "not be a sin."[181]

With the Moscow City Council of Deputies' Executive Committee calling for draining wetlands and making significant cuts in the territory of Elk Island, Moscow conservationists started making plans for the establishment of the national park shortly after this conference.[182] A little more than two years later, at a conference on national parks in May 1967, several organizations, most notably the VOOP advocated for the establishment of Elk Island National Park in honor of the fiftieth anniversary of the Great October Revolution.[183] The conference resolution expressed the need for the "active participation" of the Soviet public, especially members of the VOOP, the USSR Society for the Protection of Historical and Cultural Monuments, the Architectural Union of the USSR, the Geographical Society of the USSR, and the Botanical Society of the USSR.[184] However, without a law that would allow the RSFSR or any other union republic to establish national parks, the fiftieth anniversary passed without Elk Island gaining this status. It was an idea that would continue to inspire and galvanize the Moscow nature protection community, however.

The "Pearl" of Russian Nature

Few areas in Russia experienced more adverse environmental consequences from tourism than Lake Seliger. Located roughly halfway between Leningrad and Moscow, the lake, often referred to as the "central Russian Baikal," covers 260 square kilometers. Dense coniferous and evergreen forests surround the lake. It is long and narrow with deep gulfs and long turquoise stretches. It has more than 160 islands with steep rock outcroppings and golden sandy beaches, an abundance of berries and mushrooms, and excellent fishing as well as plentiful mammalian life.[185]

Two years before the outbreak of World War II, the Central Institute of Spa Research (Kurortologiia) and the USSR Ministry of Health took an expedition to Seliger to study the idea of developing the lake and its environs into a spa (*kurort*).[186] The institute shelved the project during the war, and the Seliger Tourist Base fell into disrepair. However, because of its proximity to Kalinin (today Tver), Leningrad (St. Petersburg), and Moscow, Seliger quickly became one of the RSFSR's most popular tourist destinations in the years following the war. Responding to tourist demand, the Kalinin Oblast Council of Ministers' Executive Committee made an agreement with the Central Trade Union Council for the revitalization of the Seliger Tourist Base in 1951. As the tourism facilities improved and the central press promoted the site for vacations, the number of tourists visiting the lake increased dramatically by the late 1950s.[187]

Tourists could see the harm that many industries were causing to Seliger's water quality and surrounding landscape. They complained about the stench of toxic air coming from a leather factory, which dumped unprocessed wastewater directly into the lake. By 1960, returning tourists noted that the fishing had become worse. Newspaper articles reported that visitors complained about forests pockmarked by clear cuts.[188] Tourists, unsurprisingly, also caused significant environmental damage. Without any specific posted regulations, few designated campsites, and poorly maintained trails, unregulated tourists (*dikari*) often littered the shoreline and cut down healthy trees to construct temporary bivouacs. Many fished in protected spawning areas. Seliger was, as one *Literary Gazette* article asserted, "in danger."[189]

The Kalinin Oblast Council of Ministers asked the VOOP to carry out a study of the environmental problems on Lake Seliger and to make proposals for their mitigation in 1960. That summer, VOOP representatives spent several weeks observing the site and called for ending clear-cuts, organizing the Upper Volga and Seliger into a center for water tourism, reviving fish populations, eliminating pollution from neighboring enterprises, and designating Seliger as a temporary reserve (*zakaznik*).[190] The proposal gained the support of the press, which published articles comparing Seliger's recreation potential to resorts such as Sochi and Kislogorsk.[191] In response, the RSFSR Council of Ministers passed a decree on September 27, 1962, On the Development of a Zone of Recreation and Tourism in the Region of Lake Seliger.

Even though union law did not recognize national parks, the decree nonetheless called for a national park where hunting and commercial fishing would be banned. The national park designation would demand that factories within the park's boundaries modernize their filtration equipment. The plan also called for designating individual sites as natural monuments. Later VOOP resolutions emphasized the great "economic value" of such a park.[192] The proposed park would require 22.3 million rubles of investment and would be comparable in size to the biggest national parks in the United States, except for some in Alaska.[193] Throughout the 1970s and 1980s, articles in the central press called attention to environmental degradation around Seliger and expressed continued hope that a national park could help resolve the problem.[194] In 1974, a primetime television program about tourism's damaging impact on the area around the lake featured the project for a national park on Seliger.[195] The Central Trade Union Council aggressively pushed for the establishment of a national park on Seliger, and another decree passed by the RSFSR Council of Ministers in 1974 advocated for designating a large part of the territory of Seliger a "National Park of Russia."[196] Several institutes—the Leningrad Urban Design Institute (Lengiprogor), the Union Institute of Landscape Design (Soiuzgiproleskhoz), and others—dedicated significant resources to drafting plans for the future park. Lengiprogor's 1980 plan was for the park to accommodate as many as seventy-five thousand people simultaneously.[197] However, a constellation of local forces opposing the park, especially the concerns of a local hunting society, ultimately led the government of the RSFSR and then the Russian Federation to abandon the idea in the early 1990s.[198]

Toward Consensus

Near the end of the 1960s, the efforts of the Central Laboratory of Nature Protection to promote the national park idea and the efforts of different groups to establish parks had coalesced into what could be called a national park movement. Various ministries, scientific institutes, and civic organizations were actively working to establish parks. Prominent writers sought to promote them to the wider public. On June 20, 1966, representatives of the Central Laboratory presented a report to the Section on Forestry and Nature Protection of the Central Committee of the Communist Party that stated that "nature parks" were a necessity. Remote scenic regions—Siberia, the Urals, and Kazakhstan—they argued, should receive priority.[199] The laboratory's report the following year emphasized the international significance of this task. After stressing the importance of the USSR joining UNESCO and the International Council for Bird Preservation, Shaposhnikov asserted:

> The importance and urgency of the topic have become evident, taking into account the fact that the resolution of the urgent problems of environmental protection in our country has become an integral part of the internal policy of the Communist Party and the Soviet government. It is also impossible to overlook the importance of the topic for strengthening the prestige and authority of Soviet science in the international arena.[200]

Shaposhnikov and others in the laboratory by this point understood that national park status carried high expectations among the international environmental protection community.

The attention that Seliger had received from the Central Council on Tourism, the VOOP, and the central press made Kalinin a natural place to hold the Soviet Union's first conference dedicated to the establishment of national parks. In May 1967, the VOOP, participants from the RSFSR Ministry of Culture, and the All-Russian Society for the Protection of Monuments of History and Culture organized a conference focused on the establishment of a set of "people's parks" in the RSFSR.[201] The conference passed a resolution that called for oblast, regional, and republic branches of the VOOP to take an active part in designating protected landscapes and zones of tourism. As part of this effort it demanded a propaganda division that would develop proposals for disseminating information on protected territories. It also encouraged the Moscow division of the VOOP to promote the idea of the establishment of the USSR's first people's park in the Moscow region.[202]

Soon after the conference, *Literary Gazette* dedicated a full-page spread to national parks, featuring articles by well-known environmental writers Leonid Leonov and Oleg Volkov. Leonov, whose *The Russian Forest* was perhaps the most well-known contemporary work of fiction promoting environmental protection, was no doubt flattered by the prospect of the first Soviet national park borrowing his novel's title. Calling national parks a potential "heaven" for tourists, Leonov deemed their establishment the solution to a "great patriotic and moral problem."[203]

Oleg Volkov, who had survived three stints in the gulag and then become a geologist, prolific writer, and tireless promoter of nature protection, echoed Udall's universalist sentiments at the World Congress on National Parks five years before. He asserted:

> From century to century, humanity has been giving itself more and more to industrial concerns. We erect more factories, cover the earth with networks of water pipes and cables, dig deeper, and lay down asphalt more widely. We build higher apartment buildings. And we retreat from the clear sky and stars, the smell of dewy meadows, rustling reeds in the quiet backwaters with the intoxicating chorus of birds in a spring grove.[204]

In modern conditions, Volkov wrote, people "inevitably" felt the pull to spend time around a campfire, breathe fresh air, and lose themselves on winding trails where they could escape industrial civilization. Spa resorts were no longer sufficient, especially for Soviet citizens who needed to experience "pristine" nature.

"We can certainly learn from the experience and practice of the national parks of Europe and America," he stated, "by making the necessary adjustments to the goals of national parks of capitalistic nations."[205] In addition to establishing parks around densely populated cities, Volkov asserted that designating territories in Crimea, the Southern Urals, Altai, around Baikal, Seliger, the Caucasus, the Valdai Hills, and other areas of "untouched" nature was an urgent task for the state.[206]

Problems of tourism in the *zapovedniki* and the prospects of establishing a system of national parks also received extensive coverage in *Hunting and Game Management* (*Okhota i okhotnich'e khoziaistvo*), a USSR Ministry of Agriculture publication.[207] Of these articles, one by N. Puzanov entitled "We Need National Parks" presented the most persuasive case for national parks in response to intensifying tourism pressure on the *zapovedniki.*

> In our country, we have organized many *zapovedniki,* but there are no national parks, even though we have had a need for them for a long time. This is attested to by the fact that a few *zapovedniki,* like Caucasus and the Krasnoyarsk Pillars (Stolby), have started to transform into national parks with tourist visitation steadily growing.[208]

Participants at a conference held by the USSR Ministry of Agriculture's Main Administration for Nature Protection, Zapovedniki, and Hunting, On Measures to Improve the Operation and Management of State *Zapovedniki,* two weeks after this article appeared, widely shared this sentiment.[209] More than any other event, this conference marked the turning point in the view of environmentalists that tourism in the *zapovedniki* had exceeded acceptable levels. It also marked the most comprehensive and full-throated call for the establishment of national parks to date.

Iurii Efremov, a longtime proponent of aligning the goals of tourism with the protection of nature, asserted that tourists might destroy many of the "most poetic corners" of the Soviet Union in the *zapovedniki* within ten to fifteen years.[210] He blamed the Central Council on Tourism for not doing enough to train tourists to act in ecologically responsible ways.[211] Several participants called for returning to the principle of inviolability of the *zapovedniki.*[212] Oleg Gusev, a former scientific associate of the Barguzin Zapovednik whose popular books on tourism around Baikal had done much to promote tourism in *zapovedniki,* likely had a change of heart due to several destructive fires caused by tourists during the previous years.[213] He stated, "We must with an iron will get rid of the irresponsible and undefined phrases about how *zapovedniki* are obligated to promote tourist excursions and the organization of tourism of working people."[214]

No participant openly disagreed with the opinion that national parks provided the answer to this dilemma. Aleksandr Formozov, who had called for the establishment of a national park in Moscow in 1948 and 1958, stated, "Tourism, of course, can be a great evil, which we must deal with in national parks that are under protection and close observation!"[215] Efremov reiterated this sentiment: "We must clarify where mass tourism will be allowed. We must carry out the project for a set of monuments and national parks."[216] Pointing to the profits that national parks accrued in other countries, he asserted that they would provide the best means to realize the profit-making potential of the USSR's scenic resources and exhorted Soviet economists to research tourism's economic value more extensively.[217] Boris Kolesnikov, a geobotanist and president of Ural State University in Sverdlovsk, talked about the efforts being made to establish a national park in one of the highest points in the Northern Urals, Konzhakovskii Kamen', which had become a place of "pilgrimage" for tourists."[218] Iurii Kravchuk spoke of the discussions in Moldavia SSR to form a national park.[219]

But how could the Soviet Union call its parks "national" (*natsional'nye*)? While "national" in the international parlance meant "state" park, the term "*natsional'nyi* park" in the Russian language risked suggesting some connection with the many nationalities that lived within the territory of the USSR. Moreover, the label of "national park" seemed to Soviet ears to suggest nationalism, which the internationalism of communist ideology was supposed to overcome. Would a Moldavian national park, as Kravchuk had proposed, strengthen separatist nationalist sentiments in Moldavia SSR? Even more potentially problematic were parks being designed in the Baltic Republics, whose citizens resented Soviet rule perhaps more than those of any other of the constituent republics.[220]

Some participants suggested revisiting alternative names, such as *narodnye* (people's) or *prirodnye* (nature) parks. But most participants, especially Oleg Gusev and Iurii Efremov, spoke forcefully for the use of the term national (*natsional'nyi*) park, despite any confusion and ideological questions that it might create. Efremov stated, " 'Nature park' sounds undefined; it ignores the continuation of economic activity, does not take into account the specifics of the scientific or historical value of the monuments of nature of the parks."[221] On the last day of the conference, Gusev delivered the longest and most impassioned argument for the use of the term national park. He stated:

> Many have come out against borrowing the term "national park" on the basis that we replace it with the words *narodnyi* [people's] park. National park is an international term with a definitive understanding, which has longstanding international recognition. Fighting against the expression national park and wishing to be consistent, we would need to declare war on those words like nation, nationhood, and so forth. In

> place of the question of your *natsional'nost'*, it is impossible to ask the question of our *narodnost'*, because the word *narodnost'* has long had an entirely different meaning.[222]

After a brief pause, he concluded, "Therefore, the name *narodnyi* [people's] park cannot replace the words national park. A large number of foreign terms and words have come into Russian life and become an organic part of the Russian language. These words—*natsional'nyi park*—coming from the Latin word natio—must become part of the Russian language."[223] As Gusev's impassioned statement thoroughly conveyed, Soviet environmentalists' thinking had, indeed, changed dramatically as a result of the USSR's changing relationship to the West since Stalin's death fifteen years earlier.

The terminological debate could hardly be resolved without an invocation of Lenin, especially considering that national parks had been proposed both to commemorate the fiftieth anniversary of the Great October Revolution and to celebrate Lenin's hundredth birthday. At a meeting of the USSR Main Administration for Nature Protection, Zapovedniki and Hunting in late December 1969, Iurii Efremov tried to do just that. Referring to the 1921 Sovnarkom decree "On Gardens, Parks, and Nature Reserves," he stated:

> There is every reason to conclude that national parks need to take the form of conservation primarily in the interests of recreation and tourism. Unfortunately, the question of national parks has been complicated by protracted and unfruitful discussions that were instigated by terminological issues, despite Lenin's explicit intentions.[224]

While this invocation of Lenin sought to dispel remaining ideological misgivings most in the Soviet conservation community had come to agree with the statement from the First World Conference on National Parks: "Nature takes no heed of political or social agreements, particularly those that seek to divide the world into compartments. It has—and always will be—all-inclusive."[225]

The IUCN had developed a definition for national parks that it hoped would guide countries that planned to establish them just several weeks before Efremov's comments. It defined them as large, unaltered, scenic territories in which visitors were allowed to enter under managed conditions that would help protect the environment. Moreover, national parks had to fall under the "highest competent authority" in the country.[226] Without a law passed at the union level, however, this was still not possible in the USSR. This political roadblock and, to a lesser degree, the terminological debate remained. However, borrowing foreign terms and expressions had become increasingly normalized in Soviet society in the decade and a half after Stalin's death, which made using the term national park considerably less problematic.[227] Soviet environmentalists widely agreed that national parks would reconcile tourism and nature protection, bring profits to the state, and earn the USSR more respect from the international environmental community, which increasingly emphasized that collaboration in environmental protection transcended politics.

Conclusion

The Soviet national park movement emerged out of vastly transformed conditions in Soviet society. Similar to the experiences of people living in other rapidly industrializing countries, Soviet citizens increasingly turned to wild places to fulfill a deep spiritual and psychological need during the three decades after World War II.[228] Parks promised to offer citizens more opportunities to have direct contact with nature, including in very remote areas. Soviet citizens felt increasingly comfortable in appealing to government officials who championed domestic travel as part of rising standards of living, which they asserted compared favorably to the West and would soon surpass it. Soviet environmentalists saw in national parks the opportunity to expand their system of protected territories and to preserve the ecological integrity of the *zapovedniki* by orienting them again toward the principles of "inviolability," which many staunchly defended in the 1920s.

While Soviet environmentalists became enamored with national parks as they strengthened their contacts with Western counterparts, *zapovedniki* remained somewhat obscure to their American and European colleagues. Conservative reactions following Khrushchev's ouster and the Prague Spring did nothing to dampen the sense of Soviet environmentalists that they were part of an international effort to protect the environment. With national parks becoming one of the most important priorities of nature protection, they understood that their efforts to establish parks would highlight Soviet contributions to protecting nature among environmentalists throughout the world. Thus, park supporters would experience increasing frustration at the state's delay in passing a law that would give national parks union status during the following decade.

3

Transformative Visions during the Brezhnev Era

In a 1975 *Literary Gazette* interview with Andrei Bannikov, one of Russia's most active supporters of national parks, the interviewer was perplexed by the fact that the RSFSR did not have national parks given that he "never met an opponent of the idea."[1] Indeed, few environmental protection ideas had broader backing during the 1970s than national parks. However, park supporters experienced tremendous frustration as they waited for the USSR Council of Ministers to pass a law giving them official status at the highest level. While the hopes and enthusiasm inspired by parks counter some of the traditional views of the Brezhnev era, the frustrations experienced by park supporters reinforce others.

Many historians portrayed the USSR under Brezhnev as already heading down the slope of inevitable decline.[2] However, by the late 1960s, Leonid Brezhnev had declared the attainment of "developed socialism" because the Soviet system had become more stable, affluent, and predictable.[3] In cultural and material terms, the lives of the Soviet "middle class" were starting to more closely resemble those of their counterparts in the United States and Western Europe.[4] But much of the buoyant optimism of the Khrushchev era had faded. The government continued to funnel massive amounts of capital into "projects of the century," such as the Baikal Amur Railway, which served more to assert the state's herculean power to overcome nature than an objective need.[5] Productivity was decreasing, and economic growth was slowing. Yet Soviet citizens had more leisure time and resources to travel widely, spend time with friends, and engage in various spheres where official ideology was increasingly irrelevant.[6] While censorship laws imposed strict limits on the extent to which Soviet citizens could criticize the government or the Communist Party, Soviet scientists, professors, artists, and intellectuals were able to carve out "unofficial spaces" where they sometimes conceived new ideas for restructuring aspects of Soviet society and the economy.[7]

Into Russian Nature. Alan D. Roe, Oxford University Press (2020) © Oxford University Press.
DOI: 10.1093/oso/9780190914554.001.0001

The mounting environmental problems in the USSR seem to fit the traditional narrative of a society in decline.[8] Satellite images confirmed the beginning of the Aral Sea's contraction.[9] The Baikalsk Cellulose-Paper Combine continued to send wastewater into Lake Baikal as the state ignored the warnings of concerned scientists.[10] Abandoned mining operations created lifeless, lunar landscapes on more than 5.5 million hectares of the USSR's territory by the mid-1970s.[11] The building of the Baikal Amur Railway led to frequent forest fires in the construction zone.[12] The development of massive hydroelectric installations in Siberia was rapidly inundating cultivable land, displacing inhabitants of villages, and leaving no time for the clearing of the mass tracts of forests that reservoirs of unprecedented scale would submerge.[13] Meanwhile, Soviet planners were devising hubristic schemes to reverse the Ob and the Yenisei to bring more water to Central Asia. From the Volga to the Amur, the pollution of Soviet rivers had become a serious health concern.[14] Such environmental problems prompted Ze'ev Wolfson to publish a *samizdat* book entitled *The Destruction of Nature in the Soviet Union* (1978).[15]

Nonetheless, the Soviet government understood the diplomatic benefits of "appearing green"[16] and stated that environmental protection was an urgent priority. This official position helped environmental problems resonate more broadly than ever before during the 1970s. A group of Siberian writers, known collectively as the village prose movement, was most responsible for bringing broad attention to Russian environmental concerns, while the international dimensions of environmental problems received heightened attention from the scientific intelligentsia.[17] With images of Earth from space underscoring the planet's fragility, the belief that environmental problems required global solutions strengthened.[18] Despite the belief of some Soviet observers that the Western-dominated IUCN, UNESCO, and other international environmental organizations sought to advance a neocolonialist agenda, the USSR expanded its collaboration with many countries, most importantly the United States, to address environmental problems through new bilateral agreements and increased participation in these organizations.

Just as détente between the United States and the Soviet Union had inspired creativity in Soviet social sciences and economics, it did so in environmental protection thought as well.[19] Taking their cues from the official rhetoric and increasingly influenced by Western-dominated environmental discourse, a broad cross-section of citizens, scientists, and journalists enthusiastically supported and promoted national parks, often with transformative visions. As the Estonian SSR, the Latvian SSR, the Georgian SSR, the Kyrgyz SSR, and the Armenian SSR established national parks during the 1970s that still were not recognized at the union level, park supporters believed that such parks were injecting new vitality into Soviet society by transforming the relationship of humans to nature. And yet the slowness of the USSR Council of Ministers to pass a law that gave parks official recognition, which was necessary before the RSFSR could establish national parks, reinforces the image of a system that was slow to respond to new challenges. Russian park supporters, like many intellectuals in the USSR during these years, could not help but be deeply frustrated by what seemed to be the futility of their efforts.[20]

This chapter focuses on the intellectual, social, and political developments during the 1970s that contributed to the wide-ranging support for national parks and the establishment of the first national parks in the USSR. It will also assess the ambivalent responses triggered by the borrowing of a foreign model closely associated with the United States and the multiple factors that contributed to the difficulties in establishing a law that recognized national parks at the union level. Finally, this chapter looks at the poorly crafted Model Regulation on State Nature National Parks, which left several issues unresolved that would complicate the efforts of the RSFSR to develop a functional system of national parks during the 1980s. This part of our story begins, however, with a revolution in Soviet geography that had its origins in the late 1950s when the USSR had reached new heights in technological advancement.

Recreational Geography and the "Naturalization" of the Soviet Person

As members of the USSR Ministry of Agriculture's Main Administration for Nature Protection, Zapovedniki, and Hunting were asserting the necessity of national parks, a group of geographers from the Institute of Geography was actively working on the "scientific" rationale for establishing parks and the principles around which they would be organized. In a 1969 article about developing the recreational resources of the USSR coauthored by Vladimir Preobrazhenskii, Innokentii Gerasimov, and A. A. Mints, the authors asserted:

> One of the foundational elements of this scheme will become the project of establishing national parks in the USSR. This project foresees the designation of a vast territory of different natural regions of the country and introduction of such regimes of their use, which provide for the preservation and reproduction of the foundational characteristics of natural landscapes. The experience of developing the scientific foundations in establishing a national park by Lake Baikal attests to the vast possibilities of the complex use of geographical research for solving tasks of this type. Together with that comes the necessity of

> developing the principal scientific foundation for designating territory for the establishment of national parks and the use of them for recreational goals.[21]

A particular paradox of modern life, they argued, necessitated the establishment of national parks and other recreational territories. While the "cultural level" of society progressively increased and created new needs, humanity's biological nature left it poorly equipped to cope with the urbanization, atomization, inertness, mechanization, and hyper-specialization of modern life. The authors argued that the USSR should dedicate no less than 1 percent of its territory (245,000 square kilometers) to recreational landscapes with a well-preserved wilderness appearance, which evoked a feeling of the "primitive life" of humanity's ancestors.[22]

The Institute of Geography's decision to focus on the organization of national parks was born out of a critical examination and fierce debate among geographers about how the field would remain relevant in a world that had experienced recent leaps in scientific and technological advancement. From the mid-nineteenth century to the 1930s, geographers cut an image of intrepid explorers in the Russian and then Soviet popular imagination. In mapping previously unexplored areas of the Russian Empire and the USSR, they attained high respect in the scientific community.[23] By the late 1950s, however, even tourists were helping fill in the "blank spots" on the map in areas where only explorer-geographers previously ventured. Geographers continued to fill in the details on the maps of more remote regions, but this hardly compared to the romantic exploration of previously unseen mountain ranges and parts of the Arctic, for which Soviet geographers became heroes during the 1930s.[24] Space was the new frontier, and its exploration depended not on geographers but on cosmonauts, physicists, and rocketry experts. These pioneers of the cosmos, along with chemists and cyberneticists, brought Soviet science world renown in the late 1950s and early 1960s. Space travel might have strengthened the perspective that humans occupied a small and fragile speck in the universe, but it was making earth sciences, especially geography, struggle to maintain relevance in the public eye. The day when geographers could explore and map other planets still seemed hopelessly far away.

New subfields such as economic geography became stronger in the 1950s, but the old guard of physical geographers—including the head of the USSR Institute of Geography, Innokentii Gerasimov—were slow to embrace applied approaches. Physical and economic geographers were mostly estranged from each other. Physical geographers interacted closely with natural scientists but very little with social scientists, while the opposite was true for the economic geographers.[25] In the mid-1950s, a group of economic geographers led by Vladimir Anuchin began arguing that the inseparability of the economy from the physical environment made the field's subdisciplines artificial. Known as the "integrationists," these economic geographers called for a "unified geography," which would bridge the gap between the discipline's growing divisions. Gerasimov, A. A. Grigoriev, and others of an older generation consistently rebuffed these calls for reform, and Anuchin's views became tantamount to heresy. Traditionalists actively sought to limit the influence of economic geographers in the Institute of Geography.[26] Anuchin and many others feared that the field risked obsolescence.

While specialized geographical journals followed the conflict in the early part of the decade, this debate remained mostly out of public view until *Literary Gazette* published articles by the integrationists and responses by traditionalists in the first half of 1965. Vladimir Anuchin, V. M. Gokhman, M. B. Gornung, V. P. Kovalevskii, and Iuri Saushkin—all roughly ten years Gerasimov's junior, asserted that the development of "unified geography" with clearly stated principles and goals was necessary. Otherwise, they argued, geography might become a purely academic exercise relevant only in the classroom.[27] While criticizing Gerasimov for the field's stagnation in the "descriptive" stage, the integrationists argued that geographers needed to utilize mathematical models better and conduct extensive studies on demographics and natural resources to help organizations like Gosplan determine the best distribution of productive strength for the USSR.[28] These articles also argued that Soviet geographers needed to study the economics of nature protection and the environmental protection practices of other countries.[29]

Perhaps more than the integrationists realized, the difference between the traditionalists and them was mostly a matter of priorities and emphasis. Gerasimov, David Armand, Iurii Efremov, and many other Soviet geographers had described at length a range of environmental problems afflicting Soviet society. Moreover, they argued that geographers should lead Soviet society in nature protection efforts and had called for adopting nature protection ideas—especially national parks—from other countries.[30] From 1957 to 1965, Gerasimov visited eighteen different countries. He toured several US national parks on a trip in 1962. This no doubt strongly influenced his belief that Soviet geographers should deal with issues of recreation's geographic organization, as American geographers had been doing since the 1930s.[31] After his 1962 trip, he argued that the national park idea could and should be adopted by the USSR and then adapted to Soviet conditions.[32] Three years later, he made a strong argument to that effect for the creation of a national park on Lake Baikal.[33] However, planning agencies had not given much heed to the environmental forewarnings of geographers, and national parks had no official status in Soviet law. As the economy expanded, environmental problems from pollution to deforestation seemed to worsen through the course of the late 1950s and 1960s. The integrationists' criticisms therefore stuck. Gerasimov and Armand pushed back on the integrationist argument for the establishment of a "unified geography" in their responses in *Literary Gazette*. However, they acknowledged that planning organizations seemed not to account for the negative economic impact of environmental damage, about which geographers frequently forewarned.[34]

Realizing the need to compromise, in the fall of 1966, Gerasimov wrote an article for the publication of the Geographical Society of the USSR, *Questions of Geography* (*Voprosy geografii*), in which he asserted that the dramatic scientific-technical advances of previous years demanded that geography expand well beyond its traditional orientation as a "descriptive science."[35] He called for the expansion of applied methods under the rubric of "constructive geography." Constructive geography, he argued, would help change society's "unreflective" and "consumptive" relationship with the natural world and help develop a more "constructive" and "transformative" approach to it.[36] Among the principal directions for the subfield, Gerasimov included studying and making recommendations for the changing level of the Aral Sea, locating and developing oil deposits in western Siberia, limiting the ecological damage of hydroelectric development, and protecting Lake Baikal. A national park on Baikal, he argued, would provide the institutional framework for the lake's environmental protection and a needed recreational resource for Soviet citizens, especially for the increasing number of stressed, nature-deprived urbanites.[37]

Gerasimov's attention to recreation created an opening for Vladimir Sergeevich Preobrazhenskii. Born in 1918, Preobrazhenskii developed a love for tourism on a twenty-five-kilometer overnight hike at a Young Pioneers camp in the early 1930s.[38] After graduating from Moscow State University (MSU) with a geography degree in 1941, he wrote an article on how to navigate by azimuth in the June 1941 issue of the tourist journal *On Land and on Sea* before it ceased publication following the Wehrmacht's attack on the USSR later that month.[39]

Preobrazhenskii served on the Ukrainian front in the Great Patriotic War and began working at the Institute of Geography in 1947 and Moscow State University (MSU) a few years later.[40] While working in MSU's Geographical Department, he served as the representative of the hiking section in the Department of Physical Education and carried out extensive research on the glaciers of the Kodar Mountains to the east of Lake Baikal throughout the 1950s and early 1960s. During these years, Preobrazhenskii also spent significant time in sanatoria near Kislovodsk in the Stavropol Region of the Caucasus. There he became concerned about tourism's environmental impact through the course of several meetings with the director of the Piatigorsk Spa Research (Kurortologiia) Institute. Preobrazhenskii also realized that no scientific discipline examined the best way for healthy people to spend their leisure time. Like many others, he believed that this was essential for the development of the "new Soviet person."[41] In 1966, Preobrazhenskii, Gerasimov, and others in the Institute of Geography made rough sketches for zoning "territorial recreation systems" throughout the USSR on a "scientific" basis.[42] Soviet recreational geography was born.

In a May 1966 article in *News of the Academy of Science, Geographic Series* (*Izvestiia Akademii nauk:Seriia geograficheskaia*), Preobrazhenskii and N. P. Shelemov described several organizational principles for recreation in the USSR.[43] They argued that nature had always been and would always be a vital necessity to humans. National parks, which would harmoniously develop recreational facilities and protect nature, could help satisfy this need.[44] In early June 1967, Preobrazhenskii represented the Institute of Geography at the conference on the formation of national parks.[45] In 1968, he returned to the oblast to lead an expedition in the territory of Lake Seliger to help make recommendations for the organization of the proposed national park. The expedition's participants made observations on tourism's environmental impact and used sociological surveys to determine the preferences of tourists. While such surveys had been banned under Stalin, they were becoming more widely utilized throughout Soviet society in efforts to determine consumer preferences following the 1965 Kosygin Reforms.[46] Brezhnev had explicitly encouraged the use of surveys and broader sociological analyses by criticizing those who would "limit the social sciences to a purely propagandistic role."[47] Several institutes had begun studying the sociology of leisure time use.[48]

The Institute of Geography expanded its efforts in 1969 when it passed a resolution calling for the organization of a recreation-geographical expedition, which Preobrazhenskii would organize and lead. Assigned the task of the "formation of the theoretical basis of recreational geography," over sixty specialists in physical and economic geography, climatology, and the geography of foreign countries participated in the expedition.[49]

The expedition began in the territory of Lake Seliger, where several divisions continued the previous year's analysis of the impact of recreation on the landscape, created maps for zoning recreational territories, and analyzed the region's economic and geographical characteristics. The following year, the expedition expanded to other European parts of the USSR and devoted particularly close attention to Crimea, the Caucasus, and the forests outside of Moscow.[50] From 1969 to 1972, Preobrazhenskii led groups from the institute. He collaborated with doctors, sociologists, central and regional design institutes, the Administration for Forest Parks of the Moscow City Council of People's Deputies, the Central Council on Tourism, the Crimea Pedagogical Institute, and the Nature Protection Brigades of MSU's Biology and Geography Departments.[51]

In the forests just outside of Moscow, the nature protection brigade of MSU's Department of Geography carried out studies of tourist behavior. These studies separated "recreationists" (*otdykhaiushchie*) into four categories: fisherman and mushroom gatherers, picnickers, tourists who travel by trail, and stationary tourists who leave the city for two or three days and set up camp. While "true tourists," they asserted, value solitude and quiet and demonstrate great respect and care for nature, stationary tourists often caused great damage, which Preobrazhenskii's student Nataliia Kazanskaia categorized in a five-stage model.[52] At the first stage, the forest experienced minimal pressure from tourists and other recreationists and consisted of healthy oaks, maples, and a dense understory. By the fifth stage, trees were in poor condition, and the undergrowth largely consisted of invasive species.[53] By determining "recreational capacity" and "maximum recreational impact," which would vary between landscapes, recreational geographers planned to work with landscape design institutes to "channelize" tourists and prevent these territories from ever reaching the "irreversible" fourth and fifth stages of degradation.[54] The institute proposed these principles as the basis for the organization of national parks, and the plans developed for the first Soviet national parks, founded in the Baltic Republics in the early 1970s, employed them.

In the years that followed, Preobrazhenskii, Gerasimov, and several of the others in the Institute of Geography developed a vision for national parks, about which they wrote extensively. They drew on findings from significant time spent in the national parks of Poland, Czechoslovakia, the United States, and Canada.[55] Some of their ideas, such as using mathematical models to determine the best locations for parks, reflected a somewhat self-conscious, perhaps forced, attempt to assert the young field's scientific authority. While such models were not used to determine the geographical distribution of national parks, the emphasis on "scientific principles" imbued the national park project with the sort of authority that proponents believed was essential for making a compelling case for their establishment. Similar to the definition of national parks established by the IUCN in New Delhi in 1969, recreational geographers argued that parks should be located in the USSR's most scenic territories that had experienced little anthropogenic change.[56] Their vision for Soviet parks voiced some disdain for national parks in the West, which they likely believed was necessary to ameliorate sensitivities about such clear borrowing of a Western idea. In capitalist countries, especially the United States, they wrote, national parks were oriented toward distracting tourists through inundating them with information, which transformed the interaction with nature into "superficial entertainment" while stoking feelings of "national or racial exclusivity."[57] While Soviet national parks would be profit-making establishments, they would stand out from parks in the West for their humanistic principles and environmentally sound organization.[58]

Soviet national parks, the geographers insisted, would be oriented toward the "multifaceted and harmonious development of the personality" and helping citizens overcome the stress and fatigue caused by urban life. They would also instill a stronger "ecological conscience" in Soviet citizens.[59]

Parks in the USSR would take into account the visual "consumption" of natural landscapes and animals, as well as physical activity such as gathering mushrooms and berries, hunting, and fishing.[60] Recreational geographers proposed the formation of four different kinds of parks—landscape parks for light hiking, parks for sporting tourism, hunting parks, and architectural-historical parks. "Transit parks" would form corridors to connect individual parks and form the nexus of a general system of territorial recreation systems.[61]

The particular demands and needs of the population, ascertained through sociological analysis, would determine the organizational principles of individual parks.[62] In consultation with recreational geographers, landscape architects would establish park zones based on the concepts of "recreational capacity" and "maximum recreation impact."[63] While most foresters were slow to see forests as having other uses than as a source of timber, some progressive forestry professionals would embrace these principles in conceiving recreational spaces.[64] Failure to apply these concepts correctly, recreational geographers argued, had resulted in environmental damage to the national parks of the United States.[65] Indeed, the US National Park Service's resistance to incorporating scientific principles into its management strategy was taking an increasing environmental toll, especially since the expansion of infrastructure and roads to accommodate significantly more tourists.[66]

Recreational geographers asserted that as part of territorial recreation systems national parks would spur regional economic development by strengthening the service sector and could be designed to lessen tourism's environmental impact.[67] They would propagate these ideas with slight modifications and continue to articulate the fundamental necessity for an urbanized population to experience nature.[68] In a 1981 publication, Preobrazhenskii wrote:

> The further the process of urbanization advances, the more critical it is for a person to return to the natural environment. Along with the growth of cities and their population, more and more people take off, as it is said, to nature.[69]

By that time, over 60 percent of the Soviet Union's population lived in urban areas, which made the need to experience nature through national parks, according to recreational geographers, a vital necessity.[70]

The USSR's First National Parks

Ideas emerging from the Institute of Geography had considerable influence throughout the environmental protection community, including in the Scientific

Research Institute of Nature Protection (formerly the Central Laboratory of Nature Protection). Like the institute, the Scientific Research Institute strongly valued learning from foreign examples, including national parks. Nataliia Zabelina, a young geographer working in the center, was particularly active in educating the Soviet environmental protection community about American national parks.

Born in Moscow several years before the start of the Great Patriotic War, Zabelina had decided that she would dedicate her professional life to studying the natural world after spending time in forests of the Moscow region on school field trips during the early 1950s.[71] The study of geography attracted her as it did many others with a wide-ranging interest in nature and general concern for environmental protection. After obtaining her undergraduate degree in geography at MSU in 1962, Zabelina began working for the Central Laboratory of Nature Protection. She immediately gravitated to the study of protected territories and by the late-1960s had become one of the institute's foremost experts on the subject.[72] Through correspondence with the United States National Park Service, she obtained information that allowed her to undertake the most thorough examination of US national parks by a Soviet scholar at that time. She would complete her PhD (*kandidatskaia*) dissertation on the organization and economics of national parks in the United States and Canada in 1979.[73]

Aided by Zabelina's research, the laboratory conducted a study for the organization of national parks led by two of the most well-traveled Soviet environmentalists of the day—Lev Shaposhnikov and Andrei Grigorevich Bannikov. Shaposhnikov had been the mainstay of the Soviet delegation to IUCN conferences throughout the 1960s. Bannikov, a biologist who traveled to almost every region of the USSR and several foreign countries, would serve as vice president of the IUCN from 1972 to 1978. The laboratory consulted with international experts and reviewed literature about protected territories from Czechoslovakia, Sweden, Switzerland, Senegal, Romania, Belgium, West Germany, Canada, and the United States as well as the materials from the International Commission on National Parks (ICNP) of the IUCN.[74] Bannikov and Shaposhnikov conducted surveys of different civic organizations, branches of the Academy of Sciences, and various governmental ministries. In total, they received seventy-one responses from different organizations and eleven from individual specialists with a variety of ideas about how best to organize a future system of national parks.[75]

Whether they were called "national," "nature," "people's," "regional," or "state" parks, these places would be dedicated to the promotion of nature protection and providing tourism opportunities.[76] The laboratory did not propose a complete ban on extractive and traditional—fishing, hunting, and the gathering of berries and mushrooms—uses of the land.[77] Limited mining activities would

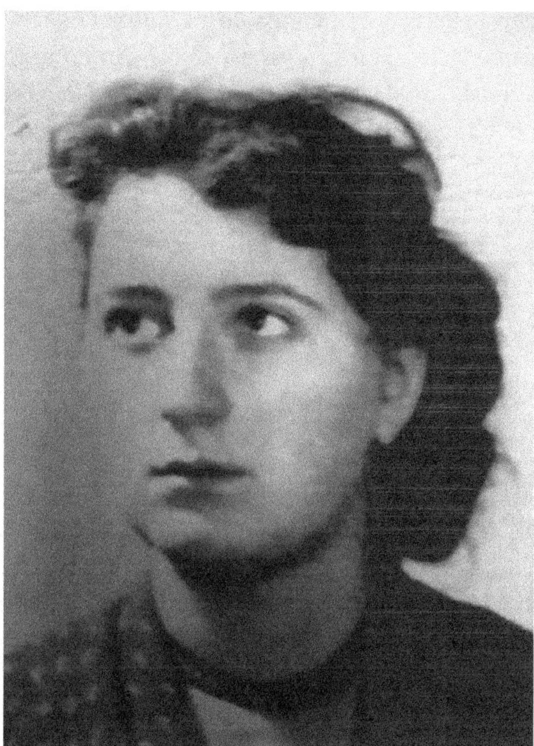

Figure 3.1 Natalia Zabelina in the mid-1950s. Photo courtesy of Natalia Zabelina.

require agreements that included provisions for reclaiming abandoned pits, and forestry activity would be limited to cuts of dead trees. Although the Central Trade Union Council proposed turning many *zapovedniki* into national parks, the Central Laboratory did not support this idea and held that Soviet parks should be a hybrid entity with characteristics of a *zapovednik* and an American national park.[78] The study presented environmental damage wrought by extensive road building and the failure to regulate the number of tourists in US national parks as something of a cautionary tale. Accordingly, it stated that infrastructure should cover no more than 3 percent of a park's territory, but it would be left to individual parks to determine the number of visitors and the specific rules for park visitation.[79] The laboratory acknowledged that the parallel goals of nature protection and providing recreation opportunities posed a dilemma in determining the department responsible for national parks.

In this study as elsewhere, the laboratory suggested that nature protection as well as providing for the well-being of Soviet citizens was an inherently socialist aim. However, the proposal did not specify what would be distinctive about national parks under socialism. Likely due to ideological concerns, some respondents still remained wary about supporting the term national. The

Estonian Academy of Sciences' Commission on Nature Protection, for example, endorsed the name state nature parks and wrote, "Indeed, in the USSR the concept of a national park does not make any sense."[80] Nonetheless, on July 1, 1971, less than two months after the Central Laboratory completed its report, the Estonian SSR Council of Ministers established the first national park in the USSR—Lahemaa National Park.

Lahemaa National Park

Located sixty kilometers to the east of Tallinn, Lahemaa National Park covers a territory of 725 square kilometers and consists of wetlands, old-growth forest, sandy seashores, and numerous limestone cliffs. Twelve rivers run through the area of the park, which lynx, brown bears, moose, and wild boar inhabit. As a border zone with numerous barbed wire encirclements, guard towers, a training facility for tracking infiltrators and areas of agricultural production, much of Lahemaa's territory hardly qualified as a "relatively unaltered" landscape, one of the IUCN's criteria for national parks.[81] Moreover, while Lahemaa's diverse landscapes, wildlife, and views onto the Gulf of Finland undoubtedly possessed an understated beauty, they lacked the sort of awe-inspiring natural features or charismatic fauna that have become associated with national parks of other countries. How and why, then, did an altered area of considerably more modest charms than many places in the USSR become the location of the Soviet Union's first national park?

The small size of Baltic republics, particularly the Estonian SSR, prevented them from harboring illusions of the inexhaustibility of their natural resources. This fact made the Baltic Republics the USSR's most amenable to nature protection. In 1958, the Estonian SSR became the first of the union republics to pass a nature protection law.[82] A 1970 *Literary Gazette* article pointed to the fact that Estonia fully reclaimed all its mines, had banned DDT, and did not allow foresters to take more than the number of cuts prescribed by the plan, praising the Estonian SSR as a model of highly developed ecological consciousness.[83] The Estonian SSR's size also made the organization of a national park a more straightforward task; Estonian scientists and government officials could go from the capital to the proposed park in forty-five minutes, facilitating the process of lobbying by park proponents.

Ivan Borodin, who first proposed a national park system in the Russian Empire, initially discussed the possibility of creating national parks in the Baltics before the Great October Revolution. Estonian scientists briefly discussed the idea again in the late 1920s.[84] The Estonian SSR Ministry of Forestry and Nature Protection revived the idea in 1968 and ordered exploratory work for the park.[85]

Figure 3.2 Lahemaa National Park. Photo by author.

The project received strong support from the head of the Estonian SSR Council of Ministers, Edgar Tonurist, who had established the Estonian Society for Nature Protection several years earlier. The Estonian SSR Scientific-Research Institute of Forestry and Nature Protection, Tatra University, and several architectural design institutes carried out preliminary design work for the park from 1968 to 1970. It is possible but unlikely that the Commission on Nature Protection in the Estonian SSR Academy of Sciences did not know these organizations intended to use the word national. More likely, the commission publicly objected to the use of the word national because it was still concerned that the term in a Baltic Republic might still raise concerns with the Communist Party.

The Scientific-Technical Council of Lahemaa National Park—a civic organization—was established to plan the park in early 1972. The council consisted of specialists in the natural sciences, history, architecture, and Estonian folk art.[86] In developing plans for the park, members of the council had toured national parks in the United States to learn about their methods in harmonizing environmental protection and recreation goals.[87] The council planned five zones: a nature reserve zone, a zone of natural landscapes, a zone of diffuse recreation, a zone of intense recreation, and an agricultural zone. While the reserve zone was off limits, tourists could visit the "zone of natural landscapes" with a guide. The park's stated goal was the protection of forests, wetlands, and historical as well as cultural monuments. It was intended to provide a base for scientific research, educate visitors on the historical relationship between humans and nature, promote the preservation of the "natural" condition of the region, and provide a place for workers to vacation.[88] As the council was working to put these principles into action, Estonia's Baltic neighbor to the south was developing plans for national parks of its own.

Gauja National Park

As tourists traveled to Latvia's Gauja River valley in increasing numbers in the late nineteenth and early twentieth centuries, it was dubbed the "Livonian Switzerland."[89] Foresters first proposed the establishment of a national park in the valley in 1928.[90] Nothing came of this effort, but shortly after the USSR took control of Latvia in June 1940, the Latvian SSR Council of People's Commissars began designating natural monuments (*pamiatniki prirody*) in forests along the banks of the river. Nonetheless, over the next two decades, the valley's ecology progressively deteriorated. Industrial development throughout the republic left its rivers, including the Gauja, polluted. On some weekends, more than fifty thousand tourists visited the valley. In just one year, the visitors totaled nearly one million. The hordes of tourists left no doubt that the valley's aesthetic value exceeded its ruble worth from lumber products, but the area lacked tourism infrastructure, even designated campsites. The mounds of trash left by tourists and the vegetation they cut down led the environmentally conscious public to call for protection for the area.[91]

The park's organization began with the Latvian SSR Ministry of Forestry and Forestry Industry and the Latvian SSR Scientific-Research Institute of Forestry Problems (LSTIFP) together setting up a working group for the park's plan in 1968. Two years later, the Latvian Society for Nature Protection and the Latvian Society for the Protection of Historical Monuments petitioned the Latvian SSR Council of Ministers to establish six national parks in the republic, including one in the Gauja River valley.[92] The Ministry of Forestry and Forestry Industry completed its report for the park organization that same year. It used published proceedings from the IUCN, quotes from Lenin, and publications of recreational geographers to bolster the argument for an expanded and "complex" approach to environmental protection. This approach would include a diverse and flexible system of protected territories that combined ecological enlightenment with recreation opportunities.[93]

Anticipating a dramatic increase of tourists coming from the Baltics and other union republics, the Latvian SSR needed to ensure that recreation had a "scientific foundation" and would not destroy natural monuments.[94] The park administration's first task, the report argued, should be to revive damaged areas by limiting the flow of tourists while simultaneously directing tourists into designated campsites. Only once this had been accomplished could the national park attempt to attract large numbers of tourists. Although the project's authors wanted Gauja to bring profits to the state, they did not want to repeat US national parks' destructive, "commercial" approach to nature.[95]

The proposed park gained the support of influential citizens. In the spring of 1972, the chair of the Plenum of the Latvian Society for Nature Protection, Peter Strautmanis, who was also former secretary of the Latvian SSR Communist Party, wrote an impassioned letter to the chair of the Latvian SSR Council of Ministers, Iurii Ruben, arguing that nature protection was the republic's "socialist duty." He also suggested that it was Latvia's responsibility to the international community:

> The ever-increasing tempo of industrialization and urbanization in countries throughout the world brings with it rapid and profound changes to natural conditions. In the scientific literature of our country and other countries, there is a great concern expressed that the *biosphere* is in danger and states must take immediate measures for nature protection.[96]

He contended that national parks, which in the future should encompass 10–20 percent of the Latvian SSR, could provide the needed opportunities for "landscape therapy" to revitalize the spiritual and physical strength of Soviet workers.[97] Within three months, the Latvian SSR Council of Ministers passed a decree that called for the establishment of a national park of thirty-six thousand hectares, which was expanded by another seventeen thousand hectares on the recommendation of the Ministry of Forestry and Forest Materials.[98]

The public response to the park reflected the growing hopes that national parks could transform the relationship of Soviet citizens to the natural world. Aldis Lauzis's article in *Science and Technology* (*Nauka i tekhnika*) captured this sentiment:

> For a moment, we can again feel a closeness to nature, the sort of closeness that we do not get enough of in the industrial, mechanical, or intellectual labor of city life. In the end, these "immaterial things" are no less important for us than material benefits.[99]

While borrowing from foreign experience, Gauja, he asserted, inspired hope that broad public opinion could be galvanized around nature protection efforts.[100] "Maybe it is still early to speak about the awareness of oneself as part of the surrounding world," an unnamed author wrote in *Soviet Youth* (*Sovetskaia molodezh'*) two years later. "We need to perceive ourselves without separating ourselves from that which is outside of us. Maybe, it is worth starting from something small—for example, ninety thousand hectares of beautiful forest, fields, valleys, and rivers—Gauja National Park."[101]

Through providing direct but mediated and controlled encounters, in which guides would teach tourists the proper relationship to nature, Gauja National Park, its supporters argued, would change the republic's moral climate. Even as journalists expressed concern about the impact of two million visitors a year to the park, they continued to express this aspiration.[102]

The project's authors echoed many environmentalist writers regarding the change of consciousness necessary to preserve the natural treasures of the USSR. Like those supporting other Soviet environmental protection projects, Gauja's progenitors and promoters championed the park as part of an international project to protect the world's biosphere.[103] They scarcely mentioned the park's role in instilling and strengthening a communist world-view. The cultivation of ecological consciousness was a task not limited to a specific political ideology. Environmental protection, for many, was a cause that transcended politics and united the Soviet individual in common cause with all of humanity.

Lithuanian National Park

While the Lithuanian SSR was the last of the Baltic republics to establish a national park, the Lithuanian SSR Council of Ministers had recognized threats to the republic's scenic resources as early as the 1950s. This threat was particularly acute in a densely forested region one hundred kilometers north of Vilnius with over 120 linked lakes, hills, and architectural monuments. By the mid- to late 1950s, tourists from Vilnius were flocking to the picturesque region and setting up "tent cities." The Engels Tour Base, the only tour base in the area, lacked the infrastructure to accommodate the visitors and offered no cultural-enlightenment projects to teach tourists proper behavior in nature. In light of tourists causing significant environmental damage and the region's expanding timber cuts, the Lithuanian SSR Council of Ministers established the Angelina Landscape Reserve and the Ažvinčiai Wood Botanical-Zoological Reserve in 1968 to mitigate the impact of tourism.[104]

Nonetheless, tourists caused progressively more damage to the reserves as they traveled to them in greater numbers. In the spring of 1974, the Lithuanian SSR Council of Ministers established the Lithuanian National Park to regulate tourism better and eliminate the timber harvest in the area. With a territory of 276,000 hectares, the park covered over 4 percent of the land in the Lithuanian SSR.[105] The park's stated goals were to ameliorate the negative environmental impact of tourism; carry out scientific research related to the region's cultural and scientific values; establish "models" of cultural landscape for forestry, agriculture, and fishing; and promote ideas of nature protection and cultural values through educational tourism.[106] The park designers divided it into permanent *zapovedniki* and *zakazniki* zones, zones of recreation, and an economic zone that allowed traditional land uses.

Over the subsequent decade, supporters of other national parks would refer to the development and citizen support of Baltic parks as examples to be emulated.[107] These parks motivated the environmental protection communities in other union republics to push for the formation of parks of their own.

Central Asia and the Caucasus

Nature protection laws passed by the Kazakh SSR and the Turkmen SSR in the early 1960s recognized national parks as official juridical entities at the republican level.[108] However, the first national park equivalent in Central Asia was the Kyrgyz SSR's Ala Archa People's Park. Located on the northern slope of the Kyrgyz Ridge, the park is located forty kilometers from Bishkek. The Kyrgyz SSR Council of Ministers established the park in 1976 to revive areas damaged by tourism, accommodate the anticipated future increases in tourist traffic, and protect the Ala Archa River's unique natural attractions and abundant plant and animal life.[109] With elevations ranging from 1,600 to 4,800 meters, spectacular river valleys, and majestic peaks, the area had long been popular among mountain climbers and trekkers, and at the time of its establishment, there were over 120 designated trails within the park and the surrounding area.[110]

The Uzbek SSR Council of Ministers established Uzbek People's Park in 1978 to protect centuries-old trees, the area's animal population, and the organization of tourism.[111] However, many popular destinations for tourists in the Uzbek SSR and other Central Asian republics had no protection. In 1978, an article in *Turist* asserted that the establishment of high mountain parks throughout Central Asia was necessary to mitigate tourism's devastating environmental impact on the region.[112]

Sevan National Park

Armenia's Lake Sevan had long been the focus for the republic's environmentally concerned public. Sometimes referred to as the "Baikal of the Caucasus," Lake Sevan suffered from the republic's breakneck pace of industrial and agricultural development in the first decades of Soviet rule.[113] During the first five-year plan, Soviet engineers transformed Sevan's main tributary, the Razanskii River, by building a series of dams to generate the power necessary to construct new industries and expand agriculture in the republic. Powered by Sevano-Raszdanskii Cascade, which provided 95 percent of the Armenian SSR's hydro-electricity, the republic built chemical, machine tool, and car factories.[114] From the 1920s to the 1960s, the population of the Armenian SSR nearly doubled, and production grew a hundredfold.[115] Economic growth, however, came at the expense of an eighteen-meter drop in the lake and a contraction of its area by 41 percent over the same period.[116] These changes disrupted Sevan's ecological balance, leaving harmful algal blooms visible in many parts of the lake.[117]

The consequences of the lake's changing level drew the public's attention to other ecological and aesthetic problems, especially the increasing impact of recreation. Sevan had become a popular tourist destination during the 1950s and 1960s and suffered the same problems as other tourism-intensive regions throughout the USSR. The haphazard construction of recreation bases and boarding houses as well as littering made for an unsightly shoreline. In 1966, an *Izvestiia* article suggested that economists had not adequately investigated the economic losses caused by the degradation of Sevan's scenic value. They called for a single steward to oversee the development of recreation on Sevan.[118]

The idea of a national park by Sevan was first written about in the central press by a landscape architect, L. Rosenburg, in a 1967 *Literary Gazette* article.[119] Concerned citizens sent hundreds of letters to the Armenian SSR Council of Ministers calling for the protection of the lake throughout the late 1960s and early 1970s.[120] In 1973, the Armenian SSR Council of Ministers passed a decree banning construction close to the water.[121] As engineers developed plans to raise the lake's level by carrying a portion of the Arpa River to Sevan through a forty-eight-kilometer tunnel through the mountains, radio programs and newspaper articles celebrated the future "transformation" of Sevan into a region of spas, tourist bases, and pioneer camps.[122] The central press highlighted both its natural beauty and its many sites of archaeological interest and called for Sevan to be turned into a recreational region that "would serve all Soviet citizens."[123]

After more than ten years of discussion, the Armenian SSR Council of Ministers established Sevan National Park on March 14, 1978. The park aimed to protect the natural resources of the watershed and its natural and cultural landscapes. It would be responsible for organizing tourism, promoting nature protection, and facilitating research on the biology and recreation resources of the lake. In describing the significance of the establishment of Sevan National Park, the director of the Department of Nature Protection under Gosplan of the Armenian SSR, P. Kh. Petrosian, said, "In the near future, Sevan will be reborn as a place of recreation for the laborers of our country."[124] At the same time that Petrosian was prematurely proclaiming Sevan's "rebirth," geographers, biologists, civic organizations, nature protection advocates, game wardens, and many other concerned citizens were conceiving plans for national parks in the RSFSR.

Planning the Park System and Promoting the Idea

Although the RSFSR could not yet officially have national parks, local and regional governments were already laying the groundwork for them by the early 1970s. Between 1970 and 1972, the Moscow City Executive Committee, the Komi ASSR Council of Ministers, and the Irkutsk Oblast Executive Committee passed resolutions establishing "nature" parks with the goal of each eventually receiving national park designation.[125] Throughout the decade, newspapers, journals, and books described and promoted proposals for parks in the Samara Bend on the Volga, the Altai Mountains, Lake Seliger, Tuva, Karelia, Kamchatka, the Caucasus Mountains near Sochi, the Ugra River, the Sayan Mountains, the Mari ASSR, and the Urals.[126] Actively borrowing from the concepts of recreational geographers and the Central Laboratory of Nature Protection, architectural institutes—Lengiprogor and later Soiuzgiproleskhoz—began working on some of these and other projects. The Ukrainian SSR was also working to establish a set of national parks, and in 1972 it passed a law allowing for the founding of "state nature parks."[127] The Kiev Scientific-Research Institute of Urban Design had developed plans for eight parks by mid-decade, which included parks in the Carpathians, the Shatskii Lakes, and Crimea.[128] Prominent voices in Soviet environmental protection, including Oleg Volkov, Andrei Bannikov, and Iurii Efremov, frequently promoted the establishment of national parks in articles and books.[129]

Few nature protection ideas resonated more deeply among environmentalists and garnered such widespread support throughout Soviet society. An abundance of leisure and vacation time and the USSR's tourism explosion, which accelerated in the 1970s, were most obvious reasons for the popularity of the national park idea. The average Soviet worker labored three hundred hours less per year in 1978 than in 1952.[130] While working less allowed Soviet citizens to pursue hobbies of various types, tourism was one of the most popular uses of leisure time. Several hundred tourist clubs existed in 1979 and there would be nearly a thousand before the USSR's collapse compared to only fifty of them in 1960.[131] In the five years after the passage of the Central Trade Union Council's decree on the "Further Development" of Soviet Tourism (1969), which declared tourism an "industry" of the socialist economy, state investment in vacation facilities—both tourism and spa resorts—increased from 260 million to one billion rubles.[132] By 1979, the Central Trade Union Council was providing services to over thirty million tourists and 165 million excursionists a year, and far more travelers did not use the services of trade union organizations or the Council on Tourism.[133] The number of Soviet citizens that stayed at tourist bases and spas combined reached forty million.[134] However, tourist facilities continued to be inferior to those of spa resorts.[135] While the number of tourists traveling throughout the USSR increased four hundredfold between 1952 and 1975, some planning organizations calculated that the existing infrastructure could only meet 15 percent of the demand.[136] Citizens often provided unofficial lodging and other services to travelers to compensate for the inadequacy of tourism infrastructure.[137] National parks, their supporters believed, would go a long way to resolving this problem.

With more Soviet citizens living in cities, many believed that tourism in "the bosom of nature" (*na lone prirody*) was more important for physical and psychological well-being than any other kind of tourism. While recreational geographers had emphasized the need for people to experience the "primitive life of our ancestors," psychologists began promoting "landscape therapy" as a means of reducing the stress of urban existence.[138] Environmentalists frequently referred to national or "nature" parks as "the most progressive" recreation establishment within the territorial recreation systems.[139] Given the environmental impact of tourism, concern for the preservation of places that could provide this amenity intensified.[140] Although the USSR probably had more territory to meet the recreation demands of its citizens than any other country, park supporters knew that they should not take the country's recreational resources for granted. An internal study by Soiuzgiproleskhoz, which strongly supported establishing national parks, stated, "It is not without reason that some economists believe that the earth's population will first experience a shortage in places for recreation, not food or gas."[141]

The Soviet government started paying significantly more attention to environmental protection in the first years of the decade, passing decrees that declared that protecting nature to ensure recreational opportunities was one of the state's foremost environmental protection priorities. A nature protection decree of the Supreme Soviet of the USSR passed in September 1972 stated, "The resolution of these [nature protection] tasks in socialist society is inextricably connected with the health of the population and with providing Soviet people the necessary conditions for productive labor and recreation."[142] It called on several ministries and departments to prepare for the transfer of forest territory into zones organized for recreation and tourism.[143] The Soviet public, the document asserted, carried great responsibility for the fulfillment of environmental protection tasks. The chair of the Commission on Nature Protection of the Council of Nationalities of the Supreme Soviet, V. A. Karol, reiterated this point. On September 20, 1972, he said:

> We must note the role of our public in the work of improving nature protection. Writers and scientists, teachers and doctors, agronomists, and the many-million army of members of the Society of Nature Protection should actively help in the battle for preserving and increasing the riches of the motherland.[144]

In no previous era of Soviet history had environmentalists, who were attentive to the cues of government and Party leaders, dedicated so much effort to galvanizing public support for the cause of environmental protection.

Conceiving and planning national parks became a popular means through which private citizens, institutions, and civic organizations believed that they could help constructively address environmental problems. Frequently invoking Lenin's love for tourism or Kalinin's statement that "love for the motherland starts with the fields, the forests, the rivers, and the grass," environmentalists as well as tourism promoters and professionals had long argued that tourism was the best way for Soviet citizens to develop a love for, and a desire to defend, nature.[145] By the late 1960s, environmentalists often asserted that the "protection of nature" was the "most important" aspect of the culture of tourism, and tourism clubs throughout the USSR were undertaking environmental protection projects, frequently under the rubric "For a Leninist relationship to nature."[146] Rallying student groups in geographical departments and in nature protection brigades to help plan different national parks on tourist trips suited this emerging orientation of Soviet tourism.

Under the leadership of Valeriia Chizhova, students from the Geography Department of MSU went to Kyrgyz SSR, the Central Urals, and other areas throughout the RSFSR to help plan parks.[147] Iurii Roshchevskii led the nature protection brigades from Kuibyshev State University to help plan a park in the Samara Bend. Komsomol groups from Sverdlovsk helped in the planning of Central Urals National Park.[148] Such efforts exemplified the voluntarism that Khrushchev had called for in the Twenty-Second Party Congress and that continued to expand under Brezhnev.[149] However, connections between different institutes and civic organizations working on parks were almost nonexistent, so they drew up diverse plans that often reflected different priorities. It remained unclear who exactly was leading the national park "movement"—architectural institutes, civic organizations, the Scientific-Research Institute of Nature Protection, the Institute of Geography, the State Committee on Construction and Architecture, or the Ministry of Forestry.

Figure 3.3 Турист—друг природе. Tourist: Friend of Nature. From S. T. Pasechnik, *Turistam o prirode* (Frunze: Sovet po turizmu KSSR, 1974).

Tourism's profitability and the increasing attention that economists were paying to the economics of environmental protection were also behind the popularity of the national park idea.[150] As one 1971 article in *Literary Gazette* put it, "Tourism gives pleasure to the people and revenue to the treasury."[151] By the 1970s, Soviet environmentalists also often argued that the most important aspect of environmental protection was reconciling it with economic growth.[152] In an essay in the journal *Smena* calling for national parks, the novelist Valentin Ivanov emphasized the urgent need for economists to account for the natural environment.

> Each generation inherits tangible assets—fixed assets of the state: the soil, forests, rivers, the sea, the subsoil. And even an average economist understands that the fate of the country depends on the ability of any generation to live by revenues from these assets. Either they will be able through intellect to augment their natural inheritance, or they will eat it up with the prospect of imminent ruin.[153]

National parks would simultaneously make profits and preserve this inheritance for future generations. As associates of the Scientific Research Institute of Nature Protection traveled around the world to examine national parks, they paid close attention to the revenues parks brought to the national coffers. After a 1971 tour of numerous African national parks, for instance, A. Nasimovich noted in an article in *Hunting and Game Management* that these parks produced sixteen million pounds a year for the Kenyan economy and that investment in tourism produced a return six times greater than any other sector of the economy.[154] Anticipating that recreational resources would become scarcer throughout the world in the ensuing decades, architects from Soiuzgiproleskhoz argued that establishing a functional set of Soviet national parks could draw large numbers of foreigners and bring tremendous economic benefits.[155]

More than two decades of unprecedented levels of economic growth accompanied with accelerated environmental change throughout the industrial world had given citizens of both capitalist and socialist countries more time, energy, and cause to reflect on environmental problems. At the same time, images of Earth taken from space greatly strengthened all environmentalists' sentiment that humankind shared a common home and the obligation to protect it for future generations.[156] As international concern for humankind's future on earth reached a new level, cooperation in environmental matters increased among nations throughout the world. In turn, Soviet biologists and geographers continued to strengthen their connections with Western counterparts through multiple bilateral agreements and increase their participation in international conferences, both of which strengthened interest in national parks.

To be sure, many observers, especially in the Institute of State and Law in the Academy of Sciences, expressed deep suspicion of the agenda of Western-dominated nongovernmental and intergovernmental environmental protection organizations. Their views reflected the broader conservative turn in the press that gave renewed attention to imperialistic propaganda and the West's attempts to undermine the position of socialism in the world. V. A. Chichvarin's *Nature Protection and International Relations* (*Okhrana prirody i mezhdunarodnye otnosheniia*) thoroughly reflects this mindset.[157] While Chichvarin argued that the cooperation of Soviet scientists in international environmental organizations was essential for the "prestige of the countries of socialism,"[158] he unequivocally asserted that capitalist countries had historically used nature protection agreements to "camouflage"[159] their colonial agendas that advanced the interests of monopolistic corporations. As a notable example, he called out the Convention on the Flora and Fauna of Africa in 1933, which explicitly stated the importance of establishing national parks in African colonies.[160]

Since the beginning of the decolonization process, the West, led by the United States, Chichvarin argued, had used environmental protection as a ploy to "advance the interests of American imperialism."[161]

> Senator Udall insists that the "world" environmental movement has been strengthened to establish the "world order" that is suitable for American imperialism. The US president in 1963 called on the eighteenth session of the UN General Assembly to adopt a "World Program" for nature protection, which does not stipulate any difference in the status of natural resources.[162]

Although Soviet environmentalists believed that nature protection was a universal goal that transcended political divides, Chichvarin thought that a "world program" led by the United States posed a potential threat to the sovereignty of individual nation states, particularly in the Third World. He reserved his strongest criticism for the internationalization of protected territories, such as international parks.[163] He excoriated UNESCO's plan to establish a World Heritage Trust, which was initially proposed by Russell Train in 1965.[164] He wrote:

> US foreign policy is intensively promoting "environmental protection" and by American representatives in various international organizations. For example, in the IUCN, they, in particular, are deciding on the creation of the "World Heritage Trust of Humanity" and appealing to the UN for its organization. . . . For all this attractive phraseology, it is not difficult to see in it an attack on the principle of state sovereignty over national resources.[165]

Historian Stephen Macekura has also recently suggested that the proposal was grounded in the neocolonial position that "the third world—especially African—countries were not able to manage these lands themselves."[166] Unlike the United States, socialist countries, according to Chichvarin, respected national sovereignty and recognized the principles of "peaceful coexistence," mutual benefits, progressive norms, and an atmosphere of goodwill that were needed as the basis for international cooperation.[167]

While the West, Chichvarin argued, understood the environmental crisis as the result of the "uncontrolled adoption of modern technology," he asserted that the global environmental crisis lay in the exploitative nature of the capitalist system.[168] This argument was repeatedly made in articles in the central press in subsequent years.[169] Works like Paul Ehrlich's *The Population Bomb* served as an example of "bourgeois pessimism" that was part of a "spiritual crisis" of Western intellectuals.[170] Many Western scientists, Chichvarin argued, increasingly understood that socialism's principles, which took a far-sighted approach and sought to curb individual selfishness, were stronger grounds for cooperation in the sphere of environmental protection. Ultimately, the participation of Soviet scientists, he asserted, would help lead to the "unification of humanity" and a more harmonious relationship with the natural world. Having long recognized that workers' revolutions throughout the West were unlikely, Chichvarin, undoubtedly like many others, recognized that for socialism to become dominant, it would need to enter into networks that initially formed almost exclusively among capitalist countries at a time when the USSR was more diplomatically isolated. As more Third World countries joined these organizations, he understood that nonparticipation was not an option for a country that aspired to global leadership.

Brezhnev publicly stated the necessity of such cooperation. At the Twenty-Fourth Congress of the Communist Party in 1971, he declared, "We are ready to participate in collective international projects for the protection of nature and the rational use of natural resources."[171] In 1971, the USSR signed on to UNESCO's Man and the Biosphere project, which provided for the designation of internationally recognized biosphere reserves and sought to reconcile economic development and the preservation of biodiversity.[172] Although the USSR boycotted the United Nations Conference of the Human Environment in Stockholm in 1972 because East Germany was not invited, several Soviet economists participated in meetings of the Club of Rome that produced the book *The Limits of Growth*, which was at the center of the conference discussions.[173]

After not participating in the 1962 World Conference on National Parks in Seattle, the Soviet Union was represented by several scientists at the Second World Conference on National Parks in 1972 at Grand Tetons and Yellowstone National Parks. While the proposal to make Antarctica the first world park demonstrated the extent to which the idea had traveled beyond its original American roots, the host country thoroughly emphasized national parks' rootedness in American history, and many delegates made a point of crediting the host country with the invention of the idea.[174] The "highlight" of the conference, as it was described in the proceedings, was the "rededication" of Yellowstone National Park to all the peoples of the world.[175] There, the leader of the Soviet delegation, V. V. Krinitskii, presented the administration of Yellowstone with a carving and a mount of two Russian animals as he informed them that the USSR was establishing national parks, which he later added were "modeled after the US system."[176] He also expressed his desire to see transnational, boundary, or twinned (such as the Rockies and Caucasus) parks.[177] The chairman of the IUCN's Council on National Parks, Jean Paul Harroy, brought special attention to the Soviet efforts to establish, in addition to existing *zapovedniki*, national parks around Baikal. Even though the

Second World Conference focused far more attention on protecting ecological communities than on preserving scenery for the enjoyment of tourists, Krinitskii perceptively noted a year later that most of world was not familiar with the Soviet *zapovedniki,* despite the fact that ecology had long been their focus. Moreover, he also remarked that US parks, unlike Soviet *zapovedniki,* accrued significant profit—five to six billion dollars a year.[178]

The USSR also signed bilateral agreements for exchanging knowledge and cooperating on environmental protection. For much of 1971 and the first months of 1972, Russell Train, chairman of the US Council of Environmental Quality, and Anatolii Dobrynin, the USSR's ambassador to the United States, hammered out an agreement on how the counties would cooperate on environmental protection matters. At the Kremlin on May 23, 1972, Richard Nixon and Leonid Brezhnev signed the Joint Agreement on the Protection of the Environment as part of the diplomatic visit that produced the Strategic Arms Limitation Treaty (SALT).[179] The agreement established working groups in several areas, including the preservation of nature and the organization of protected territories.[180] It called for exchanges in scientific knowledge, experience, and expertise in environmental protection, the organization of joint conferences, and the joint implementation of projects in applied science.[181] As a result, more than forty projects were established between the USSR and the United States.[182] In subsequent years, the USSR also signed similar, if less extensive, agreements with Japan, Canada, Norway, West and East Germany, Sweden, and Finland.[183]

Russell Train led a US group to the USSR for the first meeting of the Joint Commission in September of 1972, followed by the first working group on the preservation of nature and national parks meeting in the United States in October of 1973.[184] Over the course of two weeks, the US hosts took a Soviet team led by Krinitskii to Dinosaur National Monument in Utah, Rocky Mountain National Park in Colorado, the Institute of Arctic and Alpine Research in Boulder, Colorado, the Scientific Forestry Station in the Frasier Forest in Colorado, the Scientific Center for the Study of Wild Nature in Laurel, Maryland, the Assateague National Seashore in Maryland, and Chincoteague Island in Virginia.[185] Before the United States suspended all activities of the working group when the Soviets invaded Afghanistan in 1979, the group on protected territories met every eighteen months, alternating their visits between the two countries.[186] The working group planned to publish a joint collection of articles on the protected territories of the USSR and the United States, though nothing came of this effort.[187]

Throughout the decade, Soviet environmentalists also visited parks in Africa, Canada, and Sweden that were publicized in the press.[188] However, it was hardly surprising that Russian park supporters focused most of their attention on the national parks of the United States. Their views were mixed. In some instances, they stated that the USSR should model its national parks on the US system, praising its profitability and its role in engendering patriotic feelings. Yet in both articles and their internal reports, Soviet observers noted that American national parks' commercial character was wreaking great destruction upon their environment. Such criticism is hardly surprising, for Garret Hardin, whose writings Soviet environmentalists knew well, had pointed to the US National Park system as a classic case of the "tragedy of the commons."[189] Moreover, the conclusions of A. Starker Leopold and other biologists that US national parks should shift their focus away from mass tourism and toward restoring "biotic associations" and make national parks representative of "vignettes of primitive America" would have likely affirmed the position of many in the scientific community who maintained that the *zapovedniki* were a higher form of nature protection than national parks.[190]

Scientist Nataliia Zabelina concluded, "The economically profitable development of the industry of recreation in the parks has become catastrophic for nature."[191] In addition to the problem of litter, Zabelina noted that this economic rationale prompted national parks to try to eliminate the populations of "bad" animals, including wolves in Yellowstone. The National Park Service's poor management of wildlife was reflected, as one article emphasized, in their permitting the feeding of bears and advertising them as "harmless" animals, even though sixty-three bears had attacked people over a forty-year period.[192] Krinitskii and Uspenskii, the leaders of the aforementioned Soviet delegation to the US in 1973, complimented the exemplary service provided by Rocky Mountain National Park for 2–2.5 million tourists per year but observed accelerated erosion processes in some areas and an absence of animals in others. They also noted that the park did not seem to carry out any efforts to regulate the ecosystem and was not undertaking scientific research.[193]

These descriptions of American national parks aligned with the standard Soviet narrative, which acknowledged that socialist nations had ecological problems but maintained that the capitalist world's pursuit of profit had pushed it to a level of "ecological crisis" not found in the USSR. Even Western authors blamed the capitalist system for the world's ecological crisis.[194] Under Soviet conditions, national parks, their supporters argued, would educate Soviet citizens on the correct attitude toward nature and proper behavior while spending time in it.[195] They would thus help stave off the environmental crisis in the USSR that the West was experiencing.

Frustrations and Hope

While Russian national park supporters criticized the shortcomings of the US system, they still had no successes to show for their efforts to emulate and improve upon it. They undoubtedly realized that the national parks in the United States and other Western countries had saved some of their most scenic areas from resource extraction and the construction of new industry, both of which permanently altered landscapes to a greater degree than mass tourism. In the areas of many proposed Soviet national parks, especially in the RSFSR, industrial and extractive activities not only continued unabated but were in many cases intensifying.[196] Oleg Volkov expressed the frustrations that many environmentalists felt about delays in the passage of a law on national parks. In a 1977 *Literaturnaia gazeta* article, he wrote:

> Life has brought us face to face with the need to improve the organization of our system of nature reserves and to establish natural and national parks. The problem of utilizing areas for recreation and excursions and tourism is acute. One would think that everyone knows about this; there has been a good deal of writing and talk about it. Paper and time are being wasted on opinions and arguments as to whether parks should be called national parks, people's parks, or nature parks. As though that was the main problem! Let us move from words to deeds. Hasn't there been enough deliberating and scribbling as to what sort of national parks exist in the world and where?[197]

Having passionately advocated for national parks on the shoreline of Baikal, Volkov was undoubtedly impatient for the establishment of a park that would help more Soviet citizens see it firsthand.

In addition to disputes over terminology, disagreements among environmentalists about the organizational structure of national parks also prolonged the passage of the law.[198] While park supporters in the Scientific Research Institute of Nature Protection wanted areas dedicated to traditional research, just like in the *zapovedniki*, securing the principle of inviolability over a large territory, and some regulated tourism, Rostislav Dormidontov and other members of the hunting community and architectural institutes wanted parks that attracted mass and varied forms of tourism, including skiing and hunting, to maximize revenue for the state.[199] A second and closely related disagreement concerned which department or ministry would be responsible for national parks. Proponents who viewed national parks primarily as recreational establishments thought that the Council on Tourism in the Central Trade Union Council should oversee them. Supporters of the "museum of nature" approach believed that a new or existing department focused on environmental protection, such as the Ministry of Agriculture's Main Administration for Nature Protection, Zapovedniki, and Hunting, should manage national parks. However, nearly thirty different ministries had *zapovedniki* under their jurisdiction.[200] At various times, Komsomol, the USSR Ministry of Forestry, the Central Council on Tourism, and even the USSR Main Administration for Nature Protection, Zapovedniki, and Hunting had expressed that they did not want responsibility for managing national parks.[201]

The delay in passing a federal law reflected the chasm between the environmental rhetoric of the Party and the Soviet government and the realization of tangible achievements in the field of environmental protection during the 1970s. However, the tide seemed like it might be turning in the second half of the decade. At the Twenty-Fifth Party Congress in March 1976, Brezhnev reiterated his commitment to cooperation in environmental protection and called for a minimum of eleven billion rubles for nature protection in the tenth five-year plan (1976–1981).[202] Because park supporters had always acknowledged that national parks would demand significant capital investment, this promise gave the nature protection community hope that they could develop into the self-financing enterprises that they had envisioned. The following year, the 1977 Constitution of the Soviet Union codified the legal obligation of citizens of the USSR to "protect nature" while giving them the "right" to free time and establishments for quality "recreation" (*otdykh*).[203] In December 1978, the USSR Council of Ministers passed a decree that called on the Academy of Sciences, the USSR Ministry of Agriculture, the State Committee on Forestry, and other relevant ministries of union republics to carry out a study for the establishment of national parks over the course of 1979.[204] Russian environmentalists seemed to be on the cusp of realizing their decades-long hope.

The Model Regulation on State Nature National Parks

During the summer of 1980, twenty-five individuals from the Academy of Sciences, the USSR Ministry of Agriculture, and the Central Trade Union Council gathered in Vilnius in the Lithuanian SSR to iron out unresolved issues about the specifics of the law on national parks that would be signed by the USSR Council of Ministers. Additionally, members of the State Committee on Hydro-Meteorological Service (Gosgidromet), the State Committee of Nature Protection of Union Republics, Gosplan of Union Republics, and the Scientific-Technical Institute of Nature Protection, as well as administrators of national parks, attended. Soviet national parks, participants agreed, had become an objective necessity. In his report, V. V. Krinitskii's statement on their future importance could not have been more explicit: "The development of tourism in our country is a form of care for society and the health and education of those that comprise it. National parks establish the real foundation for the solution to this task."[205]

The representatives agreed that national parks would conform to the international definition established by the IUCN while adapting to "socialist principles" and the conditions of Soviet society. They would have three foundational purposes: providing recreational opportunities, protecting nature, and scientific research. The participants set a goal for every union republic to have one or two national parks by 1990. While emphasizing that the legislation would use the term "Model Regulation" to provide national parks with flexibility in management practices, the participants were emphatic about the need to subordinate national parks to one administrative body in the future.[206] However, continuing disagreement over which governmental body should be responsible for national parks prevented the participants from even including a recommendation on this matter in their draft of the Model Regulation.

The final version of the Model Regulation for "state, nature, national parks," which was signed into law by the USSR Council of Ministers on March 27, 1981, still left dilemmas about national parks unresolved. The wording itself, "state, nature, and national parks," reflected continued unease over the internationally accepted term. While the regulation provided firm ideas for what a national park should be, it lacked clarity on the specifics that would be necessary to realize this vision. Parks would be equally dedicated to nature protection and the development of recreation within their territory. The regulation prohibited the construction of buildings and industrial objects that were unrelated to the function of the park. National park status banned extractive industries from undertaking scouting activity. It banned the gathering of wild plants and mushrooms, livestock grazing, hunting and commercial fishing. In a nod of support for the vision that Krinitskii, Bannikov, Zabelina, and others had long promoted, mass sporting (including skiing) and entertainment activities were banned. Recreational activity within the territory of the parks would be limited to designated areas to mitigate the impact of tourism. These areas would have strict rules about where one could set up tents and start campfires. Parks would allow traditional forms of economic activity—handicrafts and folk crafts and the use of specific natural resources in small designated areas.[207]

Using ideas established by recreational geographers and associates of the Scientific Research Institute of Nature Protection, the Model Regulation called for the division of parks into four zones.[208] The first of these zones would be the reserve territory. In this zone, all recreational or economic activity was prohibited, so it would function as a *zapovednik*. If necessary, the park administration could add or remove areas that needed to be ecologically restored after significant impact from tourism. The second zone was one of regulated recreational use in which tourists could follow trails to various natural or cultural attractions. This area would have small shelters, fire pits, storage points for gas for stoves, overlook points, and signs and maps directing tourists to areas of interest. While the administration of the park would determine the recreational capacity of these areas, it would coordinate with the Central Council on Tourism and Excursions in organizing tourist services in them. The third zone, a service area for visitors, would have campgrounds, hotels, motels, tourism bases, an excursion bureau, information centers, public catering establishments, and trade and cultural facilities. The final zone included communities already living in the territory of the park. There, economic activities that did "not contradict the tasks of the state nature national park" could continue.[209] According to the document, collective farms, forestry districts, and other enterprises, establishments, organizations, and even private citizens would be obligated to compensate the national park for activities that caused damage to the territory.[210]

Three issues proved especially problematic in the subsequent history of the RSFSR and the Russian Federation's national parks. First, although national park proponents had stressed for years the importance of establishing a single administrative organ for managing the system of national parks, the Model Regulation created no such body. Agencies that had traditionally been responsible for the type of resource that fell within the park's territory would administer the respective parks. With the Central Trade Union Council not wanting an active part in administering the system, "recreational resources," or "scenic resources," as park supporters and environmentalists often called them, did not figure into this. Because most parks were located in areas with significant forest cover, the forestry service of different union republics, most of which traditionally had not focused on recreational development or environmental protection, took responsibility for them.

The Model Regulation made no mention of how the state would finance national parks. Park proponents had long maintained that significant capital investment was essential for parks to develop the infrastructure necessary to accrue the profits that would allow them to become self-financing institutions. At the conference in Vilnius, Krinitskii estimated that it would cost tens of millions of rubles to develop a park.[211]

Finally, the document was ambiguous about the acceptable land use by populations living within park boundaries. The document stated that communities could take part in uses of the territory "not contradicting the functions of a state nature national park." However, many of these populations were already taking part in hunting and fishing and the gathering of mushrooms, berries, and other plants, which the regulation explicitly banned. Moreover, while park administrators were responsible for preventing illegal uses of park territory, the Model Regulation did not legally empower them to punish violations. Thus, in addition to the clear potential to alienate the thousands of inhabitants living within the areas of proposed parks, the document gave park administrators the illusion of power but little ability to exercise it. Further complicating the situation was the fact that fully operating enterprises, employing thousands of people and causing numerous environmental problems, were operating within the territory of some of the proposed parks. The Model Regulation provided no guidelines for addressing existing enterprises within national park territory. All of these shortcomings would prove vexing when the RSFSR started establishing parks.

Conclusion

Renowned Russian political scientist Georgii Arbatov said after the demise of the Soviet Union that the leadership of the Communist Party was not seeking paths for renewal by the mid-1970s.[212] While the Soviet Union was hardly a picture of dynamism during the 1970s, this widely accepted notion belies a much more complex reality. Brezhnev and the Communist Party created a cultural environment that helped strengthen the voice of environmentally concerned citizens while giving them more opportunities to collaborate and feel connected to a global environmental protection community more than ever. Environmentalists, in turn, enthusiastically sought ways to reform Soviet society. Despite the frustrations of environmentalists with the state's delay in passing a law that gave national parks federal status, the Soviet government did in the end respond to the wide enthusiasm for parks by passing the Model Regulation. In an era characterized by many by some of its reactionary positions related to cultural policy, passing this law revealed that the Soviet government could be responsive to broad-based calls for progressive reform.[213]

The passage of a law that allowed for the establishment of national parks in every republic hardly constituted the triumph of the Russian or Soviet national park movement, however. Financing and developing an organizational structure for the administration of national parks that would not alienate different interest groups and at the same time achieve the central goals established by the Model Regulation would prove more difficult than passing a law that gave parks official union status. By the late 1980s, political instability and an economic crisis would make it nearly impossible for national parks to fulfill their stated functions. Nonetheless, national parks continued to fire the imaginations of the environmental protection community.

4

Disappointments and the Persistence of Grandiose Visions

On the coast of the starkly beautiful tundra landscape in Chukotka in the Russian Far East, cliffs drop off into the Bering Sea. Just fifty-five miles away sits Alaska's Bering Land Bridge National Reserve. United by the conviction that geopolitics should no longer impede interactions of indigenous groups with deep cultural and historical connections or collaborative efforts to protect a shared fragile ecosystem, a joint team of Soviet and US scientists gathered for the third time in two years in mid-August 1991 to work on planning Beringia International Park (BIP).[1] A Russian national park on the eastern coast of Chukotka and Cape Kusenstern and Bering Bridge National Monuments on the US side would comprise the international park. In addition to facilitating close collaboration with the USSR's traditional geopolitical rival, the planners envisioned that the park would jumpstart a strong ecotourism economy in the region, which they hoped would undercut extractive industries' attempts to gain a foothold in the area. Sharing the growing international concern for the rights of indigenous peoples, they believed that the park would also help revive the cultural traditions of the Chukchi and Yupik inhabitants of the park's territory.

On August 19, news from Moscow that Mikhail Gorbachev had been arrested by a group of hardliners, who claimed to be acting to "save the USSR," interrupted the meeting of the joint group. The Americans rushed to arrange a flight back to Alaska, and the Russian scientists took the first flight possible to Moscow, eight thousand kilometers away.[2]

Though hardly typical, this moment was a flashpoint in the history of Russia's national parks in the decade between the passage of the Model Regulation on State Nature National Parks and the collapse of the Soviet Union. Internationally minded members of the scientific intelligentsia who emphasized the benefits of borrowing from the West and developing closer contacts with Western colleagues had been the leaders of the Soviet park movement from its beginning.

Into Russian Nature. Alan D. Roe, Oxford University Press (2020) © Oxford University Press.
DOI: 10.1093/oso/9780190914554.001.0001

Figure 4.1 Russian-American Working Group on Beringia International Park in 1991. Photo courtesy of Natalia Zabelina.

As the Russian Soviet Federated Socialist Republic (RSFSR) established its first seventeen national parks at a time when domestic political reform increasingly allowed Soviet citizens to express their environmental concerns, the discourse around parks became more deeply intertwined with conversations about the global character of environmental problems. Efforts to establish BIP illustrate how Russian environmentalists felt more than ever before that they were "joining the path of world civilization," as General Secretary Gorbachev said the Soviet Union was doing.[3] However, with the economy collapsing and the USSR destabilizing, parks were unable to meet the high hopes of their founders, who felt that the state of its national parks reflected poorly on the Soviet Union before the world community. While national parks were far from the highest priority at this moment of political crisis, the abrupt departure from the Beringia planning meeting provided yet another reminder that political instability might undermine the transformative visions of park supporters. This chapter will illustrate this growing distance between the high hopes inspired by national parks and the myriad problems facing them as the Soviet economy cratered and the Communist Party's political authority was crumbling.

Questions of Organization

As environmentalists throughout the RSFSR and USSR advocated for the establishment of individual parks, the USSR State Committee on Forestry began working on a report entitled "on the organization of the study and use of the foreign experience on the establishment of national parks" in 1982. Different state ministries and individual parks expressed that the lack of a central administrative organ for administering parks was the biggest obstacle to establishing a functional system.[4] However, no one agreed which ministry should have jurisdiction over parks, and no ministry expressed interest in assuming the responsibility.[5]

By 1985, thirty ministries and departments on the republic level were responsible for 144 *zapovedniki* and thirteen national parks in the USSR. The RSFSR had four national parks—Elk Island in Moscow, Sochi in the Caucasus, Samara Bend along the Volga, and Maria Chorda in the Marinskii Oblast. Before the collapse of the Soviet Union, it would establish thirteen more. In 1986, the RSFSR Council of Ministers established Pribaikal'skii and Zabaikal'skii National Parks on the western and eastern shoreline of Lake Baikal, respectively. Five years later, it established Tunkinskii in the Sayan Mountains just south of Baikal. In the Kuzbass Region, it created Shorskii National Park in 1989. In the Caucasus, Prielbrus was established in 1986. In the Urals, Russia established Bashkiriia (1986), Taganai (1991), and Nizhnaia Kama (1991). In the Kaliningrad Region, the Curonian Split was established in 1987. Just north of Lake Seliger, the RSFSR founded Valdai in 1990, and in the far north of Karelia and Arkhangelsk Oblast, it established Kenozerskii and Vodlozero National Parks in 1991. By this time, the seventeen parks in the RSFSR covered 3.6 million hectares.[6] Because each park held significant stands of forests, the RSFSR Ministry of Forestry had jurisdiction over all Russian national parks, but parks were usually answerable to regional forestry administrations.[7]

Journalists and park supporters spilled much ink during these years about the lack of organizational coherence.[8] In 1990, A. Vasnetsev, a representative of the Union of Journalists; G. Vzdornov, a professor of Art History; Valentin Rasputin, a famous writer, defender of Siberian nature, and member of the Presidential Council of the USSR; and S. Iamshchikov, a representative of the Association of Restoration of the USSR wrote a letter published in *Pravda* that expressed frustration and even a bit of embarrassment over the situation.[9] They wrote:

> In all civilized countries national parks are managed by designated and competent departments, which are part of the presidential administration. We think that the RSFSR should have an analogous system. National parks are the calling cards of the country, characterizing the state's attention to the questions of nature protection.[10]

Their letter reflected the broader discourse taking place throughout educated society in which the word Soviet was often used, as the author Arkady Ostrovsky has written, "as an antonym to normal or civilized."[11]

Without a ministry dedicated to their management, Russian national parks were beset from the beginning by a lack of understanding about their central functions and purposes, even among those directly responsible for overseeing their management. Although *zapovedniki* had frequently struggled to preserve the inviolability of their territory, the ministries that had jurisdiction over them understood their purpose, even if they did not always wholly value it. National parks were new and did not make claims to "inviolability" but rather to the "complex" use of land. Regional administrators, therefore, viewed them as a hindrance to the exploitation of natural resources and were more than willing to test the new legal restrictions that they imposed on land use. Moreover, the trained foresters who often had a direct role in their management knew little about recreational development and were often little interested in protecting park lands from extractive uses as was required by law.

Violations of the Model Regulation were rampant. Appeals of the administration of Pribaikal'skii National Park to the Irkutsk Oblast Executive Committee to prevent illegal cuts in the park's territory led to foresters blatantly sabotaging the work of the national park.[12] In Sochi National Park, the Krasnodar Forestry Administration expanded the timber harvest in the park's territory in each of the years following its establishment. Relict species were reported to have disappeared.[13] In Samara Bend National Park, illegal mining within the territory of the park continued after its establishment.[14] Because of the command economy's generous rewards to ministries for fulfilling production quotas and the absence of conservation incentives, it is hardly surprising that the managers of forestry districts had difficulty adjusting to a completely new, conservation-oriented, juridical entity under their supervision.[15]

Developing recreation infrastructure and hiring qualified staff were both expensive, and national parks lacked the funds for either of these. From 1981 to 1987, national parks in the RSFSR received a small fraction of the two hundred million rubles dedicated to the staffing, maintenance, and development of protected territories. Sochi National Park, for instance, received only 150,000 rubles for recreational development in 1986 even though the Central Laboratory of Nature Protection had estimated that the development of individual parks would cost tens of millions of rubles.[16] In most national parks, recreational facilities remained undeveloped, and park administrations ignored nature protection projects. In late April 1986, a Gosplan report about the efforts to develop national parks concluded:

> The work on the construction of a set of roads, of excursion trails, of administrative-organizational buildings, of museums of nature, hotels,

> camping, and other objects necessary for realizing the enumerated tasks for them, especially the establishment of conditions for the organization of the leisure of working people, is not being carried out.[17]

Less than two weeks later, the Commission on Nature Protection under the RSFSR Council of Ministers expressed an even more critical judgment on the state of the RSFSR's national parks. It wrote:

> The development of the design work of national parks has been unacceptably delayed. Only in April of 1986 did the Ministry of Forestry review the foundational materials for the establishment of Sochi Park. For Elk Island National Park, the Moscow City Executive Committee has not approved the design documentation. The development of such documentation for Samara Bend is also dragging on. The necessary restructuring of economic activity in correspondence with the Model Regulation on state nature national parks is not being carried out. For the maintenance of parks, insufficient means are being dedicated. Most of them are being given to forestry projects. An unjustifiably large volume of cuts continues, bringing damage to the natural landscape, and the necessary work for the landscaping of the parks and the excursion work meant to serve the population is not taking place. The issues on the withdrawal from their territory of enterprises and organizations whose activities do not correspond to the established regime are being resolved slowly.[18]

The RSFSR Ministry of Forestry, in turn, argued that the "astronomically" vast territories of national parks meant that the development of parks would take far longer than their supporters and the RSFSR Main Administration of Hunting and *Zapovedniki* had wanted.[19]

In addition to the many problems enumerated by Gosplan and the Commission on Nature Protection, departmental recreation bases continued to operate despite being banned by the Model Regulation. They were frequently the sites of the most reviled behaviors of "uncultured" tourists. Parks were often severely littered. An article in *Pravda*, for instance, described Prielbrus National Park as strewn with household appliances.[20] While the failures of national parks to prevent illegal uses of their land and manage tourism were almost universal, nowhere was this more visible than in Elk Island (Losinyi Ostrov) National Park in Moscow.

The Forest in the Metropolis

Elk Island National Park provides a striking example of both the struggle that national parks faced in preventing illegal uses of their territory and meeting their stated goals to become schools of ecological education. Throughout the late 1960s, Konstantin Blagosklonov, the pioneer of Soviet environmental education and founder of the nature protection brigades (*druzhiny*), took students from the Department of Geography of Moscow State University (MSU) and the Geography Club of the Moscow Zoo to the territory of the future park and other forests in and around Moscow.[21] Blagosklonov and his students carried out studies on the impact of tourism on Moscow's forests and the recreational preferences of Muscovites in conjunction with recreational geographers at the Institute of Geography and MSU. He frequently spoke with his students about the importance of establishing a national park in Elk Island.[22]

One of Blagosklonov's students, Boris Samoilov, believed that a national park in the territory of Elk Island would make the USSR a pioneer in urban ecology. After graduating from MSU in 1968, Samoilov worked in a *zapovednik* in the Novosibirsk Oblast. He returned to Moscow in 1971 to work in the central office of the Central Laboratory of the RSFSR Main Administration for Hunting and Zapovedniki, located in the heart of Elk Island. Samoilov mentioned the national park idea to the director of the laboratory, Victor Gavrin, a biologist who had recently arrived from Belorussia SSR's Belovezhskaia Pushcha Zapovednik. Shortly after that, Gavrin proposed the idea to Viktor Vasilevich' Grishin, the head of the Moscow City Committee of the Communist Party. On July 14, 1972, the Moscow City Executive Committee passed a resolution that ordered General Plan of Moscow to develop the technical and economic foundations for Elk Island Nature Park.[23]

Samoilov's conception for Elk Island demonstrated the flexibility of the national park idea, which some Soviet environmentalists had long argued was one of its main advantages over *zapovedniki*. Although the IUCN's criteria for national parks emphasized that they should not be located in developed urban areas, Elk Island was situated in a city with a population of six million by the early 1970s.[24] As we walked around the territory of the park in the summer of 2014, Samoilov reflected:

> We believed that we must preserve wild nature not only in remote regions but also in the places next to where we live, mainly in large cities, especially a megalopolis. First off, the protection of nature—the air and the water sources—is necessary for such areas. At the same time, it is in the big cities where they make the critical governmental decisions and where government officials are educated. In a territory like Elk Island, it is more likely that they can be taught in a way that will make them care about nature.[25]

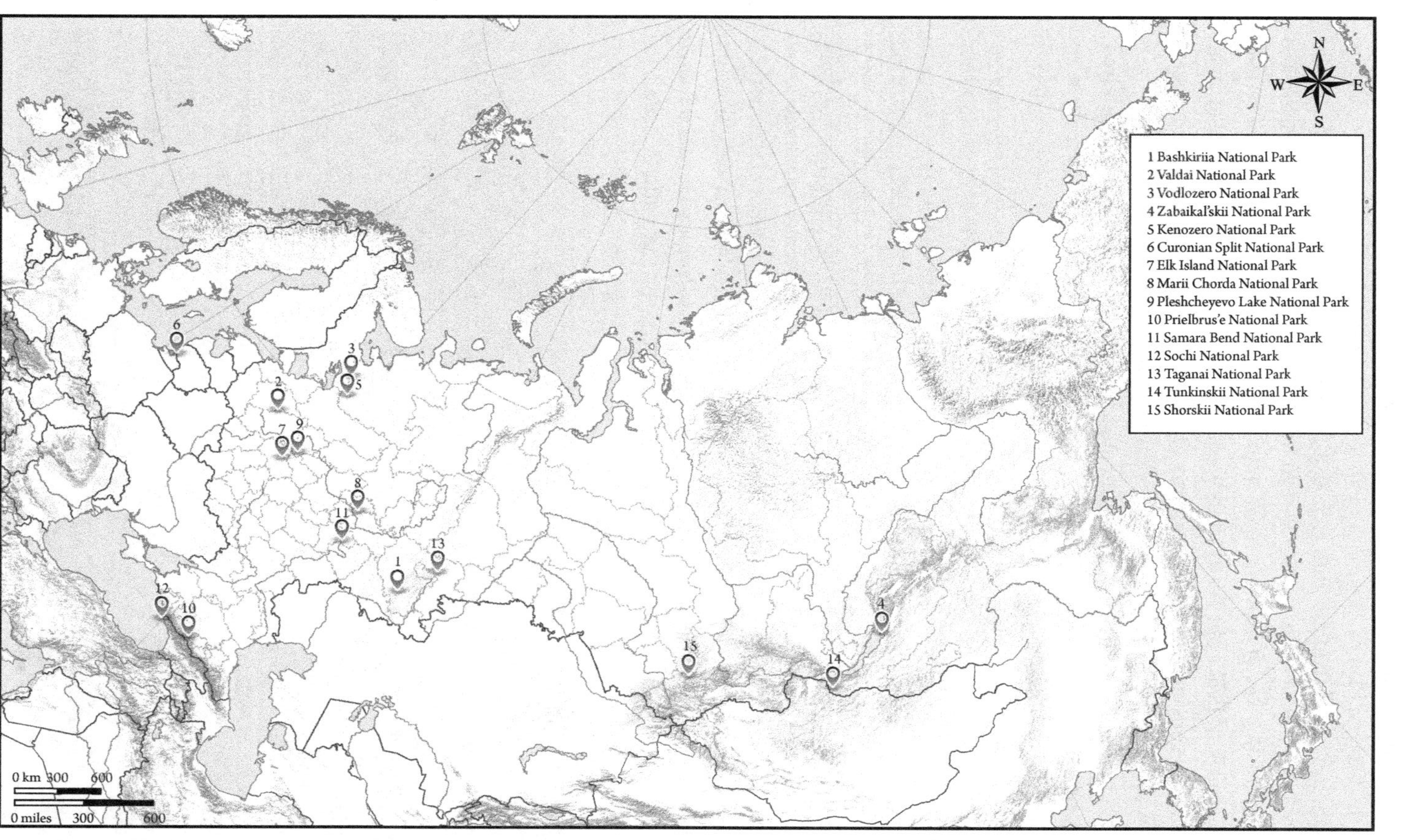

Figure 4.2 Parks prior to the fall of the USSR.

In the years that followed, while he was serving as the primary ecological consultant to the General Plan of Moscow and Soiuzgiproleskhoz (Union Landscape Design Institute), which had the joint responsibility for designing the park, Samoilov enlisted the help of soil scientists and biologists to help plan the park.[26] He invited many of the Soviet Union's most influential environmentalists—among them Oleg Volkov, Feliks Shtil'mark, and Vladimir Chivilikhin—to Elk Island in an attempt to convince them of the merits of an urban national park.[27] According to Samoilov, over the course of the decade, they gradually warmed to the idea.

Together with the landscape architects, Samoilov envisioned a hundred-square-kilometer park with trails along its periphery, which would make it accessible to all Muscovites.[28] Park goers with more time could venture deeper into the park's interior on trails that would have an explicit focus on ecological education.[29] The recreation centers, located throughout the park, would be focused on educating visitors about the territory's plants, animals, and history. Visitors would have to receive special permission to visit the reserve zone, where deer, wild boar, elk, and many other mammals not typically found in major metropolitan areas lived.[30] Every aspect of the park's design and activity, Samoilov believed, must serve its goal of being "an authentic [*podlinnyi*] ecological school that educates not simply nature lovers but patriots of the motherland who know and will protect the native soil."[31] In consultations with Samoilov and Soiuzgiproleskhoz, the Moscow City Council of People's Deputies passed a resolution in 1979 that outlined the boundaries of the park. It called for

Figure 4.3 Boris Samoilov. Photo by author.

wide-ranging restrictions and infrastructural development to be carried out in a way that would mitigate tourism's environmental impact.[32] The problem's urgency increased in the years that followed. One publication estimated that as many as three million Muscovites spent some time in and around the city's forests each weekend during the early 1980s and warned that Elk Island might be irreversibly damaged unless "immediate action" was taken.[33]

Evgeny Syroechkovskii, the former head of the Central Laboratory of Nature Protection, wrote to the Presidium of the RSFSR Council of Ministers and urged it to "accelerate the organization of the park" in the spring of 1983.[34] He called Elk Island the "most important natural attraction" of Moscow and the surrounding area and warned that the lack of organization in the proposed territory of the future park had resulted in the disappearance of different plants, mammals, various species of owls and other birds of prey, and many reptiles. Syroechkovskii concluded his letter by asserting, "We must take into account that the establishment of the first nature national park in the Russian Federation has tremendous significance."[35] Many Russian conservationists who had been skeptical about the idea of an urban national park now agreed that Russia should not waste this opportunity. Samoilov was surprised when Syroechkovskii requested the planning documents for Elk Island, which he then sent on to the Council of Ministers. On August 24, 1983, the RSFSR Council of Ministers officially established Elk Island as the RSFSR's second national park, three months after Sochi National Park became the first.[36]

Elk Island, like most national parks, was placed under the Ministry of Forestry, but the forestry districts in which the park's territory was located were responsible for managing it. Employing few qualified specialists in nature protection, the park's management regularly allowed timber harvesting in excess of the maximum "sanitary cuts" while redesignating significant portions of the "reserve zone" (*zapovednaia chast'*) as part of the recreational zone. Articles in the press commented on the indifference to conservation among the foresters working in the park.[37] With the Mityshinskii Forestry District the only body with official administrative authority over the park's territory, recreational facilities, unsurprisingly, were not developed.[38] Because the park was always understaffed, it relied on voluntary green patrols from Komsomol (Youth Communist League) divisions to protect the area against unlawful cuts and illegal hunting and fishing.[39] But there were not enough volunteers to carry out these tasks effectively. Private citizens continued cutting wood and setting hunting traps for wild boar, while others used banned fishing hooks in the park's reserve territory.[40]

As Grigorii Kozhevnikov had lamented nearly eighty years earlier, residents of areas neighboring the park cultivated personal gardens in the park's territory with impunity.[41] Five years after the park's establishment, twenty enterprises

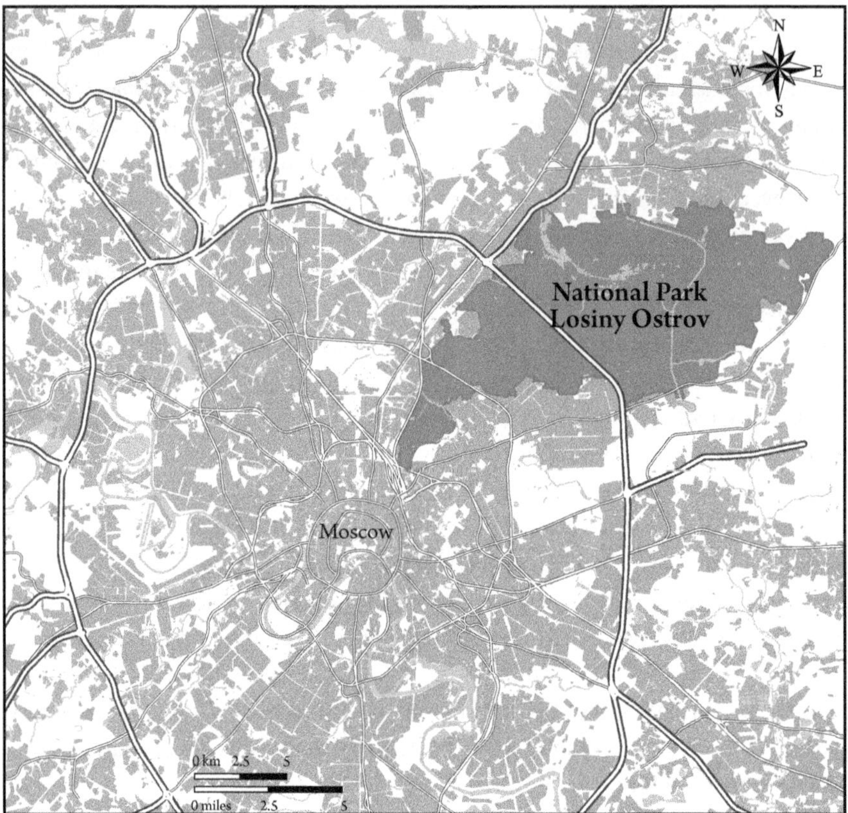

Figure 4.4 Elk Island National Park.

whose activities had no relationship to the park continued to operate within it.[42] One of these enterprises, a rubber boot factory called Red Knight (Krasnyi bogatyr'), dumped its effluents directly into the park's creeks, which flowed into the Iauza River.[43] The litter problem worsened each year despite regular voluntary workdays (*subotniki*) when "nature lovers" cleaned it up.[44] The plant and animal life continued to suffer.[45]

Soviet citizens became more concerned about environmental issues in the aftermath of the Chernobyl catastrophe in the spring of 1986. Meanwhile, the "sustainable development" discourse that started dominating discussions of global environmental problems in 1987 after the release of the United Nations Brundtland Commission Report quickly took root in the USSR.[46] In addition, Gorbachev's glasnost reforms allowed Soviet citizens to express their views, increasingly informed by knowledge about environmental protection practices in the West, more forcefully and publicly. The General Secretary's creation of the State Committee on the Environment (Goskompriroda) in

1988, for which Soviet environmentalists had lobbied many years, emerged from this growing concern for environmental problems and enabled its further spread. As citizens throughout the USSR took part in various environmental protests, environmentalists sought to pressure government officials to develop and protect national parks. National parks, in turn, frequently became rallying points for the public to address local and regional environmental concerns. Because of its location in Moscow, Elk Island National Park was uniquely positioned to become both a vehicle to address broader issues of urban health and ecology and an example of the shortcomings of Russian national parks.

Samoilov expressed particular concern about the park's failure to realize his ambitious vision and what this might mean for the national parks movement in the RSFSR. In an article in *Nature and Humans* (*Priroda i chelovek*), after sardonically suggesting that the park might need to ban all humans to ensure its protection, Samoilov wrote, "We cannot afford to reinforce the opinion of people that a littered forest can be considered a national park."[47] He continued: "The first impression that one has of Elk Island is that of an indifferent relationship to nature." He believed that the current condition of Elk Island was "discrediting the goals and tasks of a national park."[48] Newspapers, journals, and television programs regularly covered the park's problems in articles with such titles as "Our Home under the Bulldozer," "Clouds over Elk Island," "Do You Love Elk Island?" and "Will Elk Island Survive?"[49] Letters from citizens concerned about the park's fate flooded the mailboxes of the USSR and RSFSR Council of Ministers, the Moscow City Council of People's Deputies, the Moscow Oblast Executive Committee, the Moscow Oblast Council of the All-Russian Society for the Protection of Nature (VOOP), and the editorial boards of numerous publications.[50] One letter, signed by over a thousand residents of Moscow's Kaliningrad district, located just north of the park, accused the district's executive committee of misinforming the public about their "barbaric attack" on the park, which included an attempt to appropriate over a thousand hectares of the park for various construction projects.[51]

Elk Island also became a focal point in the battle against the construction of the Northern Thermal Electric Station. The plant, which would have been the largest of its kind in Europe, would have emitted sulfur gas, nitrogen oxide, and other dangerous pollutants that would threaten the park's forest cover.[52] In January of 1989, a segment on the television program *The News of the Day* (*Novosti dnia*) showed images of wild boar, elk, red squirrels, and other animals in the park's territory juxtaposed with images of abandoned industrial equipment in the park. It then showed protesters holding signs objecting to the construction of the electric station, while the narrator said, "The construction of

Northern Thermal Electric Station continues as if there was not an outpouring of the public sentiment against it. Of course, the station is necessary for the enterprises that will be constructed. But why must this be done right next to a national park?"[53]

In the spring of 1989, nearly sixty thousand residents of the Kirov, Babushinskii, and Timiriazev regions of Moscow and the Mytish Region in the Moscow Oblast signed a collective letter to Nikolai Ryzhkov, the chair of the USSR Council of Ministers, stating, "The people's mood has darkened because the belief in the bright future is being lost, knowing that an ecological bomb is being planted in Moscow."[54] The plant's proximity to Elk Island, they argued, was among the many reasons that it should not be constructed. In the two months that followed, seventy-four people's deputies signed a letter calling on the USSR Council of Ministers to address the problems surrounding the park.[55] Responding to the public outcry and the pleas of government officials, Ryzhkov and Lev Zaikov, secretary of the Central Committee of the Communist Party, visited the park in late July.[56] On August 31, 1989, the USSR Council of Ministers passed the decree On Saving and Further Developing the State National Park Elk Island, which called for the resettlement of people living within the park's territory, the removal of more than forty enterprises, and the re-cultivation of damaged land. Most importantly, the RSFSR Council of Ministers canceled the plans to construct the Northern Thermal Energy Station.[57]

This victory for Elk Island, however, proved short-lived. By the following winter, none of the enterprises had been removed, the recultivation efforts were not taking place, construction had resumed, and citizens' renewed letter-writing campaign was to no avail.[58] The city administration argued that the station was necessary to avert an energy crisis.[59] With the national economy collapsing and the government sinking into administrative paralysis, measures to improve the condition of Elk Island went unrealized, and national parks throughout the RSFSR mostly existed in a state of neglect. At a meeting of Goskompriroda on November 29, 1990, one participant stated:

> We establish national parks on paper. We have three national parks in the Baltic, but the others exist only on paper. For example, look at Elk Island National Park. We don't yet have a document about land use in it. How can we say that is a national park?[60]

The park's visibility was indeed educating the broader public about national parks, just not in the way that Samoilov had hoped. At the same time, it was reminding the environmental protection community about the many shortcomings of national parks.

Stopping Extraction, Loving Nature

Despite growing concerns about the state's inability to provide for already established parks, the enthusiasm for new parks gained strength amid the rising tide of environmental concern and the state's expressed commitment to addressing environmental problems.[61] By the late 1980s, the recreational geographers in the Institute of Geography argued that 10 percent of the country's territory and 30 percent of the European part of the country should be devoted to tourism resources. Much of this, they believed, should be national park territory.[62] Led by Nataliia Zabelina, the scientists from the Scientific Research Institute of Nature Protection spent significant time in Kamchatka, Chukotka, the Tadjik SSSR, the Georgian SSR, the Azerbaijan SSR, and the Kyrgyz SSR on trips planning national parks throughout the decade. Environmental protection was not just an issue of narrow scientific interest but also one of conscience and morality. In 1985, the institute completed its twenty-year plan for the development of national parks, which was published in Zabelina's book *National Park* (*Natsional'nyi park.*)[63] The institute planned for the establishment of up to fifty national parks by 2000.[64] The book conveyed the many benefits the parks could bring. She wrote:

> The natural values of a national park are capable of psychologically orienting the personality toward a particular style of mutual relationship with wild nature. The methods of a national park educate tourists on how to be careful in nature.[65]

Much like Samoilov, Zabelina argued that national parks would become incubators of environmentally oriented civic activism.

While national parks did in some cases help to rally the general public around environmental problems, this was not because they had successfully developed environmental education programs that fostered environmental civic consciousness. Instead, widespread notions about what a national park should be emerged from the environmental protection community's broader understanding of national parks in other countries, especially those in the United States. National parks in Russia, after all, were still in the nascent stages, and the costly plans of the architectural institutes Lengiprogor and Soiuzgiproleskhoz, both of which had been working on national parks since the 1970s, remained unimplemented. However, along with the reputation of parks in other countries, the efforts and the expanding literature promoting a national park system encouraged different interest groups throughout Russia to conceive and push for the establishment of parks. Calling for the creation of national parks, in turn, became a popular form of grassroots environmental advocacy and an increasingly compelling argument for alternative visions of economic development in the RSFSR during the final years of the USSR.

The projected profits from tourism, which had long been one of the primary justifications for national parks, meshed with the emphasis on self-financing and market-based incentives in Gorbachev's economic reform agenda.[66] National parks, therefore, were championed both for their potential to transform the relationship between humans and nature and also as an economic rationale for blocking industrial projects and the expansion of extractive industries. Existing and proposed national parks strongly informed some of the most contentious environmental debates of the Gorbachev era. Three examples in Siberia and the Far East—in the Altai Mountains and on the Kamchatka and Chukotka Peninsulas—are particularly illuminating.

The "Altai Alternative": Hydroelectric Development versus Tourism in the Altai Mountains

The movement to establish a national park in the Katun River valley of the Altai Mountains demonstrated a seismic shift in the perception of large-scale river transformation projects in the Soviet Union.[67] From the 1950s to the 1970s, Soviet planners prioritized large-scale hydroelectric projects to provide the energy to turn relatively backward regions of Siberia into powerhouses of industry. The Bratsk, Krasnoyarsk, Saiano-Shushenskaya, and Ust'-Ilimsk Hydroelectric Stations (GES) all became symbols of the Soviet system's capacity to alter the natural world. Soviet propagandists boldly asserted that only socialist economic systems could achieve such feats. The stations' construction proved socialism's superiority to capitalism.[68]

Large dams were iconic symbols of economic and industrial progress and, in turn, were seen as an enormous benefit to society for decades. Valentin Rasputin's *Farewell to Matyora* (1977), which portrayed the tragic resettlement of a village on an island in the Angara River awaiting inundation, began to change the accepted narrative about hydroelectric development.[69] Never before had an influential public figure so publicly illustrated the adverse consequences of dam construction for traditional rural communities.

Rasputin's book, however, probably resonated less with hydroelectric engineers than it did with the average Soviet citizen. In the late 1970s, Gidroproekt and other institutes nonetheless resurrected an idea for damming the Katun River to transform the "backward" and mountainous Altai Region. The project became part of the official party program at the Twenty-Sixth Party Congress in 1981.[70] In the years that followed, central newspapers celebrated

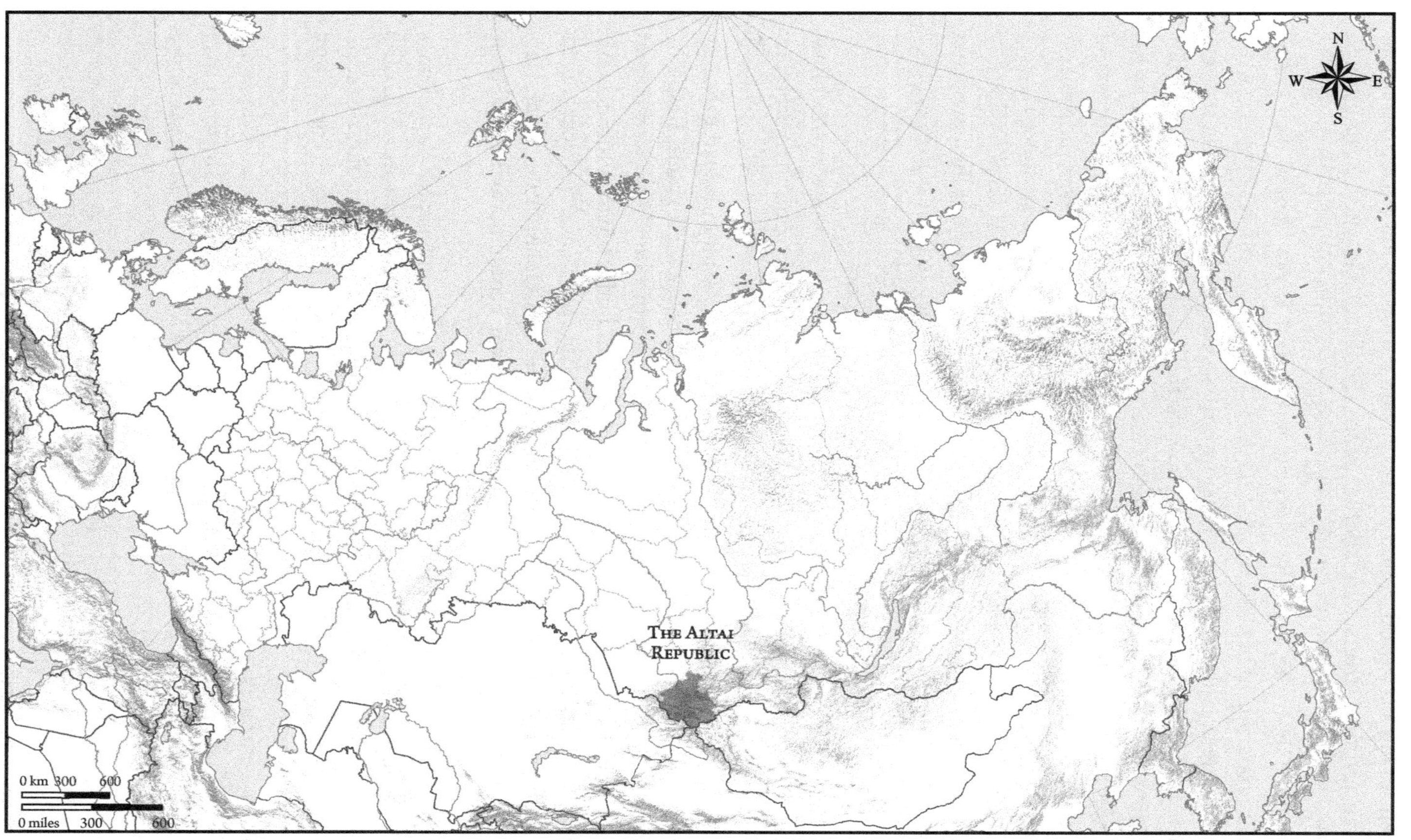

Figure 4.5 Altai Republic.

the economic growth that the dam would bring to the region while barely mentioning ecological consequences.[71] But the celebratory narrative about "transforming" rivers took another more significant hit when Rasputin and other writers led a national campaign against the plan to redirect the north-flowing Ob, Irtysh, and Yenisei Rivers to the Aral Sea in Central Asia.[72] This idea was dropped in 1986.

That year, Gidroproekt and other institutes were preparing to begin the construction of the first of a series of dams on the Katun. But environmental disaster was on many people's minds after Chernobyl, and scientists throughout the USSR became increasingly concerned that a Siberian dam could be the source of a future catastrophe. They believed that Gidroproekt had not taken the project's potential ecological impact on the region into account. On December 1, 1986, Iu. Vinokorov, the head of the laboratory of ecology in the Siberian Division of the Institute of Geography, and A. Vitovtsev, a journalist from the newspaper *The Altai Star* (*Zvezda Altaia*) called for a conference to discuss the proposed Katun Hydroelectric Station in light of the adverse ecological consequences caused by big dams in Siberia in the previous three decades.[73]

The regional press would cover the issue extensively in the years to follow. Articles raised concerns about the potential for mercury poisoning, the loss of architectural heritage, and the dangers of building a dam in a seismically active zone. Famous cultural figures such as Valentin Rasputin helped galvanize opposition to the dam.[74] In regional radio and television programs, Rasputin, who had also been active in fighting for Baikal's protection, gave such memorable statements as "Wherever an armada of dam builders passes through, nature is left incurably ravaged."[75] In meetings with the Second Secretary of the Communist Party of the Gorno-Altai Autonomous Oblast, Valerii Ivanovich Chaptynov, Rasputin emphasized the long-term economic and therapeutic value of preserving scenery.[76]

Residents of Bisk, a city of about two hundred thousand located on the banks of the Biia River into which the Katun flows, were particularly worried. In early 1987, the Biisk Literature Association, the Council of Veterans, the city committee of Komsomol, the Biisk division of the VOOP, the Biisk Local History Society, the Biisk Club of Tourists, and the Biisk Travel and Excursion Bureau of the Central Trade Union Council formed an initiative they called "Mountain Altai—national park of the country!"[77] In a collective letter, signed by more than 1,500 people and printed in *Komsomol Pravda* (*Komsomolskaia Pravda*), the authors wrote:

> Is it possible you ask, after the catastrophe of Sevan, the misfortune in the Ob Sea, where now only one turbine works and not at full power, the appearance of terrible ecological conditions after the construction

> of the Bratsk and Krasnoyarsk Hydroelectric Stations that we will destroy the most vulnerable parts of the Altai?[78]

In an editorial printed alongside the collective letter, S. Brovashov called for the end of the "war" against Siberian rivers and stated that public opinion "must be taken into account."[79] Citizens' groups also formed in Moscow, Leningrad, Novosibirsk, and Barnaul to protest the dam.[80] Among concerned groups, the "Altai alternative"—the creation of a national park—became arguably the most important rallying cry in the public fight against the proposed Katun GES.[81] In the months following the proposal of the national park, the local press printed several articles in support, with one even stating that tourism in the region would grow threefold to nearly five million people a year by 2000.[82]

Siberian scientists continued to dedicate significant attention to the problem. In July 1987, the Presidium of the Siberian Division of the Academy of Sciences called for the development of a "complex territorial scheme" for the development of natural resources in ways that did not damage the region's ecology and raised the question of the advisability of creating a recreation zone and *zapovedniki*. While the scientific community gave recommendations without prescribing specific courses of action, much of the public emphatically opposed the dam and supported a national park. The dam, its opponents argued, would deprive the region of the immense profits accrued through tourism services in a national park. Writing in *Tourist* (*Turist*) in the summer of 1987, Feliks Shtil'mark stated:

> For the mountainous Altai to become a national park not just in our dreams but also in reality, we need institutional and economic restructuring [*perestroika*], as well as the restructuring [*perestroika*] of people's minds. To confront the technocratic approach to nature use successfully, we must merge nature conservation with tourism, the care of our health, and recreation. We must not spare any effort and means to protect such places as Lake Baikal and the Altai Mountains.[83]

As a self-financing and profitable institution, the national park, Shtil'mark argued, was much more sensible from an economic standpoint, especially in the context of perestroika reforms, than an expensive hydroelectric installation whose development depended on central planning.

Scientists warned of the ecological consequences of the dam, and civic organizations, institutes, and individuals voiced their support for the national park in the form of petitions and articles in both the regional and central press. Meanwhile, supporters of the hydroelectric station painted them as alarmists who were peddling misinformation.[84] Influenced by the wave of ecological concern, the Presidium of the Siberian Division of the Academy of Sciences became more critical of the proposed project with each subsequent "expert commission" from 1987 to 1990. The vice president of the Academy of Sciences warned the chair of the USSR Council of Ministers, Nikolai Ryzhkov, about the danger of creating a "man-made" (*rukotvornyi*) region of ecological disaster. Dmitrii Likhachev, perhaps the most important figure in the cultural preservation movement and one of the country's most revered moral authorities, asserted that the project threatened the very "existence" of the indigenous populations.[85] With the overwhelming majority of letters to central organs speaking against the project, Gosplan RSFSR, the Main Commission on State Expertise, and Goskompriroda called the project inadvisable in the summer of 1989. In a clear indication of the strength that environmental protection had accrued, even the Ministry of Energy and Electrification acknowledged the inadequacy of ecological research by Gidroproekt.[86]

The discussion about the dam, however, continued, with opposition becoming even more intense. The national park won unlikely supporters. Different parties presented their work on the issue at the Siberian Division of the Academy of Sciences in Akademgorodok in April of 1990. An overwhelming number of participants strongly opposed to the dam; predictions of the ecological consequences had become increasingly dire; and some participants argued that the establishment of a national park provided the framework for the complete economic and cultural transformation of the area. N. N. Amshinskii of the Siberian Scientific-Research Institute of Geology, Geophysics, and Mineral Raw Materials gave perhaps the most unreserved support. He asserted:

> The Altai Mountains are a place in western Siberia of unique natural beauty. It has long deserved national park status. Inept economic management in this beautiful oasis has not yet fully destroyed nature but has nonetheless led to the impoverishment of its economy and the decline of culture. We must save Altai as a pearl, which can provide huge profits. Livestock, lapidary art, mining of ores of rare metals and decorative stones, maral breeding, beekeeping, resorts, the tourism industry: this is the path to further development of the Gorno-Altai Autonomous Region, which will take place in the context of the status of the Altai State National Park.[87]

As a representative of a geological research institute, Amshinskii was undoubtedly most worried that the dam would inundate territory with valuable minerals. Nonetheless, he understood the resonance of environmental protection arguments and the widespread appeal of the national park proposal. Several participants further asserted that the territory needed to be protected not only by the USSR but also by the international environmental community. The Soviet Union ratified UNESCO's World Heritage Convention on September 12, 1988, and many of the supporters of the project were now pushing for World Heritage Natural Site designation and closer coordination with international organizations such as the Food and Agricultural Organization (FAO) and UNEP.[88] Although the conference resolution did not specifically mention a national park, it discouraged the construction of the Katun GES while repeatedly referring to "alternative" courses of economic development, which by this time had become synonymous with the national park.

In the months that followed, David Brower's Friends of the Earth, the Association of Siberian Cities, the civic-scientific association Ecological Alternative, and many other organizations wrote urging government officials to prevent "the destruction of one of the earth's most beautiful valleys"[89] and to establish a national park. Influenced, evidently, by the strengthening global discourse about "sustainable development," they also called for a system of "ecologization" for the Soviet economy, which would place "environmental sustainability" on par with economic growth in planning decisions.[90] Responding to the broad public interest, the RSFSR Supreme Soviet established a parliamentary committee to address the issue.

Convening on September 5, 1990, the committee included the RSFSR Ministry of Energy; members of protest movements against the GES from Tomsk, Novosibirsk, Barnaul, Gorno-Altaisk, Biisk, and other cities; and people's deputies of the RSFSR. After their meetings concluded, committee members voted unanimously against the construction of the Katun GES.[91] They also recommended that the Ministry of Energy reclaim parts of the landscape that had suffered as a result of construction work and called for developing plans for finding alternative sources of energy and for devising a complex plan for utilizing the productive strength of the Altai region until 2005. In its final point, it recommended establishment of a nature national park and putting the Katun Valley on the list of Soviet sites deserving the designation of a World Heritage Natural Site under UNESCO.[92] The following month the RSFSR Council of Ministers approved the recommendations of the parliamentary committee and advised "alternative" means of economic development in the Gorno-Altaisk Oblast.[93]

In the public debate about the national park, almost no attention was given to how the Altai people might understand this designation. However, by 1990, it became clear to members of the Scientific Research Institute of Nature Protection that they understood from the term "national" (*natsional'nyi*) that they would have more control over the administration of the territory.[94] When the local indigenous Altai population learned that this term meant federal control, they turned against the idea. Consequently, Katun Zapovednik was established in part of the territory of the proposed national park in 1991. Six years later, by which time nature parks under regional administrations had legal status, Belukha Nature Park was established adjacent to it.[95]

Even though no national park was established, the idea of one that would transform the economy galvanized unexpected groups in defense of the Katun River and was partially responsible for blocking the construction of a large, potentially destructive dam. Increasing numbers of Soviet citizens viewed ennobling, not conquering, the natural world as the measure of a nation's level of civilization. Accordingly, internationally recognized protected territories, many believed, were the best chance to save the nation's most pristine landscapes from destruction by inefficient ministries. One place deserving such protection was the Kamchatka Peninsula.

Kamchatka

Kamchatka encapsulated the ambivalence felt by many Soviet supporters of environmental protection regarding the growth of tourism in the 1960s and 1970s. There were few regions where tourism could do more to instill patriotic feelings derived from pride in "native nature." At the same time, perhaps nowhere in the RSFSR was the fear about tourism's potential adverse environmental impact more significant than in Kamchatka's celebrated Valley of Geysers. But after Kronotskii Zapovednik banned tourism in 1974, plans for the peninsula's development increasingly took the peninsula's unique appeal to tourists into account.

As a territory the size of California but with under 350,000 people and few roads, Kamchatka was something of a blank economic slate onto which different interest groups could project their visions for the region's future. In 1977, a journalist suggested the formation of a 170,000-square-kilometer national park on the Kamchatka Peninsula.[96] The park would cover 63 percent of Kamchatka's territory. The Kamchatka Oblast Section of the VOOP, the Central Laboratory of Nature Protection, the Kamchatka Branch of the Geographical Society of the USSR, and journalists took up the question in the early 1980s.[97] Even the director of the Kronotskii Zapovednik acknowledged that the ban on tourism in that reserve denied the Soviet Union an important opportunity to instill pride about their country's nature in its citizens.[98] In turn, he proposed the establishment of a national park next to the *zapovednik*, which would allow strictly regulated visitation to the Valley of Geysers. In 1982, Nataliia Zabelina began leading trips to the Valley of Geysers and the surrounding area with the Scientific Research Institute of Nature Protection to plan this park.[99]

Several documentary films showing the Valley of Geysers reminded Soviet citizens that one of its most spectacular natural treasures was off-limits to the broader public.[100] In one 1982 episode of the popular show *Club of Film Travelers* (*Klub kinoputeshchestvenikov*), the host Yuri Senkevich visited geyser fields in Iceland and New Zealand as well as the Valley of Geysers and asked if it was time to replace the Kronotskii Zapovednik with a national park that opened the valley to the public.[101] One writer noted that Whakarewarewa National Park in New Zealand, which had a significantly smaller and less spectacular geyser field, had over 270,000 visitors per year.[102] While almost every article on the Valley of Geysers pointed out the great injustice that only highly placed officials had access to it, journalists sometimes also commented on the dangers of opening the valley to mass tourism.[103] Journalist A. Paperno's proposal of a rail line from Petropavlovsk to the *zapovednik* to capitalize on the economic potential of foreign tourism, for instance, was met with alarmed responses.[104]

The Valley of Geysers was, as print journalism and television programs both noted, hardly Kamchatka's only natural wonder that would attract hordes of tourists. In late 1987, another episode of *Club of Film Travelers* named Kamchatka the most interesting place on the planet.[105] Kamchatka was home to twenty-eight active volcanoes, numerous geyser fields and thermal springs, spectacular rock faces in inlets of the Pacific Ocean that were populated by humpback whales, difficult-to-access regions where Koriak and Itelmen still herded reindeer, and other unique attractions. With nearly 25 percent of the spawning Pacific salmon population and over thirty thousand brown bears, few areas in the world were more attractive to anglers and hunters, especially wealthy foreigners.[106] Meager tourism infrastructure, however, meant that the economic benefits of Kamchatka's attractions could not be realized.[107]

Mikhail Gorbachev fueled the hopes of those who argued that the economic future of the peninsula lay in the tourism industry. In 1986, the general secretary delivered what became known as the Vladivostok Speech on a trip to the Far East. He asserted that the USSR should strengthen trading ties with Asian countries because civilization was "moving toward the Pacific Ocean."[108] Further, he stated, "Without a familiarity with your enormous and beautiful region, there cannot be a full presentation of the motherland, its history, its present, and future. The Far East must become a significant center of domestic and international tourism."[109] The peninsula's potential opening to foreigners and new market mechanisms moved the debate over tourism on Kamchatka beyond the longstanding opposing viewpoints of access or preservation. Instead, both tourism supporters and the nature protection community argued that expanded tourism on the peninsula, even in previously protected areas, provided an alternative to resource extraction.[110]

Mineral discoveries coupled with the economic downturn threatened this vision. Geologists had discovered large deposits of oil off the peninsula's western

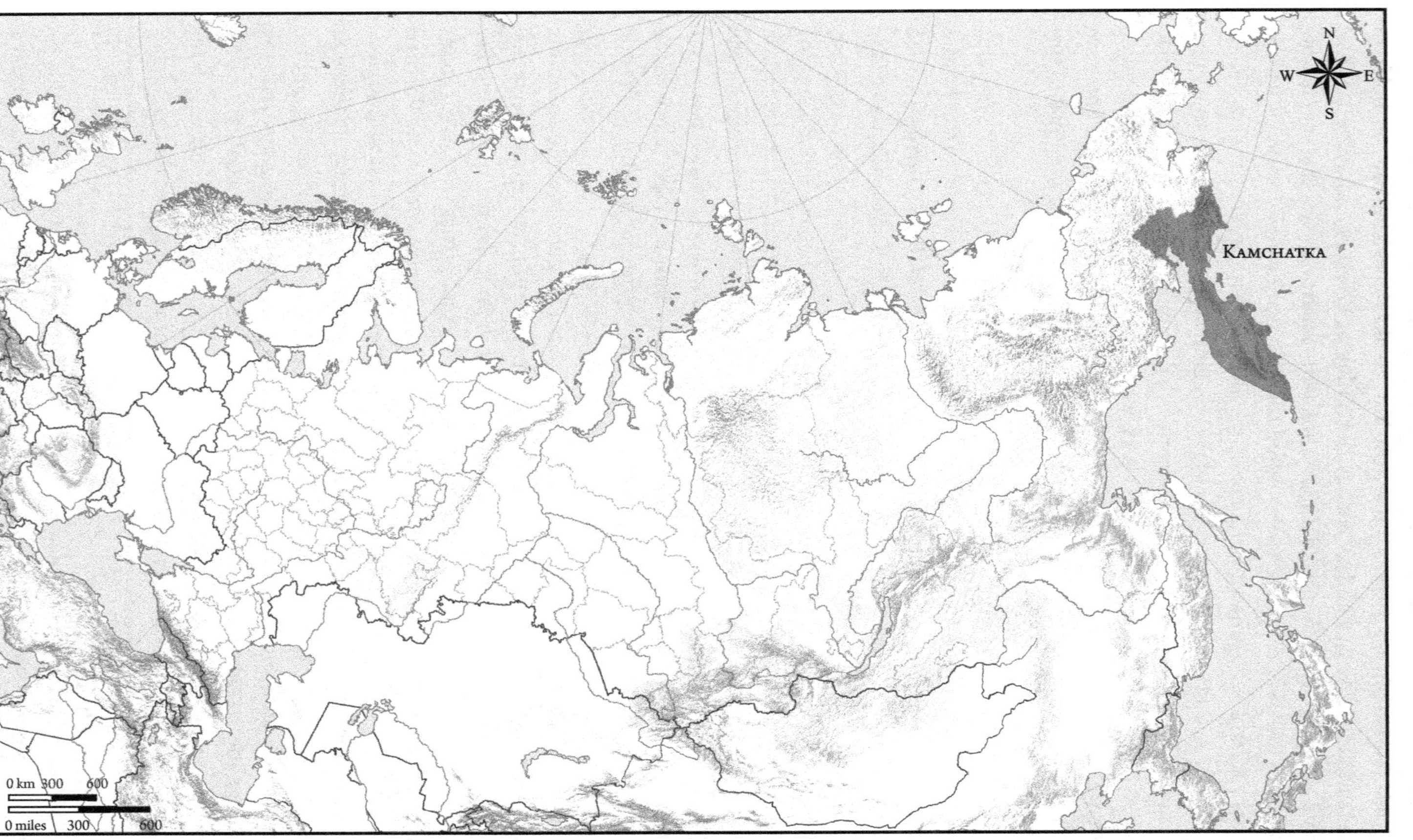

Figure 4.6 Kamchatka Peninsula.

coast in 1980 and found large deposits of gold throughout the peninsula during the decade.[111] While panning for gold had long taken place in Kamchatka's streams, geologists were proposing open-pit cyanide heap leach mining, which could cause catastrophic losses in fish populations. Tourism's proponents argued that the damage caused by rogue "uncultured" tourists (*dikari*) paled in comparison to scalping mountaintops and allowing sodium cyanide runoff into rivers. One article in *Turist* about tourism in Siberia and the Far East, including Kamchatka, described tourists as "lovers of nature" and people working in agency offices as "barbarians."[112] Another article in the journal *Nature* (*Priroda*) argued that Kamchatka risked going the way of the shrunken and polluted Aral Sea if the Soviet Union did not develop the tourism economy and gave free rein to extractive industries.[113]

Few believed more strongly in Kamchatka's future as a center of Soviet and international tourism than Vladimir Semenov and Vitalii Men'shikov. Born in Vitebsk in present-day Belarus in 1905, Semenov, who trained as a refrigeration engineer, moved to Kamchatka to work at a fish processing plan in 1938.[114] The peninsula's expanses of unmapped, unexplored territory captivated Semenov upon his arrival. Over the next four decades, he charted over one hundred previously untraveled hiking routes and made forty first ascents of Kamchatka volcanoes. In 1963, he became the first chair of the Oblast Council on Tourism while also working on the executive council of the Kamchatka Oblast Branch of the Geographical Society of the USSR. Two years later, he established the Gleb Travin Club of Tourists. From the 1960s through the 1980s, he delivered lectures promoting tourism and the local history movement at tourist seminars and rallies, schools, and youth organizations. From 1977 to 1980, he served as the chair of the Oblast Commission on Local History (Kraevedenie) and Tourism within the Kamchatka Branch of the Geographical Society, and he served as its assistant chairman of beginning in 1980.[115] From the early 1970s to the late 1980s, he wrote five books that were both guidebooks and travel narratives.[116]

Semenov had come to fear the peninsula's possible future as a center of resource extraction by the late 1980s. As he noted in his journal and articles for the regional press, the claims of the inexhaustibility of Kamchatka's resources rang hollow for him after observing threefold drops in the catches of herring, cod, flounder, salmon, and crab during his fifty years living on Kamchatka.[117] While mining, he acknowledged, might provide benefits that would last for twenty-five to thirty years, it would eventually destroy the region's "pristine" nature, its most sustainable and potentially profitable resource.[118] He wrote:

> The time will come when all the useful minerals will be dug out, the slopes and valleys dug up, the hot springs exhausted. Materially, but

> only materially, one, a maximum of two, generations will benefit, but the damage will be to all future generations of our motherland, millions of people, from whom we will deprive the possibility of falling in love with the exotic nature of Kamchatka. From this, there is only one conclusion to be made. The mining industry, which is destructive to nature, is entirely incompatible on the Kamchatka Peninsula with its biological and recreational resources and their future development.[119]

He asserted that mining activities should instead be expanded in the Magadan Oblast, the Amur region, and the Circumpolar Urals of the Komi Republic, where the prospect of gold mining was already threatening the establishment of a national park.[120]

Vitalii Men'shikov shared these concerns. Men'shikov came from Leningrad in 1968. During his vacation time, which was considerably longer in northern areas like Kamchatka, he traveled extensively throughout the peninsula. Having worked at the Valley of Geysers Tour Base in the early 1970s, Men'shikov maintained good relationships with the staff of the Kronotskii Zapovednik. After the closure of the base, he received special permission to bring independent tourists to the Valley of Geysers. Independent tourists, scientists, and high-placed government officials continued to visit the *zapovednik*, and without the tour base to maintain the tourism infrastructure, as it had in the past, tourists continued to have an adverse impact on the valley. He concluded that Kamchatka needed to reopen the Valley of Geysers and closely regulate tourism and establish national parks in other areas to soften tourism's impact. Profitable tourism, he also believed, would weaken the argument that natural resource extraction was necessary for the region's economic development.[121]

Men'shikov and Semenov agreed that national parks provided the best means to reorient the peninsula's economy toward tourism. The Soviet Union's increased openness, they and many others believed, made the task not just possible but potentially tremendously profitable. However, developing mass tourism without the adequate infrastructure would be, in the words of Semenov, "criminal" because of the damage it would cause to Kamchatka's environment.[122] He acknowledged that development would be more difficult given the economy's downward spiral. Given the limits of domestic investment, Semenov thought that the peninsula's administration should work hard to attract foreign capital and foreign tourists. He wrote:

> This analogy with the USA speaks to the enormous potential benefits that foreign tourism can bring to Kamchatka, even under a system of limited entry and the truncated tourist season. However, for this we need, firstly, to establish the entire infrastructure for service and the

Figure 4.7 Natalia Zabelina in the Valley of Geysers in the mid-1980s. Photo courtesy of Natalia Zabelina.

> transportation of tourists, to organize trails, and secondly, to protect nature. Without this, foreigners will not come here. This will demand foreign investment and organization.[123]

He continued: "Domestic and international experience speaks to the fact that, thanks to the unique nature of Kamchatka, tourism can take on such a size that it may become one of the leading if not the leading part of the economy of the oblast."[124]

Semenov and Men'shikov called on tourist clubs, the Geographical Society, the Institute of Volcanology, and other civic organizations to push the Kamchatka

Oblast Executive Committee to rally support for designating temporary reserves (*zakazniki*) throughout the oblast. They hoped that the RSFSR Council of Ministers would then convert these into permanent national parks.[125] Semenov called for designating *zakazniki* on 130 thousand square kilometers, which would amount to 30 percent of the territory of the oblast and 50 percent of the peninsula, in his book *In the Region of Hot Springs* (*V kraiu goriachikh istochnikov*, 1988).[126] Since national parks would cultivate in visitors the "proper" relationship to nature, Semenov believed that the problems of the late 1960s and 1970s could be avoided, even as Kamchatka's wonders lured hordes of tourists from all of Russia and overseas. Meanwhile, Natalia Zabelina and others from the Scientific Research Institute of Nature Protection and scientists from the Far East Branch of the Academy of Sciences continued to research their territories.[127] Many shared his enthusiasm for national parks, and one journalist even proposed national park designation for the entire peninsula.[128]

Despite this support, the RSFSR Council of Ministers did not establish national parks on Kamchatka before the collapse of the Soviet Union. While Semenov still occasionally put on a backpack and took multiday hikes, at nearly eighty he lacked the vigor to continue to lead the campaign, and Men'shikov would assume responsibility for the push to establish parks on the peninsula in the 1990s.

Beyond the National: Beringia International Park

Meanwhile, American and Soviet scientists were envisioning a plan to the north of Kamchatka more transformative than what had been called for by Semenov. The inescapable physical reality that ecological zones and natural geographic features do not conform to political boundaries was the basis for the international park idea. The governments of the United States and Canada established the first international park, Waterton-Glacier, in 1932. Two more were subsequently created on the US-Canadian border, and numerous parks were proposed on the borders of African nations.[129] By the mid-1980s, the Scientific Research Institute of Nature Protection had begun working on plans for several international reserves and peace parks. These parks dovetailed with Gorbachev's principle of "new thinking," which emphasized increased engagement with the outside world, especially with the West led by the United States. Explaining the rationale for these parks in a report, Nataliia Zabelina wrote, "The deployment of a network of specially protected natural territories on national borders marks a return to a single biosphere and the human understanding of our place in it."[130] She continued: "From the political point of view, the attention that states give to nature protection measures on borders is an additional factor in trust, stability, and the humanization of international relations."[131]

The Scientific Research Institute of Nature Protection proposed parks with neighboring client states and former rivals. During the late 1980s, it worked to establish joint nature reserves with Poland, Mongolia, and China.[132] Zabelina and the institute proposed the establishment of Kuril Bridge International Park with Japan for the protection of marine mammals, rare and disappearing species of animals and plants, and fish spawning grounds as well as for the development of ecological tourism and environmental enlightenment activities. Zabelina asserted that this park could prove "one of the most effective means of resolving the territorial debate" sparked by the Soviet Union's occupation of the islands after World War II.[133]

Soviet environmentalists recognized that the Arctic provided an unprecedented opportunity for environmental collaboration with the United States given the shared history, ecology, and culture in eastern Chukotka and western Alaska. About fifteen-thousand years ago, North America's first settlers traversed a land bridge connecting Chukotka and Alaska that formed during the last Ice Age. Eskimos—Yupik and Inupiat peoples of Chukotka and Alaska respectively—were trading with one another when Russians arrived in the eighteenth century, and the languages of natives of the two regions still resembled one another. Moreover, because their environments were almost identical, they had similar lifestyles that revolved around fishing, reindeer herding, and hunting large marine mammals.[134] Inupiat continued to visit trade fairs in Chukotka following the sale of Alaska to the United States in 1864.[135] While these exchanges became less frequent during the first three decades of Soviet rule, Alaskan Eskimos continued to come to Chukotka for festivals until 1948, when anti-Western cultural policies fueled by growing tensions with the United States prompted the USSR to terminate the passage rights of natives.[136]

When representatives of indigenous groups from North, Central, and South America, Scandinavia, Greenland, Australia, and New Zealand met in British Columbia at the first World Council of Indigenous Peoples Conference in 1975, Soviet indigenous peoples could not attend.[137] They were also not able to participate in discussions about the United Nations' proposed Declaration of Rights of Indigenous Peoples, which began in 1982. Gorbachev's reforms allowed Russia's indigenous peoples to participate in this international dialogue on human rights for the first time.[138] Having suffered from policies that sought to eradicate many of their traditional cultural practices, the Yupik and Chukchis of Chukotka were finally able to address their grievances.[139]

After scientific cooperation in the Arctic was suspended following the USSR's invasion of Afghanistan, warming relations between the two superpowers led to the revival of joint environmental projects in 1986. That year, the Soviet Union and the United States set up a working group, Conservation and Management of Natural and Cultural Heritage, dedicated in large part to improving the lives of indigenous peoples on both sides of the Bering Sea. The project sought to encourage more joint scientific efforts and facilitate exchanges of indigenous peoples. The "ice wall," as many called it, broke in 1989 when a group of twelve Yupik, Inupiat, and Chukchi, as well as Russians and Americans from outside these regions, took part in the Bering Bridge Expedition. For two months, the group traveled over 1,600 kilometers from Chukotka to Alaska by dogsled, skis, and boat.[140] During the expedition, Mikhail Gorbachev wrote to the team, "The name [Bering Bridge] is not just a symbol for me. This name represents my true feelings. You are truly helping to build friendly cooperation between Chukotka and Alaska as well as between the Soviet Union and the United States. We are united by common challenges, such as preserving northern cultures, protecting the Arctic ecosystem, and, of course, the most important challenge, the strengthening of peaceful relations among all countries of the world."[141]

Initially proposed in the late 1960s by the director of the National Center for Atmospheric Research, Walter Orr Roberts, the establishment of Beringia International Park (BIP) many hoped, would become the most critical step in melting the ice wall.[142] This region received attention at the Second World Conference on National Parks as part of a larger discussion about conceptualizing areas of a "global commons" where cooperation between countries was necessary to preserve fragile ecosystems.[143] The idea of the park re-emerged on numerous occasions during the early to mid-1970s as part of the working group on Arctic regions in the Soviet-American Joint Working Group.[144] At its seventeenth session in 1988, the IUCN General Assembly congratulated the United States and the Soviet Union on their joint effort and encouraged them to give the region a special status that would help revive the cultures of the natives.[145] The Soviet press enthused about the region serving as a model for the complex collaboration between Soviets and Americans in the sphere of environmental protection.[146] In September of 1989, three months after the successful completion of the Bering Bridge Expedition, a joint Soviet-American planning team undertook a ten-day assessment of the "proposed" park lands in Russia and a trip of equal duration to northwest Alaska.[147]

The proposed park included Bering Land Bridge National Preserve and Cape Krusenstern National Monument on the Alaska side and a national park that the Soviet Union promised to establish in Chukotka. In November 1989, the US National Park Service published its report *Beringia Heritage: A Reconnaissance Study of Sites and Recommendations.*[148] Through a standard set of land use policies, a unified international park, the report argued, could develop a more rational system for environmental management. The park would facilitate joint scientific studies, the development of ecotourism, and the exchange of indigenous groups, for whom geopolitical rivalry had always meant little.[149] The plans

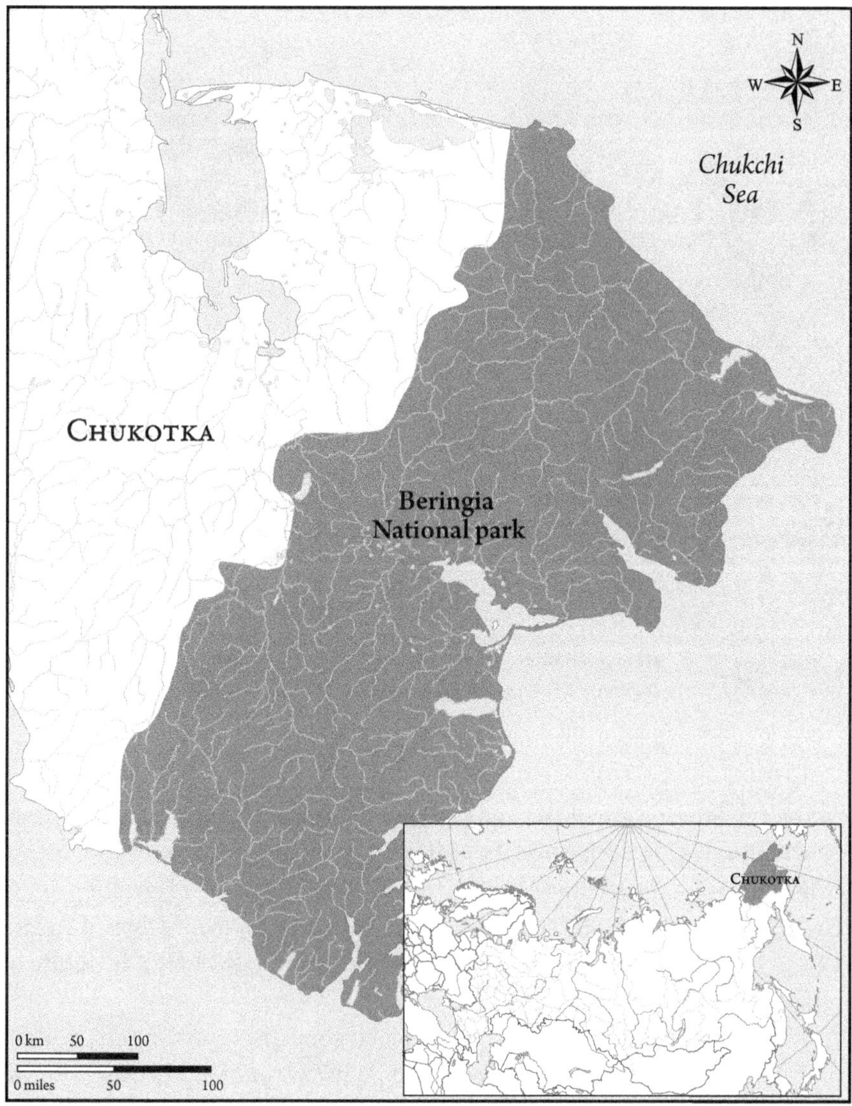

Figure 4.8 Proposed Russian Side of Beringia International Park

and joint report for the park illustrated the growing emphasis on the natural world serving as a means of overcoming Cold War politics as the report's introduction summed up:

> In order to come together, people must see each other through the walls erected by politics and understand that beauty is not the exclusive property of states but the common property of all of the inhabitants of the earth. Nature is a potential means of mutual understanding.[150]

Figure 4.9 Beringia International Park. Photo courtesy of Natalia Zabelina.

At the US-Soviet summit the following year, George H. W. Bush and Mikhail Gorbachev signed a declaration that called for joint Soviet-American expeditions to help organize the territory of the park in 1990 and 1991. At a meeting of the United States and USSR Trade and Economic Development Council in late 1990, Gorbachev said that it was Chukotka and Alaska that hold "the future of relations between our two countries."[151]

While Gorbachev and others were optimistic about the region's future, by 1990 the USSR was in an economic tailspin and politically unstable. Lacking a single steward and with limited resources, national parks still seemed like stepchildren to the departments that managed them. Moreover, the Soviet Union had no experience administering similar international territories, let alone coordinating management with its main geopolitical rival. US mining and oil companies had begun scouting the region. Perhaps the most complicated aspect of the park's organization, however, was the fact that indigenous populations lived within the borders on the Soviet side and had increased expectations about what the park could do for them based on territorial claims made by groups around the world.

The Chukchi and Yupik of Chukotka viewed the park as a means of overcoming past injustices, asserting greater control over their lives, and preventing future environmental problems. On many occasions, they expressed their overwhelming support for the park and their desire to be closely involved in its organization and management. While expressing their anger about the USSR's "predatory" relationship to the natural resources of the area, they also repeatedly critiqued the Soviet government's longstanding attempts to eradicate their cultural heritage.[152] With the region opening up to foreign natural resource companies, they worried about the continued destruction of their land and were already observing the "looting" of their historical sites by unorganized tourists.[153] A resolution of the Society of Eskimos of Chukotka in the summer of 1990 stated: "We find ourselves on our land a minority and are forced to watch powerless the heartless [*bezdushno*] predatory relationship to nature that is killing our land and its peoples."[154] The international park, they asserted, should strengthen the cultural heritage of the native groups—folklore, songs, dance, and crafts—and promote their traditional economy. Many believed that it should eliminate all scouting for and exploitation of valuable minerals and strengthen the historical rights of Chukchi and Yupiks to the land and water of Beringia.[155]

In its plan for the organization of the park, Lengiprogor prioritized the interests of native populations above all. With the full support of other organizations involved in the planning, it called for a new legal definition of the national park's territory—a protected "ethnic territory." Such a territory would aim to preserve the natural and cultural heritage of indigenous peoples (Chukchi and Yupik) as well as to develop a new socioeconomic foundation for nature use.[156] The ethnic territory, Lengiprogor's Technical Economic Basis (TEB) for the park stated, would provide "favorable conditions for the self-definition of the indigenous population" while giving them the authority to "make decisions about their economic and social problems."[157] The plan acknowledged that alcoholism afflicted a significant portion of indigenous residents, most of whom had little education. Nonetheless, it asserted they would be educated and professionalized so that they could actively take part in scientific research and manage ecological tourism, without giving any details. The appropriate management of tourism, the report stated, would prevent the growing problem of uncontrolled looting by unorganized tourists.[158] By involving the indigenous population and reviving the traditional economy based on hunting, reindeer herding, fishing, and crafts, the TEB argued, the park could eradicate unemployment.

Gorbachev's reforms had elevated the hopes of the park's champions and Chukchi and Yupiks even though the material conditions of indigenous peoples were declining and the park remained a dream. The abrupt departure of the Moscow working group cast a cloud of uncertainty over their aspirations.

Conclusion

The expressed commitment to environmental protection by Soviet leaders and the RSFSR's establishment of many national parks made the Gorbachev era a heady time for Russia's park supporters. However, nothing gave them more optimism than Gorbachev's stated aim for the Soviet Union to "join the path of world civilization." This enabled them to collaborate extensively with foreign colleagues without the pretense, which environmentalists frequently maintained disingenuously in previous eras to placate those in power, of the inherent superiority of the socialist system. Moreover, by becoming more open to the outside world, the USSR stood to gain significant profits from foreign tourism. However, the expectations for parks among their supporters were rising just as the prospects that the state could help diminished. "Joining the path of world civilization" would, as a result, come to mean aggressively seeking out external support to compensate for state neglect.

PART II

NATIONAL PARK HISTORIES

Many Russian national parks have long histories. These histories demonstrate the strong and determined efforts of individuals and groups to bring meaningful economic social, economic, and cultural change to different regions against great odds. This part will include four of these stories: the efforts of various organizations located in different parts of Russia to establish national parks on Baikal's shoreline; the efforts of environmentalists of Kuibyshev to establish a national park in the territory of the Samara Bend—a peninsula-shaped formation caused by a hairpin turn in the Volga near the cities of Tolyatti, Kuibyshev, and Zhigulev; the work of scientists of the Komi Scientific Center to protect an area in the Circumpolar Urals about half the size of Switzerland; and the efforts of a young idealistic college student to protect a large swathe of the taiga of Karelia and the Arkhangelsk Oblast. In each case, the lofty expectations of these park visionaries crashed against the realities of a political and economic collapse that left their plans mostly stillborn.

5

The "Shield" of the Sacred Sea

National Parks around Lake Baikal

> High hills and exceedingly high rocky cliffs are all around it—over twenty times one thousand versts and more have I dragged myself and nowhere seen any like these. Exceedingly many birds, geese, and swans swim upon the sea covering it like snow. It hath fishes—sturgeon, and salmon, starlet, and omul, and whitefish, and many other kinds. The water is fresh and hath great seals and sea lions in it: when I dwelt in Mezen, I saw nought like unto these in the big sea. And the fishes there are plentiful: the sturgeon and salmon are surpassingly fat—thou canst not fry them in a pan, for there will not be nought but grease. And all this hath been wrought by Christ in heaven for mankind so that, resting content, he shouldst render praise unto God.
>
> Archpriest Avvakum, 1662

Described as a "miracle of nature," "the blue heart of Siberia," the "sacred sea," and the "blue eye of Siberia," Lake Baikal has captivated Russians with its beauty and natural riches since Avvakum's journey. Baikal holds 20 percent of the world's freshwater and is home to more than a thousand species of plants and 2,500 species of animals, eighty percent of which are endemic to Baikal.[1] Numerous mountain ranges—the Barguzin Ridge, Khamar Daban, the Kodar, and the Sayan—either hug the shoreline or are visible from the lake. In many places, the translucent water, which in some parts is so clear that one can see to depths of forty meters, shows the reflections of snowcapped peaks and dormant volcanoes.

During the first three decades of Soviet rule, Baikal's distance from the European part of the USSR and the region's low population density limited industrial development and the extraction of raw materials in its environs. However, central planners anticipated dramatic postwar economic growth, which they believed necessitated tapping the vast natural resources of Siberia, especially Baikal and the Angara River watershed. In the late 1950s, much of the Soviet scientific and environmentally concerned public came to Baikal's

Into Russian Nature. Alan D. Roe, Oxford University Press (2020) © Oxford University Press.
DOI: 10.1093/oso/9780190914554.001.0001

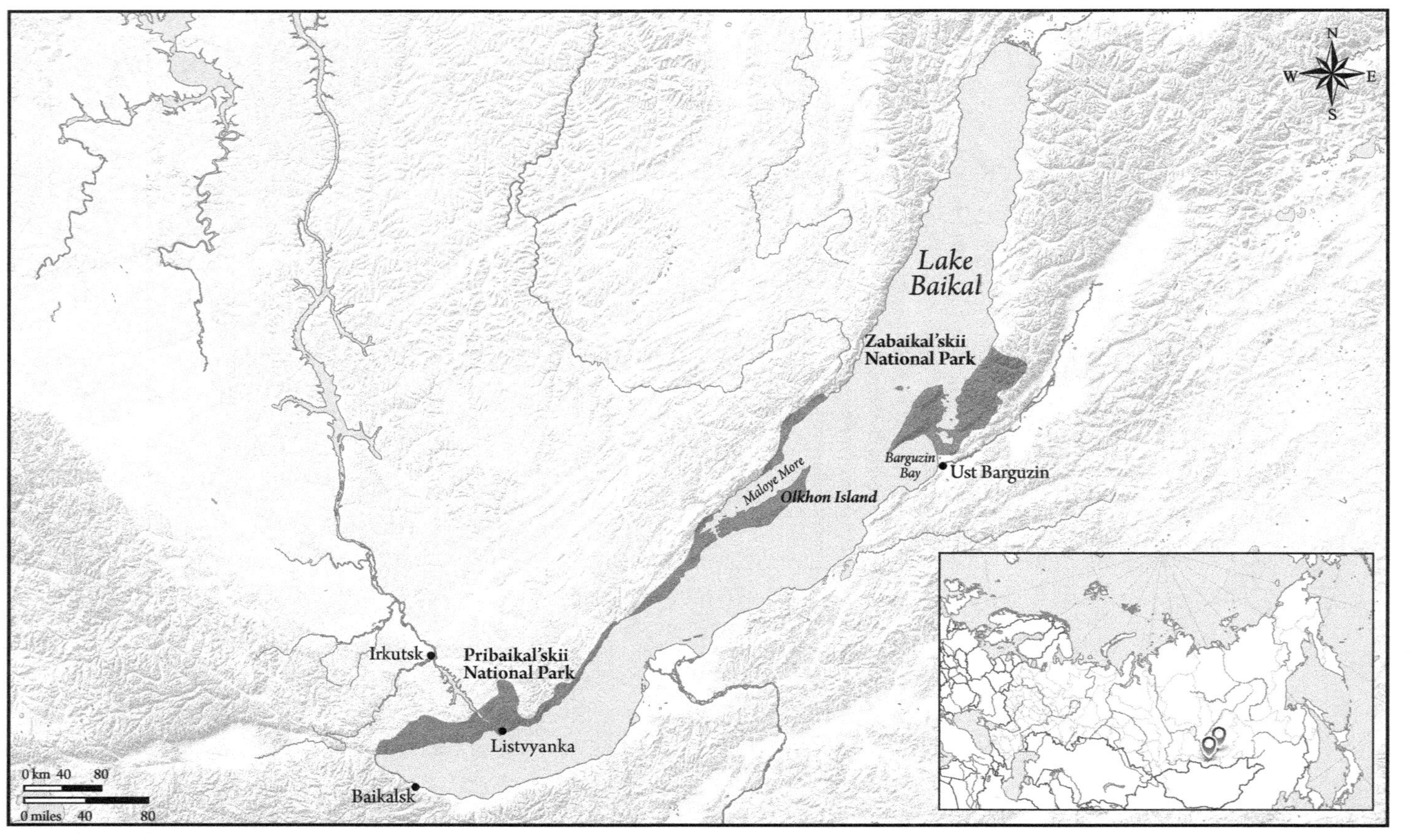

Figure 5.1 Lake Baikal and adjacent national parks.

defense in response to plans with the potential to inflict severe damages on Baikal and its environs. Game management professionals, landscape architects, workers in nature reserves, and other interested Soviet citizens called for the establishment of national parks (or a single park) on Baikal's shore and in the surrounding territory. Projecting large profits from domestic and international tourism, they argued that these parks would counter industrial development on the lake's shoreline and earn Russian environmental protection efforts international recognition.

The hopes among park supporters that Baikal's parks would be a model for Soviet national parks and help preserve a natural feature significant to "all of humanity" were frustrated soon after the founding of Pribaikal'skii National Park (henceforth PBNP) and Zabaikal'skii National Parks (ZBNP). Jurisdictional rivalries, lack of support from Moscow, and resentment from the local populations compromised the ability of these parks to function from the time of their establishment. These problems only intensified after the collapse of the Soviet Union. With many Russian and foreign environmentalists hoping that Baikal would become one of Russia's first World Heritage Natural Sites the lake became a testing ground for concepts of "sustainable development" among international environmental NGOs. Park supporters hoped that international support might compensate for state neglect, only to be disappointed. By the end of the 1990s, the lake's defenders were disillusioned about the prospects of Baikal's parks and embarrassed by the Russian Federation's failure to prioritize Baikal's protection and develop the national parks established to advance that goal.

Making Baikal's Protection Economically Viable

As the USSR looked to Siberia's vast stores of natural resources following World War II, Soviet planners called for the development of industrial projects of an unprecedented scale that would transform vast tracts of "pristine nature" into industrial oases with modern cities, unified electrical grids, and state-of-the-art enterprises.[2] Soviet planners and government officials believed that the greater Baikal region, including the Angara River watershed, surpassed all areas of Siberia in industrial potential. At the 1947 Conference for the Development of the Industrial Strength of the Irkutsk Oblast, participants recommended constructing a series of dams on the Angara, the "daughter of Baikal," which would provide the energy for the region's economic and industrial transformation.[3] Belief in the river's transformative potential and its iconic role in the "battle" to "conquer" Siberian rivers gained traction with the completion of the Irkutsk and beginning of the construction of the Bratsk Hydroelectric Stations in 1950 and 1956, respectively.[4] No idea seemed too fantastical. At the Conference for the Development of the Industrial

Strength of Eastern Siberia in 1958, N. A. Grigorevich, an engineer at the institute Gidroproekt, proposed detonating twenty-five thousand tons of TNT at the Angara's origin to increase the river's flow and thereby its energy potential. This proposal and the plan to construct a factory on the lake's southern shore, which would use Baikal's "pure" water for the production of rayon cord for airplane tires, transformed scientific concern for the fate of the "sacred sea" into a national environmental cause.[5]

An influx of tourists accompanied the region's economic transformation, and from the beginning tourism was at the center of discussions regarding Baikal's protection. During the 1950s, Vasilii Skalon and Ia. M. Grushko wrote tourist guidebooks celebrating the landscape of Baikal and its environs.[6] Following the 1958 conference, Skalon called for the establishment of a reserve on Baikal that would be among "the greatest of nature reserves of the world."[7] A month later, Grushko was one of many signatories on a collective letter to the Supreme Soviet of the USSR calling for a nature reserve on Baikal.[8] In early 1959, Frants Taurin, editor of the literary journal *Angara* and popular fiction writer, argued that a Baikal Nature Reserve should include tourist bases, houses of recreation, spas, and a sanitarium.[9] Over the next two years, Grigorii Galazii, director of the Limnological Institute of the Siberian Branch of the Academy of Sciencs, and Oleg Gusev, who had worked in the Barguzin Zapovednik for years and hiked over two thousand kilometers of Baikal's shoreline, also made proposals for a reserve in which tourism would play a prominent role.[10] Almost everyone who publicly advocated for designating new protected territories on Baikal realized that the lake's tourism value made its shoreline less suitable for *zapovednik* (nature reserve) designation.

In 1965, the Baikal Cellulose and Paper Plant (BTsBK) started operating on Baikal's southern shore. Concern about this plant motivated some geographers in the Soviet Institute of Geography to apply the field to organizing tourism on Baikal, which they belived would undercut the argument that lake should be used for industrial purposes. Moreover, they thought it would fit in well with the efforts of geographers to provide "constructive" input on major economic questions in the USSR.[11] The task was made more urgent by the Irkutsk Oblast Council admission of the inadequacy of its tourism infrastructure and the incompetence of workers (referred to as "spiritually dead" at one meeting of the Irkutsk Oblast Council on Tourism) at tour bases on Baikal.[12] In February, 1965, Innokentii Gerasimov, the head of the Institute of Geography, gave a presentation entitled "The Problem of Baikal" at a meeting of the institute's Bureau of the Department of Earth Sciences. He proposed the "Baikal National Nature Park," which would encompass the entire shoreline, have more authority over its resources than any national park in the world, and harmonize economic development with environmental protection.[13]

Gerasimov convinced prominent members of the Siberian division of the Academy of Sciences, such as the geologist Andrei Alekseevich Trofimuk and Limnological Institute director Grigorii Galazii of the park project's enormous potential. There was widespread agreement throughout interested ministries and institutes that the "Siberian Switzerland," as some came to call Baikal, would become the most attractive Soviet tourism destination.[14] Later in 1965, Gosplan USSR, Lengiprogor, the Novosibirsk-based Institute of the Economy and Organization of Industrial Production, and the Siberian Branch of the Institute of Geography began collaborating on designing national parks in the Baikal region. As it expressed concern about BTsBK's wastewater going into Baikal and the impact on the intensification of timber harvesting in the region, the central and regional press praised these efforts to transform Baikal into both a destination for tourists spending time at spa resorts (*otdykh*) and those undertaking outdoor recreation (*turizm*).[15]

Lengiprogor's director, I. A. Evlakhov, reiterated Gerasimov's claim that a Baikal national park's functions would far exceed the authority of any other national park in the world.[16] The park would assume responsibility for the development of tourism, publicizing and enforcing laws related to the use of Baikal's shoreline, and coordinating between ministries responsible for different uses of Baikal. While maintaining that Baikal's water could still be used for industrial purposes, this plan called for the scientists working for the park to help factories monitor water quality and make sure that their equipment remained up to date.

In the following years, the initial ambitious vision for the park to serve as Baikal's single steward gave way to a more directed focus on its role in developing and regulating tourism. Lengiprogor's plan evolved to include five separate parks on and near Lake Baikal's shoreline, which would cater to different types of tourists. The proposed parks in the Buryatia Republic to the east of Baikal were all tentative in their design and plans. Located on the western slopes of the Barguzin ridge, adjacent to the Barguzin Zapovednik, Barguzin National Park's 362,000 hectares would cater primarily to backpackers. Just to the south, Chivyrkuiskii National Park would occupy a territory of 155,000 hectares from the Sviatoi Nos ("Holy Nose") Peninsula and up the shorelines of the Chivyrkuiskii and Barguzinskii Bays. This park, which would also include the Ushkanikh Islands, frequented by nerpa (Baikal seals), would host many forms of mass tourism. To the south of the lake in the Buryatia Republic, Khamar Daban National Park—the only park not touching the shoreline—would occupy the southwest part of the Khamar Daban Ridge with peaks of 2,400 meters. This park would be oriented exclusively to mountaineering, backpacking, and backcountry skiing.

Parks in the Irkutsk Oblast, which would host the majority of tourists spending time on Baikal, were oriented to mass tourism. Olkhon National Park would encompass all of Olkhon Island's 175,000 hectares, which are known for dramatic rock faces, archaeological monuments, unique cliffs, and large caves. Lengiprogor developed more extensive plans for Angarskii National Park than all the others. The 219,000-hectare park would be located to the east of the Irkutsk reservoir and extend to Lake Baikal. Primarily mountain taiga landscape, the proposed park included ridgelines at three hundred meters, numerous caves popular among spelunkers in Irkutsk, important archaeological sites where prehistoric humans lived, and varied views of the lake along the shoreline. The territory would include heavily trafficked areas—Listvianka and Sand Bay (Bukhta Peschanaia). In consultation with recreational geographers in the Institute of Geography, Lengiprogor determined that the proposed park could host forty-five thousand tourists in one day. State investment would be necessary not only to construct infrastructure (including hotels, cafeterias, restaurants, and boat docks) needed to accommodate the hundreds of thousands of tourists, perhaps even millions, that would come every year but also to restore degraded landscapes. Park administrators would enforce a maximum visitation capacity in different areas, and rangers would regularly patrol to look for signs of "ecological regression."[17] Upon observing degradation, the park administration would close one trail and redirect traffic onto a parallel path. There would be shelters and tent sites next to the trail for tourists who wanted to take multiday trips.[18]

The Institute of the Economy and Organization of Industrial Production developed economic projections for Lengiprogor's model. Founded in 1962, this institute was one of the most important centers of reformist economic and socioeconomic research in the USSR.[19] It put more energy into the economic questions related to the development of tourism than perhaps any other institute in the USSR.[20] Director Abel Aganbegian strongly believed that the shortcomings of the Soviet economy lay in its continued reliance on "Stalinist methods." Under his direction, the institute developed, in the spirit of the Kosygin reforms, models that encouraged enterprise autonomy, rational prices, and other marketizing steps.[21] Frequently relying on foreign statistics about the Soviet economy, which he believed were more reliable than official Soviet statistics, Aganbegian believed that the Soviet economy suffered from its small volume of foreign trade.[22]

The economic model for the park reflected these philosophical positions. While the institute argued that tourism could provide a springboard for economic development throughout Siberia and the Far East, its economists believed that the potential of Baikal and its environs surpassed all other regions.[23] The flow of tourists to Baikal from more developed economic regions would infuse the regional economy with capital that would help modernize airports, improve roads, and construct restaurants, movie theaters, and hotels, and landscape cities. They would also help to revive natural and cultural monuments, protect forests, and clean up polluted bodies of water.[24] The institute argued that development of tourism resources would have a far higher return on investment than forestry, gold mining, or cellulose production. With the average foreign tourist spending more than one thousand dollars on a trip to the USSR, the institute's report estimated 10,000 foreign tourists a year would spend $10 million.[25] The institute predicted that the park would serve 560,000 Soviet citizens who would pay 100 rubles each by 1980."[26] By then, they estimated that the park would bring the USSR 216 million rubles a year when taking into account tourism's indirect economic benefits.[27] Such profits depended on the intensive infrastructure development envisioned by Lengiprogor's designs.[28]

When Vasilii Skalon returned to Irkutsk in 1968, he quickly became alarmed not only by tourism's increasingly detrimental impact but what he was learning about Lengiprogor's plans.[29] Although he understood tourism's profitability could make landscape protection more appealing to government officials, Skalon feared that a single-minded vision for maximizing profits, as he believed Lengiprogor wanted, would result in worse problems than unregulated tourism.[30] Referring to Lengiprogor's plan, he wrote, "I am confident that haste

Figure 5.2 Vasilii Skalon.

in this task and aspirations of gigantomania are very dangerous."[31] With this concern in mind, he independently carried out a study, "On the Development of the Scientific Basis of a Scheme of Nature Parks, Nature Reserves, and Temporary Nature Reserves in the Watershed of Lake Baikal."[32]

Skalon argued passionately for the establishment of a single national park that would encompass all territory within five kilometers of the lake's shoreline. He wrote:

> It must be recognized that for Lake Baikal it is not enough to establish one isolated national park, but rather a park on THE ENTIRE SHORELINE OF THE LAKE. This, the shoreline, is a united [*edinoe*], whole [*tseloe*], and natural phenomenon of world significance. There is no possibility, or need, to establish a few small parks on portions of the shoreline as a few authors have proposed.[33]

Countering Lengiprogor's plans, Skalon believed that the park's expenses should be minimal because tourists mostly wanted "to observe nature in its natural state" and did not need a massive infrastructure to visit.[34] "Tourists," he wrote, "are attracted by the wild beauty of nature, not the beauty of the city that they are accustomed to at home. THIS 'wildness' must be saved in full."[35] In one letter (the recipient was not identified), he wrote in all capital letters to emphasize this point: "For one and all I emphasize: TOURISTS SEEK THE PLACES WHERE NATURE IS PRESERVED IN ITS WILDERNESS FORM. THE MORE WILD THE LANDSCAPE, THE FEWER TRACES LEFT BY THE ACTIVITY OF HUMANS, THE MORE PEOPLE WILL WANT TO SPEND TIME IN IT."[36] Park regulations, he believed, should therefore prohibit the construction of roads for automobiles. Footpaths not visible from the shore should be the only transportation networks. While park regulations would allow no constructions of an "urban type," tourists could stay in taiga huts. "It is important," he wrote, "that they observe the backcountry lifestyle."[37] Any signs—trailheads, mileage markers, and other markings—should be "extremely modest."

Skalon believed that appealing exclusively to tourists drawn to wild places would mitigate the environmental damage to the shoreline and the surrounding areas. In contrast to what he and others were observing on Baikal, he stated that in Switzerland tourism was organized so well that one finds "no broken branches, not a single piece of paper, not a single ruined anthill . . . in tourist regions there."[38] Moreover, tourism in Switzerland provided a "seemingly infinite source of income."[39] The creation of an intelligently designed and a well-regulated national park would bring profits and help preserve the landscape, whereas "wild and feral tourism" would bring "destruction to the landscape." He warned: "On Baikal right now that is the only sort of tourism that there is" and asked, "What remains of the wild beauty of the lake and its shores to attract someone when they are turned into a dump?[40] "Biological deserts," as he described them, would continue to spread if tourists came to the "miracle" lake before the state had established the appropriate administrative and regulatory regime.[41]

Skalon had more restrictions in mind. He proposed imposing strict standards for visitation per unit of territory, enlisting the help of the local population in nature protection efforts, banning the entry of independent tourists into the national park, and recruiting game wardens to carry out monitoring. He also called for the strict prohibition of tourist visitation to individual *zapovedniki* within the territory of the national park during the peak tourist season from May to September when tourists "storm Baikal."[42] Naturalists would educate tourists on the "Baikal type of nature use" and teach them to become careful stewards of the natural world.[43]

Skalon's vision exemplified the growing belief that urbanized Soviet citizens sought wildness to cope with unprecedented levels of "anxiety" and "psychological stress." Moreover, his vision demonstrated the hopes of many that tourism in national parks could prove one of the best ways to cultivate a love for Russian nature.[44] However, at a time when economic concerns seemed to supersede others and the profitability of national parks was increasingly recognized throughout the world, the maximalist, utilitarian vision of Lengiprogor and the Institute of Economics and Industrial Production resonated more with the economic ministries. When the Irkutsk Oblast Executive Committee passed a decree that called for the establishment of a national park on Baikal's shoreline in 1971, it appeared that Lengiprogor's model, which would be published for the broader public to see in 1976, would be chosen for its framework. The USSR Council of Ministers' seeming disinterest in passing a law that would allow the Russian Soviet Federated Socialist Republic (RSFSR) to establish national parks ended up putting both plans in jeopardy.

Parks That Would Stand Above All Others

The attention that the Irkutsk Oblast Executive Committee, the USSR Council of Ministers, and the Central Committee of the Communist Party gave to Baikal's protection elevated the sense of the task's importance among a broad cross section of Soviet society throughout the 1970s. The lake's defenders continued to express concern about the cellulose and paper mill operating on Lake Baikal's southern shore, which was seeking to modernize its filtration system, and the environmental problems caused by unregulated tourism.[45] Russian national park proponents looked to parks or a single park on Baikal's shoreline as the cornerstone of a Soviet national parks system.[46] But this would remain a dream until the USSR Council of Ministers passed the Model Regulation.

"There is a dream. Let everything in and around Baikal be saved as it is," wrote an angler to *Literary Gazette* in 1980. He continued:

> Let a hundred years pass, two hundred, and let it be as it is now. May the forest not be cut, and the glorious sea and everything around it be clean. . . . It is imperative that we have such untouched places.[47]

In this article, Frants Taurin, who had first proposed national parks on Baikal in 1959, incorporated the letters written by miners, farmers, children, writers, and academics advocating for national parks on Baikal's shoreline. With hundreds of thousands of tourists coming to the lake independently each year, Oleg Gusev, one of the lake's longtime defenders, continued to support the late Skalon's proposal for the establishment of a unified national park and argued that this was the most critical task for saving the lake.[48] In a 1984 article, he admitted that much of the enthusiasm around the park had not been based on shared understandings of the form that it would take. But he asserted that the lake was a universal gift to future generations:

> No cosmic travel to the dead craters of Mars, but a walk along live Baikal has become a justification of our existence for our descendants. We will not be forgiven for a corrupt relationship to nature.[49]

While space travel had demonstrated the fragility of earth and helped foment global concern for the environment during the 1960s, two decades later, it had become abundantly clear that humans would not settle other planets in the foreseeable future, leaving humans no option but to protect earth's life-giving resources vigorously.

As the RSFSR was establishing parks after the USSR Council of Ministers signed the Model Regulation on State Nature National Parks into law in 1981, citizens from all over the USSR wrote to central ministries pleading for parks to be established around Baikal. These letters were read at the all-people's discussion at the Twenty-Sixth Party Congress in 1984.[50] The number of tourists coming to Baikal had doubled in the previous fifteen years, and some journalists suggested that "wild" tourism had become as big a problem as industrial emissions.[51] Skalon's hope for a unified park lived on, most notably within the Council of Ministers of the Buryat Autonomous Soviet Socialist Republic (ASSR). Noting that 80 percent of the shoreline and 60 percent of Baikal's catchment area was in Buryat ASSR, the Buryat ASSR government wrote to party officials calling for a unified national park with the administrative center in Ulan-Ude in early 1984.[52]

Not wanting to cede control of land to the Buryat ASSR, the Irkutsk Oblast Executive Committee passed a decree in November 1984 that again called for the establishment of a national park on Baikal's southwest shoreline. The 170,000-hectare park would include the territories of Lengiprogor's proposed Olkhon and Angara National Parks. The executive committee sent the decree to the working group on the protection of the environment and the rational use of natural resources under the RSFSR Council of Ministers, which circulated it to all interested agencies and ministries. Except for the Ministries of Forestry and Agriculture, both of which feared losing some control of land under their jurisdiction, the decree received unanimous support.[53]

While many would continue to push for a united Baikal national park in subsequent years, this possibility effectively died when the RSFSR Council of Ministers passed a decree that established Pribaikal'skii National Park (PBNP) on 418,000 hectares in the Irkutsk Oblast on February 13, 1986.[54] With the park under the authority of the Irkutsk Oblast Administration, the Buryat ASSR passed a decree for the establishment of Zabaikal'skii National Park (ZBNP) under its authority on Sviatoi Nos, Chiuviriskii Bay, Barguzin Bay, a portion of the Barguzin Ridge on the lake's eastern shore, and the Ushkanikh Islands. Despite the outside perception of an "all-powerful," centralized Soviet state, national parks on Baikal and throughout the RSFSR remained mired in poorly

Figure 5.3 Olkhon Island, Pribaikal'skii National Park. Photo by author.

crafted legislation, which placed them under regional administrations. Such jurisdiction would call into question the meaning of the term "national park."

While ZBNP, as some journalists remarked, was perhaps the more scenic of the two parks, it was in a much less populated and more remote area. Its conflicts with the local population were therefore less numerous, and far fewer tourists visited it.[55] Because PBNP was frequently visited and had many people living in it, journalists more often referred to its fate in conjunction with the larger issues of nature protection on Baikal. The tensions between PBNP and many of the fifty-four communities located in it exemplified, often in dramatic ways, land use conflicts created by many national parks in the RSFSR and the Russian Federation.

While PBNP experienced difficulties born out of the deteriorating economic and political situation of the late 1980s, its stated goals clashed with jurisdictional complexities, uncertainties over its boundaries, and local populations concerned with continuing their traditional uses of the land. The park's stated goals were "preserving the unique nature of the watershed of Lake Baikal, propagandizing its protection, and establishing the conditions for the development of a zone of organized leisure."[56] The park's territory lay in eleven different forestry districts and was under the authority of the Irkutsk Oblast Forestry-Territorial Production Association (LKhTPO). Mining was banned, and

Figure 5.4 Zabaikal'skii National Park. Photo by author.

forestry activity was limited to cuts of dead trees that posed a fire hazard. The decree forbade independent tourism and allowed hunting only with payment to the park. Locals resented paying and asking the park's permission to hunt, and convincing forestry professionals not to cut the forest was a difficult sell. Moreover, locals would be accountable to the park administration for keeping land on and near their villages up to national park standards. Designating the borders as "tentative" created fault lines along which different interested parties would aggressively push for their respective interests. And in contrast to the hopes that it would have "more authority" than any national park in the world, the park had no power to arbitrate between these different interests. The Irkutsk Oblast Executive Committee and RSFSR Ministry of Forestry would finalize the borders while Soiuzgiproleskhoz and Lengiprogor developed the "general scheme" of the territory of PBNP.[57]

PBNP's establishment inspired the hopes of an environmentally concerned public, among whom Gorbachev's reforms had already fueled great optimism.[58] Referring to PBNP as "the national park of the Soviet Union," A. A. Trofimuk, an eminent geologist, asserted that the park's future profits would offset lost jobs from closing BTsBK and other industrial enterprises.[59] Another article referred to the national park as "the lifeline of Baikal."[60] "We must feel our guilt for the impoverishment of nature," one writer wrote in *Soviet Youth* (*Sovetskaia molodezh'*) "the responsibility for it, as for a child. It is in our power to destroy much in nature, but to revive it, to bring it back to life, is much more difficult. The national park has been established to prevent this destruction. And so too it is also our responsibility."[61]

Following the USSR's ratification of UNESCO's World Heritage Convention in October 1988, talk of making Baikal the USSR's first UNESCO World Heritage Natural Site solidified the sense of Baikal's importance to "all humanity" among many of the lake's longtime supporters.[62] One quixotic proposal particularly illuminated the extent to which some Soviet citizens were viewing Baikal as a "sacred" international space. In it, over one hundred thousand Soviet citizens, united by the Baikal Fund, signed a letter calling for the Soviet government to immediately close BTsBK and declare Baikal a "neutral zone of nonproliferation" in the event of future global conflicts.[63] The concerned public hoped the USSR Council of Ministers' decree in 1987, which called for turning BTsBK into a less environmentally damaging furniture factory by 1993, portended a transformation in the state's relationship to nature.[64]

While perestroika kindled the dreams of Baikal's defenders and the Russian environmental community more broadly, the USSR's economic freefall compounded the difficulties created by the poorly conceived decree that established PBNP. Winning the trust of people in the communities located within the park's territory proved to be one of the most intractable problems.[65] Such conflicts, present in several areas of PBNP, were most intense on Olkhon Island, perhaps the park's most scenic area. Before the park's establishment, residents of Olkhon supplemented their income by selling thirty to forty tons of omul, an endemic fish, a year.[66] The decree establishing the national park made this practice illegal. Moreover, PBNP's hunting restrictions made it difficult to rely on what could have been another valuable lifeline for the residents during this time of economic difficulty. In a 1988 article in *East Siberian Pravda* (*Vostochno-Sibirskaia Pravda*), a journalist wrote:

> What do we have today? The situation is, to say the very least, becoming burdensome for the local population living in the territory of the national park. It must be said directly that the people native to the region do not need the national park. It infringes on their economic use of the territory.[67]

Residents within the park's territory were indifferent to tourist opportunities for Muscovites, the lake's international significance, and the quixotic fantasies of Baikal becoming a designated site of neutrality in the event of future global conflicts. As their economic situation worsened, they were mainly concerned with survival.

The park administration recognized these tensions and proposed that the RSFSR Ministry of Forestry designate a "zone of traditional land use."[68] Petr Abramenok, the park's third director in as many years, hoped that this would encourage Olkhon residents to help the national park.[69] In the meantime, Olkhon residents continued to sell fish and hunt without permission in defiance of park regulations. With the park administration unequipped and understaffed, the Olkhon Executive Committee took advantage of new business opportunities allowed by perestroika and established the Sarminskii Hunting Society, as a commercial enterprise that sought to attract both Soviet citizens and foreigners. Letters flooded into newspapers from the Baikal Branch of the Geographical Society of the USSR, the Soviet Academy of Sciences, the Fund of Baikal, the VOOP, and other civic organizations, as well as private citizens, almost all asking "Can Baikal be sold?"[70]

A lack of familiarity with the national park idea among locals and their longstanding traditional land uses combined with the era's expectations for environmental protection made it seem nearly impossible for interested parties to find common ground. At a 1988 conference, which brought together officials of the Irkutsk Oblast Administration, the administration of PBNP, and locals to discuss the ongoing conflicts, I. P. Orkhonov of the Olkhon District Executive Committee insisted that traditional land uses should not be compromised and that the national park should have to pay rent to the Olkhon District.

The patronizing response of most of the conference participants undoubtedly intensified local resentment. Some participants criticized residents of Olkhon for their "parochial interests" and their harmful relationship to nature.[71] The head of the Irkutsk Oblast Committee of Nature Protection, O. I. Vasil'ev, stated:

> I don't understand whether the question under discussion is the protection of nature or the protection of traditional land uses that have impoverished nature. I think that we need to place priority on the protection of nature.[72]

Despite the sensitivities that he had previously expressed for the plight of the local population, Abramenok called for the immediate acceptance of the general scheme for the national park. As the Irkutsk Oblast Executive Committee debated the general scheme with seemingly no urgency in the years to follow, Abramenok pleaded that it reject the demands of Olkhon residents, who would call for making the entire island a "special zone of free enterprise."[73] Abramenok argued that this would violate UNESCO criteria for World Heritage status.[74]

While Olkhon residents felt marginalized, the indifference of administrators in the Irkutsk Oblast Executive Committee and the hostility of the Irkutsk LKhTPO crippled the park. In an interview with *East Siberian Pravda* in early 1990, Abramenok said:

> It is revealing that for the entire time that the park has existed not one of the members of the executive committee has shown interest even in the idea of establishing PBNP—its tasks, problems, or future development. The executive committee, and more specifically its leaders, are interested in one question: What can the national park give to the region? The question, as it has been posed, is interesting, but it is a pity that a second question does not follow: What should the region give to the park, and how can it help preserve the nature of Baikal?[75]

PBNP did not receive funding to construct the infrastructure necessary to accrue revenue from tourists. The Irkutsk Oblast Administration rarely met the park's regular requests for more equipment.[76] During the four years following the park's establishment, it only managed to construct two campsites and renovate one tourist base.[77] It had become uncertain what sort of structures should be built. This was also true for ZBNP, where unorganized tourism brought significant environmental damage.[78] Plans drawn up in the late 1960s and early 1970s were ignored as the Landscape Design Institute, Soiuzgiproleskhoz, and Lengiprogor created new design plans.[79] Complaining about the lack of development in a letter to the State Committee on Forests, Abramenok stated that "the significance of Lake Baikal and PBNP is acquiring union but also world significance."[80] With the relationship between the park and recreational entities that existed before its establishment not specified, Abramenok, desperate for resources, started to ask existing tour bases to pay rent to the park.[81] In 1990, the park administration decided to introduce entry fees despite having almost no services to offer. Tourists complained that they were being asked to "pay for air."[82] Some expressed doubt that the entry fees would go to infrastructural development, insinuating that the administration was corrupt.[83]

While the Irkutsk Oblast Executive Committee largely neglected the park, the eleven forestry districts under Irkutsk LKhTPO treated it with contempt. Of the foresters working in the territory of the park, Abramenok stated, "They are busy with economic tasks: they are responsible for felling and growing the forest. They have never worked on nature protection."[84] The constant "harassment" (in Abramenok's words) of the park administration by the Irkutsk Oblast LKhTPO culminated in an illegal "audit," which Abramenok described as being led by a "pirate brigade."[85] At the end of September 1991, workers of the LKhTPO raided and closed the offices of the national park for four days.[86] In a letter to the head of the Irkutsk Oblast Committee, Abramenok wrote, "No normal person can work in these conditions."[87]

Land use laws in the territory of the park continued to carry little weight. Foresters regularly allowed unlawful timber cuts while allowing illegal fishing with nets and the construction of *banias* (bath houses) in the protected zone. Illegal large-scale agricultural enterprises continued to use banned pesticides within the park's boundaries. Small-scale industrial enterprises took no steps to modernize their filtration equipment. Mining enterprises were pushing the executive committee to allow new quarries for mining marble within the park's boundaries. The litter problem became so bad that the park was forced to spend 40 percent of its budget on cleaning it up.[88] With the park and the country's future appearing especially bleak in the summer of 1991, Abramenok wrote to the Irkutsk Oblast Executive Committee, "The position is best described as catastrophic. In and around Baikal, irreversible processes are developing. The establishment of PBNP as a 'shield' in defense of Baikal demonstrates nothing more than hypocrisy: over the course of five years, only five million rubles have been spent on the park. At the present rate, the park will be constructed in seven hundred to eight hundred years."[89]

If the park was going to be the "lifeline" of Baikal, as one article had stated, then it would also need to find a lifeline of its own.[90] Experience had shown the Irkutsk Oblast LKhTPO to be an unlikely candidate.[91] Abramenok requested the park be put under the direct control of the RSFSR Ministry of Forestry as early as 1988 and would later propose putting it under the control of the State

Committee on the Environment (Goskompriroda).[92] He also, like so many others, called for the establishment of a new governmental department akin to the United States National Park Service.[93] But the government of the RSFSR and then the Russian Federation never realized this hope, and the park was not transferred to federal control until after the Soviet Union's collapse. The park's near catastrophic financial situation forced it to seek private donations. However, by 1990, the fund created from those donations held less than five hundred rubles. As one journalist ruefully noted, Lahemaa National Park in Estonia had a private fund of five million rubles, 250,000 of which was given by the Estonian Society for the Blind.[94]

The success of the Estonian SSR, the smallest union republic, in establishing and developing a national park amplified the sense of backwardness that Russian environmentalists felt. Moreover, the hopes that Gorbachev inspired by making an improved environment an essential part of his broader reform agenda were giving way to disillusionment that environmentalists no longer had to disguise.[95] In this context, international support, which the politics of "new thinking" (*novoe myshlenie*) made possible, seemed the best hope for the park and the lake to many, including some at the heights of power. The head of the Ministry of Foreign Affairs, Eduard Shevardnadze, called for UNESCO to name Baikal as the USSR's first World Heritage Natural Site explaining that "the convention is based on the principle that some natural monuments are the responsibility of all of humanity."[96] For their part, UNESCO aggressively courted prominent Russians, including Andrei Sakharov, about the prospect of Baikal becoming the Soviet Union's first World Heritage Natural Site despite some concerns that Soviet officials did not fully understand what this responsibility meant.[97] Other than among some marginalized Communist Party hardliners, previous warnings, such as those by V. A. Chichvarin, that World Heritage designation was part of America's attempts to dominate the Third World resonated much less in this era. "Ecological problems," the Soviet Foreign Minister wrote in *Literary Gazette* later that year, "do not know national boundaries."[98] While Soviet leaders had long emphasized the universality of the goal of nature protection, these statements had a profoundly different resonance in an era when the USSR increasingly looked to Western ideas and institutions. On a Baikal fishing trip with Shevardnadze in July 1990, James Baker, the US secretary of state, reaffirmed US cooperation in many environmental protection endeavors, including the joint commitment to a program for preserving Lake Tahoe and Lake Baikal.[99] The park administration described this agreement as "an expansion of the environmental movement for saving the planet earth."[100] That fall, UNESCO completed a report of a fact-finding mission for assessing Baikal's suitability for World Heritage Natural Site designation.[101]

International collaboration and the expanding debate about UNESCO designation left the park's administration increasingly sensitive to how far short

PBNP fell of international standards.[102] Abramenok corresponded with national park officials in the United States, Czechoslovakia, and Austria and environmental organizations such as Greenpeace, and he hired American firms as consultants on the development of tourism in the park.[103] In February 1991, the park issued a memorandum of mutually beneficial cooperation with the California State Committee on Ecology. That summer, Abramenok and several other workers from PBNP spent several days in Denali National Park to learn about nature protection laws in Alaska, and Russian and American participants in the first program of the Tahoe-Baikal Institute constructed ecological trails and a center of environmental education in PBNP.[104] Even in the aftermath of a failed coup on August 11, Baikal's defenders continued to enjoy new foreign collaborative opportunities. In the subsequent weeks, Francis Macey, Gary Cook, and David Brower, the former head of the Sierra Club and perhaps the most influential American environmentalist, visited PBNP and ZBNP to help with an ecotourism plan for the two parks.[105]

One day after the Soviet Union dissolved on December 25, 1991, Abramenok effusively complimented his American partners in a letter to the Irkutsk Council of People's Deputies. Soviet people, he opined, needed to think about what should be done to "avoid ecological catastrophe." While Brezhnev and others had boasted of how the lake's ecological condition compared favorably to the Great Lakes nearly two decades earlier, Abramenok, without seeming to understand the magnitude of what had just occurred, suggested that looking to the American example might provide the right guidance needed to save the "sacred sea."[106]

Baikal's National Parks in the First Years of the Russian Federation

Following the Soviet Union's demise, the young government of the Russian Federation was keenly aware of the international perception of the USSR's environmental mismanagement and its failure to achieve its stated goals in environmental protection.[107] Boris Yeltsin, in turn, proclaimed environmental protection as one of the Russian Federation's foremost priorities.[108] In June 1992, the Russian Federation signed onto the Rio Earth Summit's Agenda 21, and in the years that followed would commit itself to fifteen international environmental agreements.[109] As the political scientist Laura Henry has noted, Russian environmentalists used their strengthened connections with Western colleagues as a source of leverage in attempts to force the state to address environmental problems.[110] The Russian sociologist Oleg Ianitskii has referred to this dynamic, the designation of protected territories under UNESCO World

Heritage designation, and the increasing financial dependence of Russian environmentalists on Western foundations as the "Westernization" of the Russian environmental movement.[111]

Baikal's environmental problems were conceived in global terms more than those of any other Russian place during the 1990s. No one conveyed this better than the poet Evgenii Evtushenko. In the late summer and fall of 1990, Evtushenko's friend Paul Winter, a famous American saxophonist known for seeking inspiration in wild places, and Peter Matthiessen, one of America's most renowned nature writers, took a trip to Baikal. After visiting some of the lake's most scenic locations and meeting with many of its defenders, most notably Valentin Rasputin, Mathiessen published a book, *The Sacred Sea of Siberia* (1992), for which Evtushenko contributed a foreword. Having expressed admiration for his American friends and their hopes to "rescue" Baikal, Evtushenko wrote:

> People of the so-called capitalist and socialist worlds have come face to face with the same tragedy—the deficiency of freedom. In capitalism, this deficiency is less apparent because it is masked by the illusion of freedom, while that which was called socialism has collapsed just because of the degrading visibility of this deficiency. Absolute freedom isn't possible—indeed, it would be criminal, for a man who has become completely free becomes free from his conscience and from a sense of beauty, and that is fascism. But there is a grand sense of freedom preserved in feeling the preciousness of space, in feeling the uniqueness of each blade of grass on which the dew gleams like tiny eyes of the earth. Precisely because we die with rapture before the wide-open lap of the Grand Canyon, and before Baikal, which seethes in anger and caressingly licks its shores in moments of tenderness, we are in this instant neither Russian nor American, but heirs of the indivisible treasure of all humankind: nature.[112]

He concluded his foreword: "Dostoyevsky once wrote: 'Beauty will save the world.' But who will save beauty?"[113]

Russian environmentalists hoped that a government more open to international cooperation and meeting the expectations of Western democracies would lay a solid foundation for Baikal's protection. The early signs were promising. Following a government decree in December 1991 that made national parks exclusively federal property, the government of the Russian Federation moved the park's jurisdiction from the Irkutsk Oblast LKhTPO to the Federal Forestry Service of the Russian Federation.[114] Federal jurisdiction better matched expectations for a "national" park and offered hope that PBNP would not be vulnerable to parochial concerns and regional political machinations. A law signed two weeks earlier reaffirmed that park land could not be used for economic purposes counter to the Model Regulation on national parks. However, the gap between law and practice and between aspiration and reality quickly became apparent.

Meanwhile, the park administration lacked the finances to build new infrastructure. If the park's problems with litter did not worsen, it was only because far fewer tourists had the time, resources, or energy to travel there. On the other hand, as was the case in protected territories throughout much of the Russian Federation, poaching became even more common within the park's boundaries, as game animals were a reliable food source at a time when residents' incomes plummeted, runaway inflation made buying food difficult, and the park lacked the funds to enforce its rules.[115] While Abramenok sought to win over the local population by stressing the benefits of environmentally conscious stewardship, the Irkutsk Oblast Administration portrayed Abramenok as an imperious landlord aspiring to consolidate a private fiefdom.[116] Among many other grievances, locals complained that the park prevented them from gathering berries, mushrooms, and firewood.[117]

Jurisdictional disputes continued to undermine the park. The Irkutsk Oblast Administration had permitted individuals and enterprises to construct private dachas and bases of relaxation within the park territory during the Gorbachev era. This illegal practice increased dramatically during the two years following the USSR's collapse despite Abramenok's multiple appeals to the arbitration court of the Irkutsk Oblast.[118] Although the national park was now legally under the Federal Forestry Service, in late 1992 the Irkutsk Oblast Administration established a commission to redraw the park's boundaries.[119] As the oblast administration argued that the national park impeded the interests of the local population, the park administration maintained that federal control best served local interests. In 1993, a research associate for the park wrote in the regional newspaper, *Sovet Youth*:

> We are not selling Baikal to Moscow. Putting the national park under federal, and not oblast, jurisdiction, although at first glance it might seem paradoxical, is to protect the interests of the local population.[120]

He continued: "It is possible that people simply do not understand that only the regime of the national park can save the shoreline of Baikal."[121] Not surprisingly, most of those living within the territory of the park did not appreciate being told what was best for them. That spring, ignoring the pleas of the park and independent ecological expertise, the Irkutsk Oblast Administration appealed to the government of the Russian Federation for the immediate removal of 112,000 hectares of the park's land.[122] The conflict between the park, the Irkutsk Oblast Administration, and those living within the park's territory received wide coverage from newspapers, civic organizations, radio, and television.[123]

Operating under the jurisdiction of the federal government did not protect the park from these attacks. The first assistant to the head of the Irkutsk Oblast Administration and the heads of the Olkhon and Sliudianka Districts wrote a letter to the Federal Forestry Service in June 1993 that criticized Abramenok and the government of the Russian Federation while questioning an undeveloped park's right to retain so much territory. Other than interfering with the livelihoods of local populations, the three officials asserted that Abramenok had done little to distinguish the activities of the park from an ordinary forestry district. Moreover, the letter suggested that the government of the RSFSR and then the Russian Federation completely neglected the park.[124] They wrote:

> PBNP has not developed; its material foundation has not been established, and the national park practically does not exist. The federal organs have no control over the work of the park.[125]

If the park did not, for all practical purposes, "exist," the authors seemed to suggest, why should the Irkutsk Oblast not use its territory as it saw fit?

Following months of pleas by the park and the reports of the Irkutsk Committee of Nature Protection, which showed that the Irkutsk Oblast Administration was brazenly breaking nature protection laws, the government of the Russian Federation confirmed the illegality of the Irkutsk Oblast Administration's removal of 112,000 hectares from the park's territory.[126] A month later, the directors of seven national parks and four nature reserves, as well as representatives of many environmental protection organizations, wrote an open letter to the Irkutsk Oblast Administration, the Irkutsk Oblast Council of People's Deputies, the Federal Forestry Service, and the population living within the park's boundaries.[127] After accusing the Irkutsk Oblast Administration of trying to "discredit the system of national parks and protected territories of Russia," they called for the organization of "international ecological monitoring" to protect it from government officials.[128] Seemingly oblivious to the vehement opposition of its residents to the park, the letter argued that this system would serve their interests. They never seemed to consider that local populations might be even more resentful toward foreigners bringing more "enlightened" practices to the park than they already had been about control from Moscow.[129]

For much of 1992 and 1993, the government of the Russian Federation appeared unable either to stop the Irkutsk Oblast Administration from giving away portions of the park or to provide material support for the park's development.[130] Baikal's defenders were increasingly putting faith in international support.

On March 6, 1992, George H. W. Bush and Boris Yeltsin signed an agreement that called for the United States and Russian Federation to work together to "save the unique ecosystem of Baikal."[131] That same year, the Federal Ministry of Environmental Protection of Germany and the Ministry of Environmental Protection and Natural Resources of Russia signed an agreement for collaboration on the development of ecotourism. In late 1992, representatives of the World Bank came to Baikal to discuss financial support for the development of recreational and environmental programs.

Baikal's longstanding role in mobilizing citizen protest within a system that banned independent organizations inspired environmental organizations and democracy proponents from around the world who saw fertile ground to promote the "rebirth of civil society" in the Russian Federation.[132] International organizations viewed the lake as a testing ground for ideas of sustainable development that the Rio Earth Summit had promoted, and the park reciprocated by reaching out to international NGOs. Funded by the US Agency of International Development (USAID) and led by the forester and former executive director of the Wilderness Society George D. Davis, the NGO Ecologically Sustainable Development brought Americans to Olkhon Island, where they helped Russians construct interpretive walking trails, restore traditional architecture, and develop environmental education programs.[133] A group from the Sierra Club came to Baikal each year during the early 1990s to take part in recreational planning; constructing bridges, shelters, and trails; and cleaning up the territories of ZBNP and PBNP. The administrations and several workers from both parks took part in annual exchanges with the national park services of the United States and Canada from 1992 to 1994.[134] In 1993, David Brower's Earth Island Institute established Baikal Watch, which sought to coordinate training for Russian park officials while lobbying international organizations, such as the World Bank, to provide financial support for Baikal's parks.[135]

With environmental activism ebbing throughout the Russian Federation as the economic situation worsened, international efforts to protect Baikal offered hope while causing some embarrassment within the Russian environmental protection community. Speaking of the establishment of Baikal Watch, a journalist wrote in *Pravda of Buryatia* (*Pravda Buryatii*):

> It seems that the foreign ecologists know better than us what is happening in our country and are more concerned about the fate of our forests and lakes. We are just learning how to orient ourselves toward

> nature. Through direct communication with these foreign ecologists, we can see their high level of culture and bring their experience to our country.[136]

Scientists from around the world brought their "experience" to Baikal in the subsequent years through numerous conferences hosted on Baikal's shores. NATO's scientific affairs division called for it to become a "model territory for the world."[137] Participants in these gatherings advocated for new designations of "national rivers" in the Baikal Basin, the immediate closure of BTsBK, and the implementation of a Concerted Tourism Management (CTM) program that could reconcile the interests of tourism operators, national parks, and the local population.[138] In 1994, the World Wildlife Fund began a project named Conserving Russia's Biodiversity, which provided for a $17.5 million investment in conservation projects in the Russian Federation and $1.5 million for the conservation of Baikal and its environs.[139] To lay the groundwork for UNESCO World Heritage Status, the US government under the auspices of USAID developed a land use plan for the Baikal watershed.[140] In total, from the collapse of the USSR to 1998, international working groups carried out forty projects on Baikal at the cost of more than $20 million.[141] Local communities eking out a living were largely absent from the working groups that brought together concerned citizens of different countries who could marvel at the breathtaking beauty that surrounded them.[142]

UNESCO named Baikal and the volcanoes of Kamchatka World Heritage Natural Sites on December 4, 1996. Both Russian and foreign environmentalists had placed high hopes on UNESCO World Heritage status as both a tool for environmental protection and an attraction for tourists. However, Mikhail Grachev, the director of the Baikal Limnological Institute, warned Bernd von Droste, the head of the World Heritage Committee, that World Heritage Status might come to be resented by the local population if it threatened some economic activities. Moreover, he asserted in the same letter that tourism posed a potentially greater threat than industry to Baikal's environment.[143]

In May 1996, two years before he was fired for "mismanagement," Abramenok lamented the general situation in *East Siberian Pravda*.[144] He wrote, "It is shameful that in our country until this time it is not clearly understood what is meant by the term national park."[145] On the one hand, PBNP had survived the attempts of government officials in the Irkutsk Oblast to reduce its territory, which the lake's defenders argued would "discredit" Russia's national park system. However, as Abramenok's comment revealed, PBNP, and for that matter ZBNP, had not protected the Baikal region in the ways hoped for by Oleg Gusev, Innokentii Gerasimov, Vasilii Skalon, or even the architects of Lengiprogor.

Conclusion

In 1987, Valentin Rasputin wrote, "How we resolve today our painful questions surrounding Baikal will be an example of our relationship to nature as a whole."[146] Since the late 1950s, no area in Russia had weighed more heavily on the consciences of Russian environmentalists. They increasingly emphasized that Baikal's protection was important to "all of humanity." By the late 1980s, leaders of environmental protection throughout the world were more concerned about Baikal than any other place in Russia. While international help gave brief hope to Russia's environmentalists who had long fought for Baikal's protection, this optimism had dimmed significantly by the end of the century. To many, it seemed that different international organizations had spent millions of dollars on the Baikal region's development and protection primarily to allow these experts to come and marvel at the lake's beauty.[147]

Evtushenko believed that beauty could bring humanity together in this new era. People came together, certainly. No longer separated by rival geopolitical camps, they met in one of the world's most beautiful landscapes. They could find common ground and speak openly without fears of political reprisal. But Baikal's environmental problems seemed no closer to resolution and its parks in no better condition than when Rasputin expressed this sentiment or when Russian environmentalists looked to the West following the USSR's collapse. Rasputin and other environmentalists were concluding that nothing had changed in their state's relationship to nature, and without that occurring in the future "foreign intervention" would yield limited results.

6

Paddling Upstream

Samara Bend National Park and the Transformation of Citizen "Environmentalism" from Soviet to Post-Soviet Society

In the summer of 1890, a teenaged Vladimir Ulianov took a four-day boat trip, the Zhigulevskaia Krugosvetka, which flows through one of the most scenic and morphologically unique parts of the Volga River, the Samara Bend—home to the Zhiguli Mountains.[1] Reflecting on this trip much later in life, Ulianov, now known as Lenin, reportedly said, "In Switzerland it is good, but it is better in the Zhiguli."[2] A peninsula-like formation, the Samara Bend is shaped by three sharp turns in the Volga; after flowing south from Kazan for about two hundred kilometers with occasional meanderings to the east and west, the river takes a hairpin turn and then flows west for eighty kilometers. Just beyond the village of Shiraevo, the river begins an arc to the south before turning west just beyond Samara.[3] After flowing west for 130 kilometers, the Volga turns south and then maintains a much more direct course to the Caspian Sea.

Since the early twentieth century, the Samara Bend and the Zhiguli Mountains have attracted the attention of geologists, biologists, and geographers. In 1927, the establishment of the Zhiguli Zapovednik put the Zhiguli Mountains under protection.[4] As the region became one of the USSR's fastest developing hubs of industry after World War II, the *zapovednik* was liquidated in 1951, re-established in 1958, and then liquidated again in 1961. With the future of environmental protection in the region still in doubt, members of the All-Russian Society for the Protection of Nature (VOOP) used the development of tourism as the rationale to expand protection to almost all the land within the Samara Bend in the form of a national park.

The movement for the establishment of Samara Bend National Park (SBNP) grew out of citizen activism led by the scientific community. As the park's indefatigable supporters in the Kuibyshev Oblast galvanized the region's environmentally concerned public and gained the support of influential scientists

Into Russian Nature. Alan D. Roe, Oxford University Press (2020) © Oxford University Press.
DOI: 10.1093/oso/9780190914554.001.0001

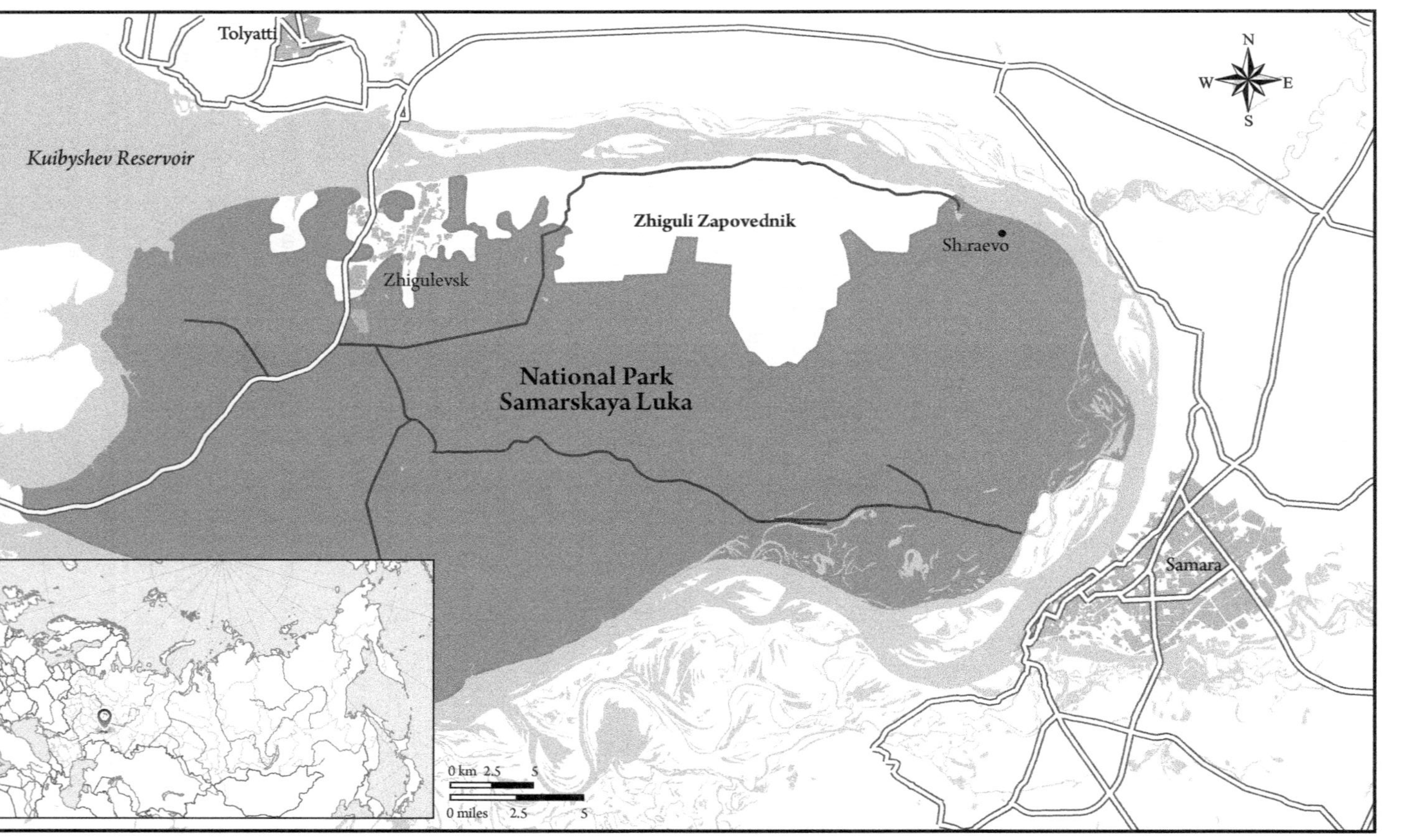

Figure 6.1 Samara Bend National Park/SBNP.

in Moscow, industries expanded their foothold, factories and other places of work built houses of recreation, and high-placed individuals built private dachas within the territory of the proposed park. While extractive industries and numerous enterprises proved much more difficult to dislodge after the park was established than park supporters had imagined, the park administration struggled to sell its vision for regional economic transformation through the development of tourism. Following the Soviet Union's collapse, emboldened by their newfound freedoms, a group of radical environmentalists, led by 22-year old Sergei Fomichev, staged a protest against mining in the park, which met violent retaliation. As illegal mining continued and the park's infrastructure remained undeveloped in the years after these clashes received national attention, the park's early supporters became more disillusioned about the its prospects with each passing year.

This story of hope followed by disillusionment illustrates the limited success regional actors had in pushing Moscow to pass environmental legislation during the USSR's final decades. At the same time, this history demonstrates their weak position in pressuring the government of the Russian Soviet Federated Socialist Republic (RSFSR) and then the Russian Federation to enforce the country's existing environmental laws.

From Visions of Transformation to Hopes for Protection

With the same technocratic optimism that led to calls to transform the Angara River and make the Baikal region "work for communism," Communist Party leaders and central ministries planned to make the area around Samara Bend one of the USSR's largest industrial centers. As part of the Great Stalin Plan for the Transformation of Nature, in 1950 the USSR began the "Big Volga" project. This project planned a series of dams to produce the energy that would allow for dramatic economic growth while making it easier for freight ships to navigate the river.[5] Upon its completion, the Kuibyshev Hydroelectric Station (GES), which would inundate the territory where the Volga turns sharply to the east just north of the Samara Bend, was the largest hydroelectric station in the world. As it was being constructed, journalists and propagandists celebrated the "conquerors of the Volga" and the "assault" on the river.[6] Kuibyshev GES, they frequently noted, was superior to Grand Coulee, Hoover, or any other dam in the United States.[7] One journalist described the completion of the Kuibyshev GES, which would produce six times more energy than all energy stations before the 1917 revolution combined, as the "incarnation of a dream" that once seemed "utopian."[8]

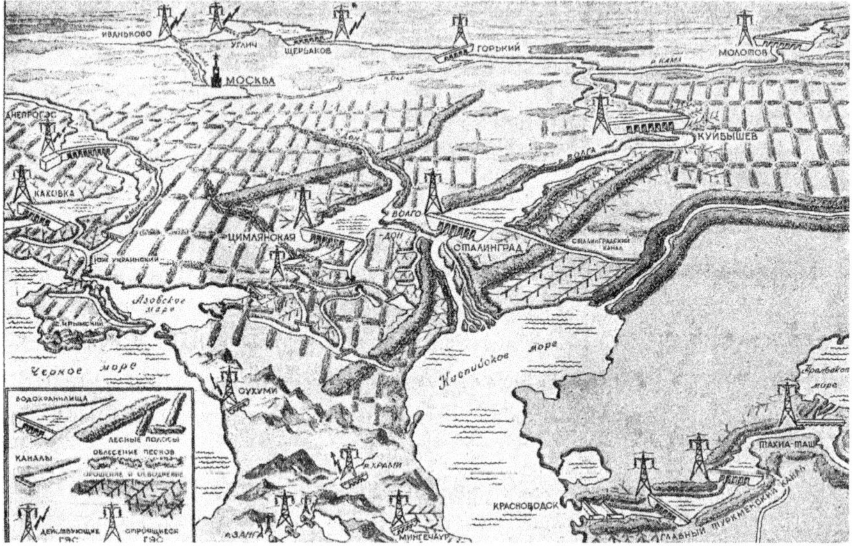

Figure 6.2 The Big Volga Project. From *Literaturnaia gazeta,* May 12, 1951.

The "conquest" of the Volga would help the USSR move toward the Khrushchev-era dream of a socialist society in which cheap energy would propel economic growth through the production of consumer goods.[9] The new industrial region at the Samara Bend would include fertilizer plants, petrochemical and electronics factories, and the USSR's largest automobile plant.[10] The Kuibyshev GES, these new industries, the model socialist city of Tolyatti, and the residential housing in the rapidly growing industrial region required tremendous amounts of limestone, and the Zhiguli Mountains of the Samara Bend had an abundance of it. After the Zhiguli Zapovednik was closed in 1951, the state mining industry started extracting large amounts in the former reserve.[11]

As the central press focused more attention on environmental problems throughout the USSR, the Zhiguli became an object of particular concern. Although the *zapovednik* had been reestablished in 1958, mining activities continued. A *Literary Gazette* article in December of that year article painted a bleak picture.

> The new plant crumbles, crushes, and explodes the slopes of the Zhiguli, and it will only be a few dozen years when nothing remains of the charming, pristine beauty of the mountains, which have inspired generations of poets. Already, the right slope of the Zhiguli has been transformed into a sea, which causes a joyless impression. There are fallen trees, heaps of rubble, and colossal mining pits.[12]

The author exhorted readers: "Daily, hourly, we must think about the Soviet person. It is for him that cities and miracle seas are constructed. It is for him that we must protect the nature of the motherland!"[13]

Tourists were coming to the area in higher numbers, and some were observing the environmental damage to the Zhiguli. In 1955, teams from forty-two oblasts in the RSFSR came to the Samara Bend for the Second All-Russian Tourist Rally.[14] In 1963, two years after the Soviet government liquidated the *zapovednik* again, a group of twenty-two students from the Krasnoyarsk Pedagogical Institute traveled by boat around the Samara Bend. After the trip, they wrote to the Kuibyshev Oblast Council of Ministers:

> We Siberians, having spent time on the Volga, were inspired by the beautiful nature of the Zhiguli Mountains, which are no less impressive than the landscapes of the Krasnoyarsk Pillars [Stol'by]—the unique *zapovednik* of Siberia. Therefore, we were surprised to learn that these beautiful places are not protected and are being predatorily destroyed: forests are being cut, mining is taking place, although there are other areas to do this in the oblast. We are members of the Society of Nature Protection, and we consider it our duty to say a word in defense of the Zhiguli and request the restoration of the Zhiguli Zapovednik.[15]

Increased travel throughout the USSR was, indeed, giving Soviet citizens a much better sense of environmental problems outside their home regions.

The residents of the Kuibyshev Oblast were the most concerned about the fate of the Samara Bend and the Zhiguli. The two centers of the growing environmental concern in Kuibyshev were the Nature Protection Section of the Local History Museum and the oblast section of the VOOP. These two organizations, working together, collected numerous petitions for the reestablishment of the Zhiguli Zapovednik. Even after the RSFSR Council of Ministers did so in 1966, many concerned about the area remained anxious about the *zapovednik*'s future, since the state had already liquidated it twice.[16] Moreover, they knew that the USSR's largest automobile plant, beginning its operations just across the river in Tolyatti, would put further demands on the area's natural resources.[17] Writing about the Zhiguli in the Kuibyshev newspaper *Volga Commune* (*Volzhskaia kommuna*) less than a year after the RSFSR Council of Ministers reestablished the *zapovednik*, the journalist I. Egorov wrote, "In many places, mining is turning the banks of the Volga into a dusty, stone wasteland."[18] In an *Izvestiia* article in 1968, another journalist described the *zapovednik* as "a weak establishment" and a "small island surrounded by oil drills, towers, quarries and crossed by power lines."[19] It had no scientific workers and almost no dormitories to house its few employees. *Izvestiia* quoted the chief forester of the *zapovednik* as saying, "This is a typical picture in the Zhiguli. They blow up the mountains, take away the forest, and fulfill the plan."[20]

Some concluded that a national park was necessary to save the Zhiguli and the surrounding area. In 1961, the Commission on Nature Protection had discussed the formation of a national park in place of the recently dissolved *zapovednik*.[21] In 1965, the Kuibyshev branch of the VOOP established a working group called the Protection of Significant Places and Natural Monuments, which planned to map the best locations for protected territories in the oblast. They argued that scenic areas were essential for the residents of the rapidly industrializing region. In early 1966, Aleksei Zakharov, a member of the working group and one of the progenitors of the idea for SBNP, stated:

> Nature is not only for the people in the sense of the resources it provides. We cannot forget that nature is an essential factor in the health of our people, and from this point of view we must remember natural monuments are places of mass recreation for working people.[22]

The local press touted the prospects of the region for health resorts and tourism as visitors increased each year.[23] Beginning in 1968, citizens from different parts of the USSR would come to the area every year for the Grushin Festival of Tourist Songs.[24] That same year, the Central Council on Tourism designated the Zhigulevskaia Krugosvetka as an "all-union route."

Architects came up with proposals for a park that threatened to undermine the restorative qualities of the area's nature that Zakharov and others believed were increasingly necessary. In late 1968, the Central Scientific-Technical Council of Landscape Design completed a preliminary plan for a "nature park," which called for extensive infrastructural development, including high rise hotels. In October 1969, the Executive Committee of the Oblast Council passed a resolution that called for the establishment of a " nature park of republic significance," which would include the Zhiguli Zapovednik and create four new temporary reserves (*zakazniki*).[25] However, it did not indicate what form the park would take, and the architectural community seemed to be shaping the debate.

In December, *Volga Komsomol* (*Volzhskii komsomolets*), a Kuibyshev newspaper, published a long article describing the future national (no longer referred to as nature) park. Writing that the "landscape of the Zhiguli is under the threat of destruction," the article asserted that the preservation of the Zhiguli and its environs was possible only through the creation of a national park that regulated tourism and prevented natural resource extraction.[26] While the author, L. Iarkaia, described the forest as "attraction number one," he stated that the national park would need a health resort, apartments, boat clubs, beaches, and tourist bases. The park would include a forty-story hotel and would be able to accommodate

180,000 people simultaneously.[27] Since tourism's environmental impact was becoming a prominent subject of conversation, the oblast's environmental protection community was hardly comforted by such "gigantomania."

Galvanizing Public Support for the Park

The landscape architects' vision perhaps concerned no one as deeply as Tatiana Tezikova. After working for a few years as an agronomist, Tezikova became a research associate at the Kuibyshev Museum of Local History (kraevedenie) in 1956. There, she helped establish the museum's "nature section" in 1965 and became its first director.[28]

As head of the section, Tezikova taught, among other subjects, the natural history of the region, the plant and animal world, water resources of the Kuibyshev Oblast, and nature protection.[29] She organized expositions on the natural attractions of the region and a television program, *Our Region* (*Nash raion*), along with the Society for the Protection of Historical Monuments.[30] Her lectures, which she presented at the museum, different educational

Figure 6.3 Tatiana Tezikova. Photo courtesy of Valerii Erofeev.

establishments, and factories throughout the oblast, articulated her uncompromising vision for protecting the most scenic and historically significant places of the Samara Bend. During these years, she became the area's most passionate and uncompromising defender. As she was described by one colleague, "When it came to nature, she spoke frankly and demanded that the law be followed regardless with whom she was talking."[31] Her passion, persistence, and uncompromising positions helped engender strong environmental protection values among a generation in the Kuibyshev Oblast.

The growing regional interest is evidenced in the letters from concerned citizens that flooded the Kuibyshev Oblast branch of the VOOP and the Local History Museum in 1969 and 1970.[32] In 1970, a group of young people from Tolyatti wrote, "We demand that the architects leave the Zhiguli Mountains wild. For the sake of humanity and science, do not kill this beautiful place."[33] A week later, the Kuibyshev Oblast branch of the VOOP held a meeting that included different civic organizations and representatives of universities in Kuibyshev, Tolyatti, and Zhigulevsk. They discussed establishing a regional land use plan that focused on preserving the Zhiguli Zapovednik and protecting the shoreline of the Samara Bend by establishing a park. They passed a resolution that called for immediately declaring the territory of the Samara Bend a single *zakaznik* of "republican significance."[34] Signed by representatives of several universities, institutes in the Academy of Sciences, and local history museums, the resolution stated: "As a nature-historical complex and unique corner of Russian nature, the Samara Bend must be preserved forever in its natural form."[35] Tezikova and V. V. Lebedev, the chair of the Scientific Technical Council of the Kuibyshev Oblast branch of the VOOP, wrote a letter appealing to the Central Council of the VOOP.[36] Nikolai Alekseevich Gladkov, a renowned ornithologist and a member of the Central Council, called Samara Bend the "equal of Baikal." The Central Council passed a resolution calling for a "national nature park."[37]

Over the next few years, Tezikova and other park supporters wrote tirelessly to government officials, party members, and the scientific community about the proposed park. From 1970 until the park's official establishment in 1984, Tezikova sent letters to writers, journalists, scientists, local organs of power, the RSFSR Supreme Soviet, the government of the USSR, and high-ranking Communist Party members at the level of the Kuibyshev Oblast and the USSR.[38] Within a few years after it was proposed, the idea had already received support from a wide cross-section of the Soviet scientific community in the Kuibyshev Oblast and beyond. Influential scientists, such as Grigorii Nikol'skii, Valeriia Obedientova, and Aleksei Yablokov, wrote to the high-ranking party members and the USSR Council of Ministers calling for the establishment of the proposed park.[39] In 1974, Yablokov, who would eventually serve as Yeltsin's ecological security advisor, sent an open letter published in the magazine *Labor* (Trud) signed by many renowned scientists. He wrote, "There is a great unease when we speak of the Zhiguli, on the shore of the great Russian river—the beautiful Volga."[40] He continued: "The fate of Samara Bend is an evolutionary problem, which has theoretical (for the theory of evolution and biogenesis) and practical significance. The destruction of the ecology of Samara Bend, without any doubt, will irredeemably impoverish our science and our people."[41]

Yablokov and others believed that the plans for mass tourism posed as significant a threat to the region's nature as extractive industries. Viktor Timofeev led a group of environmentalists in pursuing a middle path that sought to address the regional economy and the protection of Samara Bend. A professor at Kuibyshev Pedagogical University and a member of the VOOP, Timofeev is an example of how a deeply rooted love for nature close to home inspired local Russian actors to counter the environmentally destructive economic agendas of central ministries. Born in St. Petersburg in 1912, Timofeev moved to Kuibyshev in 1932 after finishing Semipalatinsk Agricultural Technical Institute. In 1933, he enrolled in the Kuibyshev Agricultural Institute to earn a PhD in botany. After fighting in the Red Army, in 1946 he began working as an assistant professor at Kuibyshev Pedagogical University.[42] Throughout the 1950s, Timofeev took long treks by foot, bicycle, and motorcycle in the territory of Samara Bend. By 1960, he had become an active member of the Kuibyshev Oblast branch of the VOOP and developed extensive contacts with Moscow environmentalists. Along with Tezikova and others, he worked tirelessly for the reestablishment of the Zhiguli Zapovednik.

Timofeev sought to enlist science in planning the park. Supported by the Kuibyshev branch of the All-Russian Design and Scientific-Research Institute (Gidroproekt), Timofeev began a study in 1974 called "The Scientific Basis for the Use and Protection of Samara Bend." During the summers from 1974 through 1976, he and a group of geobotanists and zoologists from Kuibyshev Pedagogical and Kuibyshev State Universities took groups ranging from twenty to fifty students to visit. Most of the participants were enthusiastic members of nature protection brigades (*druzhiny*).[43] The professors consulted with the VOOP to work out plans for dividing the park, which they decided not to call "national" because they thought it might alarm some government officials, into different zones with varying levels of protection.[44] The final report consisted of the study of the biogeography of the proposed park, an inventory of the flora and fauna, nature protection zoning, and recommendations for nature use and protection.[45]

The project report emphasized the fundamental human need to experience the sort of unaltered nature that was quickly vanishing from the region. They wrote:

> Samara Bend will serve as an additional place of recreation where people can relax in communion with pristine [*pervozdannyi*] nature and receive particular emotional-aesthetic pleasure away from the stress of life in industrial cities and crowded civilization.[46]

By alleviating stress, they argued, workers would become more productive.[47] The natural beauty and the area's good weather, Tezikova and Zakharov assumed, would draw hundreds of thousands, perhaps millions, of people who could enjoy a wide range of recreational trails. However, all of this would be lost if the region continued to suffer damage from mining, industrial development, and the careless behavior of tourists at tourist bases and pioneer camps. Moreover, they argued that the plans of Lengiprogor, which had taken over the planning for an infrastructure-intensive park several years before, "would transform the area into a typically inhabited area" that would undermine its aesthetic appeal. While 75 percent of the park would have reserve status, the remaining quarter of the park's territory would be dedicated to recreational purposes. They envisioned the park, which they referred to as both a "green island" and a "museum of nature," as a unified decision-making center that would remove all industrial enterprises, extractive industries, and dachas as well as tourist bases and houses of recreation not under its control.[48] The report, however, never addressed the likelihood of the government acting on such a radical plan, and economic ministries and government officials were already expressing profound misgivings.[49]

The final project report and the VOOP resolution left many unresolved questions and contradictions. Human activity had already extensively shaped the territory of the Samara Bend region, which hardly made it "pristine" nature. Over twenty-five thousand people lived in the proposed park's territory, and Zhigulevsk, a city with a population of fifty-three thousand, bordered on it. Were the authors proposing to carry out projects to restore anthropogenic landscapes to their more "natural" condition? Would some of the inhabitants of the region have to leave? If not, what land use restrictions would the park impose on them? Was it realistic to assume that the service industry would provide enough work to compensate for the jobs lost through the removal of enterprises and mining? And if enough tourists did come, how would the residents of Samara Bend react to so many visitors spending their leisure time near their homes? When and where would the enterprises and industries within the park be relocated? The lack of discussion about fundamental questions illustrated the absence of cooperation between the authors of the project and the central economic ministries on which they would depend to carry it out.

Nonetheless, the project and the VOOP resolution made the park the central rallying point for the environmentally concerned residents of the Kuibyshev Oblast. Many of them had embraced an uncompromising view as to what constituted the appropriate land uses within the proposed park. Continued mining stood as the foremost threat to the area's recreation value.[50] With Tezikova leading the movement, the protection of Samara Bend had become a moral imperative for many. By the mid-1970s, the park's supporters had set themselves on a collision course with the residents and the enterprises within the territory of the proposed national park.

Industry's Expanding Foothold

The prospect of more significant restrictions on extractive uses motivated industries to enlarge their foothold in the proposed park's territory before it was officially established. The Kuibyshev Oblast Executive Committee had done nothing to enforce decrees passed in 1969 and 1973 calling for the Kuibyshev Construction Materials Administration to carry out reclamation work in mining pits.[51] In August 1975, the RSFSR Council of Ministers reprimanded the Kuibyshev Oblast Executive Committee for neglecting these decrees, the RSFSR Law on Nature Protection, and the Land Code of the RSFSR. Additionally, it called on the USSR Ministry of Construction Materials to do reclamation work.[52] Every year, mining operations took out up to eleven million cubic meters of rubble from the territory of the *zapovednik*.[53] As Timofeev and his team worked on the project for the national park, the Oblast Executive Committee was negotiating an extension of the Zhigulevsk Building Materials Plant's lease on existing quarries. Illegal timber cutting also continued in the *zapovednik*.[54]

Throughout the decade, enterprises accelerated the pace at which they gave out land to their employees, who would build dachas on it. Over ten thousand dachas were constructed between 1971 and 1984.[55] During this time, different enterprises also built more than eighty recreation bases, many of which blighted the most scenic parts of the shoreline.[56] In 1978, the administration of the *zapovednik* agreed to give land for the expansion of a limestone quarry in exchange for land of lesser value. In the early 1980s, the administration did not protest the construction of a hotel by the VAZ Auto Factory within sight of its territory and the establishment of a hog farm on the land adjacent to it.[57]

The regional press dedicated increasing attention to the environmental damage taking place in the Samara Bend. The regional paper, *Volga Komsomol* (*Volzhskii komsomolets*) published over 250 articles related to nature protection in the area during the 1970s.[58] The central press was also paying attention. The *Izvestiia* editorial board received many letters, such as one from a reader from Volgograd in June 1975:

> The Zhiguli is our pride, a region of rich nature, and it must be inviolable. We need to remove the heartless violators of nature quickly. We have heard enough formal bureaucratic replies and promises. Our descendants will not forgive us for failing to preserve what nature has created over the course of millions of years for the joy of humans.[59]

In a 1977 *Pravda* article entitled "In Defiance of Logic," Iurii Mironov described the disfigurement of the Zhiguli and the failure of the Kuibyshev Oblast Executive Committee to enforce previous decrees calling for reclamation work, and concluded, "We believe that a state-operated national park must be organized here to preserve Samara Bend."[60] Writing in *Soviet Russia* (*Sovetskaia Rossiia*) in 1981, A. Bochkarev declared, "We must utilize all of our strength to find other deposits of construction stone so that we can finally end the destruction of the Zhiguli Mountains."[61]

Establishment of the Park and Winning Friends

Even as the park inched closer to establishment, government ministries did not give promising signals that mining would end anytime soon. In 1981, Gosplan RSFSR opined that it would be "inadvisable" to stop quarry activity in the Zhiguli.[62] The park's supporters were not deterred. With the support of the VOOP and Kuibyshev State and Pedagogical Universities, Tezikova, Roshchevskii, and Zakharov put together the planning documents and materials to send to the RSFSR Council of Ministers.[63] While Tezikova and Zakharov continued to barrage government officials with letters, Roshchevskii, as Timofeev had done several years before, took members of nature protection brigades to the territory of the future park to carry out "green patrols" and continue zoning work for the future national park.[64]

After a conference brought environmentalists throughout the Kuibyshev Oblast together to talk about the best strategy for doing this, the RSFSR Council of Ministers passed a decree in May 1984 that established the park and called for it to begin operations on July 1, 1985.[65] The decree banned hunting, the collection of medicinal plants, and the use of herbicides in the park's territory. Of the park's 125,000 hectares, over half came out of the state forest fund, and fifty-six thousand were from agricultural establishments (*kolkhozy* and *sovkhozy*). The

Ministry of Forestry assigned the landscape design institute Soiuzgiproleskhoz the task of designing the park between 1985 and 1987.[66] The decree, like so many others establishing national parks, deferred the most difficult questions to the future. A resolution regarding continued work by mining and other enterprises within the park's territory, for example, would be made after the completion of the park plans.

Given the fact that various land uses irreconcilable with the definition of national parks outlined by the Model Regulation were taking place within the park's territory, it is difficult to believe that the government of the RSFSR ever seriously considered the conflicts that the park would cause. This seeming inattention to important details supports the image of an aging and sclerotic system, even as the Council of Ministers was establishing what was from the perspective of the nature protection community an environmentally progressive institution. Four quarries were located within the territory of SBNP, as well as more than ten thousand dachas and sixty short- and long-term recreation facilities. The Tolyatti Chicken Processing Plant, a hog farm, an airport, a psychiatric facility, and the Zhigulevsk landfill fell within its boundaries. The park's supporters insisted that economic ministries remove the illegal and aesthetically unpleasant enterprises.

The profits from tourism, they argued, would make it possible to close existing enterprises incompatible with the goals of the park. Tezikova believed that people living within the park's territory would open cafes, souvenir stands, shops for renting tourism equipment, transportation services, and even dance halls.[67] Describing her vision shortly after the park's official establishment in a letter to the central organs of the Communist Party, she wrote, "The social interests of the villages will merge with the interests of the national park. The villages will become an integral part of the composition of the park."[68] Work, she said, would be available to "every member of the family."[69] As Tezikova worked to convince Party officials and different levels of government to make the changes necessary to realize this vision, Iurii Roshchevskii, working as a scientific associate for the park, led the efforts to convince the residents that the existence of the park was in their interests.

The son of an officer in the Red Army during the Great Patriotic War, Iurii Konstantinovich Roshchevskii had moved to Kuibyshev in 1956. After graduating from the Kuibyshev State Pedagogical University with a specialization in teaching biology and chemistry in 1968, he taught at the Kuibyshev Pedagogical and Kuibyshev State Universities. For fifteen years, he taught courses in ecology and nature protection while leading students on expeditions to Yakutia, the Murmansk and Astrakhan Oblasts, and the Kazakh SSR during the summers. In 1975, he became the leader of the section of protected territories in the Kuibyshev Oblast branch of the VOOP. From that time, he began working closely with Zakharov and Tezikova. From the park's establishment in 1985, he served as the head of the science department and recruited many of his former students who had been active in nature protection brigades.[70]

During his ten years working for the park, Roshchevskii was SBNP's public face, as park directors, most of whom were political appointees who knew little about nature protection, came and went. Roshchevskii put together the first functioning scientific division within any Russian national park. From the beginning of its operations, according to Roshchevskii, the scientific division's conclusions were attacked by the industry lobby.[71] Roshchevskii also spent significant energy writing to anyone who he thought could help the park, including officials from all levels of government, different ministries, and leading cultural figures of the day.[72]

Educating the public about SBNP was Roshchevskii's foremost priority. Each year, he gave dozens of lectures in Kuibyshev, Tolyatti, Zhigulevsk, and small settlements throughout the area. He called for the "transformation" of the region's socioeconomic structure, with the park serving as the center for co-ordinating recreation, scientific, and economic activity.[73] He invited heads of village councils to seminars to educate them about the park's nature protection regulations.[74] He also sent letters regularly to regional newspapers, appeared on radio, and wrote a documentary film script about SBNP.

The forty-five-minute film begins with a shot of the Zhiguli Mountains from the Volga while the film's narrator relates the region's geological history and the

Figure 6.4 Iurii Roshchevskii in Samara Bend National Park, mid-1980s. Photo courtesy of Valerii Erofeev.

history of Stepan Razin and Emilian Pugachev—leaders of the most famous Russian Cossack uprisings—hiding from government officials in the caves of the Zhiguli. He then describes the area's many animals—elk, bear, wolves, wild boar, roe deer, and fox. Throughout, the narrator consistently reminds the viewer to "respect nature." The film concludes with a view from Molodetskii Kurgan, one of the most scenic points in the Zhiguli, onto the city of Tolyatti, a city constructed for the mass production of automobiles.[75] The narrator intones, "Humans need modern comfort, but nature is no less important. Without it, humans cannot survive."[76]

Roshchevskii saw the park's mission as imparting a love for Russian nature, as well as an incubator of civic consciousness. He believed that educated citizens would feel empowered to try to shape the society in which they wanted to live. He asserted that the very existence of the park was a testament to the power of civic activism, but realizing the park's potential demanded public involvement.[77] In a 1988 article in *Volga Commune,* he wrote:

> Everyone must take into account that our nature national park is the only such organization in the country, established by the initiative from the bottom up. And therefore it is for us to decide what SBNP will be like.[78]

Figure 6.5 Molodetskii Kurgan. Photo by author.

Roshchevskii did everything possible to convince young people of this vision and wrote to any organization—tourist clubs, participants of the Grushin Festival of Tourist Songs, Komsomol—that he believed would come to the park's defense. The public responded. The RSFSR Council of Ministers received over thirty collective letters supporting the park in 1988 alone.[79] Concerned citizens also sent letters to the Kuibyshev Oblast Executive Committee and different governmental departments and ministries. They wrote extensively about illegal land uses. In one such letter, a group of participants from the Grushin Festival in 1988 implored, "The unique nature, the legendarily rich history, and the original culture draws people to the Samara Bend. The establishment of SBNP was an enormous step toward saving the peninsula, but it cannot be protected without immediate resolutions on the question of removing objects not compatible with its goals."[80]

Despite the park's broad base of vocal and passionate supporters, land use practices changed little during its first years. Some collective farm (*kolkhoz*) administrators asserted that the park was an illegal entity and refused to abide by restrictions.[81] In the first two years of its existence, ninety thousand cubic meters of timber were harvested from the territory of the park.[82] Mining continued as before, and poaching was commonplace.[83] Moreover, the Kuibyshev Oblast Executive Committee continued to propose the withdrawal of protected territory for the expansion of quarries in blatant violation of the Model Regulation.[84] Meanwhile, the park lacked the infrastructure to bring in any revenue from tourism, which made its arguments for economic reorientation to the tourism industry an impossible sell.

Dachas also posed problems. By the end of the decade, there were sixteen thousand dachas in the water-protected zone near some of the most important natural and architectural monuments.[85] Participants of the Zhigulevskaia Krugosvetka frequently noted that near the dachas trash heaps containing refrigerators, radios, and other household appliances littered one thirty-kilometer stretch of shoreline.[86] One article characterized dacha owners as carrying out "chemical attacks" on adjacent lands.[87] In early 1989, the Kuibyshev Oblast Council of People's Deputies stated that they would not address the prospect of removing dachas until 1997.[88] By taking up valuable space on the more scenic parts of the shoreline, pioneer camps also impeded the development of tourism facilities.

Soiuzgiproleskhoz worked on its "general plan" as the fledgling park struggled to curb illegal land uses and develop infrastructure. The project, completed in 1989, rarely took into account input from people living within the park's territory.[89] The USSR's precarious economic situation, however, made the park plans moot; national parks were not a priority for economic ministries. Commenting on the situation, Roshchevskii wrote, "The park in actuality exists only on paper, but not on the Samara Bend."[90]

Elevated Expectations, Disappointment, and Anger

National park supporters, like environmentalists throughout the USSR, were emboldened by glasnost reforms.[91] By the late 1980s, Roshchevskii, Tezikova, and others were taking a more combative approach and speaking in a more moralistic tone, as they blamed "philistine" government bureaucrats for their "consumerist" and "barbaric" relationship to nature.[92] In one article, Roshchevskii insisted that dacha owners, government officials, and the Kuibyshev Oblast Quarry Administration were determined to destroy the national park.[93] Journalist A. Fedorov described the park land as developing into an "anthropogenic desert" and accused the Kuibyshev Oblast Administration of committing "crimes against ecology."[94]

While their early criticisms in the press focused on the failures of the Kuibyshev Oblast Administration and suspicion toward different ministries, Roshchevskii, Tezikova, and others began using the press and personal correspondence to critique the Soviet system and the Russian state more broadly. Writing to Gorbachev in 1988 about the "incorrect" relationship to nature demonstrated by Communist Party members of the Kuibyshev Oblast, Tezikova stated:

> The government of an enormous and powerful country should be ashamed of such robbery of national parks—saving mere crumbs of genuine nature, which are necessary both psychologically and physiologically, not to mention failing to meet the international obligations of the USSR to save relict and endemic species.[95]

In letters to all levels of the government and the Communist Party, she chastised "communist dachniki" (dacha owners) to illustrate the hypocrisy of well-positioned members of the Party elite taking private plots in a system that purported universal equality.[96]

Roshchevskii asserted that the problem had even deeper historical roots. In a 1988 article in *Volga Commune*, he wrote:

> From the times of the tsars, there has been the mistaken point of view that first material needs must be satisfied and only then, if there is time and energy, spiritual demands of humans, including the protection of nature and culture, can be considered. This is a dangerous path. I think that as long as productive interests stand over our spiritual interests, we cannot have an excess of objects of the first necessity and nature cannot be saved.[97]

The assertion that communism and the Russian state had done such a poor job at protecting nature raised the question of whether other systems and states had acted as better stewards of the environment. Supporters of SBNP, like other Soviet environmentalists, were concluding that they did. Writing about the park's predicament in *Volga Komsomol,* A. Fedorov wrote:

> In the West, reserves and national parks are national treasures. They receive attention and care from federal and municipal authorities. We squander and foul up everything, and everyone does whatever they want.[98]

The "imagined West" had long been the measuring stick with which different groups of Soviet citizens—dissidents, refuseniks, hippies, and others—used to pass adverse judgment on the Soviet state.[99] Internationally minded environmentalists increasingly used national parks to publicly lament the superior commitment of Western democracies to environmental protection.

Above all other issues, mining in SBNP continued to concern the environmentalist community and attract attention well beyond the Kuibyshev Oblast.[100] In 1987, the famous bard Bulat Okudzhava came to the area to protest the operation of quarries.[101] The following year the RSFSR Council of Ministers gave the park's defenders a kernel of hope when it passed a decree that called for the closure of the Mogutova Quarry in 1990.[102] Some environmentalists proposed preserving the area to serve as an uncomfortable but instructive reminder of the USSR's past destructive relationship to nature. Mogutova could be, one journalist argued, "a scary, ugly, cautionary reminder of thoughtless human actions."[103]

The park's opponents fought with no less resolve. The Zhigulevsk Quarry Administration asserted that its continued operation was a necessity during a time of economic crisis. In May 1988, the administration's chief engineer stated in *Volga Commune* that it would be impossible to fulfill the region's housing program by the year 2000 if the Zhiguli quarries were shut down.[104] In Tolyatti, an organization called Social Justice, made up of workers in different industries, defended the interests of industries under "attack" by the park. In an open letter to the local newspaper, *Zhiguli Laborer* (*Zhiguli rabochii*), the organization asserted that the closure of enterprises operating within the park's territory would cost the oblast three billion rubles a year. Moreover, the letter said that the removal of pioneer camps, tourist bases, and houses of relaxation would have "serious social consequences."[105] Inhabitants of areas in the park increasingly expressed frustrations about the stringent land use regime that the new "masters," SBNP, had imposed, and well-founded skepticism about the likelihood that tourism revenues could compensate for closing enterprises.[106] The defenders of industry and the enterprises that had long operated within the park's territory portrayed environmentalists as radicals who threatened their livelihoods.[107]

As the industry position was gaining strong support in the summer of 1989, the Kuibyshev Oblast Council Executive Committee began setting timelines for removing mining enterprises. Citizens of Zhigulevsk and surrounding towns staged protests in response.[108] The city council reconvened and assumed responsibility for, in its words, "reconciling the irreconcilable" to enable ongoing mining in SBNP.[109] Environmentalists were enraged when the city council overrode the decree of the RSFSR Council of Ministers and called for the continuation of mining on thirty-eight hectares.[110] It also advocated designating an additional fifteen hectares in the park's territory for excavating clay. Most insulting to the environmental protection community, the decree asserted that the city of Zhigulevsk was taking responsibility for the "fate" of the SBNP.[111] The council argued that the nature protection community must take into account new social and economic realities.

The park's defenders did not see matters this way. Tezikova said that continued mining would be a betrayal of "national values," which any "self-respecting state would uphold, especially in dark times."[112] If a city council could override decrees passed by the RSFSR Council of Ministers and blatantly violate the Model Regulation, what, if anything, made a national park "national"? Institutionalized state protection is what proponents of national parks had fought for in Baikal, the Samara Bend, and many other places. Reflecting ironically on the situation in an *Izvestiia* article, P. Zhigalov (likely a pseudonym) wrote:

> In other countries, national parks are under the direct guardianship of the government and the president. Will this happen at some point with us? In the meantime, at one of the meetings, a constructive proposal was heard. . . . Hang the director of the national park so he wouldn't stop the mining.[113]

Passions were reaching a dangerous level.

Environmental Radicalism Comes to SBNP

As tensions were brewing around the Samara Bend, Kuibyshev was becoming one of the country's most important centers of grassroots environmental organizing. Perestroika and glasnost reforms allowed organizations not strictly monitored by the Communist Party to form for first time in the USSR. Environmental groups were among the many of these "informal" organizations that proliferated throughout the Soviet Union.[114] New environmental organizations had names such as Green World (Kazan), Alternative (St. Petersburg), Neformal'niy (Volgograd), Green Shore (Gorky), Noosphere (Astrakhan), Pathfinders (Moscow), and Rebirth (Kaliningrad). Much more so than the nature protection brigades, these groups frequently framed their mission in the context of the larger global environmental movement. Their demonstrations frequently drew thousands, sometimes tens of thousands, of participants.[115]

Gorbachev's reforms also allowed for the creation of new political parties in the Soviet Union, which further emboldened the emerging environmental protest movement. In April of 1989, a group of green "informal" organizations of the USSR gathered along the banks of the Volga across from SBNP in Kuibyshev where they formed the Movement for and Establishment of Green Parties. The movement's founder, twenty-two-year-old Sergei Fomichev epitomized the shift in thinking among some Soviet citizens about how best to push for an improved natural environment. Born in Dzerzhinsk, Fomichev was the son of a chemist and music teacher. He started but did not complete his university degree at Kuibyshev State Cultural Institute. He continued educating himself by reading previously banned literature about the green political movement in West Germany and the anarchist writings of Murray Bookchin. And in Kuibyshev, he saw firsthand the conflict over the continued mining activity on Mognutova Mountain in SBNP.

Fomichev became involved in the Samara Union of Greens. In 1989, he took part in a protest against the canals Volga-Don 2 and Volga-Chograi just before starting the Movement for the Founding of the Green Party.[116] Two years later, he established the League of Green Parties, which he characterized as an organization devoted to the "radical reordering of the existing social structure."[117] With Bookchin's teachings as Fomichev's guide, the program of the league rejected both the capitalist and socialist models of industrial society and called for a "third way" (*tretii put'*), in which power was organized on the local level.[118] The anarchist orientation of the group rejected a centralized structure that would make the league members and component organizations subject to a single agenda.[119] Instead, the league would provide a framework for independent organizations to get support on the informational and, to a lesser extent, material level.[120]

Fomichev had already established one such organization, the Rainbow Keepers, in 1989.[121] From its inception, that organization, modeled after Greenpeace, took part in the sort of radical ecological protest common in the West but previously unheard of in the USSR.[122] Environmental protest precipitously declined throughout the USSR in late 1990 and 1991, and there were even fewer protests in the Russian Federation's first years, but the

Rainbow Keepers remained active and became more uncompromising in their tactics.[123] The Rainbow Keepers felt empowered by several successes, and Fomichev's familiarity with the Samara Bend region made SBNP a natural choice for him to stage a protest. Although the Samara (formerly Kuibyshev) Oblast Executive Committee had ruled in 1989 that mining work could continue only in the form of reclamation, rubble was being removed at a rate double that of the years before the oblast administration's ruling. Moreover, the quarry operators continued carrying out earth-shaking explosions even though the State Geological Committee had recommended many other areas in the Samara and Saratov Oblasts where such mining could take place.[124] Fomichev published a letter in the international ecological journal *Eurasia* in which he invited people from all countries to join an "international ecological camp dedicated to the preservation of nature in SBNP."[125] In an interview, he stated, "If the government does not have the power to prevent illegal actions, then the broader public must do it." [126]

Some oblast residents had already started realizing that international attention might help protect the park. Months before Fomichev and the Rainbow Keepers set up their camp next to Mognutova Mountain in the summer of 1993, the regional press had discussed UNESCO World Heritage Natural Site designation.[127] The protestors, who came that summer from Russia, Belarus, Ukraine, and the United States, included a representative of Greenpeace and several anarchist organizations and shared an understanding of Samara Bend as international space.[128] Jennifer Adibi, a recent Russian studies graduate from Brown University, said, "Russian nature is the heritage of humanity, and therefore for

Figure 6.6 Fomichev at SBNP in 1993. Photo courtesy of Valerii Erofeev.

us, it is not a question of why I am here. The issue is saving a part of our shared planet earth."[129] During the protest, an article in *Volga Commune* asserted:

> What significance does nationality have when somewhere a treasure of nature for all generations is being destroyed barbarically? This treasure belongs to all of humanity, and not to an evil quarry.[130]

While environmentalists from different countries had long emphasized the protection of nature as a universal striving, for the participants it seemed initially that the end of the bipolar world would allow citizens from around the world to join together to save nature for the common good.

With many Russians struggling to make a living, animosity toward environmentalists, including those in the Samara Oblast (renamed from Kuibyshev Oblast in 1991), became stronger in the early 1990s.[131] Because SBNP had been resented even before the broader souring of the Russian public on environmentalism, Fomichev had chosen a particularly explosive place to stage a protest. After setting up camp on July 8, the demonstrators immediately blocked off sections of the hillside, seized drilling rigs, and lay down next to dynamite-filled holes.[132] Quarry workers responded with threats of violence. On July 12, the police arrested six protestors, including Iurii Roshchevskii, who offered material, informational, and technical support during the protest. The police threatened protestors that they would be forced to compensate the quarry for any financial losses and liquidated the protest camp the next day.[133]

Fomichev immediately made contact with the oblast prosecutor's office, which confirmed that the quarry was operating in violation of the law. After the protesters reestablished the camp on July 14, unidentified assailants (in all likelihood quarry workers and perhaps, it was suspected, the police) stormed the camp and assaulted several of the protestors. During the night of July 16, a group tore down the tents, forced members of the protest onto buses, and threw them out of the vehicles while going at high speed. Less than a week later, explosions in the quarry resumed. After negotiations between the protestors, the oblast administration, and the director of the quarry, the oblast administration called for the suspension of explosions until the completion of an "ecological review" on August 12.[134] The cessation of operations proved short-lived. In the ensuing months, the official report concluded that the blasting "was not criminal."[135] Once again, the law on national parks in the Russian Federation seemed to mean little.

Fomichev, by his own admission, was much more interested in developing a robust activist-minded culture in the Samara Oblast and the growth of the Rainbow Keepers than he was concerned about damage to SBNP.[136] His motives were thus fundamentally different from the park's early defenders, who had been driven by their love for their home region. But Fomichev's approach did not discourage Roshchevskii from supporting him for the duration of the protest.[137] In an interview with the ecological magazine *Beringiia*, Roshchevskii said:

> I have never considered myself a follower of radical movements. But reflecting after the protest of the Rainbow Keepers, I came to the unambiguous conclusion: in our country, where there is not a semblance of respect for the law, for ecological problems, and for nature protection, radicalism must become part of the activity of the public.[138]

While Roshchevskii had believed that citizen efforts would transform the regional economy and the relationship of the average Soviet citizen to nature, he and the park's stalwarts were losing hope that the park could fulfill the most rudimentary nature protection tasks common to national parks throughout the world.

The park was making little progress on other fronts. Infrastructure remained undeveloped. Much of the shoreline was littered. In many cases, it remained unclear what property belonged to the inhabitants within the park's territory, and residents of the many population points regularly complained to government officials about the park impeding their use of the land. The Federal Forestry Service was barely interested in the park, so SBNP received a fraction of the funds needed to carry out its essential functions.[139] In 1996, the park had to cut its staff significantly and closed a meteorological station that had been operating since 1894 as well as the museum of local culture.[140] With all of these problems, the area had little chance of being designated a UNESCO World Heritage Natural Site despite earlier hopes.[141]

Roshchevskii's continued public criticisms of the "barbaric destruction of nature" in SBNP led to him being fired in 1996.[142] In a public lecture two years later, he said, "People have become convinced that the most dangerous thing for nature is the government bureaucrat [*chinovnik*] who can clothe any unsightly action in the law."[143] Tezikova became equally disillusioned. Her letters to government officials became increasingly angry and embittered, with one accusing the Forestry Service of actively "trying to destroy SBNP."[144] In 1997, the Federal Forestry Service asked that its workers cut off all communication with her.[145] By the end of the decade, the Rainbow Keepers had disbanded.[146] Nature protection brigades faded into memory. Reflecting on the fate of SBNP at a 2001 conference, Iurii Roshchevskii said:

> The hopes of the public and its euphoria in regard to the establishment of SBNP turned out to be naive. As might be expected, the region's national treasure could not take care of itself.[147]

In the summer of 2013, he expressed his disappointments, especially the failure of the park to help engender ecological consciousness among students. "I thought that the person of the future would be formed out of this student movement, that previous generations did not have this mentality. Now, I have become somewhat cold to this idea."[148]

Conclusion

Although regional actors had limited ability to push the state to change economic policy or drastically alter highly damaging uses of the land during the Brezhnev era, they still dreamed of doing so. The story of SBNP belies two Russian historians' recent characterization of Soviet citizens during the Brezhnev era as having "adapted so well to the current reality that the previous decade's relentless hope for systemic change seemed to belong to a different world altogether."[149] Contradicting this view, Valerii Erofeev, who participated in the nature protection brigades that actively planned SBNP, said:

> The young activists of the nature protection movement (they were all then between seventeen and eighteen) did not know anything about stagnation. And therefore they decided to dedicate their full effort to lessen the ecological crisis that was effecting the entire country, including the Samara Oblast.[150]

And yet even though Tezikova, Roshchevskii, Timofeev, and many others could dream, plan, and successfully push the government to establish a national park that they hoped would both transform the regional economy and protect its environment, SBNP fell far short of their vision.

In retrospect, the idea of SBNP seems quixotic from its very conception. While Soviet citizens enjoyed greater freedom to conceive social and economic models as everyday life became increasingly de-ideologized during the Brezhnev era, the distance between SBNP's supporters and the economic ministries undoubtedly contributed to the unworkability of their vision. Making SBNP conform to the Model Regulation would have required regional transformations that the state never considered seriously. This supports the widely accepted notion that the USSR often passed environmental laws and regulations without much commitment to enforcing them.[151] However, realizing the vision of the founders by enforcing the provisions of the Model Regulation would have undoubtedly caused much greater suffering among the local population than they were already experiencing as a result of Russia's political and economic crisis of the late 1980s and 1990s. SBNP's failure to live up to the grandiose plans of its founders might have been a personal tragedy for them, but a much greater tragedy for the many people living within the park's territory might have unfolded had the founders realized all of their impractical goals.

7

Protecting the Pechoran Alps?

The Unmet Promise of Iugyd Va National Park in the Nether-Polar Urals

Located in the northwest of European Russia, the Komi Autonomous Soviet Socialist Republic (ASSR) felt strong winds of change during the Khrushchev era. In the years just before and after World War II, the Soviet government opened three Gulag labor camps dedicated to the extraction of coal in the eastern part of the republic in the Nether-Polar (*pripoliarnyi*) and Polar Urals. The hundreds of thousands of prisoners who were sent there undoubtedly had little energy to reflect on the beauty of the mountainous tundra landscape, which would soon start attracting tourists not long after nearly two hundred thousand inmates were released from these camps.[1] With environmentalists in the republic seeing firsthand the dramatic impacts of the liberalized cultural climate, they saw an opportunity to bring attention to a variety of problems mounting in the republic, including deforestation, the pollution of rivers, and overfishing. They also sought to instill environmental concern among the population while emphasizing the need for Soviet citizens to experience the country's beautiful landscapes.[2] Publicly, however, they remained silent about a threat to some of the most breathtaking scenery in the Urals that had high-level institutional support.

For decades Soviet engineers had been devising plans to divert the Pechora and Vychegda Rivers to the south, which would have inundated large expanses of land adjacent to the Nether-Polar Urals. Adolf Bratsev, a geographer at the Komi Scientific Center in Syktyvkar, became particularly concerned that this would be catastrophic for the Komi ASSR during the 1960s as regional environmental concern continued to grow. Along with two other colleagues, Vladimir Gladkov and Vladimir Balibasov, Bratsev established the Commission on Nature Protection, which focused almost exclusively on the establishment of a national park in the Nether-Polar Urals. Though not stating so directly, he hoped to undermine the rationale for the rivers' diversion project by convincing government

Into Russian Nature. Alan D. Roe, Oxford University Press (2020) © Oxford University Press.
DOI: 10.1093/oso/9780190914554.001.0001

officials that the spectacular scenery of the Nether-Polar Urals would attract hordes of tourists, which he believed would bring economic benefits to the republic that would be lost if much of this area was inundated.

The commission made speculative and grandiose claims about the project's economic potential to bolster their case. Their prediction that millions of tourists would come to the national park was always unrealistic, but it proved utterly fantastical when the Iugyd Va National Park (IVNP) was established in 1994 amid political chaos and economic contraction. Even after this had become evident, park supporters hoped that its designation along with Pechoro-Illychski Zapovednik (PIZ) as Russia's first World Heritage Natural Site (the Virgin Komi Forests) would elevate Russia's sense of moral obligation to protect it. Critics of the park accused the founders of making false promises about tourism's potential economic benefits and accused its supporters, who the critics argued were more concerned international prestige than the lives of the inhabitants of Komi, of "ecological blackmail."

Both the river diversion project and the founders' original vision are largely forgotten, and tourism in IVNP has never been more than a trickle of what the founders hoped. The mining industry has in turn repeatedly questioned the need for maintaining such a large park when the founders' vision has been, in their view, invalidated. Environmentalists, on the other hand, have long pointed to the Russian Federation's wavering position on the park's boundaries as yet another example of the Russian Federation's weak commitment to protected territories and to honoring its international obligations.

Early Proposals and Fantastical Plans

The first proposal for a national park in the Nether-Polar Urals came in 1929 from the Pechoro-Ilych Expedition, led by Frants Shillinger and sponsored by the All-Russian Society for the Protection of Nature (VOOP). Following this survey of the territory of the Northern and Nether-Polar Urals and the headwaters of the Pechora River, Shillinger stated, "I can personally say that in terms of beauty and uniqueness there is no better landscape in the Urals."[3] Following the expedition, the VOOP sent a questionnaire to gauge interest in protecting the territory to different government bureaucracies, scientific organizations, and interested specialists. The VOOP journal *The Protection of Nature* (*Okhrana prirody*) published some of these responses in the spring of 1930.[4] Respondents stated that the reserve would "compare favorably" to national parks in the United States, would gain renown throughout the entire Soviet Union, and would become a "self-sustaining" enterprise by charging entry fees.[5] However, when it received official legal status within the RSFSR

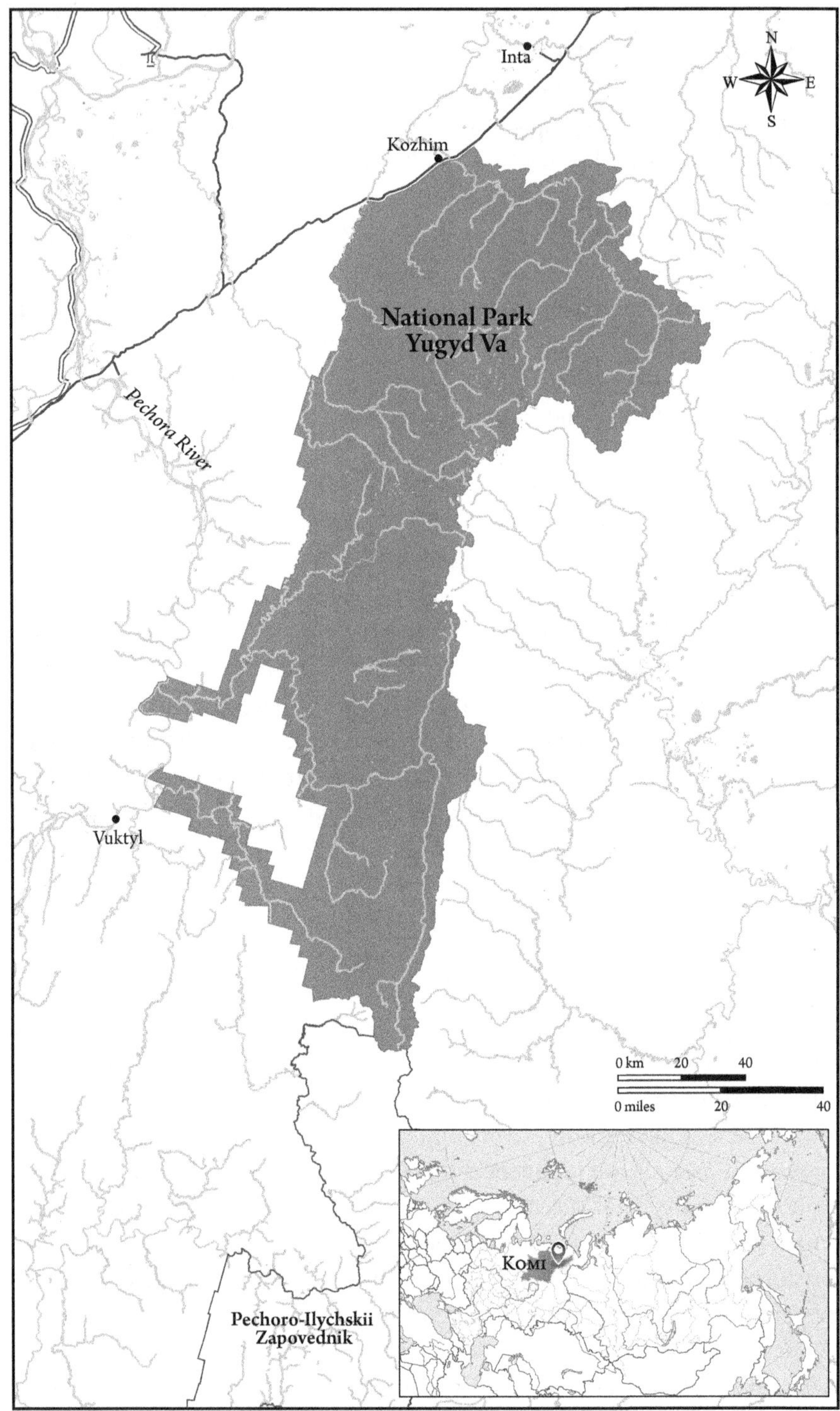

Figure 7.1 Komi and Nether-Polar Urals/IVNP.

in 1930, the Pechoro-Ilychskii Zapovednik's explicitly stated purpose was to protect the region's declining sable population.

By the mid-1950s, the PIZ and the scenic territory north of it were in danger. From 1934 to 1936, the Leningrad branch of the All-Russian Design Research and Scientific-Research Institute (Gidroproekt) proposed improving internal navigation by reversing the Pechora and Vychegda Rivers through a series of reservoirs and canals that would divert the water into tributaries of the Volga. One of the reservoirs would have inundated parts of the *zapovednik* and much of the area adjacent to it.[6] The outbreak of war in 1941 interrupted this project, but engineers had found a more compelling rationale for continuing it by the mid-1950s.[7] From 1929 to 1955, increased use of the Volga's water for agriculture, along with some natural fluctuation caused by tectonic activity, lowered the level of the Caspian Sea by 2.4 meters and shrunk its surface from 114,000 to 84,000 square kilometers. By channeling more water through the Volga to the Caspian, engineers believed that they could stabilize the Caspian fishing industry, preserve its role as an important shipping hub, improve agriculture, and expand hydroelectricity throughout the Volga River valley. The net economic gains, the project's authors argued, would pay for the project's costs in three to four years and would eventually have a net benefit of 562 million rubles a year, or about 5 percent of Soviet military expenditures at that time.[8]

The PIZ was reduced to one-tenth of its previous size as part of the 1951 decree that eliminated eighty-eight *zapovedniki* at the time that Gidroproekt was discussing diverting the republic's largest rivers. Although the USSR Council of Ministers had reestablished most of the liquidated reserves and restored PIZ to its previous size by 1960, Khrushchev's attack on the *zapovedniki* raised further alarm.[9] While a growing contingent of environmentally concerned scientists in the Komi ASSR was undoubtedly relieved that the PIZ had been spared, they and others in the environmental protection community remained uncertain of the future status of the *zapovedniki*.

As concerns about the rivers' diversion continued and the fate of PIZ remained uncertain, Khrushchev's release of Gulag prisoners widened the range of the republic's future economic possibilities. During the late 1930s, the Soviet government started sending large numbers of convicts to the republic to open the vast deposits of coal in the Pechora River basin. The first camp—Vorkutlag—opened in the Polar Urals in the far northeast of the republic in 1938.[10] The Soviet government opened two more camps in the Nether-Polar Urals—Rechlag and Mineral'nyi (Minlag) in 1948. Neither camp operated for more than ten years, with Rechlag closing in 1954 and Minlag three years later. More than two hundred thousand prisoners were released from the three camps from 1953 to 1958, but many areas, which would become part of a future park, were not cleaned up.[11] And with spur railroad lines planned to make extraction more efficient, central planners were calling for more extensive resource extraction in the Republic, even as Khrushchev's liberalizing reforms had allowed the public an unprecedented opportunity to publicly discuss environmental problems, which were becoming more evident in Komi ASSR.[12]

In 1960, the Komi Branch of the VOOP held its first republic conference on nature protection. Participants warned of increased deforestation, the pollution of rivers, and widespread poaching. They emphasized the importance of Soviet citizens developing a love of nature by taking part in tourist treks throughout the Komi ASSR.[13] Grigorii Chernov's *Tourist Treks in the Pechoran Alps* (*Turistskie pokhody v pechorskie Al'py*, 1959) described the area's terrain and encouraged tourists to protect the scenic areas, making the Nether-Polar Urals more accessible for tourists than ever before.[14] However, much of these areas would be lost if the diversion project was realized.

One of the scientists researching the project to divert rivers of the Komi ASSR was Adolf Petrovich Bratsev, a member of the rapidly growing Komi Branch of the VOOP, a hydrologist and research associate of the Komi Scientific Center of the Academy of Sciences.[15] He believed that the proposed project could cause a variety of unforeseen ecological problems. Bratsev was also concerned that the creation of a reservoir would cost the Komi ASSR its most valuable scenic resource at a time when economists and geographers were making persuasive arguments about the potential economic value of scenery.[16] With increased flights to the republic and the completion of the Kotlas-Vorkuta railway line, thousands of tourists were arriving in the Nether-Polar Urals each year by the late 1960s.

Bratsev believed that proposing a profitable national park adjacent to and overlapping with the territory targeted for inundation could weaken the rationale for the river diversion project. However, the Komi Scientific Center did not have a department that could address the creation of a national park. After establishing the Commission on Nature Protection in the Komi Scientific Center with two younger colleagues, Vladimir Gladkov and Vladimir Balibasov, in late 1968, Bratsev proposed that the commission develop plans for the national park as its first task.[17] While Bratsev criticized the shortsighted policies of economic managers who neglected issues related to the "protection" and "rational use" of resources, he and his younger colleagues agreed that the economic and quality-of-life arguments central to the formation of a national park would resonate more deeply than scientific arguments with the public and high-ranking government officials.[18]

A gifted writer and the head of the division of media relations for the Komi Branch of VOOP, Gladkov led the public relations campaign for the establishment of the park.[19] In August 1970, he made a case for the national park to readers of the Syktyvkar newspaper, *Red Banner* (*Krasnoe znamia*).[20] Asserting that the Komi ASSR was the best place to serve the fundamental need to escape industrial civilization in European Russia, he stated that a failure to act would allow the depletion of the most "unaltered" areas of the Komi ASSR.[21] Tourism and scientific research, he argued, constituted the only acceptable uses of the land of the future national park. He concluded the article with an impassioned plea for readers of the newspaper to make their opinions known. Tourists and environmentally minded citizens responded by sending numerous letters of support. A doctor from Syktyvkar wrote:

> The proposal must be argued for in an even more affirmative way: the entire country needs the national park in our republic. Specialists, on the one hand, have already positively decided this question, and no less importantly, the thousands of tourists who have already judged the fantastic beauty of the Pechoran Alps have decided it.[22]

Another letter called for similar parks throughout the USSR.[23]

As Gladkov rallied public opinion, Gidroproekt proceeded apace with its plans to divert the Pechora and Vychegda. In order to construct a sixty-five-kilometer canal to connect the basins of the Pechora and Kama Rivers, the latter of which flows into the Volga, the institute had planned 250 nuclear detonations. The first of these ("Taiga"), which took place in March 1971, created a radioactive lake.[24] This explosion undoubtedly increased the sense of urgency to protect the territory of the future park. Through the Commission on Nature Protection's strong lobbying and public relations efforts, the idea gained strong allies in Vladislav Podoplelov, the representative of the Komi Scientific Center to the Komi ASSR Council of Ministers, and Ivan Morozov, head of the Komi ASSR Communist Party. After Podoplelov agreed to the proposal, the Komi ASSR Committee of the Communist Party and the Komi ASSR Council of Ministers passed a resolution, On the Organization of the Nature Park in Komi ASSR, on May 28, 1971.[25] Encompassing the Nether-Polar Urals in the Komi ASSR and the Pechora River watershed, the designated territory was 20,500 square kilometers. The park would prohibit all industrial development. Regulated tourism would be the only acceptable economic use of the park's territory. Because there was no government ministry designated to serve as the steward of "nature" parks, the decree assigned the Komi ASSR Ministry of Forestry jurisdiction over the park, even though this new designation would threaten the prerogatives of the timber industry.

The Commission on Nature Protection began surveying geographical, biological, hydrological, climatological, and geological characteristics of the planned park in 1972. In describing the organization of the park, the authors

Figure 7.2 Iugyd Va National Park. Photo by author.

Figure 7.3 Iugyd Va National Park. Photo by author.

employed the terms and theories of recreational geography.[26] While only 1,500 registered tourists and perhaps five thousand unregistered tourists from over fifty cities in the USSR came to the territory of the proposed park in 1972, the report unrealistically projected that the park would eventually be able to host three million tourists a year, most of whom would be taking part in outdoor recreation.[27] Overly cultivated and developed areas, they argued, did not meet the needs of people living in densely populated, polluted, and noisy urban industrial centers who yearned to return to more "pristine" and "undeveloped" landscapes.[28] While Siberia was also replete with such areas, the Komi ASSR's "proximity" (undoubtedly overstated by the project's authors) to population centers in the European part of Russia made it more likely to attract large numbers of tourists.[29]

The commission continued developing the project without support from the forestry or mining ministries, both of which had much to lose. Although the park would have territories that functioned as more traditional *zapovedniki* where tourism was strictly prohibited, the commission publicly sought to assuage the concerns of different groups by explicitly emphasizing that the area would be dedicated to "intensive economic use" in the form of organized tourism.[30] Operating on the principle of "self-sufficiency," the national park would accrue revenue through entrance fees, rental of tourist equipment, souvenirs and literature, hunting and fishing licenses, and eventually hotels that the park would later construct. This revenue would fund the development and maintenance of infrastructure as well as the salaries of park workers.

Frequently referring to the profitability of US national parks, the authors argued that there was "no other branch of industry in the Komi ASSR that can pay off capital investment as quickly as tourism."[31] However, the authors did not want to carry out the intensive infrastructural development that had allowed US national parks to draw large numbers and accrue significant revenue. Both distance and an approach that emphasized "minimum comfort and maximum wild nature" made their projections of future visitors wildly unrealistic.[32] Yellowstone, for example, was within a two-day drive of several metropolitan areas with populations of over a million people each and had a well-developed infrastructure to accommodate large numbers of paying visitors, but it had just over two million visitors at the time.[33] The project's authors never seemed to consider seriously the willingness of the average Soviet citizen to travel to such a remote location.

As the union republics in the Baltics, Central Asia, and the Caucasus established national parks during the 1970s, the Komi Commission on Nature Protection continued the public relations campaign at the levels of the Komi ASSR, the RSFSR, and the USSR. The park received attention from the regional newspapers—*Youth of the North* (*Molodezh' Severa*) and *Red Banner*—while appearing in central newspapers and journals such as *Komsomol Pravda* (*Komsomol'skaia pravda*), *Forest Industry* (*Lesnaia promyshlennost'*), and *Literary Gazette*.[34] The articles emphasized the territory's spectacular scenery, its uniqueness as a completely "pristine" area in Europe, and its relative "proximity" to major cities. Additionally, Gladkov organized an exhibit at the Exhibition of Achievements of the National Economy (VDNKh) in Moscow to promote the park. In 1977 the Komi Scientific Center published a book, *Nature Park in Komi ASSR* (*Prirodnyi park v Komi ASSR*), which publicized the research conducted by the Commission on Nature Protection.[35] This book, the *Literary Gazette* article, and an article two years later in *Forest Industry* implored the RSFSR Council of Ministers to give the park legal standing as soon as possible. Otherwise, they argued, industrial expansion and unregulated tourism would bring tremendous harm to the area.[36]

As was the case for park enthusiasts throughout the RSFSR, supporters of this park were frustrated by the fact that the government did not seem to share their sense of urgency.[37] In articles and personal correspondence, Gladkov expressed frustrations about the slow push for the establishment of the proposed park.[38] Less than a year after the USSR Council of Ministers finally passed the Model Regulation on State Nature National Parks in 1981, he again called on the Komi ASSR Council of Ministers to appeal to the Central Committee of the RSFSR.[39] As the RSFSR Council of Ministers established parks throughout the 1980s, Gosplan RSFSR maintained that the remoteness of the Nether-Polar Urals, the inadequacy of design plans, and the potential damage to the forestry industry made the plan for a park in the Komi ASSR unfeasible.[40] Experts from Lengiprogor asserted that the Tyumen Oblast and the Komi ASSR were the least suited regions in European Russia to accommodate large numbers of tourists due to their poor transportation systems.[41] Three years later, the RSFSR Central Scientific Research Design Institute recommended that the RSFSR establish the park no earlier than 2000.[42] Gladkov had a different opinion about the proposed park's accessibility. In a 1989 letter to Gosplan, he emphasized that remoteness was one of the most important criteria for national parks internationally. Exasperated, he sarcastically replied that Gosplan would recognize the accessibility of these areas "if they would look at a geographic map."[43] Accordingly, neither Lengiprogor nor other design institutes made efforts to design the future park until the end of the decade.

Fearing the expanded intrusion of extractive industries into the area of the proposed park, Bratsev, Gladkov, members of the VOOP, and other environmental activists took measures to protect the territory of the proposed national park and other scenic areas of the Komi ASSR through the creation of temporary reserves (*zakazniki*) and natural monuments (*pamiatniki prirody*). Thanks to the lobbying efforts of Gladkov and others, the Komi ASSR Council of Ministers placed 202 areas, which encompassed 2.3 million hectares, under official protection. This area covered 5 percent of Komi ASSR's territory, which gave the Komi ASSR perhaps more protected land than any other part of the RSFSR. By the end of the 1980s, the republic administration had put 44 percent of the proposed park under the status of temporary reserves and natural monuments.[44]

Throughout the 1970s, natural resource industries, fearing future reductions in their resource base, expanded activities in territories of proposed parks in different areas of the RSFSR, including the proposed park in Komi ASSR.[45] In 1975, the RSFSR Council of Ministers designated the forests in the watersheds of Bol'shaia Synia and the Shugor River as part of the resource base for a prison camp (PL-350) that would focus on timber extraction. From the mid-1970s to 1988, the timber industry cut over five million cubic meters of timber and thirty-five thousand hectares of forest in the territory of the proposed park. Meanwhile, a vague 1976 decree of the RSFSR Council of Ministers, which had acknowledged that a park would be established at some point in the future, assigned the RSFSR Ministry of Forestry as the future park's official steward.[46]

The mining industry also opposed the creation of the national park. Geologists undertook surveys in all the major watersheds within the territory of the proposed park during the 1970s. They discovered that the Kozhim watershed had rich deposits of gold and other valuable minerals, perhaps as much as one-third of the hard metal potential in the Komi ASSR.[47] In 1977, the cooperative Pechora, later known as the Kozhim Mining Company, began mining alluvial gold deposits. Along with other parties, it mined the area intensively until the late 1980s. By decade's end, mining had destroyed much of the plant cover along the Kozhim River, which became increasingly turbid.[48]

The pollution of the Kozhim River decreased the food base for fish by 20 percent. With the prime feeding territory of salmon reduced and their spawning grounds diminished, the salmon population had dropped by nearly 30 percent from the late 1960s to the late 1980s. Populations of some species, like the Siberian grayling and char, declined, and many rare animals—the pika, osprey, golden eagle, erne, sable—were disappearing from the area. Ecological damage, Gladkov lamented, would reduce the territories' recreational significance. With no explanation, in 1990 he made the sensational and unsupported claim that the loss of one species was worth an estimated 32–64 million rubles.[49] Here, in the park plans and on other occasions, the obsession with proving the park's economic value, often on dubious grounds, undermined the credibility of the founders' vision.

The Failure of the Economic Defense

The growing environmental concern throughout the USSR during the Gorbachev era was shared by the citizens of the Komi ASSR.[50] Scientists, writers, and concerned citizens rallied around "saving" the Pechora River, for which, many argued, the establishment of the national park was essential.[51] Increased public pressure seemed to be working. Commissioned by the Scientific Research Institute on Nature Protection under the USSR Ministry of Agriculture, the institute Soiuzgiproleskhoz started the design work on the national park in Komi ASSR in 1989. On September 28, 1990, the Komi ASSR Council of Ministers again passed a resolution for the establishment of the park—this time using the term national, not nature, park. The established park would be 1.9 million hectares, have a buffer zone of nearly three hundred thousand hectares, require the removal of the Ministry of Internal Affairs prison camp PL-350, and request that the RSFSR Ministry of Forestry provide the park with the resources needed for infrastructural development. The realization of this final point seemed doubtful given the lack of interest and support from the Ministry of Forestry. Mining companies rushed to expand their activities in the area before the park's official designation.

While new opportunities to amass profits invigorated capitalists, the government of the Russian Federation's championing of genuine democracy following the USSR's collapse emboldened environmentalists of the Komi Republic, even as environmental activism declined throughout the Russian Federation. On the other hand, the park's growing number of opponents argued that economic hardship made ambitious environmental protection plans impractical, prompting them to argue for a scaled-down version of the park. Meanwhile, newly formed environmental organizations, such as the Social Economic Union (founded 1988), the Committee on Saving the Pechora River (1989), the Center for Wild Nature (1989), and organs of the regional press, especially the Vuktil newspaper *Northern Lights* (*Siianie Severa*) made moralistic and patriotic appeals for preserving the park's original boundaries.[52]

As business interests intensified lobbying efforts, ministries and committees began working on projects to expand resource extraction in the Komi ASSR. In 1991, the Komi Committee on Transport and Communication proposed a project "on the organization and development of mining valuable metals, minerals, and mammoth bones and its realization in the Komi ASSR" to the Komi ASSR Council of Ministers. Three of the proposed mining sites were in the territory of the proposed park. Toward the end of the year, a member of the Inta City Council sent a letter to a representative of the Komi ASSR Council of Ministers, in which he proposed removing the watershed of the Upper Kozhim River from the park because of its importance to the mining industry.[53] Now, with a president (Yeltsin) who recently stated that the regions should "take all the autonomy they can swallow," extractive industries had grown more circumspect about new territorial designations that would by definition give Moscow greater authority over the natural resources of the Komi Republic.[54] Gold mining, one Inta City

Council member stated, would provide the base for the "economic sovereignty of the Komi Republic." He believed that setting aside two billion dollars in potential minerals would constitute "an economic crime against the Komi Republic."[55] Thus the new, genuine federalism helped adversaries of a national park policy find arguments and gain momentum.

Succumbing to the mounting pressure, the Komi Council of Ministers passed a resolution on March 31, 1992, that ordered the Komi State Committee on Ecology (Goskompriroda) and Polar Ural Geological Bureau (Poliaruralgeologiia) to prepare a proposal for "adjusting" the national park's boundaries, taking into account the opportunities for the "complex use" of the Kozhim watershed.[56] During the summer of 1992, the Komi Union of Entrepreneurs sponsored a Public Expert Commission to discuss the proposed boundaries of the still unestablished park. The commission, which claimed to be independent, included representatives from the forestry-lobbying group Komilesprom, the Institutes of Biology and Geology of the Komi Scientific Center, the Committee on the Rebirth of the Komi People, the Commission on Ecology of the High Council of the Komi Republic, and the administration of the cities of Inta and Pechora. However, the director of the Polar Ural Geological Association, Ivan Granovich, served as the leader of the committee, giving it a definite bias toward industry.[57]

The commission argued that the level of expertise for the organization of the park had been low and that its executive functions were poorly defined.[58] It also asserted that a speculative methodology, which incorrectly viewed recreation and extraction as mutually exclusive, underscored assumptions about the area's recreational potential. Furthermore, it argued that the proposed project did not estimate the damage that the national park would cause to productive economic activity, reflect the loss of future profit from reduced mining, or take into account the expenses of future nature protection projects.[59] The commission claimed that the costs involved in the park's development would likely total sixty billion rubles, but might even exceed one hundred billion rubles.[60] Finally, the commission stated that park planners had underestimated the potential profits of mining in the watershed one thousandfold. Contending that withdrawing the Kozhim River Valley from economic activity would "cause irreversible damage to the economy of the Komi Republic," the commission concluded, "The national park must be based on a sensible plan that is economically realistic. Therefore, a fundamental reworking of the project with all interested agencies is necessary."[61] On December 8, Granovich wrote to V. I. Khudiev of the Komi Republic Council of Ministers:

> We believe that in the growth of unbridled national self-definition the Komi ASSR Council of Ministers made a decision that was based not

> on rationality or economics but on emotions. Yes, we need a nature/national park. But why must the territory of the protected lands of our republic be five times larger as a whole and fifty times larger than any national park in the Russian Federation? Yes, we need a nature, national park. But why do we need to protect the watersheds of four rivers that have practically identical characteristics? Yes, we need a national park. But why, without any serious scientific basis for such a vast territory, are we taking out of economic use more than 2.2 trillion rubles, or more than eighteen billion dollars, in the values of the first half of 1992?[62]

With even fewer tourists coming to the territory than when the Komi Commission on Nature Protection proposed the park, its defenders could hardly press the economic argument of its founders.

As debate about the park's boundaries continued, the newly formed, Moscow-based Institute of Cultural Heritage became involved in arguing for the necessity of the park's establishment. Its final report emphasized the need to borrow from the experiences of Western Europe and the United States.[63] However, the report characterized the Komi Scientific Center's projections on future tourist traffic as "wildly" inflated.[64] At the same time, it insisted that mining and other extractive industries had no place in the national park. But with the park's foundational economic rationale in question, extractive industries were ready to argue for more profitable uses of the area. Bratsev had little interest in political battles, and Gladkov's declining health prevented him from participating in the public debate over the park. A new generation of environmental activists used moral and ecological arguments as well as appeals to Russian and Komi patriotism in their defense of the park. Despite the significant decline in environmental concern among most Russians, many residents of the Komi Republic expressed strong support for the park and condemnation of the predatory environmental policies now associated with the Soviet Union and the corruption of the early 1990s.

The regional press referred to the still unnamed national park as "the island of hope," "the future of the inhabitants of the Komi ASSR," and "the pride of the nation."[65] On July 30, 1992, *Red Banner* published an open letter signed by people's deputies of the Russian Federation and the Komi Republic as well as leaders of social movements and government departments that focused on nature protection. They wrote:

> For twenty years, hundreds of millions of cubic meters of timber have been cut out of our republic, hundreds of billions of tons of oil taken from the ground, and much more. Have we really become richer

from this? Have our lives become easier or happier? Can we just sit here thinking of the future that we are giving to our children and grandchildren? Will we really be more prosperous if we dig out, ruin, and sell this last unique corner of our motherland—the nature, national park of the Komi Republic?[66]

In an article from January 23, 1993, in the regional newspaper *Spark* (*Iskra*), N. Bratenkov, a former Communist Party official who was active in the Committee on Saving the Pechora, stated, "Whoever has seen the ruined, wounded, almost dead Kozhim, will say: Stop! No more is necessary."[67] Two months later, an open letter in *Northern Lights* from "Young Ecologists and Teachers of the Republic Station of Naturalists" stated:

We are very worried about the problem of the national park of the republic. We know that many honest and good people are agonizing about its fate. We children do not decide the fate of nature in our republic. However, we understand well that in a few years we will become society's leaders. We want concrete measures to protect our natural riches. And today it is imperative to protect our unique natural environment from the different assaults on the future national park, which is gradually being destroyed by gold mining and poaching with the approval of the republic's government and industry.[68]

Another commission to discuss the boundaries of the park had formed the month before this plea from the Young Ecologists and Teachers. The head of the Ministry of Natural Resources of the Komi Republic, Alexander Borovinskikh, who had previously served as head of the Committee on Geology of the Komi ASSR, led the commission. Undoubtedly emboldened by the indications that the government of the Komi Republic was sympathetic to industry, on June 8, 1993, the former state farm Saranpaluski, now private, made an agreement to rent out one hundred thousand hectares of land in the territory of the future national park for the purposes of "developing tourism" with the mining company Oniks. A cover for mining, the agreement would allow Oniks to "engage in the production of local raw materials and benefit from the natural bounty of the region."[69] The city of Inta confirmed the agreement two days later in a resolution that guaranteed the city no less than 15 percent of the Oniks' profits, a classic case of corruption in the Russian Federation's early years.[70]

After the national park and the Komi Committee on the Environment complained to the city of Inta, saying that any lease longer than five years was unacceptable, the city sent a curt reply that an arbitration court where the original agreement was made—Inta—would take up the issue.[71] Despite appeals from the Komi Committee on the Environment to nullify the resolution passed by the city of Inta, the Komi Council of Ministers confirmed the city's resolution on January 4, 1994. Eventually, it reneged and reduced the lease to five years as the Komi Committee on the Environment continued to exert pressure.[72]

As the boundary debate continued, interested government bureaucracies sent their recommendations on the national park to the government of the Russian Federation in late 1993 and through the first part of 1994. In the decree that established Iugyd Va National Park (IVNP) on April 23, 1994, the government of the Russian Federation called for the State Committee on Environmental Protection and the Federal Forestry Service to form a commission to determine the park's final boundaries.[73] While the commission worked to resolve the issue, a new federal law on protected territories that passed in the spring of 1995 reaffirmed the ban on extractive economic uses within national parks and stated that only the federal government could redraw their borders.[74]

To many environmentalists, international help and recognition now seemed the best bet in light of the state's inability to commit resources to environmental protection. In Kamchatka, around Baikal, and at the Samara Bend, the Valdai Lakes, the Altai Mountains, and many other regions, environmentalists were arguing that UNESCO World Heritage designations might provide the best chance to preserve Russia's natural treasures in pristine form. Expecting that Yeltsin would not be reelected and that the next administration would not be as eager to cultivate a progressive image before the international community, Greenpeace Russia pushed aggressively to nominate as many Russian sites as possible. In 1994 and 1995, it collaborated directly with the Ministry of the Environment in forming the final list that was sent to UNESCO, which included IVNP and PIZ.[75] On December 9, 1995, UNESCO designated "Virgin Komi Forests," which included IVNP and PIZ, as the first World Heritage Natural Site in the Russian Federation.[76] While this designation did not impose specific criteria for how the Russian Federation could use this land, it put the park under much closer international scrutiny.[77]

The people and the government of the Komi Republic had a poor grasp on what UNESCO designation meant. Moreover, by the summer of 1995, PIZ and the IVNP had practically exhausted their funds. Like most protected territories in the 1990s, both were chronically understaffed. The infrastructural development in IVNP was not taking place, and the biological reclamation of areas along the Kozhim River was still incomplete.[78] Meanwhile, the government of the Russian Federation subdivided the Federal Ministry of Environmental Protection and Natural Resources into the Ministry of Natural Resources and the State Committee on Ecology. This diminution of environmental protection's status in comparison to natural resource extraction emboldened extractive industries to challenge existing environmental protection laws.[79]

Throughout the Russian Federation, regional and local governments often allowed activities of natural resource industries that violated the laws on economic uses of protected territories.[80] Perhaps no case was more brazen than what transpired in IVNP. Without approval from the Russian Federation, on January 9, 1997, the president of the Komi Republic, Iurii Smorodinov, illegally excised two hundred thousand hectares from IVNP through an executive order.[81] Eventually overturned by the High Court of the Komi Republic, Smorodinov's decision demonstrated how weak governmental support for the park had become in the Komi Republic. The UNESCO World Heritage Committee repeatedly urged Mikhail Fedotov, the representative of Russia's permanent delegation to the committee, to "inform the authorities of the Komi Republic of the status of the site."[82] The government of the Russian Federation formed yet another commission for a "redefinition" of the borders of the park. In late 1998, the commission, which was made up of thirteen people (doctors, biologists, geologists, and engineers), presented their conclusions. Stating that because "the proposal on the redefinition of the boundaries was not a 'redetermination' but a cardinal redrawing of the boundaries of the national park," it decided that the legislative process was the only way to make any boundary changes.[83]

The government of the Komi Republic expressed disappointment, and three members of the commission wrote minority reports. Each of these reports expressed concerns that in a time of economic hardship neither the Komi Republic nor the Russian Federation could afford not to exploit such a rich source of minerals. Igor Burtsev, a PhD in geological-mineralogical sciences at the Komi Scientific Center, presented this viewpoint most vigorously. With few Russians traveling in the early 1990s, he argued that the projections for the growth of tourism in the region were baseless, which made capital investment in the park senseless.[84] Burtsev criticized the "ignorance" of Greenpeace workers who did not understand the particular circumstances of the Komi Republic and the UNESCO designation, which he believed compromised the Komi Republic's autonomy and was of no interest to those living in it. In concluding his report, he stated, "Some biologists and ecologists are working on the question of IVNP on behalf of those who will not compromise, and worse yet, are on the side of those engaged in ecological blackmail."[85]

Conclusion

IVNP, like many other national parks, was initially planned without any coordination with central economic ministries or architectural institutes. In the absence of such cooperation, the founders' quixotic vision might have seemed entirely plausible to them, but it was unlikely to ever be accepted by the central ministries. Although Adolf Bratsev firmly believed that nature protection without an economic rationale was "empty noise," the wildly optimistic predictions of the Commission on Nature Protection of the Komi Scientific Center about the future park's profitability gave extractive interests ample material to undermine the park during the economic crisis of the 1990s.[86]

In 2004, the park's director characterized the relationship between the state and the park's supporters as "an ongoing war between the government and the greens."[87] From 2000 to 2009, the city of Inta and the Council of Ministers of the Komi Republic made six additional attempts to reduce the size of IVNP.[88] Finally, in 2010 the Russian Ministry of Natural Resources sidestepped the legal process and gave the company Gold Minerals a license to carry out mining on 1,900 hectares in the Kozhim River watershed, located in the park's territory. While Gold Materials had carried out limited activities for years, this decision threatened to intensify them considerably and posed a much larger environmental threat.[89] At the Thirty-Fifth Session of the Committee of World Heritage Sites, UNESCO released the following statement:

> We express our extreme concern in connection with the changes to the boundaries of the northern part of the World Heritage Site. We consider that what has been carried out at the World Heritage Site, and the support of gold mining at the Wonderful [*Chudnoe*] site presents a potential threat to the exceptional universal value and integrity of the site.[90]

In turn, UNESCO threatened to give the Virgin Komi Forests the status of a World Heritage Natural Site in Danger.[91] In 2015, the Supreme Court of the Russian Federation ruled that removing this area was illegal and established that any further attempts would be as well. The Ministry of Natural Resources, however, has not stopped trying as of 2019.

IVNP today is the second largest national park in the Russian Federation, but it has fewer than seven thousand visitors per year.[92] Given its significant distance from major population centers, estimations of IVNP's potential profitability were always fantastical. Indeed, while the Komi Scientific Center's relative independence from Moscow in the planning process allowed it to imagine a beautiful dream, coordination between the center and central ministries might have provided a stronger foundation for the park. Since the park's establishment to this day (2019), the park's opponents accuse the park of stunting the economic development of the region.[93] A moderately profitable national park, which would have undoubtedly required improved transportation and infrastructure development, would in all likelihood have gained stronger support from high-level officials who would have been more dedicated to curbing the appetites of extractive industries in national park territory. As with many other Russian national parks, this counterfactual cloud hangs over the history of IVNP.

8

The Vision and the Reality in the Taiga of Karelia and the Arkhangelsk Oblast

Oleg Cherviakov and Vodlozero National Park

"In transforming nature," Maksim Gorky famously wrote, "man transforms himself."[1] Gorky's phrase reflected the Promethean worldview of Stalinism and the Communist Party's belief in the malleability of the human spirit, but he wrote these words specifically about the convicts who dug the iconic Baltic–White Sea (Belomor) Canal and cut vast swathes of forest in the Karelian Autonomous Soviet Socialist Republic (the Karelian ASSR), which borders Finland and is the most densely forested part of European Russia. While the canal proved too difficult to navigate for productive economic use, central planners increasingly oriented the economies of the Karelian ASSR and the neighboring Arkhangelsk Oblast toward the exploitation of its forests in the decades following the canal's completion. By the late 1980s, the Karelian ASSR alone accounted for 15 percent of the USSR's timber harvest.[2]

Despite decades of aggressive cuts in the Far North, the Ileks River valley and the territory around Vodlozero Lake in the Arkhangelsk Oblast and the Karelian ASSR was still the largest stand of old-growth forest in all of Europe in the late 1980s. As national parks were being established and new ones proposed throughout the RSFSR to block potentially damaging extractive uses of scenic areas, a young, idealistic college student from the Ukrainian SSR named Oleg Cherviakov took a fateful trip down the Ileks River into Vodlozero Lake. Entranced by the beauty of the area and wistfully romantic about Orthodox Christian traditions of pre-Revolutionary Russia, which the USSR had tried to eradicate, Cherviakov envisioned, lobbied for, helped plan, and became the first director of Vodlozero National Park (VNP). He believed that this park would not only protect the forests of this area but would bring

Into Russian Nature. Alan D. Roe, Oxford University Press (2020) © Oxford University Press.
DOI: 10.1093/oso/9780190914554.001.0001

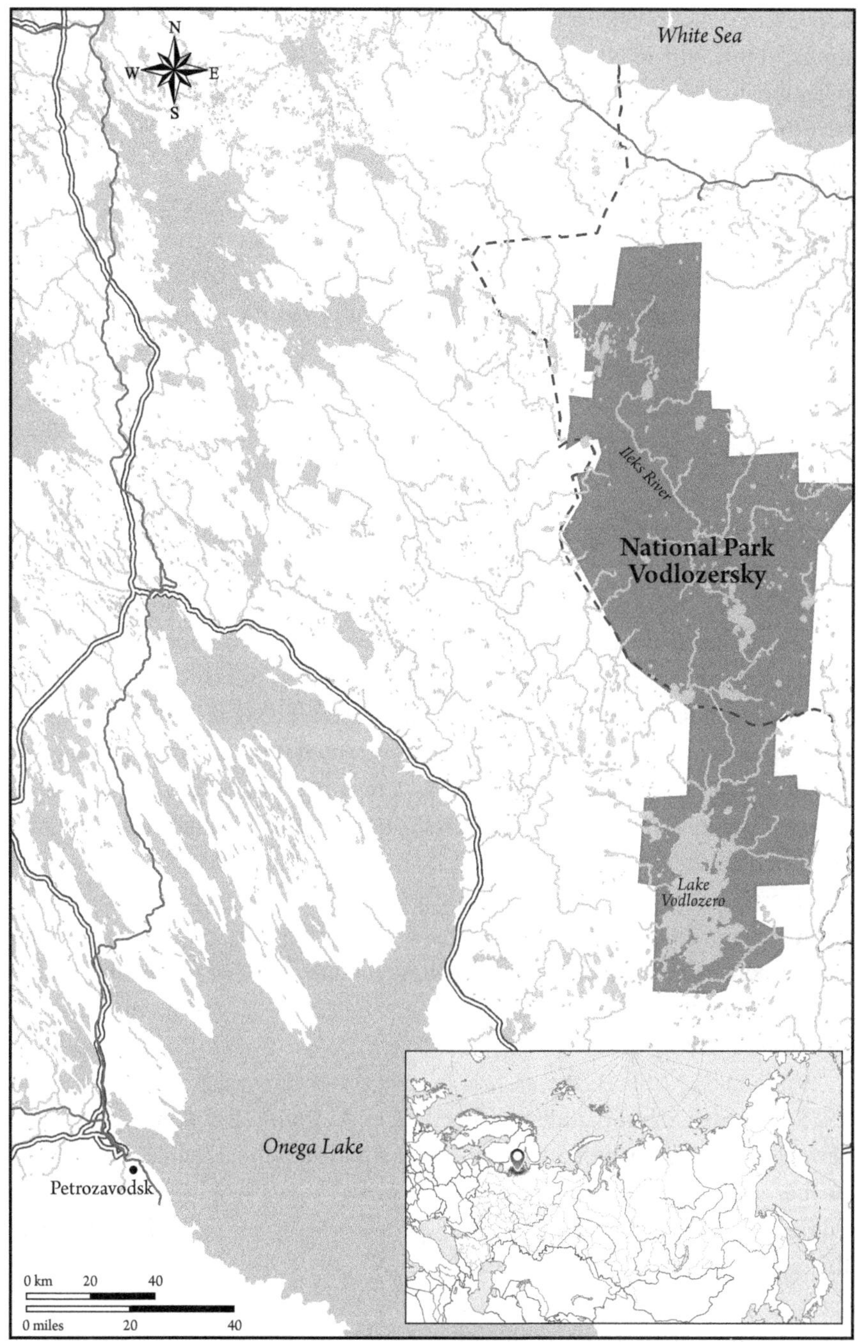

Figure 8.1 Ileks and Vodlozero/VNP.

about a regional religious revival, which would engender a stronger environmental ethic in the region and beyond. Ultimately, to his profound disappointment, he realized that no one wanted to go back to the old ways and that tourism's economic benefits, which had initially intrigued the struggling local population, would never materialize when few tourists wanted to come to this region and with the state little interested in developing the park's infrastructure. While many Russian park founders made lofty claims, VNP's history marks perhaps the apotheosis of utopian proposals for parks and the depths of disappointment caused by a park's failure to bring the regional transformation that it had promised.

A Love of the Forest

Through the early twentieth century, Russian writers romanticized northern forests as a broad discussion about the destruction of forests animated Russian intellectuals and scientists.[3] Although Soviet foresters did successfully lobby for the creation of large forest reserves to protect watersheds during the Stalin era, the "forest question" was more muted in public discourse in the USSR's first decades.[4] Timber harvests increased throughout the USSR, and the Karelian economy was increasingly oriented toward forestry.[5] Leonid Leonov's novel *The Russian Forest* (1953), however, strongly criticized Soviet forestry practices, which spurred larger debates over making forestry more sustainable in a less repressive political environment.[6] In the ensuing decades, deforestation became one of the most talked about issues among the environmentally concerned community. As the forests of Karelia and the Arkhangelsk Oblast continued to make up a disproportionate share of the Soviet timber harvest, Soviet environmentalists and foresters in the region worried deeply about their fate.[7]

While taking trips to the eastern part of the Arkhangelsk Oblast in 1984–1985 as a high school student, Cherviakov witnessed and grew deeply concerned about timber harvesting in the North. The oblast's traditional villages further away from significant forestry enterprises, however, left an equally strong impression on him. There, he met with people who, to his mind, lived in much the same way as before the revolution.

> They lived in harmony with nature. I saw that the level of spiritual development and the level of knowledge exceeds ours many times. With time I came to understand that it was based on a special relationship to the earth as mother and in the belief in God. These two bases made this traditional world of the village of the Russian North.[8]

Cherviakov's passion for the forest continued to grow stronger after he enrolled in the Kharkiv Physics Institute. His yearning for the ideal forest led him back to the North during his summer breaks. During the summers of 1987 and 1988, he led a group of fellow students to Solovki to help restore a monastery. After finishing his work, he undertook his fateful, month-long, 150-kilometer boat trip down the Ileks River into Vodlozero. He found in this area the ideal forest that he had long sought.

While different branches of the VOOP and other civic organizations had been proposing national parks for Karelia and the Arkhangelsk Oblast since the 1970s, the conversation gained momentum in the Gorbachev era when Cherviakov was spending so much time in the region.[9] Many Karelians felt a particular urgency to protect its landscapes. While this area accounted for 15 percent of the RSFSR's timber harvest, only 0.3 percent of its territory was under protection.[10] With places in Karelia having become increasingly popular with tourists in the previous years, the Karelian Institute of the Forest (founded in 1957) expected tourism to increase two- or threefold by 2000. In response, it began working on plans for six national parks, including one on Kizhi, an island in Lake Onega, and Valaam, which was the site of a large monastery under restoration.[11] It called for bringing 5 percent of the Karelian ASSR under protection by 2000.[12] In 1988, scientists from Moscow, Leningrad, Arkhangelsk, Vologda, Petrozavodsk, and Syktyvkar met in Arkhangelsk for a conference dedicated to establishing national parks in northern regions—the Murmansk and Arkhangelsk Oblasts, the Komi ASSR, and Karelian ASSR.[13]

The previous year, a group of scientists from the Biology Institute of the Karelia Branch of the Academy of Sciences, led by wetland scientist Vladimir Antipin, had designated eighty-six thousand hectares a *zakaznik* (temporary reserve) around Vodlozero.[14] While *zakazniki* were often established at the republic, oblast, or krai level in anticipation of federal *zapovednik* or national park status, the designation was usually more permissive regarding extractive interests. In late February and March 1988, the Pial'mskii Forestry District cut a road through the *zakaznik* directly to the lake to open the area to limited logging, with the permission of the Karelian ASSR Council of Ministers. The road alarmed many among the environmentally concerned public. Describing its construction as a "national calamity," the journalist L. Peregud wrote two months later in the newspaper *Banner of Labor* (*Znamia truda*):

> In Karelia, very few untouched corners remain. One of them is Vodlozero, especially the northeastern part of this corner of our Pudozh land. Here we need to organize not only a *zakaznik* but also a *zapovednik* or a national park.[15]

Cherviakov learned about the recent intrusions of the Karelian Timber Cooperative (Karellesprom) into the protected zone as well as larger issues of protected territories in the Karelian ASSR when he visited the Institute of the Forest in Petrozavodsk after his river trip. En route back to Kharkiv, he stopped in Moscow and found Nataliia Zabelina's recently published book *National Park,* which outlined the Scientific Research Institute of Nature Protection's plan for creating a system of national parks in the USSR.[16] Zabelina's assertion that parks could transform the human-nature relationship resonated deeply with Cherviakov. At the time, he was reading Mikhail Prishvin's *In the Place of Fearless Birds* (*V kraiu nepuganykh ptits*). This work of historical fiction is based on the semiautonomous economic and political center—Vygorets, which united several Old Believer monasteries in the North from the seventeenth to the nineteenth centuries.[17]

> I thought it would be possible to create such an alternative today in a society that is so hostile and aggressive to nature. If Andrei Denisov [the founder of Vygorets] did it in the eighteenth century, why couldn't it be done in the twentieth century? For Denisov, it was a religious idea. I thought about what sort of idea could be a basis for that sort of republic today.

Cherviakov understood his accidental discovery of Zabelina's book as a sign, perhaps from God, that he was destined for something different than a life of physics research.

The Campaign

When he returned to Kharkiv, Cherviakov published an article, "Desert or National Park," in the Karelian newspaper *Komsomol* (*Komsomolets*).[18] He asserted that a *zakaznik* could not prevent Karellesprom from penetrating into the "last ecologically clean region of the republic." [19] "I have seen how these loggers work," he wrote. "They have no mercy on the forests, nor the wetlands. One is left with a depressing impression upon seeing the hundreds of hectares of ruined forest."[20] After asserting that a national park could transform the regional economy by reviving handicrafts and attracting tourists from throughout the USSR and even abroad, Cherviakov stated that the establishment of the park would also "clarify the moral health of society."[21] "The logic is simple: empty souls will produce a deserted wasteland around them; rich souls will produce national riches," he argued.[22]

The Karelian public responded positively to the idea, but the editor of *Communist Youth* told Cherviakov that nothing would come of it if the effort did not have a leader. There had, after all, been different proposals for a national park for Vodlozero and the surrounding area in the previous fifteen years.[23] Cherviakov's primary academic advisor, Vladimir Volovik, was intrigued and encouraged him to spearhead the effort while he completed his thesis. He even fueled Cherviakov's imagination by proposing a name for the park that would encapsulate its transformative vision—a noosphere park.[24]

The idea of the noosphere was put forward by the renowned Russian geographer Vladimir Vernadsky (1863–1945) during the 1920s.[25] Presaging present-day geological debates about the Anthropocene, Vernadsky argued that human societies throughout the world were not only the agents of biological destruction but also the shapers of the geological environment. The noosphere was the sphere of collective human (societal) cognition. Vernadsky asserted that the application of intellect and ingenuity in the name of material progress had caused vast destruction. But he also believed that humans could direct their intellectual energy toward a harmonious and sustainable relationship with nature. The Soviet environmental community had rediscovered Vernadsky's ideas during the Brezhnev era, and the noosphere had become a common trope in Soviet nature protection discourse by the time of perestroika.[26]

Cherviakov returned to Petrozavodsk to rally support for the idea of establishing a national park just after the New Year holiday in 1989. His youth, charisma, enthusiasm, and tireless public outreach helped him win many supporters. Among them were the Karelia State Committee on Nature Protection and the director of the Institute of Biology, S. N. Drozdov, who would make a case for the park's establishment to the Karelian ASSR Council of Ministers.[27] Cherviakov met with officials from the Karelian ASSR branch of the Ministry of Forestry, leaders of newly formed environmental protection organizations, and governmental representatives of the Pudozh District, the most populated area in the territory of the proposed park. He also organized meetings with village councils and called for members to write petitions to officials at the local, state, and union level of government.

Calling forestry "Karelia's lifeblood," the Karelia Forestry Cooperative opposed Cherviakov's proposal and emphasized to both the public and the Karelian ASSR Council of Ministers the economic harm that its establishment would cause.[28] However, the press largely reported widespread support from the twelve villages in the areas in and adjacent to the park, which were home to 3,500 people. Throughout the first few months of 1989, the local newspaper *The Pudozh Messenger* (*Pudozhskii vestnik*) received over 750 local letters of support, with many stating that the park would create new economic opportunities.[29]

Because Cherviakov insisted that these villages and their "authentic" culture were essential to the park, they did not fear forced removal. The population, which had been forced to accept the dictates of central economic ministries for decades, was clearly energized by the prospect of having more say in its future.

The park also needed the support of local leaders. The most influential supporter of the park in the Pudozh community was Andrei Beckman, the director of the region's largest employer, the fish canning factory Ekodar. Beckman was sociable and widely trusted throughout the community.[30] In an article published in the newspaper *Lenin's Pravda* (*Leninskaia pravda*) on October 20, 1989, "How to Revive Vodlozero," he stated, "Not only is the national park needed for our distant descendants, but firstly it is necessary for us, those living now."[31] Embracing the era's renewed emphasis on civic engagement and perhaps concerned about the country's stability, he continued: "In protecting the unique historical and natural watershed of Vodlozero and the Ileks River we affirm in our civic-mindedness, our responsibility for the fate of the fatherland."[32]

Cherviakov raised the proposed park's profile throughout the RSFSR by writing articles in the widely circulated magazines *Forest gazette* (*Lesnaia gazeta*) and *Nature and People* (*Priroda i chelovek*).[33] These articles described the region's forestry practices as "colonial plunder" led by "looting central agencies" that were out of step with perestroika's emphasis on regional economic self-accounting.[34] He argued that tourism would become the largest sector of the Karelian economy.[35] Calling for "rational" and "complex" use of Karelia's forest, Karelian journalists characterized it as a common resource that industry had monopolized at the republic's expense.[36] Of the two million cubic meters of timber cut each year, factories in the republic only processed two hundred thousand, resulting in a net loss of thirty to thirty-five million rubles a year.[37] Tourism, the park's proponents argued, would provide a much more sustainable, diversified, and independent basis for the future of the Karelia's economy. Cherviakov and others were still vague in their descriptions of the types of tourism that would take place in the park. They would develop these ideas over time.

Cherviakov's Vision

Having formed a close relationship with Nataliia Zabelina and influential individuals working in the RSFSR Main Administration for Hunting and Zapovedniki, Cherviakov was offered a position by the head of the main administration that would provide him with needed financial support and a place to work. He would live in the Kostomushskii Zapovednik on the Finnish border, about six hundred kilometers northwest of Lake Vodlozero, and his sole responsibility would be to plan the national park. Cherviakov, with the help of his advisor Vladimir Volovik, assembled a planning group for Vodlozero National Noosphere Park, drawing on scientists from the Karelia Institute of the Forest, the Ural Division of the Academy of Sciences, the Geographical Society of the USSR, Rostov State University, and Tambov State University.

Cherviakov met with the team of biologists and geographers in the territory of the proposed park during the summer of 1990. They provided the descriptions of the physical territory for the park project in a report entitled "The Economic-Ecological Basis for VNNP." Sixty-three percent of trees in the more than four-thousand-hectare proposed park were more than two hundred years old, which made it the largest old-growth taiga forest in Europe. Wetlands within the forests that made the territory especially appealing to a variety of birds would make the road construction for expanding timber harvesting extraordinarily costly and damaging. The abundance of black bears, moose, deer, wild boar, rabbits, and squirrels, Cherviakov believed, might make the park particularly attractive to foreign hunters.

Much of the transformative vision presented in "The Economic-Ecological Basis for VNNP" would have been inconceivable in previous eras of Soviet history. Cherviakov believed that his conception of a national noosphere park would lay the foundation for environmental sustainability in the region.

> These parks provide a symbiosis of protected natural areas and economic development of areas where industry, agriculture, forestry, hunting and fishing, recreation, and other types of the use of nature are based on closed processes and comprehensive use of the local natural resources without any environmental risk.[38]

The revival of "traditional culture," which he largely defined as Orthodox Christianity, would help achieve this ecological harmony and revive the socioeconomic life of the region.[39] Cherviakov argued that this plan would preserve the area's "natural evolutionary development" without seeming to consider that the Soviet command economy and the state's hostility toward religion had already profoundly disrupted the continuity of the region's "natural" development.

"Restoring ancient temples," he wrote, "Il'inskii churchyard, deserted monasteries, and their full inclusion into the life of society will contribute to the revival of spiritual life in the province and return to the high cultural and moral values of Christianity."[40] The return to such a moral atmosphere, in turn, would cultivate a culture in which people valued their work and would foster greater creativity.[41] Just as Vygorets had been a quasi-independent center of commerce within an increasingly centralized state, Cherviakov believed that VNNP would begin a movement that would allow the Russian North to develop a vibrant and independent culture grounded in a strong sense of place and local control.

Harvesting and processing of fallen wood as well as wild edible and medicinal plants, fishing and fish processing, and agricultural production would help offset economic losses that the logging industry would suffer from the protection of forests. The profitability of US national parks demonstrated that tourism, especially foreign tourism, could become a tremendous source of revenue.[42] Cherviakov planned the development of paddle tours to the lake's different islands, cross-country skiing trips, and excursions by foot and horseback. Tourists could also take excursions focused on the area's local history and literary traditions, environmental education, and "guest tourism," in which visitors would stay with locals and take part in the collection of berries, mushrooms, and medicinal plants to learn about traditional rural life.[43]

Cherviakov asserted that the principle of the "ecological economic unit" would inform all decisions about the area's development. This model held that the principle of "ecological stability," which he never clearly defined, must serve as the basis for all decisions about the region's economic development. While the park administration would determine these "units" through defining coherent ecosystems, such as watersheds, Cherviakov explained that a system of monitoring and mathematical modeling could precisely determine the impact of different types of land use.[44] He wrote, "So if the scenario does not satisfy the most ecologically acceptable form of development" (Cherviakov does not clearly define this in the report), "the option is not allowed for consideration."[45] This principle of economic organization, he believed, would make VNP a model.

> Resources and effort must first be concentrated on model regions most suitable for these goals, transforming them into ecological-economic zones and only then can this system expand to the entire territory of the republic. The impact would extend beyond the boundaries of Karelia.

According to Cherviakov, the "ecological economic unit" was "a task of global, or in any case European, scale."[46]

These ambitious plans ignored some obvious realities. Organized tourism was still almost nonexistent in the area of the proposed park, which was far from large population centers.[47] Infrastructure, qualified staff, improved transportation to the park, and marketing would require significant investment. Cherviakov stated that the park could not rely on state investment given the economic situation in the USSR at the time, but he seemed to assume that the park infrastructure could be built through partnerships with foreign firms.[48] Moreover, he never seemed to question how commercialism might undermine cultural "authenticity." Could an authentic culture truly be revived and grow "organically," as he frequently stated, when it sought to profit from its appeal to outsiders who wanted a glimpse of the "exotic?" If Cherviakov had spent much time in capitalist countries, he would have reflected more on how selling an image of "authenticity" to paying tourists can undermine the values long held in a particular place and often devolves into self-caricature.[49]

Some of Cherviakov's other ideas demonstrated a profound naiveté concerning the relationship between money and power and between the economy and culture. He claimed that local power with "high levels of professionalism and competence" would shape the region's managerial priorities. His ideas about competence, however, were based on a particularly narrow and absolutist vision of the proper uses of park territory. Despite his emphasis on local control, he repeatedly argued that the virgin forests of Karelia and Arkhangelsk were "universal property" (*obshchechelovecheskoe dostoianie*).[50] It followed that the park would attract the interest of international organizations and investors.[51] He called for cooperation with the IUCN, UNEP, and World Wide Fund for Nature and compliance with "proper ecological standards" established by the IUCN and the United Nation's World Conservation Strategy.[52]

Cherviakov never hinted at the fact that such standards might interfere with local autonomy and initiative. He also never seemed to consider that outside investors might be empowered to alter his original vision or influence local decision-making. His vision reflected the sense of infinite possibility for the future born out of the Soviet public's questioning of the USSR's philosophical and economic foundations and the strengthening of the international discourse of "sustainable development."[53] At the same time, he demonstrated the trait of economic illiteracy that was not uncommon among environmental protection advocates of different countries but was particularly pronounced in the USSR after decades of a centralized and top-down approach to economic decision-making.

Establishment and Disappointment

Cherviakov proved more adept at persuasion than developing a realistic plan. From the publication of his article that had set everything in motion to the park's establishment in 1991, he forged relationships not only with scientists, academics, and advocates for cultural preservation but also with influential government officials whose support was necessary for the park's establishment. "He had," Nataliia Zabelina said, "a way of crawling into one's heart."[54] While the Ministry of Forestry and the State Committee on Forests made official objections to the proposed park to the special commission on the subject formed by the USSR Council of Ministers, Cherviakov successfully rallied support from ministries, civic organization, and influential environmentalists.[55] In a letter supporting the park, Alexei Yablokov struck an alarmist tone in warning the USSR Council of Ministers that Karelia would exhaust its timber reserves in ten to thirty years.[56] Dmitrii Likhachev, perhaps the USSR's strongest voice for preserving cultural heritage and church restoration efforts in the North, also expressed strong support and visited the site of the proposed park.[57]

Cherviakov also benefited from idiosyncrasies within the Soviet system of allocating forest cuts, which pitted the interests of the Arkhangelsk Oblast and the Karelian ASSR against one another. Even though the entire Ileks River and its surrounding old-growth taiga forests were in the Arkhangelsk Oblast, the Karelian Forestry Cooperative had the rights to cut these forests.[58] The Arkhangelsk Executive Committee realized that allowing the Karelian Forestry Cooperative to harvest them would bring no economic benefit to the Arkhangelsk Oblast. Moreover, by designating a *zakaznik*, the oblast administration would reach its yearly quota for assigning new protected territory set by the RSFSR Main Administration for Hunting and Zapovedniki. Accordingly, toward the end of 1990, the Arkhangelsk Oblast Executive Committee declared the 274,000 hectares of the proposed park in the oblast a temporary reserve (*zakaznik*).[59] The Karelian ASSR Council of Ministers had been vacillating in its support for the national park in large part because of the projected economic benefits that timber cuts in this region would bring to the republic. Now, with the largest portion of the proposed forests inaccessible regardless of whether the RSFSR Council of Ministers established the national park, Vladimir Razonov, who became chair of the Karelian ASSR Council of Ministers in early 1991, expressed his support for the park.[60]

Establishing the park required only the signature of the head of the deputy chair of the RSFSR Council of Ministers, Vitalii Trifonovich Gavrilov, if it gained unanimous support from the State Committee on Ecology (Goskompriroda), the Ministry of Economy, the State Committee on Forests, and the Ministry of Finance. If any of these agencies opposed its establishment, the park would need the signature of the head of the RSFSR Council of Ministers, Ivan Silaev. Stating that the creation of a national park would cost the Karelian Forestry Cooperative half of its harvestable territory and result in the loss of two thousand jobs in the Karelian ASSR, the Association of Workers of the Wood Processing Industry, an RSFSR-wide organization, expressed strong opposition to the park.[61] The Ministry of Economy and the State Committee on Forests shared these concerns. After receiving signatures from Goskompriroda and the Ministry of Finance, Cherviakov depended on Gavrilov to secure Silaev's signature and feared that if he did not provide it immediately, he might reconsider his support. Cherviakov waited for three days as a strike by miners from the Kuzbass region of western Siberia was preoccupying Gavrilov. Knowing that Silaev would be leaving the country the following day, Cherviakov prayed as he never had before on the night of April 19, 1991. On April 20, as Silaev was preparing to board the plane, Gavrilov obtained his signature, which officially established the park. To this day, Cherviakov attributes this success to something more powerful than luck.[62]

While the RSFSR Council of Ministers had established the 490,000-hectare park, Cherviakov's vision for it remained in his head and on paper. Because he despised the USSR for its attempts to eradicate religious belief, among other things, its fall in late 1991 intensified Cherviakov's sense of mission and purpose. Moreover, for Cherviakov, the strengthening discourse of "sustainable development," which was the foundational principle of the Rio Earth Summit of 1992, seemed to confirm to him that the park was at the vanguard of a new epoch in world history. Local support remained strong for the first year and a half after the park's establishment. One journalist, perhaps with some exaggeration, asserted that "all residents" of the region supported the park.[63] Others wrote confidently that interest in the park would "grow headlong" in other countries and that it would become a national park "of the highest category."[64]

This enthusiasm and hope for the park had little undergirding it. Over this period, the state provided almost no funding for infrastructural development, and few tourists visited. Moreover, as the state divested itself of many of the responsibilities it had under socialism, the park became responsible for many essential social services for the region, such as kindergartens, electricity, and water, all without receiving the necessary funds from an increasingly dysfunctional and financially crippled government.[65] The park also inherited all of the area's agricultural enterprises without receiving subsidies from the Ministry of Agriculture. Moreover, the fish-canning factory Ekodar went bankrupt in early 1993, which left the majority of the working population unemployed. Andrei Beckman, who had long been one of the most influential community members and a strong supporter of the park, moved away to Petrozavodsk.[66] While the population was increasingly looking to it as a source of employment, the park was accruing almost no revenue and could not expand its personnel. Although there could not have been a better time than perestroika for Cherviakov to inspire others with his transformative vision, the economic collapse that followed created the worst possible conditions for him to realize it.

While Cherviakov was able to sell his vision, he seemed uninterested in the everyday social interactions necessary to build and sustain healthy relationships and trust with members of the community. They increasingly viewed him, according to articles in the press, as imperious and uncompromising. While many had initially regarded the park as a means of asserting independence from Moscow, the local press began describing it as another imposition from the center.[67] Although Cherviakov had emphasized empowerment of the local population, many inhabitants of the territory in and around the park accused Moscow of sending "incompetent people" to govern the region.[68] Moreover, as was the case throughout the Russian Federation, the worsening economic situation made environmental protection seem like an unaffordable luxury to many.[69]

Cherviakov sought to obtain territory adjacent to the park to establish a buffer zone without input from the area's inhabitants, according to the community. Meanwhile, locals expressed their frustration that the park had not brought the promised economic benefits. They also expressed skepticism that foreign "moneybags" would ever want to visit, doubt about whether the state would ever fund infrastructure, and sympathy for the forestry industry, which most had strongly criticized in the lead-up to the park's establishment.[70] At a meeting of the Kugavalanok Council on March 30, 1993, one participant, ignoring the park's new responsibilities for supporting different social services, stated that the national park had not given "a kopeck" to the region and that the village's residents would not realize the economic benefits for at least fifteen years.[71] Another attacked the "science" behind the national park while suggesting that its propagandists had deceived residents of the region. Echoing the suspicions of local populations toward some national parks outside Russia, he stated:

> The national park has its professional writers, who can prove whatever they want. But the heart of the matter is that the national park wants to be the master of the region. In deciding the question concerning the life of the region, only one side is present. We have received nonobjective information. The creeping annexation of the territory of Kubovski and Pial'mskii Forestry District is underway, all in the name of science. My relationship to science is that whoever pays more will have science prove what they want.[72]

This skepticism about science reflected the local population's longstanding alienation from regional decision-making processes, which for decades had been controlled by "experts" from outside the region. In many ways, the current situation seemed little different in that respect. The deputy of the Kugavalonok Council, N. D. Durov, succinctly expressed the growing distrust between the people and the park: "The interests of the region and the interests of the national park are quite different."[73]

Cherviakov and others in the park administration sought to reassure the local population that it would bring many new jobs and that a "flood of tourists thirsting for the beauty of wilderness" would soon begin.[74] However, Cherviakov did not always seem to understand the impact of his words, and his occasional tactlessness made it difficult for such appeals to the future to calm the nerves of an anxious public. In early 1994, he remarked, perhaps truthfully but insensitively during a radio program called *Hostage to the Village,* that the park had inherited not only an "unprofitable enterprise" and a "destroyed economy" but also a "demoralized collective."[75] One of the park's strongest supporters in the local press, L. Peregud, seemed to take offense at this remark and retorted in the newspaper *Northern Messenger,* "It turns out that the park has it bad because of the village. But what does the village get from the park?"[76]

A Vision Unrealized

National parks throughout the Russian Federation found themselves hamstrung by a lack of funds. However, no national park had presented such a transformative vision, and few others had assumed so much responsibility for the livelihood of the surrounding population as VNP. The funding situation worsened throughout the 1990s. Park employee wages hovered at subsistence levels. Cherviakov noted in 1996 that the park had tattered infrastructure, no good roads, and a transportation fleet that was hardly functional. He estimated that the park needed over 225 million rubles more than it received from the state that year to fulfill its essential responsibilities.[77] There was no state money for infrastructural development, the absence of which he believed had prevented the park from becoming a popular destination for foreign tourists. At mid-decade, fewer than three thousand tourists visited the park annually.[78] Frustrated, he reflected: "It all seemed as though we were moving against the current. It seemed that we were walking in place."[79]

Cherviakov did successfully establish foreign contacts and raised the park's international profile, which he had always maintained was necessary for its development. In early 1993, he established a cooperative relationship with the United States National Park Service through which he visited several American parks and hosted superintendents of several US national parks.[80] He received a grant of 2.5 million dollars in 1997 from TACIS (Technical Assistance to the Commonwealth of Independent States), which the park used to establish an office with an ecological education center in Petrozavodsk, build an ecological trail, initiate the restoration of old churches and chapels, and develop an extensive strategic plan and system of ecological monitoring.[81] However, accessibility remained a problem, and tourism infrastructure remained rudimentary. In 1998, a UNESCO delegation visited the park to determine if it would be designated a World Heritage Natural Site.[82] While that did not happen, it was named a UNESCO biosphere reserve in 2001.

While Cherviakov led an international team in planning several more national parks in the Republic of Karelia and the Arkhangelsk Oblast in 1998, these parks

Figure 8.2 Restored Monastery in Vodlozero National Park. Photo by author.

remained proposals, and VNP was still mostly undeveloped as the end of the millennium approached. Demoralized, he commented:

> I came to the understanding that it was a dead end. Most of what existed were just plans and documents. We developed ecological trails, including a forty-kilometer trail. We made booklets and carried out landscape planning, but it is not interesting to anyone. Tourists are only interested in throwing out a fishing line and drinking vodka.[83]

While the Soviet tourism movement incorporated a broad range of leisure activities from outdoor recreation to visits to spas, Cherviakov in his disappointments could only see the interests of tourists in more limited terms.

As Cherviakov successfully restored small chapels, a monastery, and the small abandoned village of Varishpel'da where he and his wife Natasha live, he became increasingly devoted to his religious practice (he was ordained as a priest in 1992) and more pessimistic about the park's prospects. Moreover, as he sought to live out his ideal of a life in harmony with the natural world, he was becoming resigned to the fact that "local residents don't want to return to the motherland of their ancestors," which for him meant the restoration of the locally based economy and deep devotion to Orthodox Christianity.[84] In 2005, realizing that he would never realize his utopian vision, he left his official position as head administrator of the national park. The new administration continues to

Figure 8.3 Oleg CheVodlozero National Park. Photo by author.

support the development of tourism and educational outreach programs to the extent that its resources allow, but it has abandoned Cherviakov's transformative vision.[85]

Conclusion

Oleg Cherviakov hoped that VNP would provide the springboard to move Karelia from an extractive economy to one increasingly focused on tourism. However, timber and wood processing industries remain by far the largest sector of the Karelian economy. With nearly 765,000 tourists visiting Karelia every year, the tourism industry accounts for almost 5 percent of the Republic of Karelia's economy.[86] Though hardly insignificant, tourism has not brought about the economic transformations expected during the late 1980s, and, with VNP hosting only seven thousand visitors a year, its role in the republic's tourism economy is small.[87] Its meager infrastructure and poor prospects for its development make it unlikely that it will play a larger economic role in the future.

Today, the forests in VNP undoubtedly have far more protection than if Russia had never established the park. In this sense, it must be considered a success. Stopping the ongoing destruction of northern forests, after all, had initially been Cherviakov's foremost concern. However, because his broader vision was not realized, Cherviakov, ever the idealist, sees the park largely as a failure, one that he understands in a broader and apocalyptic context of a morally depraved world heading towards ecological destruction.[88] Sobered by disappointment, Cherviakov now seems to acknowledge that reclaiming an idealized version of a "traditional" past was as unrealistic as the Communist Party's aspiration to engineer human souls, as Gorky put it. Living out these ideals provides him with some solace for the fact that few others wanted to do the same.

PART III

THE CRISIS OF RUSSIA'S NATIONAL PARKS

In the early 1990s, park supporters and environmentalists strongly hoped that expanded contacts with the West and democracy would result in a stronger government commitment to the development of Russia's national parks. By decade's end, they were deeply disappointed. Their disillusionment has deepened over the last twenty years. Part III gives a broader view of Russia's general neglect of national parks and other protected territories from the fall of the USSR to the present. It also assesses how park supporters have understood what they see as their government's failure. This part also reflects on Russia's national park story in the context of the global history of national parks and the broad appeal that wild places have long had for Russians and people of other industrialized countries.

9

The Crisis of National Parks in the 1990s

The fall of the USSR gave hope to environmentalists that democracy and a closer relationship to the West would help Russia overcome its backwardness in environmental protection. In January 1992, Aleksei Yablokov said in a *Los Angeles Times* interview, "At last, now there is someone who listens. There is a possibility of accomplishment. If you can get the ear of Yeltsin or Burbulis [the deputy prime minister], things get done."[1] Yablokov was no doubt making an implicit appeal to Western environmentalists to focus their attention and perhaps resources on Russia. But Yeltsin's environmental diplomacy would continue to give hope to his and others' optimism. The Russian president signed the Russian Federation on to Agenda 21 at the Rio Earth Summit a few months after Yablokov's interview and committed the country to numerous international environmental agreements in the years to follow.

Four months before Rio, several Russians represented their country at the IUCN's Fourth World Conference on National Parks in Caracas, Venezuela.[2] The Caracas Declaration that came out of the conference set the goal of having 10 percent of the world's surface under protection by 2000.[3] With Yeltsin understanding that appearing to work toward international environmental protection goals helped Russia's image, the government of the Russian Federation established more parks than in any other period in Russian or Soviet history over the next several years.[4] Originally intended as one national park, Meshchera and Meshcherskii National Parks were formed in 1992 in the Vladimir and Ryazan Oblasts, respectively. In April 1992, Smolensk Lake (Smolenskoe Poozer'e) National Park was established in the northern part of the Smolensk Oblast, an area with many lakes and wetlands. After three years of joint work between Karelian and Finnish scientists, the government established Paanajärvi National Park in the northern part of Karelia along the Finnish border.[5] During this time, the government of the Russian Federation also established Chuvash Varmane in the Chuvash Republic (1993), Russian North (Russkii Sever) in

Into Russian Nature. Alan D. Roe, Oxford University Press (2020) © Oxford University Press.
DOI: 10.1093/oso/9780190914554.001.0001

the Vologda Oblast (1993), Pripyshminskiye Bory in the Sverdlovsk Oblast (1993), Ziurtukul in the Chelyabinsk Oblast (1993), Khvalynskii in the Saratov Oblast (1994), Iugyd Va in the Komi Republic (1994), Orlovskoe Poles'e in the Oryol Oblast (1994), Shushenskii Bor in the Krasnoyarsk Region (1995), and Smolnyi National Park in the Republic of Mordovia (1995). By 1995, the Russian Federation had thirty-one national parks.

Officially designating parks was easier than garnering support for them among local populations or committing federal resources toward their development. Privatization, weakened central authority, and economic crisis often made parks seem to many like an unjust and irrational imposition during a time of economic despair and federal overreach in light of Yeltsin's promises to empower regional administrations.[6] Further, as previous chapters have shown and this chapter will expand on, the government of the Russian Federation did not adequately protect park territory or finance parks' most basic functions, which made it impossible to realize the profits that park proponents had promised. In 1995, Feliks Shtil'mark, who argued that the Russian Federation was establishing national parks mainly to win prestige, reflected: "Sometimes the establishment of a park meant little more than a new signboard, since the protection regime hardly changed and even forest clearance went on regardless."[7]

With Russian park supporters concluding that the state was unwilling or uninterested in developing national parks, they tried to leverage their strengthened international contacts to gain needed material support for parks and pressure the government of the Russian Federation. However, foreign NGOs and international organizations, such as the IUCN and UNESCO, had limited ability to influence the Russian government, and foreign financial assistance proved more limited than expected. Realizing that international support was no panacea, environmentalists came to view the Russian Federation's inability to protect and support its scenic treasures as a failure of responsibility to the Russian people as well as the entire world.

This chapter is divided into four parts. The first two parts each focus on a case studies—Meshcherskii National Park in the Ryazan Oblast and the proposed Beringia International Park (BIP) in Chukotka and Alaska. Each of these cases illustrate the intense local opposition to establishing parks amid economic hardship and weakened central authority. The third part will show how Russian national parks' struggles pushed Russian park supporters and administrators to more aggressively appeal for help to their international partners. Although the hopes they placed in international support and pressure largely met disappointment, the fourth part of this chapter illustrates a rare exception—Nalychevo Nature Park in Kamchatka—to this general trend. Nalychevo proved that parks—nature (managed at regional level) or national—could be established and successfully developed through the combination of international support and citizen participation, even in a climate of weakened central power and economic instability.

Resistance in All Directions: Meshcherskii National Park

The Meshchera Lowlands are a 23,000-square kilometer forest-wetland valley located within the Moscow, Ryazan, and Vladimir Oblasts. The area has coniferous and mixed forests that are home to 850 plant, 170 bird, fifty mammal, thirty fish, and ten amphibian species. In his novella *Kordon 273,* Konstantin Paustovskii, who frequently advocated in newspapers for stronger nature protection measures, said of the region's Pra River, "I have seen many wild and scenic places in Russia, but I have probably never seen a river as pure and mysterious as the Pra."[8]

During the 1960s and 1970s, unorganized tourists flocked to the region in such great numbers that it appeared as if tent cities had been set up along the banks of the Pra and nearby rivers.[9] From the early 1960s to the late 1970s, tourism in the Oka Zapovednik alone grew six hundredfold.[10] The region bore increasing scars from the volume of visitors, but the establishment of a national park for the Meshchera lowlands, which might have mitigated the damage, was not yet possible. However, less than a year after the passage of the Model Regulation on State Nature National Parks in 1981, the nature protection brigades of MSU and the Ryazan Oblast revived the issue.[11] From 1982 to 1985, members of the Geographical Society of the USSR and associates of the Oka Zapovednik along with the nature protection brigades carried out numerous joint projects in the region of Meshchera to establish the "scientific basis" for the formation of a national park.[12] One of the park's supporters, V. Pankratov, wrote in 1983 in *Priokskaia pravda* that a future park with well-developed trails and campsites would allow it to accommodate 160,000 people simultaneously.[13]

In 1986, the RSFSR Main Administration for Hunting and Zapovedniki called for the establishment of Meshchera National Park in its plans for new national parks and *zapovedniki* by the year 2000. With V. N. Tikhomirov, an environmental educator from MSU leading different groups on land surveys in the years that followed, the VOOP, the Ryazan Division of Komsomol, the Youth Council of MSU, and numerous civic organizations offered their backing for the project. The idea gained even broader support when plans were proposed to build a sewage canal through a floodplain of the Oka River. A large protest against its construction led over fifteen thousand people to sign a collective letter in the summer of 1988.[14] *Priokskaia pravda* and *Komsomol of Ryazan*

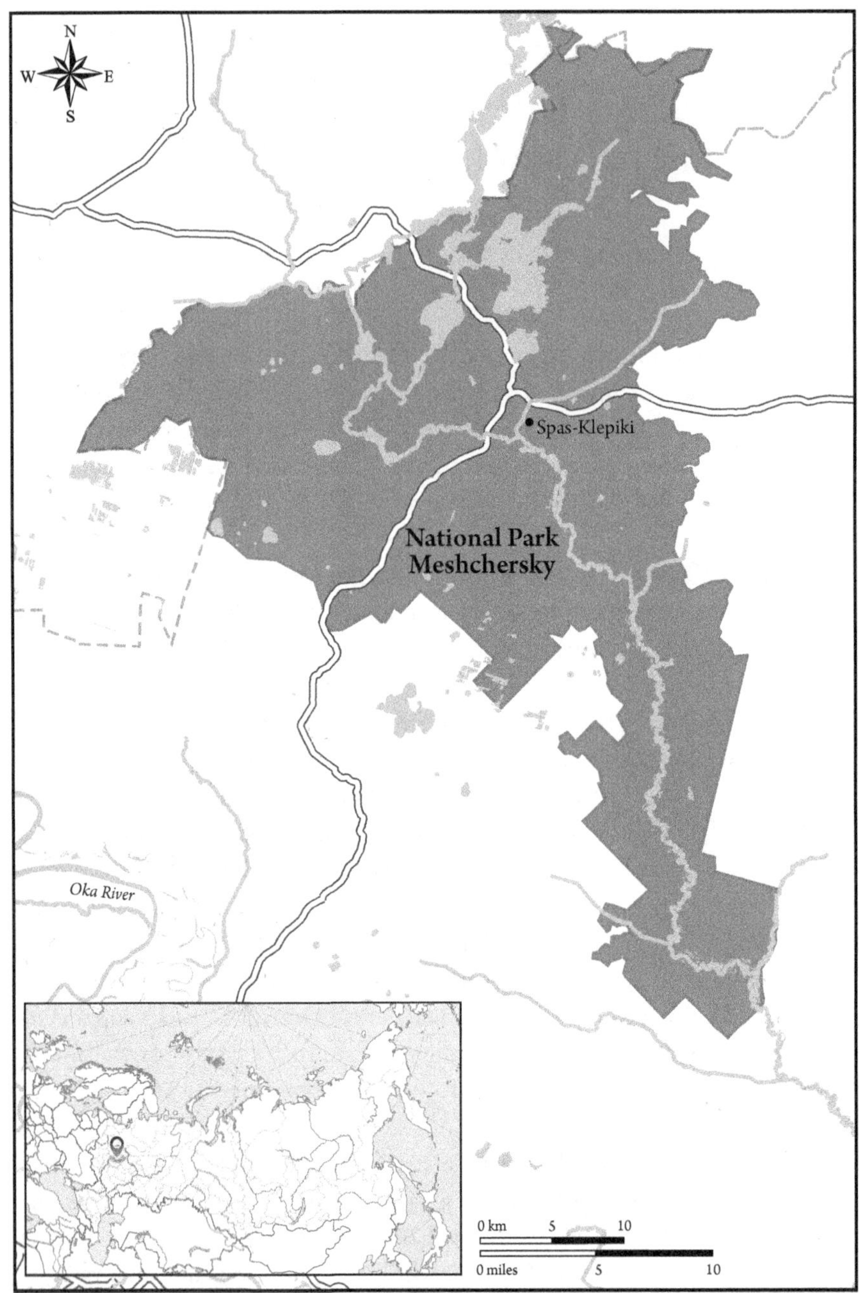

Figure 9.1 Meshchera Lowlands / Meshcherskii National Park.

Figure 9.2 Pra River. Photo by author.

(*Ryazanskii komsomolets*) actively promoted the idea for the park, and the latter solicited thoughts and opinions from readers about what form it should take, resulting in dozens of letters to the editorial board.[15] Some of the most important figures in the protection of the RSFSR's natural and cultural legacy, such as Aleksei Yablokov and Iurii Vedenin, also spoke in favor of the park.[16]

The Scientific Research Institute of Nature Protection had taken a particularly strong interest in the project by the end of the decade. More than 20 percent of the waterfowl in Central Russia nest in the lakes and wetlands of this region, and around 50 percent pass through it on their migration routes.[17] But their habitat was severely threatened by longstanding efforts to drain these wetlands. Moreover, doing this also made it more vulnerable to severe flooding.[18] To address the problem, the institute strongly believed that a single park in the Ryazan, Vladimir, and Moscow Oblasts under federal control was necessary. However, this effort was derailed by local concerns in the Ryazan Oblast.

Residents of the Klepikov Region in the Ryazan Oblast were concerned about new land use restrictions that the national park might impose. Especially worrisome was a possible ban on hunting. The Meshchera Lowlands were among the most popular regions for hunters not just of waterfowl but of wild boar and moose as well.[19] The Klepikov Regional Council of People's Deputies, in turn, strongly conveyed its opposition to the Scientific-Technical Institute of Nature Protection and the Ryazan Oblast Administration.[20] In turn, the Ryazan administration proposed to the government of the RSFSR that it should have jurisdiction over the all the park's territory that fell within its oblast.[21] After months of correspondence between the Ryazan Oblast Administration and different levels of the government of the RSFSR and then the Russian Federation, the Supreme Soviet of the Russian Federation established two national parks—Meshchera and Meshcherskii—on April 9, 1992, with the latter located only within the territory of the Ryazan Oblast.[22]

The decree, which barred "economic activity that countered the tasks of the national park," hardly assuaged concerns of the Ryazan Oblast Administration and residents of the Klepikov Region. Residents believed that the decree's language put the park's interests above the twenty thousand people living within it, despite its promise to "ensure the optimal combination of the interests of the local population, tourism, and nature protection."[23] They had no idea if they could practice agriculture, graze their sheep and goats, gather berries, hunt, or even fish. Moreover, the decree did not specify how the park would be financed or under which department it would operate. If the government failed to invest in tourism infrastructure, there would be nothing to offset the economic shortfall caused by closing enterprises within the park's territory. Moreover, joblessness was rampant, and residents worried that they might be unable to survive with the new restrictions on their use of the land.

The administration of the Klepikov Region called for meetings to be held in different villages where participants took part in referendums on the park.[24] In April 1992, hardly anyone spoke in favor of the park, and the opposition was vehement. Villagers repeatedly expressed the fear that a national park would ban them from gathering mushrooms and berries. Some even stated that park regulations would prevent them from entering its territory.[25] At one meeting, a resident expressed concern that the park designation would give the federal government authority to force him to turn over his firearms.[26]

When the votes were tallied, the result was overwhelmingly negative. In the Bolon'skii Agricultural Council in Surgun, 268 residents voted against the park and only one for it. In another district, the results were 299 against and two for the park.[27] At the meeting of the citizens of Kuzino and Krasnaia Gorka of the Kaldevskii Agricultural Council, 307 participants voted against it, and only nine voted for it. Following the referendum, the Ryazan Oblast Administration wrote a letter to the government of the Russian Federation expressing its opposition. It concluded by stating, "We would like to remind you that in our difficult times when much of the population, including us, is living below the poverty line and has a shortage of food products, money should be invested in a much more promising direction than the organization of a national park."[28]

The Ryazan Oblast Administration treated the park as if it did not exist, even though the referendums could not overturn its legal status. While the Supreme

Soviet would accuse it of peddling misinformation to turn the local population against the park, neither the Ryazan Oblast Administration nor the residents within the territory of the park had been informed of exactly how and where the restrictions would be imposed. The oblast administration began giving land allotments for the construction of boat docks, camps, and recreation bases and for various commercial operations.[29] Given the lack of funds they received from Moscow and the suffering of the population, it is hard to blame the oblast administration for trying to make economically fallow land profitable. The government of the Russian Federation could not do anything to stop its illegal actions. Meshcherskii National Park essentially existed only on paper. Meshchera and Meshcherskii National Parks were united into a single park in late 2015. As of 2019, the Ryazan Oblast Administration illegally rents out more than 60 percent of the territory as hunting grounds to different legal entities.[30]

The Limits of Transnational Cooperation: The Failed Effort to Establish Bering International Park

Russian environmentalists' enthusiasm for international parks illustrated their cosmopolitan orientation and sense of the global dimensions of Russian nature protection. With the federal government incapable of developing and exercising authority over a park less than 250 kilometers away from Moscow, it is hardly surprising that the grandiose plans for international parks in the Far East fell flat. In early 1992, the Russian Federation dropped the proposal for the formation of Kuril Bridge International Park, because Japan would not agree to the establishment of the park until the Russian Federation acknowledged Japanese sovereignty over Iturup, Kunashir, and Shikotan Islands, which Japan had lost after World War II.[31] The effort to establish Beringia International Park (BIP) in Chukotka and Alaska illustrated, as much as any Russian park proposal, the challenges of formulating a vision that could foster effective collaboration between local, regional, national, and international levels.

BIP aimed to empower Chukotka's indigenous populations of Yupik and Chukchi, to protect the area from extractive industry and orient the regional economy toward tourism, to reestablish regular contact between indigenous groups of Chukotka and Alaska, and to strengthen Russia's ties with the United States through joint environmental protection projects. While Russian and American scientists did little work on the proposed park for nearly a year after the attempted coup in August 1991, Boris Yeltsin and George H. W. Bush signed another accord reaffirming the joint commitment of the countries to develop it on June 16, 1992. The agreement stated that the Russian government, together with local authorities, would finalize the plan for the Russian side of the park within two months. It assigned the administration of the Chukotka Autonomous Okrug the responsibility for taking immediate measures for the protection of the territory, in which looters were undertaking illegal excavations.[32] However, no one had the money to complete the planning.[33] Moreover, the governor of the Chukotka Autonomous Okrug, Aleksandr Nazarov, had been building a patronage system that gave him more independence from Moscow.[34] He viewed the park as an unwelcome impediment to the extraction of gold and offshore oil reserves, which he believed was potentially much more valuable than tourism.[35] In turn, he informed the government of the Russian Federation that he intended to form a "regional nature park" directly under the okrug's jurisdiction.[36] By spreading rumors that control from Moscow would result in bans on hunting walruses and seals, the administration of the Chukotka Autonomous Okrug turned much of the Chukchi and Yupik communities against control from Moscow. Realizing that it might play a greater role in the organization of a regional nature park, the Far East Branch of the Academy of Sciences, based in Magadan, supported Nazarov.

The Moscow-based scientific community was deeply alarmed at the prospect of the area being controlled by regional interests that marginalized the groups that the park was supposed to help and viewed gold and oil extraction as the economic future of the region.[37] A group from the Academy of Sciences in the capital, which included Iurii Vedenin and Larisa Boguslavskaia, wrote to the government of the Russian Federation in October 1992, accusing the administration of the Chukotka Autonomous Okrug of unspecified "authoritarian actions."[38]

> Now, most residents, who have been disappointed by the delayed progress on the establishment of the park and their lack of participation in it, are indifferent to the idea of the park. A few are coming to the point of view of their fellow tribesmen in Alaska that the park is a task of white people and is only needed by them.[39]

They also raised alarms about the okrug administration's desire to create a "free economic zone" where foreign and Russian firms could freely exploit the region's mineral riches. The letter concluded by expressing hope for renewed involvement of the region's indigenous population in park planning in 1993, which the United Nations declared the year of indigenous peoples.[40]

The frustrations with progress on the plan and increasing distrust of Moscow scientists would have been understandable even without the machinations of the administration of the Chukotka Autonomous Okrug. Having for decades endured Soviet policies that sought to erode their traditional cultural identity, they were naturally skeptical of new transformative projects, regardless of their stated intent.[41] Emboldened by the Association of the Peoples of the North's Declaration of Free Development of the Peoples of the North, which asserted the rights of indigenous peoples to "self-determination" and the ability to "define their relationship to the state," the park's indigenous residents were ready to assign blame for delays in establishing the conditions needed for their material improvement.[42]

Influential leaders of these native communities sent a joint letter in November 1992 to the Academy of Sciences and several government ministries expressing their frustration. While the Moscow scientists claimed to be supporting the interests of native groups, this letter asserted that they had never met them and expressed resentment for having "long taken orders from Moscow." [43] The indigenous leaders claimed that over half the members of the commission established by the administration of the Chukotka Autonomous Okrug were from indigenous groups. They blamed Boguslavskaia and other Moscow scientists, "who knew nothing about the region," for adopting the "pretense of concern for indigenous populations" to finance their travels to Chukotka and Alaska.[44] They continued:

> Convinced of the righteousness of our position, we protest against such politics of expansion. We do not need any commissions from Moscow, especially now, when our people, having acquired independence, are forming a community and farming economy. We do not need interdepartmental bureaucratic groups, which are proposed by a group of scientists. And we know about the old style of management and order from Moscow, which forced us to write this letter.[45]

Suspicious that these Moscow scientists were like the resented government inspectors from Soviet times, they insisted:

> Tell scientists from Moscow to leave us alone. We assure the government of the Russian Federation that the project will be fulfilled, but with our active participation here on Chukotka and certainly with enough financing for carrying it out in the territory of Beringia. The government of the Russian Federation has not guaranteed us anything, and it has not given one ruble project to the Beringia International Park.[46]

The park's promises of economic revival and cultural rejuvenation rang hollow to groups that had expressed great enthusiasm just one year earlier.

As the Ministry of Environmental Protection and Natural Resources (established out of Goskompriroda in 1992) continued to insist that the park would be under the jurisdiction of the federal government, the president of the Far East Division of the Academy of Sciences, G. B. Eliakov, sent a scathing letter to Yeltsin making similar claims to those in the letter of the representatives of native groups. Asserting that the Far East was not an "intellectual backwater," Eliakov argued that his office's proximity to the park made it a more logical choice to coordinate the park's scientific work than Moscow. He continued:

> We know in the history of our country many examples of deficient "grandiose" projects, prepared and realized under pressure of central agencies "for the benefit" of the territories, located many thousands of kilometers from Moscow and St. Petersburg, and the people who regularly live in them.[47]

Environmentalists in different regions often thought of national parks as a means of countering Moscow's grandiose plans for economic development and the transformation of the natural world. Here, the regional administration characterized Moscow scientists as similarly imperious.

The Chukotka Autonomous Okrug never threatened to separate from the Russian Federation as some administrative territories in the Far East did.[48] Nevertheless, governor Nazarov's next steps exemplified the tensions that emerged in many parts of the Russian Federation.[49] Without agreement from the Russian Federation Council of People's Deputies, the administration of the Chukotka Autonomous Okrug established Beringia Regional Nature Park on January 27, 1993, even though Russian law did not yet recognize "nature parks" as an officially protected territory. In a referendum on the decision, 83 percent of residents of the Providenskii Region and 68 percent of the residents of the Chukotka Region voted for the park to remain under the jurisdiction of the Chukotka Autonomous Okrug.[50] Following the vote, Nazarov wrote a letter that he sent to heads of several government ministries and the Council of Ministers: "Such a complex area with lots of native villages requires control outside Moscow. This is what the population wants."[51]

The following months would demonstrate that the population, in fact, was willing to support whoever it thought could improve their lives. Their desperation was understandable. While the vast majority of Russia's population struggled in the 1990s, the situation in Chukotka was much worse. In Soviet times, salaries had been significantly higher in Chukotka and other sparsely inhabited regions with harsh climates. While wages did remain higher during the 1990s, the cost of living in Chukotka increased to more than three times the average in the Russian Federation.[52] Indigenous groups suffered the most and were left with the fewest resources to draw on, as the anthropologist Patty Gray has asserted.[53]

Native Chukotkans bought into the idea that an ethnic territory could offer economic relief, protect their interests, and revive their culture. With strong inherent distrust of Moscow, they quickly became disillusioned when Moscow failed to deliver immediate results. However, they had continued to believe that the okrug administration would carry out this idealistic vision, even as Nazarov's administration were clamping down on native Chukotkan cultural expression, as he came to fear expanded demands.[54] Meanwhile, Nazarov instituted an okrug border zone law that made foreign tourists increasingly subject to harassment by government officials. [55] The xenophobia that he encouraged countered the spirit of the international park.

By 1994, Chukotka's indigenous population again sought federal help on a variety of issues.[56] When they realized that Nazarov's inaction on the park and continued authoritarian behavior augured ill for the park's future, they turned back to Moscow. In a letter to the assistant chair of the Interdepartmental Commission on Affairs of the Arctic and Antarctica, D. K. Zotov, the Regional Society of Eskimos, and the Organization of Native Residents of the Providenskii Region claimed that the administration of the Chukotka Autonomous Okrug established the regional nature park "behind the back of the local population."[57] Calling Beringia "the heritage of all humanity," they argued that history proved that indigenous groups fare better under federal than regional administrations. An international agreement with the United States, the letter argued, would grant them even stronger protection. They then expressed surprise at the "lack of interest" on the part of the Ministry of Environmental Protection and Nature Resources in the "fate of a unique region and its indigenous peoples" and their readiness to cooperate with scientists from Moscow and Leningrad and with all "who were worried about the fate of our region."[58]

Concern over the fate of the region and Russia's reputation within the international community had in fact become widespread in the Russian environmental community. On July 22, 1993, the Central Council of the VOOP wrote to the Council of Ministers and the government of the Russian Federation:

> The delay in the realization of the project, many times agreed upon by the USSR and then Russia with the government of the United States, is undermining the international authority of our country and is bringing the destruction of the unique flora and fauna of Beringia, its rich ethno-cultural legacy, acknowledged by international public opinion.[59]

A follow-up letter three months later again warned of the damage to Russia's international prestige.[60] The US side had also hoped that reputational interests might push Yeltsin's hand. Peter Berle, the director of the Audubon Society, which had helped with the US effort, had said the previous year, "Throwing his [Yeltsin's] weight behind the national park plan will be a low-cost way for him to protect a joint Russian-American interest and to send the fast-greening world a signal that he cares."[61]

Federal ministries and institutes seemed to be losing hope toward the end of 1993, as Yeltsin's grip on power appeared increasingly imperiled. His dissolving of parliament delayed the passage of a new law on protected territories, which called the government's commitment to BIP and national parks in general increasingly into question. Writing to the Council of Ministers in December, the Ministry of Nature Protection and Natural Resources asserted that while federal status would be "the most correct" for the park, the establishment of a "nature-ethnic park" on a regional level would not violate existing law.[62] While Yeltsin's call for the regions to take "all the autonomy they could swallow" was most likely a statement of political expedience, Moscow seemed less able to impose its vision with each passing month.

Yeltsin signed the federal act On Specially Protected Natural Areas, which recognized "regional-nature" parks under regional (krai), republic, or oblast jurisdiction, on March 14, 1995.[63] With less potential linguistic confusion after the dissolution of the USSR, national parks dropped the words state (*godudarstvennyi*) and nature (*prirodnyi*) from their official names. Less than two months later, the Federation Council Committee on Northern Affairs and Indigenous Peoples held a parliamentary hearing to discuss the organization of the "nature-ethnic" park Beringia. The acknowledgment of the status of the "nature-ethnic" park under okrug jurisdiction effectively ended the efforts to establish the international park.

With the euphoria of the idea of cooperating with a longtime rival having worn off, critics pointed out that the USSR's portion of the park was more than four times larger than the US area. Moreover, they pointed out that no indigenous populations resided in the territory on the proposed US side. Finally, they asserted that the government of the Russian Federation never carefully thought through potential threats to Russia's territorial integrity that would emerge from creating such a park with its former rival.[64] Even though the Cold War was supposedly over, the fear that the United States wanted to use international environmental organizations and institutions to assert global dominance, as was expressed by V. A. Chichvarin nearly twenty-five years earlier, lived on among some. The dream of a BIP died due to the weakness of the federal authority and the ambitions of regional government. Longstanding geopolitical suspicions re-emerged whenever the idea was resurrected.

The establishment of Meshcherskii National Park and the failure to establish BIP demonstrated the strong opposition to national parks among various interest groups in the years after the collapse of the USSR. Both parks' histories support Laura Henry's argument that "haphazard decentralization" undermined the government's attempts to carry out environmental protection initiatives.[65] Successfully developing, managing, and protecting national parks proved even more difficult than establishing them.

Broken Models: The Dysfunction of Russian National Parks and a Plea for Help

Low budgets, local land disputes, conflicts between federal and regional administrations, and underqualified staffs stunted the development of Russia's national parks in the wake of the USSR's collapse. These problems were almost universal. While *zapovedniki* were under the jurisdiction of the Ministry of Environmental Protection and Natural Resources (Minpriroda), national parks were under the Federal Forestry Service. Although national parks were supposed to be under the control of the ministry's central organs, all but three remained under regional—oblast, krai, and republic—level forestry organizations in 1995.[66] In addition, executive authorities in the Komi Republic, Dagestan, Khabarovsk Krai, Voronezh Oblast, and Sakhalin Oblast all made attempts to reduce the size of protected territories unilaterally.[67]

Despite the dramatic increase in the number of *zapovedniki* and national parks in the Russian Federation's early years, their total budget had fallen by more than 90 percent from 1990 to 1994 when adjusted for inflation.[68] Limited budgets prevented parks from hiring the qualified specialists necessary to develop educational outreach to the local populations, which were frequently unaware of the purpose of the national park in which they lived.[69] Workers of both national parks and *zapovedniki* often lived below the poverty line and lacked basic equipment—uniforms, transportation, communication equipment, computers, firearms—needed to carry out their essential tasks.[70] Making between one hundred and two hundred dollars per month, many employees practiced agriculture on park and reserve territory to help feed their families.[71] With populations in and adjacent to national parks also struggling to survive, they especially resented being told by parks that they now could not hunt in areas where they had previously had no restrictions. But underequipped park and *zapovednik* workers could do little to stop what was now considered illegal poaching.[72] National parks had no funding to build the infrastructure that could attract Russian or foreign tourists, earn revenue from them, and make parks the self-financing institutions that their supporters long claimed they would be. On a trip to Great Smoky Mountains National Park, the deputy director of Smolensk Lake National Park said to a reporter from the *Knoxville News Sentinel*, "The government does not sponsor parks. Unfortunately, that was not what was planned and we are still trying to educate [the people] to a national park concept."[73]

To the dismay of many in the Russian environmental community who continued to want *zapovedniki* to strictly limit tourism, more *zapovednik* managers were allowing tourism under the rubric of "convergence" of national parks and *zapovedniki*.[74] However, for Russian tourists who could travel, journeying to new countries was both more alluring and more prestigious than visiting the most attractive landscapes in Russia, especially given the end of largely subsidized domestic tourism. The Central Trade Union Council and the Central Council on Tourism, which might have supported trips to national parks, were disbanded after the collapse of the Soviet Union, and most tourist clubs had shut their doors. The Russian Federation's growing reputation as a place of corruption and lawlessness undoubtedly scared off many would-be foreign tourists. Most parks seemed unable to handle the ones who did visit. In more heavily trafficked parks, such as Samara Bend, Valdai, and Pribaikal'skii National Parks, the small staffs made public outreach difficult and organizing tourism almost impossible. On top of that, the almost nonexistent infrastructure to accommodate unorganized visitors led to a significantly worsening litter problem.[75] In a 1993 television program on environmental problems in Moscow, a five-minute segment featuring Elk Island National Park showed abandoned industrial equipment, chopped down trees, and illegal private gardens throughout the territory of the park. After saying that the park could be a "true salvation" for Muscovites, the program's narrator laments, "Alas, *dikari* [unregulated tourists] have overrun this green island. The evidence of this is everywhere."[76]

As had been the case in most parks in the 1980s, regional forestry administrations, governors of oblasts, krais, and republics, and private businesses continued to disregard the land use regulations of many national parks. In Sochi, residents went to the press on multiple occasions to report on the clear-cuts of oak and chestnut trees within the territory of the park.[77] Because of their poor level of organization, some government ministries expressed strong sympathy for such use of park land. In a June 1992 letter to Prime Minister Yegor Gaidar, who was the architect of the Russian economic reforms known as "Shock Therapy," the Ministry of Industry, for instance, stated, "As practice has shown, withdrawn from economic use, the material and financial resources are not used by the national parks, and they become ownerless."[78] Eighteen percent of the Sochi National Park's territory was being rented out for the establishment of a *zakaznik* dedicated to hunting trips for high-placed officials.[79] The director of Prielbrus National Park accused the village of Elbrus of turning the local population against the park and the oblast administration of permitting various illegal uses of national park land.[80]

While a large environmentally concerned public had rallied to the establishment and protection of national parks in the 1980s, a small subset of the Russian population shared this concern after the Soviet Union's collapse. In *Independent Gazette* (*Nezavisimaia gazeta*), one journalist wrote in April 1994 about past ecological concern as if it had taken place decades, not years, earlier: "Ecological slogans that used to seem like a reflection of the legitimate human right to a normal environment are today being assessed by the same population as green extremism."[81] Nonetheless, enthusiasm for international environmental cooperation had never been higher among the Russian environmental community following the Rio Earth Summit in 1992.[82] The government of the Russian Federation hoped, as previous chapters have explored, to benefit from this development and established ecological funds that it anticipated would be financed with foreign support.[83] By the late 1990s, Western organizations provided nearly five times more financial support for environmental protection programs in Russia than the government of the Russian Federation.[84]

While Baikal most clearly illustrates this dependence on the West, national parks and *zapovedniki* throughout the Russian Federation increasingly relied on international generosity. Audubon, the World Wildlife Fund, the Sierra Club, and numerous other NGOs began carrying out assistance projects to national parks and *zapovedniki*.[85] From 1990 to 1995, four hundred people took part in exchanges between the US and Russian national parks as part of the Ecology and Education program.[86] National parks and *zapovedniki* throughout the Russian Federation regularly competed for foreign grants. Russian environmental leaders were even mentioning international intervention to government officials. Writing in early 1994 to the director of the Ministry of Environmental Protection and Natural Resources, Victor Danilov-Danilian, Aleksei Yablokov described a dire situation on Elk Island National Park. He wrote:

> In regard to the preservation of Elk Island National Park, if it is not positively decided soon, we will be forced to go for help from international intergovernmental organizations and nongovernmental organizations, including UNESCO, UNEP, and Greenpeace.[87]

Not long afterward, Iurii Efremov wrote that the Russian Federation risked their national parks becoming a "national disgrace" before the international community.[88]

While threats of "international intervention" might have given environmentalists an illusory sense of leverage that they lacked in Soviet times, they as well as park administrators nonetheless knew, as they had said many times in the past, that the protection and development of a national park system required significant capital investment that only the state was likely to provide. Although the government had committed in early 1994 to creating forty-two new national parks and seventy-two new *zapovedniki* between 1994 and 2005, the directors of national parks were much more concerned about the development of the existing system.[89] Feliks Shtil'mark referred to the government plan as a sort of gigantomania more focused on winning prestige than actually protecting nature.[90] Directors of national parks and *zapovedniki* could not help but to doubt their government's commitment to environmental protection and protected territories when the Ministry of Environmental Protection and Natural Resources informed them in late November 1994 that it was stripping the parks of the right to manage their finances. On top of that, they also learned that their already meager budgets would be cut significantly in the following year.

To address this and their many other concerns, the directors of Russia's national parks and *zapovedniki* gathered at Sochi National Park in December. At the conclusion of the meeting, they wrote a collective letter to Boris Yeltsin and other government officials. It began:

> We, the managers of the federal *zapovedniki* and national parks of Russia, turn to you with great alarm about the fate of our national system of *zapovedniki* and national parks. Attempted measures for their preservation and development are on the verge of collapse, while in your decree of October 2, 1992, Number 1155, On Specially Protected Territories, this direction was proclaimed as a priority in the government's environmental policy of the Russian Federation.[91] The system of protected areas of Russia was formed over a period of eight decades and today includes eighty-nine federal nature reserves and twenty-eight national parks, preserving natural and cultural heritage from the Arctic to the Caucasus. The uniqueness of this system is recognized throughout the world.[92] In all civilized nations, similar nature conservation lands are supported by the government; their operation is maintained by a distribution of enough governmental financing. In Russia, however, *zapovedniki* and national parks have felt like the stepchildren of the government and more recently the situation has become unbearable. It is impossible to preserve our protected areas without any help from the government relying only on the enthusiasm of individuals who consider this their life's work.[93]

The letter then highlighted many of the myriad difficulties caused by the lack of governmental support. It complained that many experienced professionals had already started leaving the *zapovedniki* and national parks because of the untenable situation.

The letter concluded with a request for increased funding for 1995 and the establishment of a Department of Nature Reserves within the Ministry of Environmental Protection and Natural Resources as well as a Division of National Parks within the Federal Forestry Service. They requested that these new departments carry out all of the vital management functions, including planning, financing, and construction.[94] This, the writers hoped, would be a partial solution to the lack of a single state ministry in charge of national parks, about which park supporters had spilled much ink during the previous two decades.

Rather than this serving as the beginning of a constructive dialogue, the minister of Environmental Protection, Victor Danilov-Danilian, replied with a dismissive letter that criticized the effectiveness of the directors of protected territories.[95] Having received no response from Yeltsin after a few weeks, the directors appealed to the international environmental community. They wrote:

> We have yet to hear a response from President Yeltsin. The situation requires immediate international intervention. Russia's protected territories are too significant a part of world natural heritage for the rest of the world to stand witness as they are destroyed by neglect. We believe that economic assistance now pouring into this country should be conditioned by the Russian government's provision of aid to its own nature reserves. We believe that attention and pressure from western organizations and agencies could make a difference in bringing a change to the dire situation.[96]

Not long afterward, Aleksei Yablokov stated, "We can save them [*zapovedniki* and national parks] if we find a partner somewhere in North America for each."[97]

As Russian environmentalists became more connected to international environmental networks, they were deeply influenced by international efforts to promote national parks and by the discourse that held that national parks were the "heritage of humanity." Now, the Russian environmental protection community believed that the government of the Russian Federation had demonstrated that it was an "uncivilized" country for failing to make good on its international obligations. And yet there was a profound ambivalence among some of them about international aid and support and even a sense that Russia had imported a model unsuitable for Russian circumstances in national parks. Several years earlier, for instance, at a meeting of Goskompriroda, the botanist and longtime supporter of protected territories V. N. Tikhomirov stated:

> We frequently look at the foreign experience, especially the United States. But we can't forget, and we must be in agreement, that our reserve system is much more developed than those of other countries. *Zapovedniki* as they were conceived present a higher form of conservation.[98]

Some believed that the national park idea was corrupting the concept of "inviolability," which some in the scientific community still held up as a model for protected territories, by making tourism more acceptable in the *zapovedniki*.[99] Moreover, by being oriented to development projects, international aid, some believed, further threatened Russian nature protection traditions. Writing in 1995, Feliks Shtil'mark asserted:

> International contacts between specialists are of course to be welcomed, but excessive efforts at unthinking importation onto Russian soil of experience from across the sea, while at the same time rejecting our own traditions, would undoubtedly damage the *zapovednik* system. The histories, traditions, and ways of life of our countries differ too widely.[100]

Shtil'mark's sentiments reflected the anxieties that came with the increasing tendency within the Russian environmental community to judge itself by the standards of the West.

To be sure, the government of the Russian Federation did acknowledge the problem and the damage to its reputation in the international environmental community. On March 14, 1995, it passed Law on Protected Territories, which distinguished between regional "nature" parks under regional (krai), oblast, or republic authority and "national" parks under federal jurisdiction. A government decree of April 25, 1995, called for 1.3 trillion rubles of investment in the system in the following decade and emphasized the necessity of establishing national parks and *zapovedniki* to meet the state's "international obligations" under the International Convention of Biodiversity signed at the Rio Earth Summit. It stated, "As world practice has shown, only full state financing allows for the preservation of nature reserves and national parks, and also for the successful resolution of the tasks standing before them."[101] The order called for the federal government to provide 83 percent of the investment in the program. The Russian Federation's weakness made its government eager to show that its values were evolving to resemble those of Western democracies. But that same weakness often proved to be the biggest obstacle to funding the institutions that would help it achieve this.

Even though the state could recognize the problem and prescribe a solution for Russia's national parks and *zapovedniki,* the supporters and administrators of protected territories remained skeptical about the state's ability to follow through in doing so. The Yeltsin administration's removing "environmental protection" from the Ministry of Environmental Protection and Natural Resources and creation of the State Committee on Ecology the following year undoubtedly intensified this skepticism.[102] More than ever, international support seemed a necessity. Throughout the late 1990s, the Center for the Protection of Wild Nature modestly raised awareness of Russian national parks domestically and internationally with its annual fundraiser and walk, March of Parks, which spread to all countries of the former Soviet Union.[103] With the center's assistance, Russian *zapovedniki* and national parks sought help from Western philanthropic organizations, such as the Mott Foundation, the Trust for Mutual Understanding, the W. Alton Jones Foundation, the Robert Wood Johnson Foundation, and the MacArthur Foundation. [104] At the same time, the Russian Federation was repeatedly pressed by UNESCO to pay annual dues and denied a representative to the World Heritage Committee.[105] Meanwhile, different groups throughout the Russian Federation lobbied for various areas to receive UNESCO World Heritage Natural Site designation.[106] While international support and UNESCO World Heritage status often seemed to make little difference in the development of national parks, it was especially critical in helping an enthusiastic group of volunteers led by Vitalii Men'shikov on the Kamchatka Peninsula.

Kamchatka's Nature Parks

In the wake of the Soviet Union's collapse, the twin threats of privatization and the expansion of the mining and oil industry in Kamchatka increased the sense of urgency to establish parks. In 1991, private companies began drilling for oil off the Kamchatka coast. That same year, a Kamchatka entrepreneur, Vladimir Kovalev, started investing his resources in developing the proper tourism infrastructure—boardwalks, helicopter landing pads, temporary shelters, and other infrastructural development—that would allow the Kronotskii Zapovednik's Valley of the Geysers to be opened once again to tourists in 1993. While the decision sparked some unease, this apprehension paled next to the fears of the harm that extractive industries backed by international capital might do to Kamchatka's natural wonders.[107] Earning profits from domestic and international tourists seemed the best argument against opening Kamchatka to resource extraction. However, most of Kamchatka's celebrated tourist regions lacked official protection to mitigate the environmental impact of tourism and allow those regions to be profitable. Tourism's most vocal proponents continued to believe that the establishment of national parks would provide the best means of achieving this.

Vitalii Men'shikov, who had worked at the Valley of the Geysers Tour Base in the 1970s, took full leadership of the movement for Kamchatka national/nature parks in the early 1990s. He recalled:

> I believed and argued that it was the future of Kamchatka. When there are no more fish, when they have dug all of the gold out of the ground, the parks will remain and will give bread to those living on Kamchatka. I believed that tourism was the economy of the future.[108]

Working as head of the recently formed Kamchatka Recreation Expedition, Men'shikov concentrated his efforts on the establishment of a park in the Nalychevo Valley, which had breathtaking surrounding mountains and hot springs that had long attracted Petropavlovsk tourists. His public outreach helped the idea gain the interest of a broad cross-section of the Russian scientific community. Men'shikov hosted a Russian Open University conference in the summer of 1992 in the territory of the future park that brought in scientists from all over Russia.[109] Their discussions centered around the question "Can recreational tourism save Kamchatka as a unique region?"[110] Indeed, many participants asserted that the peninsula had no analogs in the world.

Kamchatka's spectacular and unique scenery was undoubtedly critical for Men'shikov in gaining international support, while its existing vibrant tourism culture helped him rally local residents around the park idea. He corresponded with UNESCO, which was considering designating specific spots in Kamchatka as World Heritage Natural Sites, and with Greenpeace and other environmental organizations. He also garnered the help of the Kamchatka branch of the VOOP, in which he was a deputy, and members of the Gleb Travin Club of Tourists—one of a small number of Russian tourist clubs that continued to flourish in the 1990s—to take part in a petition drive. In their door-to-door campaign in Petropavlovsk and Elizovo, club members obtained 1,500 signatures in support of protecting the Nalychevo Valley.[111]

By that time, anticipating the passage of a law that would recognize regional nature parks, Men'shikov had decided that this designation was more suitable than a that of a national park because of the bureaucratic challenges that he expected would come with dependence on Moscow.[112] Moreover, he believed that his work would be simplified if he knew the government officials with whom he would coordinate his efforts. Men'shikov used his position on the oblast soviet and was able to get support from all interested government ministries except for the Ministry of Geology. Seeing the broad base of local, regional, national, and international support for the proposal, the governor of the Kamchatka Oblast agreed to establish Nalychevo Nature Park in 1994. After the passage of the long expected law on protected territories, which granted regional nature parks official status, the Kamchatka Oblast Administration established Nalychevo Nature Park, Bystrinskii Nature Park, and South Kamchatka Nature Park on August 11, 1995.

Men'shikov realized that Russia's political and economic challenges meant that for Kamchatka's nature parks to thrive, they would require significant international support. Following the founding of the nature parks, a German delegation came to Kamchatka to determine the best places for UNESCO World Heritage Natural Site designations. Serving as their guide, Men'shikov led the group on helicopter tours to the three parks, the Kronotskii Zapovednik, and the South Kamchatka Zakaznik (Kuril Lake). UNESCO designated these areas together, which accounted for 8 percent of the territory of the Kamchatka Peninsula, as a World Heritage Natural Site called Volcanoes of Kamchatka in December of 1996.

Men'shikov understood that legal protection and UNESCO designation would not ensure the successful development of Nalychevo or other nature parks. The governor of the Kamchatka Oblast had explicitly told him that the oblast administration would support the parks but was in no position to dedicate financial resources to them.[113] Following the formation of the park's administration, its thirteen employees worked for five months without pay. Men'shikov continued to court international organizations assiduously, and in 1996 he organized an expedition of members of the WWF to come to Kamchatka to study bear populations. During the expedition, Men'shikov proposed that the organization help with the construction of the park. The following March, Prince Philip, the Duke of Edinburgh and the president emeritus of the WWF, came to Kamchatka. In September, a WWF delegation from Germany awarded Nalychevo and Bystrinskii Nature Parks a $800,000 grant for infrastructural development and the development of environmental education programs over a five-year period.[114] However, Men'shikov's ability to personally lead the effort of developing Nalychevo, which was much closer to Petrazavodsk than Bystrinskii, and ongoing pressure from the mining industry to mine for gold near Bystrinskii resulted in most of these funds being used by Nalychevo.[115] Beginning in the summer of 1998, Men'shikov led groups of volunteers from Petropavlovsk and Elizovo, most of them members of the Gleb Travin Club of Tourists, to the territory of Nalychevo, where they would construct guest houses, a museum, a bathhouse next to hot springs, and trails.

Despite an environment of increased economic uncertainty following the August 1998 debt default, Men'shikov garnered more Russian volunteers, as well as volunteers from Germany, the United States, Great Britain, and other countries. After working during the day, they would gather around the campfire, prepare their dinner, and sing at night. "I believe," Men'shikov reflected, "these were some of the happiest moments in many of our lives."[116] By the end of the summer of 1999, the volunteers had built over thirty structures. When the president of the WWF saw the work they had accomplished, he said to Men'shikov, "We did not give you that much money."[117] In subsequent years, volunteers returned to continue working on the park infrastructure. As a result of their labor, Nalychevo Nature Park has an unusually high level of infrastructure for Russian national/nature parks.

In reflecting on this accomplishment, Men'shikov noted, "This was a rare case in Russia. Change in Russia before and after the revolution has traditionally come from above. Ours was a movement from below."[118] To be sure, the

Figure 9.3 Nalychevo National Park. Photo courtesy of Aleksandr Tereshchenko.

history of the establishment of other national parks in Russia and the Soviet Union demonstrates that civic organizations, scientists, private citizens, and the press could establish movements that led to the legal protection of territories. These movements demonstrated the ability of non-state actors to conceive original plans and successfully lobby for national parks in the late Soviet era. However, the development of functional protected territories and maintenance of good relations with local communities almost always proved far more difficult. By creating a nexus of cooperation at the local, regional, national, and international levels, Men'shikov and others accomplished something highly unusual. By 2006, according to Men'shikov, the park was largely self-financing.[119] Although its revenue is undoubtedly modest compared to many other countries'national parks, Nalychevo has shown that achieving a profit from environmental protection in Russia was in fact possible.

Nalychevo Nature Park's success begs comparisons to the many other parks discussed in this book. The area's spectacular landscape undoubtedly helped it attract international financial support, but this was true of Baikal as well. Men'shikov had rallied strong support at the grassroots level, but Roshchevskii and Timofeev had done the same for Samara Bend before the Soviet Union's collapse. Nalychevo, however, did have some distinct advantages. Unlike the territories of Samara Bend, Iugyd Va, and many other national parks, extractive industries had not gained a foothold in the territory of Nalychevo before its establishment. While Pribaikal'skii, Samara Bend, Meshcherskii, Vodlozero, and many other national parks were in areas with numerous local populations, the territory of Nalychevo Nature Park was completely uninhabited. Kamchatka's numerous other spectacular landscapes and recreation opportunities—fishing, hunting, whale watching, and more—gave the region a particular exotic appeal, especially for foreigners, who could not travel there until perestroika.

One final difference is particularly illuminating. Most parks in this study were established after years of lobbying and public calls for their formation. There had always been the assumption that strong support from Moscow was necessary to develop the infrastructure needed to attract tourists and thus make parks profitable. During the 1990s, park supporters often lashed out at the government's neglect of the park system. Their reaction was understandable but in the end amounted to fruitless hand-wringing before a government that did not have the resources to make good on its promises. These hopes and expectations for government action probably produced a disincentive to organize locally. Men'shikov, on the other hand, did not expect federal support; moreover, the governor of the Kamchatka Oblast told him directly that he would not receive funding from the oblast administration. Without any expectations that he would receive government support, Men'shikov focused on the grassroots and gained the support of a passionate community of tourists based out of a functional tourist club. In large part, Nalychevo Nature Park owed its success to the Kamchatka tourists, who exemplified the idea, promulgated by the nature protection community since the 1950s, that a tourist should be a "friend of nature."

Stepping Back

Iugyd Va, Samara Bend, Pribaikal'skii, Vodlozero, and Elk Island National Parks' problems were much more representative of the national/nature park movement in the Russian Federation than the success of Nalychevo Nature Park. By the decade's end, environmental protection efforts accounted for only 0.02 percent of the federal budget.[120] The funding for the federal program State Support of State Nature Reserves and National Parks dropped from a meager \$2.6 million in 1996 to an insignificant \$496,000 in 2000.[121] Some prominent environmentalists, such as Aleksei Yablokov, expressed concern that the word "ecological" might soon disappear from the vocabulary of governmental officials.[122] In 1999, the Russian Federation's parks were funded at just 25 percent of the level necessary for them to carry out their essential functions.[123] Only 40 percent of their budgets came from the government, despite its stated plans to fund 83 percent.[124] Sixty-five percent of the international funding for environmental protection projects in the Russian Federation was going into plans that were never carried out.[125] UNESCO's World Heritage Committee had repeatedly expressed deep concerns about proposed or ongoing activities in all of the Russian Federation's World Heritage Natural Sites—The Virgin Komi Forests, Lake Baikal, Volcanoes of Kamchatka, and the Golden Mountains of Altai.[126]

Writing in early 1999 to the head of the Federal Forestry Service, E. F. Shatovskaia, the director of Kenozero National Park in the Arkhangelsk Oblast, which many consider one of the Russian Federation's most successful parks, said:

> Unfortunately, national parks, for the most part, have found themselves in such a situation that they do not have the funds from oblast and republic budgets or from forestry profits for the investment in tourism, which should be the foundational source of equity.[127]

In developing the "conception of protected territories" that summer, the Russian office of WWF requested feedback from the workers of national parks and *zapovedniki*. A. M. Volkov, who worked in the Bashkirskii Zapovednik, presented an even bleaker picture than Shatovskaia had. "Many of our *zapovedniki* and national parks as organizations are extremely ineffective, having in essence transformed into social funds for supporting their little-qualified staffs and also retirees and locals living in protected territories and on their outskirts."[128] Then, after asserting that expecting state help in resolving the problem was "senseless," Volkov wrote, "Today the system of protected territories must find a new place in the social and economic life of the country. Otherwise, they await destruction."[129]

But what place could national parks find? The idea of national parks gained traction as the number of tourists traveling throughout the USSR skyrocketed, but Russians were more interested in international travel during the 1990s. With drastically reduced demand for internal tourism and the country's economy sputtering throughout the decade, it is hard to see why the government of the Russian Federation would prioritize national parks. The limits of international support for environmental protection in the Russian Federation had become apparent by the latter part of the decade. At the same time, the Russian environmental community increasingly judged their state's efforts to protect the environment using the benchmarks of environmental protection in other countries. By the turn of the century, their verdict was harsher than ever before. Any hopes they had for improvement would soon be dashed.

Conclusion

Russia's Forgotten Parks and the Crisis of Environmental Protection in the Russian Federation

It was difficult for Russian environmentalists not to smirk when in early 2016—the one hundredth anniversary of the establishment of the first Russian *zapovednik* under federal protection—Vladimir Putin announced that 2017 would be the "Year of Ecology." Less than two weeks before his death on January 10, 2017, Aleksei Yablokov, who had been Russia's best-known environmentalist for decades, expressed his skepticism. He wrote: "It would seem that the government of the country has finally become serious about ecology. But this impression would be deceiving. Conversations 'about ecology' will do nothing to solve ecological problems."[1] The "attack on protected territories" was one of many ongoing problems highlighted by Yablokov.[2]

Few if any knew the plight of Russia's protected territories better than Vsevolod Stepanitskii. Stepanitskii had worked with protected territories in different administrative roles over the past three decades. In 2013, he decided to go on a "grand tour," visiting different national parks and *zapovedniki* and meeting with their managers. Several months after his return, he left his post in the Ministry of Natural Resources in April 2017. Explaining this decision in a blog post, he wrote:

> In the time of my four years of travel by car from the Briansk Forest to Kamchatka and back, dedicated to the one-hundred-year history of protected territories in Russia, I asked one question to colleagues dozens of times: What do you consider the main problem? In different versions, I heard the same response: the main problem is weak federal administration of protected territories.[3]

Into Russian Nature. Alan D. Roe, Oxford University Press (2020) © Oxford University Press.
DOI: 10.1093/oso/9780190914554.001.0001

Explaining the ongoing exodus of experts who had worked in protected territories, he wrote: "In the bowels of state politics and environmental regulatory organs, there were many authoritative specialists, who did everything that they could do to support the vitality of federally protected territories. But during the one hundredth anniversary of protected territories, they could no longer maintain that front."[4]

It had been difficult for Stepanitskii and others to maintain that front since Vladimir Putin's first years in power. In the spring of 2000, several months after he became president, Putin eliminated the State Committee of Ecology and the Ministry of Forestry. Protected territories were put under the Ministry of Natural Resources. In the years that followed, it stripped *zapovedniki* and national park administrators of the ability to appoint their staffs and occasionally threatened the elimination of some "ineffective" protected territories.[5] From early 2003 to mid-2005, the ministry transferred national parks and *zapovedniki* to different departments on four separate occasions. NGOs would continue to make futile appeals to Putin to establish a department with the exclusive responsibility for administering protected territories.[6]

Although park supporters had realized by the late 1990s that international support was no panacea, they continued to court it. Seeing international NGOs and foreign funding of Russian NGOs as both a stain on national dignity and a political threat, Putin made this increasingly difficult. In late 2012, after years of railing against the subversive motives of foreign NGOs, he signed what has been commonly referred to as the "Foreign Agent" law, which required NGOs receiving funding from abroad to register as foreign agents.[7] Within several months of the law's passage, over twenty environmental NGOs were forced to register.[8] These included the World Wildlife Fund (WWF), Greenpeace, and the Center for the Protection of Wild Nature—all of which had been leaders in fundraising for protected territories and lobbying the government to dedicate more resources to their development.[9] Continued government pressure has led international organizations that had long funded Russian protected territories, such as the C. S. Mott Foundation and the MacArthur Foundation, to close their Moscow offices.[10] Following Russia's annexation of Crimea in 2014, collaborative projects with the US National Park Service, including the Beringia Heritage Program, also ceased. While the Russian Federation did finally establish Beringia National Park—now the biggest in Russia—the termination of this program in 2014 effectively ended hopes for the international park.

With a stronger economic situation than in the 1990s, the Russian Federation has had greater capacity to support national parks since Putin came to power. Moreover, in recent years, Putin has shown an awareness that state support for high-profile environmental protection initiatives can bring prestige. In 2013, he approved the establishment of the Amur Tiger Center—a joint effort between the largely state-supported Russian Geographical Society and several large Russian corporations. While many Russian environmental NGOs have barely functional websites, the Amur Tiger Center has a state-of-the-art website that highlights its varied, often capital-intensive, projects for protecting the Amur Tiger.[11] Not coincidentally, the Russian Federation has established several *zapovedniki* and four national parks in the Khabarovsk and Primorsky Krais over the last decade and a half. After establishing Call of the Tiger (Zov Tigra) National Park and Udegeiskaia Legenda in 2007, the government established Land of the Leopard (Zemlia Leoparda) and Bikin National Park (the third largest in the country) in 2013 and 2016, respectively. While the Primor'e area of the Far East was the region with the least territory under protection at the turn of the century, today it has the most, with 16 percent of its territory protected in what has been called a "tiger stronghold."[12] In 2018, Putin said in a letter addressing the participants of the annual Tiger Day in Vladivostok: "Much is being done for the development of national parks and *zapovedniki*; comfortable and safe conditions are being made for Amur tigers to live in. Such fruitful work deserves sincere recognition and support."[13] Just as the Soviet Union often invested heavily in symbolic, highly visible showcase projects to demonstrate its progressiveness to both its citizens and the outside world, tiger protection seems to fill a similar role today in the Russian government's attempts to portray itself as a concerned and dedicated environmental steward.[14]

Russia established sixteen national parks in addition to those focused on tiger protection from 2006 to 2019. However, as Stepanitskii and Yablokov noted, establishing national parks and *zapovedniki* is a far cry from protecting and effectively managing them. The Russian government has turned a blind eye to illegal uses of the land in many parks since they were established, including illicit logging activity in national parks and *zapovedniki* in the Far East.[15] Moreover, many parks face ongoing threats of dissolution or significant size reductions from the Russian government. The boundaries of Sochi National Park were redrawn to develop facilities for the 2014 Olympic Games.[16] A law proposed in 2015 would allow the state duma to change the boundaries of *zapovedniki* and national parks if they lost their "nature protection value" without defining what this might mean. Critics argued that the government could use such a law as a pretense for cutting off some areas in national parks that had long been controversial, including in Samara Bend, Iugyd Va, and Pribaikal'skii.[17] Although this law did not pass, the proposal echoed threats made to administrators of "ineffective" protected territories in 2005 and the liquidation of the *zapovedniki* under Stalin and then Khrushchev. Government officials have proposed reducing the size of Elk Island National Park in Moscow several times in recent years.[18]

Threats to reduce the size of or legalize previously illegal uses of the land in protected territories are not unique to Russia. Since the beginning of

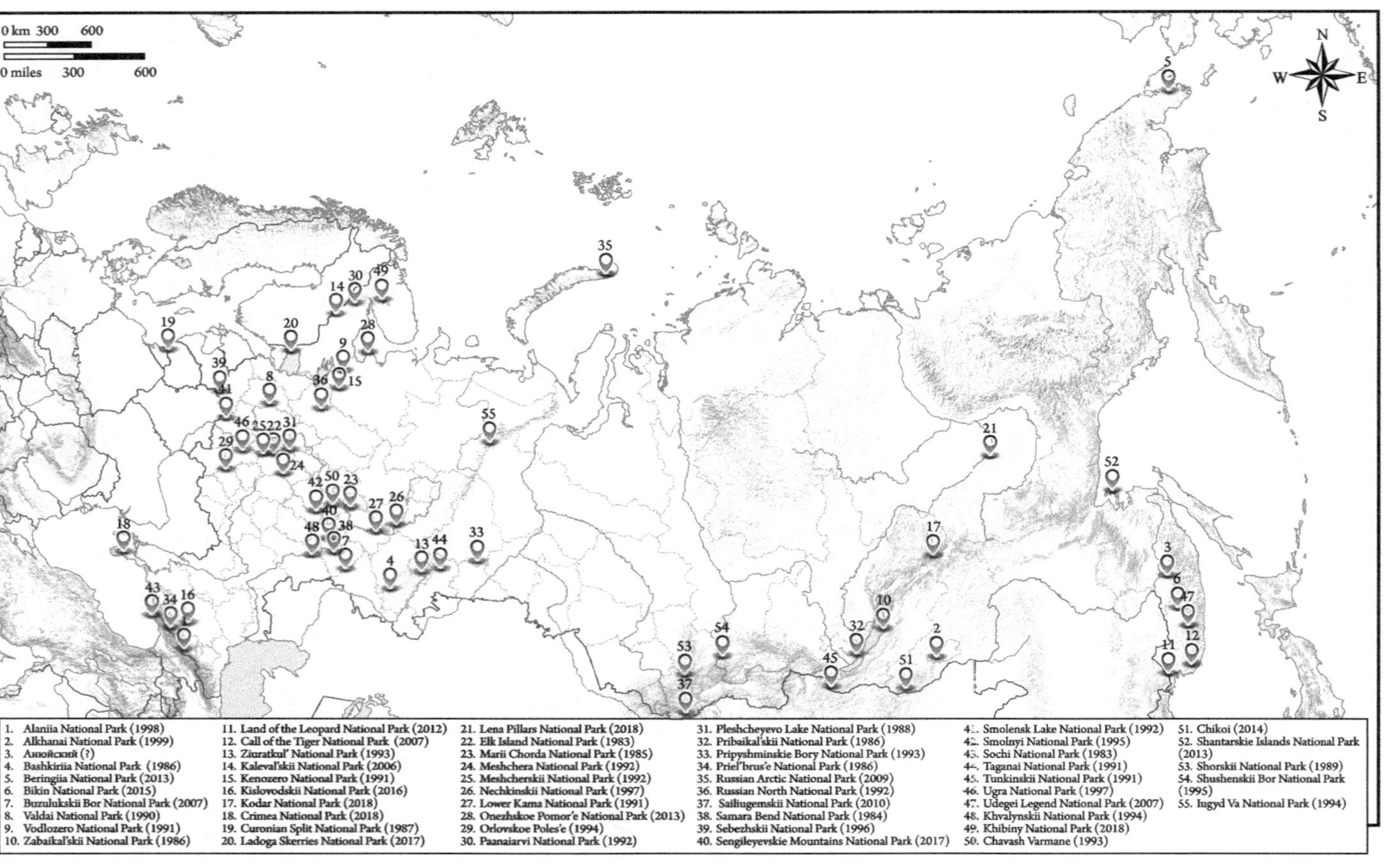

Figure C.1 Russian national parks.

the twentieth century, there have been dozens of documented cases of this occurring in different countries.[19] In 2017, the US government reduced the size of Bears Ears National Monument by 85 percent to allow for uranium mining and Grand Staircase Escalante National Monument by nearly 40 percent to allow for coal mining and oil and gas drilling.[20] Threats of oil drilling have long loomed over Alaska's Arctic National Wildlife Refuge (ANWAR).[21] However, environmentalists in the United States and most other countries that Russian environmentalists have historically invoked when trying to push the state to make meaningful improvements in environmental protection usually take hope in looking to the next election cycle. Russian supporters of protected territories have little expectation of changing the situation through the ballot box. Alfred Runte might have been right when he characterized the national park idea as "landscape democracy" in action.[22] That the idea has struggled to take root in Russia should perhaps not be too surprising.[23] As environmental historian Donald Worster and others have convincingly argued, authoritarian regimes have generally proven less interested in protecting wild places than societies that profess democratic principles.[24] Just as the Russian Federation's citizens see their elections as a half-hearted, almost farcical measure by the government to proclaim that it is a democracy, Russian environmentalists see its poorly funded and shambolic system of protected territories as a disingenuous attempt by the Russian government to claim to Russians and the world that it is interested in environmental protection. While Soviet citizens understood that their system was not a democracy, environmentalists in Russia had more optimism in the USSR's last decades than today that government officials might one day back up their lip service to environmental protection with meaningful action.

The Russian Federation has invested little financially in national parks. In addition to the state's weak commitment to environmental protection, this represents the Russian government's tepid support for developing domestic tourism. The demand for domestic tourism infrastructure dropped dramatically during the 1990s when many Russians could not afford to travel and most of those who could preferred to go abroad.[25] By 2012, Russian tourists were spending nearly sixty billion dollars outside of the Russian Federation, which ranked fifth in the world in tourism dollars spent by tourists outside their home country.[26] While this number has dropped significantly in recent years, Russians continue to spend stupendous sums on foreign holidays relative to the overall size of the Russian economy.[27] Russia's tourism revenue from international arrivals, on the other hand, was only $15 billion in 2017, compared to $250 billion in the United States.[28] While Putin has acknowledged the economic importance of tourism, state investment suggests that it remains a low priority. While services directly and indirectly related to travel and tourism account for 10.4 percent of the global GDP, in Russia they account for less than 5 percent. At less than 2 percent, Russia's capital investment in tourism as a percentage of the entire economy ranks 172nd in the world.[29] The World Economic Forum ranked the quality of Russia's tourism infrastructure 116th out of 136 ranked countries.[30]

Putin has in recent years touted the economic potential of developing tourism in protected territories. At a 2010 cabinet meeting, he noted, "Yellowstone National Park is visited by 2 million tourists [annually], while we in Kamchatka have only a few thousand people visiting each year."[31] The following year, the Russian government revised the 1995 Law on Protected Territories to allow for skiing complexes and other previously banned mass tourism facilities in protected territories.[32] This law also opened the *zapovedniki* to more tourists, much to the chagrin of environmentalists who long held they should serve different functions. In fact, the Russian government was planning in 2011 to invest more in tourism development in *zapovedniki* than national parks with the possibility of reprofiling some of them as national parks.[33] Advocating a $77 million investment between 2011 and 2013, the plan's supporters argued that both national parks and *zapovedniki* would eventually become self-supporting from the profits brought in by tourism.[34]

While the Russian government has increasingly blurred the distinction between *zapovedniki* and national parks by promoting tourism in both, the state has not developed tourism infrastructure on a level anywhere close to what the government called for in 2011. Putin signed an order in late 2017 to promote the development of private entrepreneurial tourism ventures in protected territories, in part to compensate for continued meager federal support.[35] That year, the entire budget for the Russian system of protected territories was seven billion rubles, or $116 million, as compared to the US National Park Services' operating budget of $3 billion. While US national parks received 318 million visits in 2018, Russian national park and *zapovedniki* receive fewer than ten million visits a year (less than Great Smoky Mountains National Park alone), and more than 80 percent of these are to Elk Island and Sochi National Parks.[36] Many Russians continue to confuse parks and *zapovedniki,* while some are entirely unaware of the existence of the country's national parks. On numerous occasions while doing research in Russia, when I told someone that I was writing a book on Russia's national parks, I was met with the response of "Do you mean *zapovedniki*?"

Even the more frequently visited parks have failed to regulate existing tourism to minimize environmental damage. In a 2018 article in *Rossiskaia gazeta,* Vsevolod Stepanitskii asserted that national parks had not developed genuine "ecotourism" and that the environmental destruction wrought by tourists in them contradicted "the very ideology of national parks that had developed throughout the world over a one-hundred-year period."[37] He expressed particular dismay at the "terrible damage" inflicted by tourists to Olkhon Island in Pribaikal'skii National Park.[38] This matches my personal observations during my time spent on Olkhon. Far from serving as a model for nature protection in Russia, as Vasilii Skalon had wanted, the national park territory on the island has litter scattered throughout and mounds of trash that have accumulated over the years in some places. A project named Protected Baikal, which was led by the Ministry of Natural Resources, cleared more than twenty tons of trash in the spring of 2019.[39] While no doubt a positive development, this effort thoroughly demonstrates the degree to which Pribaikal'skii has long been underequipped to deal with this ongoing problem.

Baikal's national parks are hardly the only ones that have failed egregiously in dealing with the litter problem. When I took part in the Zhigulevskaia Krugosvetka, the popular boat trip on which Vladimir Lenin became enamored with the Samara Bend, every campsite that we stayed at had trash that had collected over many years, and the shoreline still had ramshackle, waste-strewn recreation bases in no way affiliated with Samara Bend National Park. Recently, after years of complaints by people from communities within SBNP, the government of the Samara Oblast finally acknowledged the presence of an illegal dump with trash that had amassed in plain view since the 1980s.[40] As Russia prepared for the 2014 Winter Olympics in Sochi, part of Sochi National Park was used as a dump for trash accumulated in constructing the facilities for the games.[41] This park, unlike many, collects entry fees, which the administration has recently started to return to tourists who are willing to haul trash out of the park.[42]

While neglect has been disastrous for more visited parks, for those with few visitors, state inattention might not be a bad thing. I was reminded of this in the summer of 2012 when I did an eight-day backpacking trip with a group of nine people in Iugyd Va National Park in the Nether-Polar Urals. After our guide, Aleksei Popov, met us in the morning at the train station in Inta, we traveled 120 kilometers in seven hours in a large KAMAZ truck on an uneven, overgrown, and potholed dirt road. After strapping on our backpacks at the entrance to the park, we rarely saw another person for the next several days of hiking. On the fifth day, one of our companions, Andrei Konstantinov, departed from the group to venture off on another three weeks of solo hiking. He did this every year in Iugyd Va. He said that he needed these periods of solitude in "pervozdannaia priroda" (pristine nature). A neglected and scarcely visited park was just what he wanted.

When the Commission on Nature Protection in the Komi Scientific Center was planning what became Iugyd Va National Park in 1994, they invoked Yellowstone to argue that the future park could host hundreds of thousands, perhaps even millions, of people each year and bring significant economic benefits to the Komi ASSR. It is easy to imagine mass tourism causing significant damage to this fragile tundra landscape where we saw no reminders of industrial civilization other than the equipment we carried. Today, fewer than ten thousand people per year visit this park, which is nearly the half the size of Switzerland. The remoteness of the park made the projected number of visitors wildly unrealistic. However, the state has invested almost nothing in infrastructure, and had it done so and promoted the park aggressively, there would likely be far more visitors to Iugyd Va than there are today. Many Russians much prefer spending time in an area that seems little touched by the hand of humans than in parks developed for industrial tourism. At the same time, the negligible impact that such parks have on economic development has strengthened and will continue to reinforce the argument of extractive industries that such land in parks should be used for more profitable purposes.

From its establishment in 1916, the US National Park Service made extensive efforts to make parks profitable through expanding their infrastructure to cater to automobile tourists.[43] The national park lobby and early directors of the NPS acknowledged that more tourists in existing parks strengthened the case for creating new ones and effectively rebuffed criticisms about more potentially profitable uses of park territory.[44] The intensive road and infrastructural development as well as the dramatic increase in visits to national parks in the interwar years—from one million visitors in 1920 to sixteen million in 1940—alarmed many environmentalists who wanted to preserve the opportunity for hardy travelers willing to strap on a backpack and experience majestic scenery without the comforts or artifice of civilization.[45] They argued that such places would serve the deep psychic need of many citizens of a country with a national character formed out of a closeness to nature and their desire to relive the "frontier" experience of their ancestors, even for just a short time.[46] In the decades after World War II, improvements in outdoor equipment made wilderness travel easier and the expansion of highways made parks more accessible.[47] While many Americans were discovering backcountry areas away from national parks, the National Park Service further increased its efforts to develop infrastructure, causing much wider alarm than it had in the 1930s.[48] Popular parks were often littered extensively in the 1950s and the 1960s, leading some writers to opine that park visitation should be drastically curtailed, and one to suggest that they should be closed altogether.[49] While infrastructural improvements helped national parks deal better with expanding tourism, in recent years many national parks have been overwhelmed by the increases in visitors.

Many US citizens preferred and continue to prefer spending time in spectacular nature away from crowds and without signs of modern industrial civilization. The desire to keep large tracts of nature "wild" and the related criticisms of overdevelopment laid the intellectual foundation for the passage of the Wilderness Act of 1964. This act designated roadless areas in national forests so that hardy souls who wanted to venture into wild places without signs of civilization would enjoy the opportunity to do so in perpetuity.

Environmental historians, literary critics, activists, and many others have argued about the meaning of wilderness and this idea's impact on different groups.[50] While the debate began with American understandings of wilderness, scholars have more recently sought to understand the idea's relationship to other parts of the world. Strikingly, Russia, a country with more area that could be characterized as wilderness than any other in the world, has been missing from this discussion.[51]

Many scholars have argued that the establishment of the first national parks and the movement for establishing wilderness areas reflected a peculiarly American relationship with nature.[52] They assert that in America an ahistorical dichotomy between "wilderness" and civilization was deeply imprinted on the national consciousness. Critics of this understanding of nature, the American idealization of wilderness, and the export of the idea made some good points. They have drawn attention to the fact that proponents of wilderness have used false assertions that some areas were always unsettled to undermine indigenous claims to the land.[53] Some historians have astutely pointed out that the harm caused by Western wilderness champions imposing their ideas of wilderness on Third World countries in Asia and Africa.[54] Other historians have pointed out that an obsession with the sanctity of wilderness might have distracted environmentalists from other more impactful environmental issues.[55] Indeed, in an era of global warming and mass extinction, the protection of circumscribed areas away from industrial civilization seems marginally relevant to staving off climate catastrophe and severely limited in its capacity to slow biodiversity decline. The climate crisis highlights the long-held fallacy that the backcountry traveler was an environmentally benign actor.[56] Travel to remote, protected territories requires extensive use of fossil fuels, and the vast array of modern outdoor recreation equipment available to backcountry hikers requires the resource extraction that wilderness enthusiasts sometimes moralize against.

However, some of the critiques of wilderness recreation seems particularly misplaced. Environmental historian Hal Rothman asserted that "those determined to leave mainstream society" on backcountry trips were "scripted into believing" that they were a "rare breed, somehow morally and intellectually above other tourists."[57] In his much-debated article "The Trouble with Wilderness," William Cronon wrote: "To the extent that we live in an urban-industrial civilization but at the same time pretend to ourselves that our real home is in the wilderness, to just that extent we give ourselves permission to evade responsibility for the lives we actually lead."[58] While Cronon later qualified this statement by emphasizing that he thought reverence for "wild" nature was only damaging insofar as it disincentivized us from finding the sacred in our lived environments, neither he nor Rothman acknowledged the highly individual reasons that people want to spend time in wild nature and the benefits that time in these places might bring to them and, by extension, society.[59] This need and these benefits have been perceived by people in many countries of the industrialized world.

For some, spending time away from civilization provides needed perspective on the relationships that shape their day-to-day existence and a necessary reprieve from the ubiquitous reminders of constrictive social hierarchies, which become meaningless in the presence of geological marvels millions of years old. Oftentimes, backcountry travel allows one to gain more insight into one's past and conceive of new paths for the future. Others might seek nature's spectacular beauty to soothe personal despair or come to grips with darker aspects of one's past. Still others might find in wilderness travel a personal proving ground where one can affirm one's wits, resolve, and independence in ways not possible in day-to-day urban life. Scholars of various disciplines might criticize and deconstruct the underlying motivations of wilderness sojourners. But their analyses will continue to mean little to the vast majority who seek to escape the "cares and troubles" of civilization while "standing aloof" from civilization's entanglements for a short while.[60] Many Russians, Americans, and people of other industrialized countries will continue to see it as a vital necessity. The fact that many of them will return to their everyday life more engaged and productive attests to the broader social value of "wilderness" travel.

Participants in the wilderness debate have also suggested that the desire to go to wild places is more distinctive to the American character than is actually the case. Americans undoubtedly love their wild places, and their attitudes toward remote areas have likely strengthened, or at the very least helped them explain their urge to "get back to nature."[61] Moreover, the United States' early designation of specific territories of spectacular natural beauty reinforced the belief among many US citizens that spending time in nature was a necessity. But Russians, like people in many industrial societies, sought out wild places well before territories specifically aimed at satisfying the impulse had been established.[62]

Scholars have generally pointed to Romanticism and the idea of the frontier to explain the particular American fascination with wild places. Romanticism was a stronger current in philosophy in Russia during the nineteenth century than in the United States. By the late nineteenth century, the works of some landscape artists strengthened the sense that northern forests were the quintessential national landscape and a romantic sense that Russians were closer to nature than most Europeans. But these paintings were usually nonspecific about the location and not tied to efforts to promote them as tourist destinations.[63] By the twentieth century, landscape painting had fallen out of fashion. Moreover, the sentiment that Russia's landscapes were monotonous and generally inferior to those of Europe again became common among the educated in urban areas.[64] While the romantic depictions by nature writers in the United States during this era made America's remote, rugged areas far away from civilization the country's most iconic landscapes, Russian writers were writing relatively little celebratory prose about the rugged environs of Kamchatka, Baikal, Altai, and many other of the regions that would most appeal to backcountry tourists decades later. The socialist realism movement of the 1930s had tried to quash Romanticism's influence altogether just as Soviet citizens were starting to travel much more widely.[65] By that moment, most of Russia's remote areas of spectacular beauty had still not entered firmly into the popular imagination.

Although Russia had far more open space than the United States, it had nothing akin to a "frontier myth," which historians have argued influenced Americans to seek out experiences in the "wilderness" on conscious and unconscious levels. Further, while the American word "wilderness" has undergone an etymological evolution from connoting a much reviled deserted wasteland to something of pristine, undefiled beauty, the Russian language, like Japanese, Chinese, and even most European languages, has no equivalent, and these expressions—*dikaia priroda* (wild nature) and *pustynia* (desert or deserted wasteland)—remain entirely distinct.[66] Moreover, as an ideology that focuses on industrial modernization in urban settings, Marxism did emphasize the importance of leisure, but it was hostile to the sort anti-modernism celebrated by the Romantic movement, which informed individuals and groups that sought to get "back to nature."[67]

In spite of a comparative dearth of literary tropes celebrating the country's remote places and an official ideology that paid no attention to them, Soviet authors started starkly juxtaposing "wild" places and civilization in the decades after World War II as the percentage of Soviet citizens living in cities dramatically increased. Nature was most typically identified with something "out there," in areas seemingly away from people's everyday lives in civilization.[68] With an internal transportation system that by then allowed its citizens to go to once remote places, Soviet citizens went into the backcountry in droves. Time away from civilization allowed them to revel in their country's spectacular beauty, set new challenges, and even give them more space to contemplate "higher truths" (*istina*) than during their daily lives when they were constantly hearing official ideology that few believed on television or the radio.[69]

The extensive development of US national parks since the 1930s has made the most spectacular natural areas of the United States much more accessible to Americans than Russia's spectacular landscapes are to its citizens.[70] However, from the late 1950s until the USSR's final years, the numbers of Russians who took part in backpacking and rafting trips for extended periods perhaps exceeded the numbers of those doing so in the United States. At first, many, like Vasilii Skalon, lamented that pride in the USSR's wide variety of spectacular landscapes was not a strong part of Russian or Soviet identity. However, a distinctive culture of outdoor recreation that encouraged Soviet citizens to experience the USSR's and especially Russia's wild places developed in the decades that followed. Contrasting with pre-Revolutionary Russia, pride in living in a country with such a variety of wild, beautiful, and dramatic landscapes became a strong component of Russian and Soviet identity. But the initial impulse to leave the city for wild places seems grounded in something much deeper than particular cultural associations with and understandings of those areas outside of what we call civilization. The strong pull that Russians and Americans felt to wild places suggests that there is a common yearning among those living in industrial civilization to experience more primitive conditions and that this desire might be even stronger among people in large countries with a great variety of scenic landscapes. Perhaps the wonder that both Americans and Russians seek and experience in the face of the wild is grounded more in our common biology than in something within each of our distinctive cultures.

However, culture has undoubtedly been critical in informing the development, effectiveness, and exportability of nature protection institutions. Often associated with democracy, the national park idea proved much more appealing to environmentalists around the world than pre-Revolutionary Russian nature protection ideas or those of the USSR's first years ever were. The Soviet government's responsiveness to broad demand in establishing parks demonstrates the deep international resonance of national parks. Moreover, it shows more flexibility within the Soviet system than is often acknowledged. At the same time, however, national parks likely would have become more of a priority for government officials if the idea had not been appropriated from the West and if Russia had stronger democratic institutions.

On the other hand, the United States invested little in parks during their first several decades, and the US National Park Service was not established until more than forty years after the creation of Yellowstone National Park. Although the Russian Federation could make national parks a higher priority in the decades to come, few Russian environmentalists and veterans of the park movement are optimistic about such a prospect. But less developed national parks will mean that many of Russia's parks will offer opportunities to spend long periods of time in places without visual reminders of the civilization.

Because of its geographical immensity, Russia still has more places to enjoy primitive recreation, where tourists can, as Vasilii Skalon once said, "observe nature in its natural state," than any country in the world.[71] While natural beauty is always in the eye of the beholder, Russians can make a strong claim that no other country has such a variety of beautiful landscapes. Although the state's ongoing neglect of environmental protection and protected territories has demoralized Russian environmentalists and park supporters, many Russians are justifiably proud to live in a country with so many seemingly "untouched" spectacular natural landscapes and will continue to value the temporary reprieve that these places offer from civilized life.

NOTES

Introduction

1. GAIO, fond 2844, opis' 1, description.
2. GAIO, fond R-2844, opis' 1, delo 90, 2.
3. For articles on the environmental problems caused by tourism around Baikal, see V. Sharov, "Trevoga v bukhte peschanoi," *Pravda*, August 2, 1967, 6; "Budut novye turbazy na Baikale," *Pravda*, September 28, 1967, 3. Also see V. Novgorodov, "Shchepotka zla," *Vostochno-Sibirskaia pravda*, July 31, 1968, 4; Vladas Maltsiavichius et. al, "Kto za eto otvetit?," *Vostochno-Sibirskaia pravda*, August 15, 1968, 4; Oleg Volkov, "Slavnoe more," *Literaturnaia gazeta*, October 6, 1966, 2.
4. GAIO, fond R-2844, opis' 1, delo 90, 38.
5. Ibid., 34.
6. Ibid., 52.
7. Diane Koenker, *Club Red: Vacation Travel and the Soviet Dream* (Ithaca, NY: Cornell University Press, 2013), 257.
8. Alexei Yurchak, *Everything Was Forever Until It Was No More: The Last Soviet Generation* (Princeton, NJ: Princeton University Press, 2005).
9. Interview with Nataliia Zabelina, October 15, 2013, Moscow, Russian Federation. Interview with Boris Samoilov, September 16, 2014, Moscow, Russian Federation.
10. P. Abramenok, "Sokhranit' v pervozdannosti," *Vostochno-Sibirskaia pravda*, April 13, 1996.
11. Douglas Weiner, *Models of Nature: Ecology, Conservation, and Cultural Revolution in Russia*, 2nd ed. (Pittsburgh: University of Pittsburgh Press, 2000).
12. "Otvety N. S. Khrushcheva," *Izvestiia*, April 2, 1958, 1–2.
13. Chris Miller, *The Struggle to Save the Soviet Economy: Mikhail Gorbachev and the Collapse of the USSR* (Chapel Hill: University of North Carolina Press, 2016), 71.
14. For a general treatment of environmental issues in the Brezhnev era, see Paul Josephson et al., *An Environmental History of Russia* (Cambridge: Cambridge University Press, 2013), 184–253.
15. Eugene Simonov and Vsevolod Stepanitskii, "Leaders of Russia's Protected Areas Take Desperate Measures in a Desperate Situation," *Russian Conservation News* 1 (January 1995): 3.
16. See Evgenii V. Anisimov, *The Reforms of Peter the Great: Progress through Violence in Russia* (London: Routledge, 1993); Martin Malia, *Russia under Western Eyes: From the Bronze Horseman to the Lenin Mausoleum* (Cambridge, MA: Belknap Press of Harvard University Press, 2000).
17. Martin Malia, *Alexander Herzen and the Birth of Russian Socialism* (Cambridge, MA: Harvard University Press, 1961); Laura Engelstein, *Slavophile Empire: Imperial Russia's Illiberal Path* (Ithaca, NY: Cornell University Press, 2009).

18. Yuri Slezkine, *The House of the Government: A Saga of the Russian Revolution* (Princeton, NJ: Princeton University Press, 2017), 597.
19. Michael David-Fox, *Crossing Borders: Modernity, Ideology, and Culture in Russia and the Soviet Union* (Pittsburgh: University of Pittsburgh Press, 2015); Michael David-Fox, "The Iron Curtain as Semi-Permeable Membrane: The Origins and Demise of the Stalinist Superiority Complex," in *Cold War Crossings: International Travel and Exchange across the Soviet Bloc, 1940s–1960s*, eds. Patryk Babiracki and Kenyon Zimmer (College Station: Texas A&M University Press, 2014), 19.
20. Julian Huxley, *The Conservation of Wildlife and Natural Habitats in Central and East Africa* ([Paris]: UNESCO, 1961); Roderick Nash, *Wilderness and the American Mind*, 4th edition (New Haven, CT: Yale University Press, 2014), 368.
21. Paul S. Sutter, "Geographies of Hope: Lessons from a World of National Parks," in *National Parks beyond the National: Global Perspectives on America's Best Idea*, eds. Adrian Howkins, Jared Orsi, and Mark Fiege (Norman: University of Oklahoma Press, 2016), 278–296.
22. For some recent park histories, see Jerry Frank, *Making Rocky Mountain National Park: The Environmental History of an American Treasure* (Lawrence: University Press of Kansas, 2013); Richard West Sellars, *Preserving Nature in National Parks: A History* (New Haven, CT: Yale University Press, 2009); Emily Wakild, *Revolutionary Parks: Conservation, Social Justice, and Mexico's National Parks, 1910–1940* (Tucson: University of Arizona Press, 2011); Patrick Kupper, *Creating Wilderness: A Transnational History of the Swiss National Park* (New York: Berghahn, 2014); Warwick Frost and C. Michael Hall, eds., *Tourism and National Parks: International Perspectives on Development, Histories and Change* (London: Routledge, 2015); Jane Carruthers, *National Park Science: A Century of Research in South Africa* (Cambridge: Cambridge University Press, 2017).
23. Alfred Runte, *National Parks: The American Experience*, 4th ed. (New York: Taylor, 2010); *Wilderness and the American Mind*, 4th ed.
24. Mark David Spence, *Dispossessing the Wilderness: Indian Removal and the Making of National Parks* (New York: Oxford University Press, 2000); Roderick R. Neuman, *Imposing Wilderness: Struggles over Livelihood and Nature Preservation in Africa* (Berkeley: University of California Press, 1998); Marc Dowie, *Conservation Refugees: The Hundred Year Conflict Between Conservation and Native Peoples* (Cambridge, MA: MIT Press, 2011).
25. Bernhard Gissibi, Sabine Hohler, and Patrick Kupper, ed., *Civilizing Nature: National Parks in Global Historical Perspective* (New York: Berghahn, 2015); John Sheail, *Nature's Spectacle: The World's First National Parks and Protected Places* (London: Routledge, 2010); Frost and Hall, ed., *Tourism and National Parks*; Hawkins, Orsi, and Fiege, eds., *National Parks beyond the Nation.*
26. Astrid Mignon Kirchhof and J. R. McNeill, "Environmentalism, Environmental Policy, Capitalism, and Communism," in *Nature and the Iron Curtain: Environmental Policy and Social Movements in Communist and Capitalist Countries, 1945–1990*, eds. Astrid Mignon Kirchhof and J. R. McNeill (Pittsburgh: University of Pittsburgh Press, 2019), 3.
27. For an example, see Steven J. Macekura, *Of Limits and Growth: Global Sustainable Development in the 20th Century* (Cambridge: Cambridge University Press, 2016); Joachim Radkau, *The Age of Ecology: A Global History*, translated by Patrick Camiller (Cambridge, UK: Polity Press, 2014). For a recent collection that aims to show the transmission of environmental protection ideas during the Cold War, see Kirchhof and McNeill, *Nature and the Iron Curtain.*
28. For some recent works in the field of Russian and Soviet environmental history, see Stephen Brain, *Song of the Forest: Russian Forestry and Stalinist Environmentalism, 1905–1953* (Pittsburgh: University of Pittsburgh Press, 2011); Nicholas Breyfogle, ed., *Eurasian Environments: Nature and Ecology in Imperial Russian and Soviet History* (Pittsburgh: University of Pittsburgh Press, 2018); Andy Bruno, *The Nature of Soviet Power: An Arctic Environmental History* (Cambridge: Cambridge University Press, 2016); Sarah Cameron, *The Hungry Steppe: Famine, Violence, and the Making of Soviet Kazakhstan* (Ithaca, NY: Cornell University Press, 2018); Roman A. Cybrisky, *Along Ukraine's River: A Social and Environmental History of the Dnipro* (Budapest: Central European University Press, 2018); Bathsheba Demuth, *Floating Coast: An Environmental History of the Bering Strait* (New York: W. W. Norton, 2019); Ryan Tucker Jones, *Empire of Extinction: Russians and the North Pacific's Strange Beasts of the Sea, 1741–1867* (New York: Oxford University

Press, 2014); Josephson et. al, *An Environmental History of Russia*; David Moon, *The Plow that Broke the Steppes: Agriculture and Environment on Russia's Grasslands, 1700–1914* (Oxford: Oxford University Press, 2014); Maya K. Peterson, *Pipe Dreams: Water and Empire in Central Asia's Aral Sea Basin* (Cambridge: Cambridge University Press, 2019); Douglas Weiner's two books established the field. See Weiner, *Models of Nature*, and *A Little Corner of Freedom: Soviet Environmental Protection from Stalin to Gorbachev* (Berkeley: University of California Press, 2002). For recent articles that have addressed the international dimensions of Russian environmental protection, see Laurent Coumel, "Building a Soviet Eco-Power while Looking at the Capitalist World: The Rise of Technocratic Environmentalism in Russian Water Controversies, 1957–1989,"17-35 in Kirchhof and McNeill, *Nature and the Iron Curtain*; Mark Elie, "Formulating the Environment: Soviet Soil Scientists and the International Desertification Discussion, 1968–1991," *Slavonic and East European Review* 93, no. 1 (January 2015): 181–204; Stephen Brain, "The Appeal of Appearing Green: Soviet-American Ideological Competition and Cold War Environmental Diplomacy," *Cold War History 16*, no. 4 (October 2014): 1–19.

29. Dina Fainberg and Artemy M. Kalinovsky, ed., *Reconsidering Stagnation in the Brezhnev Era: Ideology and Exchange* (London: Lexington, 2016); Benjamin Nathans and Kevin Platt, "Socialist in Form, Indeterminate in Content: The Ins and Outs of Late Soviet Culture," *Ab Imperio* 2 (2011): 301–324.
30. Yurchak, *Everything Was Forever*; Nathans and Platt, "Socialist in Form, Indeterminate in Content."
31. For recent scholarship on Soviet tourism, see Koenker, *Club Red*; Anne Gorsuch, *All This Is Your World: Soviet Tourism at Home and Abroad after Stalin* (Oxford: Oxford University Press, 2011); Anne E. Gorsuch and Diane Koenker, ed., *Turizm: The Russian and East European Tourist under Capitalism and Socialism* (Ithaca, NY: Cornell University Press, 2006); Anne Gorsuch, "'There's No Place Like Home': Soviet Tourism in Late Socialism," *Slavic Review* 62, no. 4 (Winter 2003): 760–785. For a work that looks at the connections between tourism and nature protection in socialist East Germany, see Scott Moranda, *The People's Own Landscape: Nature, Tourism, and Dictatorship in East Germany* (Ann Arbor: University of Michigan Press, 2014). For works that have looked at the connection between tourism and environmental protection, see Andrew Denning, *Skiing into Modernity: A Cultural and Environmental History* (Berkeley: University of California Press, 2014); William Philpott, *Vacationland: Tourism and the Environment in the Colorado High Country* (Seattle: University of Washington Press, 2014); Tait Keller, *Apostles of the Alps: Mountaineering and Nation-Building and Germany and Austria, 1860–1939* (Chapel Hill: University of North Carolina Press, 2015).
32. RGAE: fond 544, opis' 1, delo 40, 204.

Chapter 1

1. D. N. Kashkarov, "Natsional'nye parki Soedinennykh Shtatov Severnoi Ameriki," *Nauchnoe slovo* 3 (March 1929): 72.
2. Ibid., 73.
3. Ibid., 97.
4. Alexis de Tocqueville, *Democracy in America* (Chicago: University of Chicago Press, 2000), 395–396;
5. Christopher Ely, *This Meager Nature: Landscape and National Identity in Imperial Russia* (Dekalb: Northern Illinois University Press, 2009), 3.
6. Marjorie Hope Nicholson, *Mountain Gloom, Mountain Glory: The Development of the Aesthetics of the Infinite* (Seattle: University of Washington Press, 1997).
7. Ely, *This Meager Nature*.
8. Alfred Runte, *National Parks: The American Experience*, 4th ed. (Lanham, MD: Taylor, 2010), 13.
9. Ibid., 14–15.
10. Ibid., 18.
11. Ibid.

12. John Sheail, *Nature's Spectacle: The World's First National Parks and Protected Places* (London: Routledge, 2010), 28.
13. For a general history on Yellowstone, see George Black, *Empire of Shadows: The Epic Story of Yellowstone* (New York: St. Martin's Griffin, 2013).
14. Sheail, *Nature's Spectacle*, 45.
15. Ibid., 53.
16. Alfred Runte, *Trains of Discovery: Railroads and the Legacy of Our National Parks*, 5th ed. (Landam, MD: Roberts & Rinehart, 2011).
17. Hal Rothman, *Devil's Bargains: Tourism in the Twentieth-Century American West* (Lawrence: University Press of Kansas, 1998), 40. Some writers were calling Switzerland the "Colorado of Europe."
18. John Muir, *Our National Parks* (Madison: University of Wisconsin Press, 1981), 1.
19. Laura Engelstein, *Russia in Flames: War, Revolution, Civil War 1914–1921* (New York: Oxford University Press, 2017), xix.
20. Edith Clowes, Samuel Kassow, and James West, ed., *Between Tsar and People: Educated Society and the Quest for Public Identity in Educated Russia* (Princeton, NJ: Princeton University Press, 1991); Harley D. Balzer, ed., *Russia's Missing Middle Class: The Professions in Russian History* (London: Routledge, 1996).
21. See Frithjof Benjamin Schenk, "This New Means of Transportation Will Make Unstable People Even More Unstable: Railways and Geographical Mobility in Tsarist Russia," in *Russia in Motion: Cultures of Human Mobility since 1850*, eds. John Randolph and Eugene M. Avrutin (Urbana: University of Illinois Press, 2012), 218–234.
22. Christopher Ely, "The Origins of Russian Scenery: Volga River Tourism and Russian Landscape Aesthetics," *Slavic Review* 62, no. 4. (Winter 2003): 669–673.
23. A. B. Lebedev, *Istoriia i organizatsiia samodeiatel'nogo turizma* (Leningrad: Gosudarstvennyi institut fizkul'tury, 1988), 7–10.
24. Louise McReynolds, "The Pre-Revolutionary Russian Tourist," in *Turizm; The Russian and East European Tourist under Capitalism and Socialism*, eds. Diane Koenker and Anne Gorsuch (Ithaca, NY: Cornell University Press, 2006), 34–38; Diane Koenker, *Club Red: Vacation Travel and the Soviet Dream* (Ithaca, NY: Cornell University Press, 2013), 17; Johanna Conterio, "The Soviet Sanatorium: Medicine, Nature and Mass Culture in Sochi, 1917–1991" (PhD diss., Harvard University, 2014).
25. Evgeny Anisimov et al, "Books That Link Worlds: Travel Guides, the Development of Transportation Infrastructure, and the Emergence of the Tourism Industry in Imperial Russia, Nineteenth–Early Twentieth Centuries," *Journal of Tourism History* 8, no. 12 (2016): 185.
26. Louise McReynolds, *Russia at Play: Leisure Activities at the End of Tsardom* (Ithaca, NY: Cornell University Press, 2003), 167.
27. Lebedev, *Istoriia i organizatsiia samodeiatel'nogo turizma*, 8.
28. McReynolds, *Russia at Play*, 167.
29. Anisimov et al., "Books That Link Worlds," 186.
30. Ely, *This Meager Nature*, 225.
31. For an example of travel narrative in Siberia in the late nineteenth century, see Samuel Turner, *In Siberia: A Record of Travel and Exploration* (London: Unwin, 1905), 247.
32. For more on Muir and Roosevelt's camping trip, see Donald Worster, *A Passion for Nature: The Life of John Muir* (New York: Oxford University Press, 2009), 366–368.
33. Holt-Atherton Special Collections, University of the Pacific, Diaries: 26 of 45, http://digitalcollections.pacific.edu/cdm/compoundobject/collection/muirjournals/id/3313/rec/2.
34. For a history on the Trans-Siberian Railway, see Steven Marks, *The Road to Power: The Trans-Siberian Railroad and the Colonization of Asian Russia, 1850–1917* (Ithaca, NY: Cornell University Press, 1991).
35. Holt-Atherton Special Collections, University of the Pacific, *John Muir Papers*, reel 24, http://digitalcollections.pacific.edu/cdm/compoundobject/collection/muirjournals/id/3313/rec/2.
36. Ibid.

37. Ibid.; William H. Brennan, "John Muir in Russia, 1903: Part 2," *John Muir Newsletter* 4, no. 1 (Winter 1993–1994): 1 and 6; William H. Brennan, "John Muir in Russia, 1903: Part 3," *John Muir Newsletter* 4, no. 3 (Summer 1994): 1 and 4; John Muir, Reel 29, July 25–August 17, 1903.
38. See Stephen Brain, *Song of the Forest: Russian Forestry and Stalinist Environmentalism, 1905–1953* (Pittsburgh: University of Pittsburgh Press, 2011), 16–17.
39. Jane Costlow, "Imaginations of Destruction: The 'Forest Question' in Nineteenth Century Russia," *Russian Review* 62, no. 1 (January 2003): 95.
40. Ekaterina Pravilova, *A Public Empire: Property and the Quest for the Common Good in Imperial Russia* (Princeton, NJ: Princeton University Press, 2014), 48.
41. Douglas Weiner, *Models of Nature*: Ecology, Conservation, and Cultural Revolution in Russia, 2nd ed. (Pittsburgh: University of Pittsburgh Press, 2000), 8.
42. Jane T. Costlow, *Heart-Pine Russia: Walking and Writing the Nineteenth-Century Forest* (Ithaca, NY: Cornell University Press, 2011), 81–115.
43. Paul Josephson et al., *An Environmental History of Russia* (Cambridge: Cambridge University Press, 2013), 34–35. For more on the "forest question," see Costlow, *Heart-Pine Russia*; Pravilova, *Public Empire*, 68.
44. Josephson et al., *An Environmental History of Russia*, 37. See Pravilova, *A Public Empire*, 73. Also see Douglas Weiner, "The Predatory Tribute-Taking State," in *Global Environmental History: An Introductory Reader*, eds. J. R. McNeill and Alan Roe (London: Routledge, 2013), 288. Weiner notes that forest cover declined in European Russia from 52.7 percent to 35.16 percent from 1696 to 1914.
45. Sheail, *Nature's Spectacle*, 3.
46. Weiner, *Models of Nature*, 13–15.
47. Ibid., 12.
48. See John Oldfield and Denis Shaw, *The Development of Russian Environmental Thought* (London: Routledge, 2015), 48–77; David Moon, *The Plough That Broke the Steppes* (Oxford: Oxford University Press, 2014); Weiner, *Models of Nature*, 13–15.
49. Moon, *Plough That Broke the Steppes*, 53–61.
50. Josephson et al., *Environmental History of Russia*, 49.
51. Mark Bassin, *Imperial Visions*: Nationalist Imagination and Geographical Expansion in the Russian Far East, 1840–1865 (Cambridge: Cambridge University Press, 2006), 249.
52. Andrei Semenov-Tian-Shanskii, *Nasha blizhaishaia zadacha na Dal'nem Vostoke* (St. Petersburg, 1908), 36.
53. Weiner, *Models of Nature*, 13.
54. G. A. Kozhevnikov, "O neobkhodimosti ustroistva zapovednykh uchastkov dlia okhrany russkoi prirody," *Okhrana prirody i zapovednogo dela SSSR* 4 (1960): 97.
55. Feliks Shtil'mark, *History of the Russian Zapovedniks, 1895–1995*, trans. G. H. Harper (Edinburgh: Russian Nature Press, 2003), 109
56. Pravilova, *Public Empire*, 72.
57. Ibid., 73.
58. V. Generozov, "Ob administrativnoi organizatsii amerikanskikh zapovednikov i ikh ekonomicheskom znachenii." *Nasha okhota* 14 (1914): 4–8.
59. Shtil'mark, *History of the Russian Zapovedniks*, 17.
60. Ian Tyrell, "America's National Parks: The Transnational Creation of National Space in the Progressive Era," *Journal of American Studies* 46 (2012): 5.
61. G. A. Kozhevnikov, "Mezhdunarodnoe soveshchanie po vsemirnoi okhrane prirody," *Ornitologicheskii vestnik* 3–4 (1913): 375–380; Weiner, *Models of Nature*, 18; Patrick Kupper, "Science and the National Parks: A Transatlantic Perspective on the Interwar Years," *Environmental History* 14, no. 1 (January 2009): 63.
62. V. A. Dubianskii, ed., *Mirovaia okhrana prirody* (Petrograd: Imperatarskoe Russkoe geograficheskoe obshchestvo, 1915), 95.
63. Ibid., 96.
64. Ryan Tucker Jones, "A 'Havock Made Among Them': Animals, Empire, and Extinction in the Russia North Pacific," *Environmental History* 16, no. 4 (October 2011): 598–599.

65. I. P. Borodin, "Okhrana pamiatnikov prirody," *Imperatorskoe Russkoe geograficheskoe obshchestvo: Postoiannaia prirodookhranitel'naia komissia* 1 (1914): 6.
66. Borodin, "Okhrana pamiatnikov prirody," 6.
67. Tyrell, "America's National Parks," 7.
68. Ibid., 8.
69. Ibid., 21.
70. Robert Righter, *The Battle over Hetch Hetchy: America's Most Controversial Dam and the Birth of Modern Environmentalism* (New York: Oxford University Press, 2006); Jerry Frank, *Making Rocky Mountain National Park: The Environmental History of an American Treasure* (Lawrence: University of Kansas Press, 2013), 7; Thomas Lekan, *Imagining the Nation in Nature* (Cambridge, MA: Harvard University Press, 2005), 23.
71. Richard Pipes, *Russia Under the Old Regime* (New York: Penguin, 1995), 23.
72. See Marguerite S. Shaeffer, *See America First: Tourism and National Identity, 1880–1940* (Washington, DC: Smithsonian Books, 2001).
73. Runte, *National Parks*, 83, 96.
74. Sheaill, *Nature's Spectacle*, 125 and Runte, *National Parks*, 76.
75. McReynolds, *Russia at Play*, 189.
76. ARGO, fond 48, opis' 1, delo 317.
77. Ibid.
78. Ibid.
79. Ibid., 18.
80. Ibid., 18.
81. Pravilova, *Public Empire*, 2.
82. Shtil'mark, *History of the Russian Zapovedniks*, 29.
83. Weiner, *Models of Nature*, 22–24.
84. Shtil'mark, *History of the Russian Zapovedniks*, 30.
85. V. E. Boreiko, *Doroga k zapovednomu* (Moscow: WWF, 1996), 7.
86. Weiner, *Models of Nature*, 35.
87. Paul Josephson, *The Conquest of the Russian Arctic* (Cambridge, MA: Harvard University Press, 2014), 8, 13.
88. Andrei Semenov-Tian-Shanskii, "Svobodnaia priroda," *Priroda* 4, no. 6 (1919):199.
89. Ibid., 200. See Runte, *National Parks*, 35.
90. Semenov-Tian-Shanskii, "Svobodnaia priroda," 201.
91. Ibid., 203.
92. F. R. Shtil'mark and G. S. Avakov, "Pervyi proekt geograficheskoi seti zapovednikov dlia territorii SSSR," *Biulleten' Moskovskogo obshchestva ispytatelei prirody: Otdel biologicheskii* 2 (1977): 153.
93. Ibid., 213.
94. Sheaill, *Nature's Spectacle*, 26.
95. See Brian Bonhomme, *Forests, Peasants, and Revolutionaries: Forest Conservation and Organization in Soviet Russia, 1917–1929* (Boulder, CO: East European Monographs, 2005); Andy Bruno, "What Does It Mean to Liberate the Land?" Towards and Environmental History of the Russian Revolution," in *Russia's Home Front in War and Revolution*: Book 3, National Disintegration and Reintegration, ed. Christopher Read et al. (Bloomington: Indiana University Press, 2018), 257–277; Brain, *Song of the Forest*, 54–78.
96. For more on the social and cultural experimentation of the NEP era, see Richard Stites, *Revolutionary Dreams: Utopian Vision and Experimental Life in the Russian Revolution* (New York: Oxford University Press, 1989).
97. Weiner, *Models of Nature*, 29.
98. Shtil'mark, *History of the Russian Zapovedniks*, 49.
99. Ibid., 15.
100. Weiner, *Models of Nature*, 32.
101. Weiner, "Predatory Tribute-Taking State," 289.
102. Mark Bassin, "The Russian Geographical Society, the 'Amur Epoch,' and the Great Siberian Expedition, 1855–1863," *Annals of the Association of American Geographers* 73, no. 2 (June 1983): 242.

103. See Koenker, *Club Red,* 12–52; Johanna Conterrio, "The Soviet Sanatorium: Medicine, Nature, and Mass Culture in Sochi, 1917–1991," PhD diss., Harvard University, 2014.
104. Boreiko, *Doroga k zapovednomu,* 9.
105. Patrick Kupper, *Creating Wilderness: A Transnational History of the Swiss National Park* (Washington D.C.: Berghahn, 2014), 33.
106. Jeffrey Brooks, "The Press and its Message," in *Russia in the Era of NEP,* eds. Sheila Fitzpatrick, Alexander Rabinowitch, and Richard Stites (Bloomington: Indiana University Press, 1991), 231–253.
107. Ibid.
108. Loren R. Graham, *Science in Russia and the Soviet Union: A Short History* (New York: Cambridge University Press, 1993), 92.
109. See Bassin, *Imperial Visions.*
110. For more on Soviet nationalities policy in the 1920s, see Terry Martin, *The Affirmative Action Empire: Nations and Nationalism in the Soviet Union, 1923–1939* (Ithaca, NY: Cornell University Press, 2001); Ronald Grigor Suny and Terry Martin, ed., *A State of Nations: Empire and Nation-Making in the Age of Lenin and Stalin* (New York: Oxford University Press, 2001); Francine Hirsch, *Empire of Nations: Ethnographic Knowledge and the Making of the Soviet Union* (Ithaca, NY: Cornell University Press, 2005).
111. Weiner, *Models of Nature,* 68.
112. Shtil'mark, *History of the Russian Zapovedniks,* 41.
113. Weiner, *Models of Nature Russia,* 53–55.
114. Ibid., 61.
115. Ibid., 64–84.
116. For more on the state's priority of investing in spas, see Koenker, *Club Red,* 12–52.
117. Koenker, *Club Red,* 58.
118. "Zapovedniki na Ukraine," *Pravda,* August 5, 1927.
119. "Dom otdykha," *Pravda,* May 10, 1925.
120. A. Smirnova, "Kavkazskii zapovednik," *Vsemirnyi turist* 9 (November 1928): 266–275.
121. "Kavkazskii zapovednik," *Pravda,* July 13, 1926, 5.
122. Shtil'mark, *History of the Russian Zapovedniks,* 47.
123. For recent biographies on Stalin, see Simon Sebag Montefiore, *Stalin: The Court of the Red Tsar* (Vintage, 2005); Oleg Khlevinuk, *Stalin: New Biography of a Dictator,* trans Nora Seligman Favorov (New Haven, CT: Yale University Press, 2016); Stephen Kotkin, *Stalin: Waiting for Hitler, 1929–1941* (New York: Penguin, 2017).
124. Graham, *Science in Russia and the Soviet Union,* 94.
125. Weiner, *Models of Nature,* 87. Participants of the conference included representatives from Narkompros RSFSR, Narkozem RSFSR, Narkomtorg USSR, Gostorg RSFSR, VSNKh RSFSR, VOOP, the TsBK, the Hunter's Cooperative Union, the Academy of Sciences, zoos, individual *zapovedniki,* universities, and botanical gardens. Weiner argues that the main tension at the conference was based on generational differences.
126. Josephson et al., *Environmental History of Russia,* 57.
127. Ibid., 87.
128. Weiner, *Models of Nature,* 92.
129. Ibid.
130. Boreiko, *Doroga k zapovednomu,* 8.
131. Ibid., 8.
132. Koenker, *Club Red,* 60. For some tourism books of the era that reflected these values, see Igor' Orlov and Elena Iurchikova, *Massovyi turizm v stalinskoi povsednevnosti* (Moscow: ROSSPEN, 2010), 168. For tourism books that emphasized tourism's role in instilling the Marxist-Leninist worldview, see Iu. Vonzblein, *Otdykhaite v lesu!* (Leningrad: Leningradskaia pravda, 1929); L. Grubich, *Sotsialisticheskoe stroitel'stvo i proletarskii turizm* (Moscow: OGIZ-Fizkul'tura i turizm, 1931); O. A. Arkhangel'skaia, *Rabota iacheiki OPET po samodeiatel'nomu turizmu* (Moscow: Izdanie OPTE, 1935).
133. Koenker, *Club Red.*
134. Weiner, *Models of Nature,* 98.
135. Koenker, *Club Red,* 65.

136. Ibid., 56.
137. Ibid. For an essay on early Swiss tourism and the Swiss Alps serving as a benchmark for beautiful scenery, see Laurent Tissot, "From Alpine Tourism to the 'Alpinization' of Tourism," in *Touring beyond the National: A Transnational Approach to European Tourism History*, ed. Eric Zuelow (Burlington, VT: Ashgate, 2011), 59–78.
138. V. V. Dvornichenko, *Razvitie turizma v SSSR 1917–1983* (Moscow: Tsentral'noe reklamnoe-informatsionnoe biuro "Turist," 1985), 23.
139. Ibid., 72, 74.
140. V. N. Makarov and A. G. Giller, ed., *Trudy pervogo Vsesoiuznogo s"ezda po okhrane prirody v SSSR* (Moscow: Vlast' Sovetov, 1935), 132.
141. Weiner, *Models of Nature*, 125.
142. Weiner, "Predatory Tribute-Taking State," 296.
143. Maxim Gorky, ed., *Belomor: An Account of the Construction of the New Canal between the White Sea and the Baltic Sea*, trans. Amabel Williams-Ellis (New York: Harrison Smith & Robert Haas, 1935), 217. For a book that presents a more "holistic" approach of Soviet planners, see Andy Bruno, *The Nature of Soviet Power: An Arctic Environmental History* (Cambridge: Cambridge University Press, 2016), 76.
144. William Husband, "Correcting Nature's Mistakes: Transforming the Environment in Soviet Children's Literature, 1928–1941," *Environmental History* 11, no. 2 (April 2006): 304.
145. Weiner, "Predatory Tribute-Taking State," 290.
146. Ibid.
147. Josephson et al., *Environmental History of Russia*, 107.
148. Ibid., 74; Douglas Weiner, *A Little Corner of Freedom: Soviet Environmental Protection from Stalin to Gorbachev* (Berkeley: University of California Press, 2002), 9.
149. For more on forest conservation during this era, see Stephen Brain, "Stalin's Environmentalism," *Russian Review* 69 (January 2010): 93–118.
150. Shtil'mark, *History of the Russian Zapovedniks*, 57.
151. Ibid., 61.
152. Makarov and Giller, *Trudy pervogo Vsesoiuznogo s"ezda*, 149.
153. Ibid., 143–144.
154. Ibid., 145.
155. Ibid., 148.
156. Ibid., 122.
157. Ibid., 121–122.
158. Ibid., 185.
159. Ibid., 158.
160. Koenker, *Club Red*, 34.
161. S. Ivanov, "Zimnie marshruty po Kavkazskomu zapovedniku," *Na sushe i na more* 10 (October 1938): 24; V. Borkotova, "Belovezhskaia pushcha," *Na sushe i na more* 8 (August 1940): 14–16; A. Sheidlina, "V Krymskom zapovednike" *Na sushe i na more* 8 (August 1938): 18–20; N. Ponrovskii, A Dement'ev, F. Pronin, K. Sergeev, V. Popov, and V. Molokanov, "Kto otvechaet za turism," *Pravda*, March 28, 1937, 4; "Zapovedniki Sovetskogo Soiuza," *Pravda*, January 20, 1936, 6; A. Kol'bina, "Il'menskii zapovedniki," *Pravda*, June 14, 1935, 4.
162. Shtil'mark, *History of the Russian Zapovedniks*, 74.
163. Runte, *National Parks*, 154.
164. V. N. Makarov, *Zapovedniki SSSR* (Moscow: Sel'khozgiz, 1940), 8.
165. Emily Wakild, *Revolutionary Parks: Conservation, Social Justice, and Mexico's National Parks, 1910–1940* (Tucson: University of Arizona Press, 2010); Patrick Kupper, "Nature's Laboratories? Exploring the Intersection of Science and National Parks," in *National Parks beyond the Nation*, 118–119; Henri Hackers, "The Albert National Park," *Geographical Journal* 4 (1937): 276.
166. Kupper, "Nature's Laboratories?," 118–119.
167. Millicent Morrison, *Wild Life and Rare in National Parks and Paradises Round the World* (London: Green Cross Society, 1938), 44; Julian Huxley, *Africa View* (New York: Harper

& Brothers, 1931), 253; Bernhard Bissibl, Sabine Hohler, Patrick Kupper, *Civilizing Nature: National Parks in Global Historical Perspective* (New York: Berghahn, 2012), 2.

168. Arno Cammerer, "National Parks and New World Idealism," *The Regional Review*, vol. 4–6 (June 1940), 6.
169. Weiner, *A Little Corner of Freedom*, 49. Also see *A History of the Russian Zapovedniki*, 80–83.
170. Weiner, *Little Corner of Freedom*, 47.
171. Martin, *Affirmative Action Empire*, 309–343.
172. Boreiko, *Doroga k zapovednomu*, 29.
173. Koenker, *Club Red*, 109.

Chapter 2

1. "Otvety N. S. Khrushcheva," *Izvestiia*, April 2, 1958, 1–2.
2. Steven Harris, *Communism on Tomorrow Street: Mass Housing and Everyday Life after Stalin* (Baltimore: Johns Hopkins University Press, 2013).
3. "Otvety N. S. Khrushcheva," 2.
4. Ibid.
5. Ibid.
6. Diane Koenker, *Club Red: Vacation Travel and the Soviet Dream* (Ithaca, NY: Cornell University Press, 2013), 2. For more on the emphasis on material consumption during the Khrushchev era, see Susan Reid, "Cold War in the Kitchen: Gender and the de-Stalinization of Consumer Taste in the Soviet Union," *Slavic Review* 61, no. 2 (Summer 2002): 211–252; Susan Reid, "Who Will Beat Whom? Soviet Popular Reception of the American National Exhibition in Moscow, 1959," *Kritika: Explorations in Russian and Eurasian History* 9, no. 4 (Fall 2008): 855–904.
7. Douglas Weiner, *A Little Corner of Freedom: Russian Nature Protection from Stalin to Gorbachev* (Berkeley: University of California Press, 1999), 117–136, 288–311.
8. Denis Kozlov and Eleonory Gilburd, ed., "The Thaw as an Event in Russian History," in , *The Thaw: Soviet Society and Culture During the 1950s and 1960s*, eds. Denis Kozlov and Eleonory Gilburd (Toronto: University of Toronto Press, 2013), 18–59; Eleonory Gilburd, *To See Paris and Die: The Soviet Lives of Western Culture* (Cambridge, MA: Belknap Press of Harvard University Press, 2018).
9. See Elena Zubkova, *Russia after the War: Hopes, Illusions and Disappointments, 1945–1957* (Abingdon, UK: Routledge, 1998).
10. Odd Arne Westad, *The Cold War* (New York: Basic Book, 2016), 213.
11. Lynn Meskell, *A Future in Ruins: UNESCO, World Heritage, and the Dream of Peace* (Oxford: Oxford University Press, 2018), xv.
12. Alexander Adams, ed., *First World Conference on National Parks* (Washington: US Department of the Interior, 1962), 6.
13. Secretariat of IUPN, ed., *International Technical Conference on the Protection of Nature: Proceedings and Papers* (Paris: Lake Success 22–29 VIII, 1949), 15. Also see Martin Holdgate, *The Green Web: A Union for World Conservation* (London, UK: Earthscan, 1999), 41–43.
14. Secretariat of IUPN, *International Technical Conference on the Protection of Nature*, 51; L. G. Permiakova, "Iz istorii razvitiia vzaimootnoshenii Rossiii I UNESCO v Sovetskii period," *Vestnik Tomskogo Gosudarstevnnogo Universiteta*, no. 18 (2012): 129.
15. Secretariat of IUPN, *International Technical Conference on the Protection of Nature*, 51.
16. Ibid., vii.
17. Ibid.
18. Ibid.
19. Ibid., 153.
20. Stephen Macekura, *Of Limits and Growth: Global Sustainable Development in the 20th Century* (Cambridge: Cambridge University Press, 2016), 21.
21. Secretariat of IUPN, *International Technical Conference on the Protection of Nature*, 294.
22. Ibid., 565.
23. Ibid., 51.

24. See Zubkova, *Russia after the War.*
25. Stephen Brain, "The Great Stalin Plan for the Transformation of Nature," *Environmental History* 15, no. 4 (January 2010): 670–700; Weiner, *Little Corner of Freedom*, 88–93; Denis J. B. Shaw, "Mastering Nature through Science: Soviet Geographers and the Great Stalin Plan for the Transformation of Nature, 1948–1953," *Slavonic and East European Review* 93, no. 1 (January 2015): 120–146. For a history of Soviet science in this era, see Ethan Pollock, *Stalin and the Soviet Science Wars* (Princeton: Princeton University Press, 2008). For examples of the propaganda celebrating the plan see A. N. Akhutin, *Preobrazovanie rek SSSR* (Moscow: Voenizdat, 1950); V. A. Kovda, *Velikie stroiki kommunizma i preobrazovanie prirody* (Moscow, 1951).
26. Weiner, *Little Corner of Freedom*, 119 and 133.
27. V. N. Makarov, *Okhrana prirody v SSSR* (Moscow: Voennoe izdatel'stvo Ministerstva vooruzhennykh sil Soiuza SSR, 1949), 11 and 25.
28. Feliks Shtil'mark, *History of the Russian Zapovedniks, 1895–1995*, trans. G. H. Harper (Edinburgh: Russian Nature Press, 2003), 109.
29. Weiner, *Little Corner of Freedom*, 129.
30. Grigori Usyskin, *Ocherki istorii rossiiskogo turizma* (Moscow: Gerda, 2000), 146.
31. Vera Dunham, "The Big Deal," in *In Stalin's Time*, ed. Vera Dunham (Cambridge: Cambridge University Press, 1976), 12–23; also see Timo Vihavainen and Elena Bogdanova, *Communism and Consumerism: The Soviet Alternative to the Affluent Society* (Leiden: Brill, 2015).
32. GARF, fond 9520, opis'. 2, delo 69, l and 12; Koenker, *Club Red*, 140.
33. GARF, fond 9520, opis'. 2, delo 69, 12.
34. Ibid.
35. Juliane Furst, *Stalin's Last Generation: Soviet Post-War Youth and the Emergence of Mature Socialism* (Oxford: Oxford University Press, 2010), 22.
36. P. Vershigora, "Samyi massovyi i samyi zabroshennyi vid sporta," *Literaturnaia gazeta*, May 20, 1950, 2.
37. Ibid.
38. Boris Egorov and Ian Polishchiuk, "V storone ot turistogo shliakha," *Literaturnaia gazeta*, September 18, 1951, 2; also see "Otpusk sovetskogo truzhenika," *Literaturnaia gazeta*, May 27, 1952, 1; "Vsemerno razvivat' fizkul'turu i sport," *Izvestiia*, May 31, 1952, 1; M. Pogrebetskii, "Zavoevateli gornykh vershin i te, kto ne pomogaet," *Literaturnaia gazeta*, December 28, 1950, 2; "Za massovost': Fizkul'turnoe dvizhenie i vysokoe sportivnoe masterstvo," *Pravda*, May 26, 1950, 1; "Letnii otdykh trudiashchikhsia," *Pravda*, May 26, 1953, 1; V. Kriushkin, "V Khaborovske ne zabotiatsia o sporte," *Izvestiia*, April 18, 1953, 2; Evgenii Semenov, "Peregrady na turistskoi trope," *Literaturnaia gazeta*, September 3, 1955, 2; A. Letebet, "Fizkul'tura boret gody," *Literaturnaia gazeta*, May 30, 1953, 2.
39. GARF, fond 9520, opis' 1, d. 2524, 1.
40. Ibid.
41. For more on tourist badges (*znachki*), see M. Azarkh, *Turistskie znachki rasskazyvaiut* (Sverdlovsk: Sredne-Ural'skoe knizhnoe izdatel'stvo, 1966).
42. Usyskin, *Ocherki istorii rossiiskogo turizma*, 155.
43. GARF, fond 9520, opis' 1, delo 57, 13; Aleksandr Kemmerikh, *Puteshestvie tseloi zhizni* (Moscow: Moskovskie uchebniki i Kartolitografiia, 2004).
44. Biblioteka otchetov o sportivnykh pokhodakh, http://www.tlib.ru. This site has digitized 470 *otchety* from the 1950s alone.
45. Viktor Vitkovich, *Puteshestvie po sovetskomu Uzbekistanu* (Moscow: Molodaia gvardiia, 1951); B. Rubel', *Po Uralu* (Moscow: Profizdat, 1953); Vera Vetlina, *Krymskie puteshestviia* (Moscow: Molodaiia gvardiia, 1955); E. Zlatova and V. Kotel'nikov, *Puteshestvie po Moldavii* (Moscow: Molodaiia gvardiia, 1957); P. Luknitskii, *Tadzhikistan* (Moscow: Molodaiia gvardiia, 1951); Raisa Rubel', *Turisty Sverdlovska* (Moscow: Fizkul'tura i sport, 1957); I. Vinokurov, *Po Iuzhnomu Sakhalinu* (Moscow: Ministerstvo Prosveshcheniia, 1950); V. I. Gukov, *V kraiu netronutykh sokrovishch* (Moscow: Fizkul'tura i sport, 1959); I. A. Kirillov, *Tainy Krasnykh peshcher* (Moscow: Fizkul'tura i sport, 1959); N. Pritvits, *Saianskii dnevnik* (Moscow: Fizkul'tura i sport, 1959); A. T. Predybailo, *Po znoinoi Srednei Azii* (Moscow: Fizkul'tura i sport, 1959); A. T. Predybailo, *Krai ozer, lesov i rek*

(Moscow: Fizkul'tura i sport, 1960); Zelenko, Grigorii Andreevich, *Gde iskat' zhemchuzhinu Altaiia* (Moscow: Fizkul'tura i sport, 1957).

46. M. K. Snytko, *Turistskie marshruty po Tambovskoi oblasti* (Tambov: Tambovskoe knizhnoe izdatel'stvo, 1961), 1; I. M. Mullo, *Po rodnomu kraiu* (Petrozavodsk: Gosizdat KFSSR, 1955), 3; G. A. Zelenko, "Chto takoe turizm," *Turistskie tropy* (Moscow: Fizkul'tura i sport, 1958), 9.
47. Dmitrii Shcherbakov, *Po goram Kryma, Kavkaza i Srednei Azii* (Moscow: Geografgiz, 1954), 200.
48. Iurii Promptov, *V gorakh i dolinakh: zapiski turista peshekhoda* (Moscow: Fizkul'tura i sport, 1954), 5.
49. Koenker, *Club Red*, 265.
50. Shtil'mark, *History of the Russian Zapovedniks*, 93.
51. Ibid., 124.
52. Weiner, *Little Corner of Freedom*, 224.
53. RGAE, fond 7486, opis' 33, delo 166, 71; V. E. Boreiko, *Doroga k zapovediku: priorodookhrannaia propaganda i ekoprosveshchenie v zapovednykh ob"ektakh* (Moscow: WWF, 1996),11.
54. RGAE, fond 544, opis' 1, delo 16, 5.
55. RGAE, fond 544, opis' 1, delo 15, 69. Although Armand used the term *zapovednik* here, it is clear in this context that he is writing about national parks. At this time, supporters of the *zapovedniki* sometimes used the terms interchangeably.
56. Ibid., 211.
57. Shtil'mark, *History of the Russian Zapovedniks*, 124.
58. Ibid.
59. Miriam Dobson, *Khrushchev's Cold Summer: Gulag Returnees, Crime, and the Fate of Reform after Stalin* (Ithaca, NY: Cornell University Press, 2009).
60. For works that present the social and cultural climate after the Twentieth Party Congress, see Liudmilla Alexeyeva and Paul Goldberg, *The Thaw Generation: Coming of Age in the Post-Stalin Era* (Pittsburgh: University of Pittsburgh Press, 1990); Vladimir Zubok, *Zhivago's Children* (Cambridge, MA: Harvard University Press, 2011); Donald J. Raleigh, *Soviet Baby Boomers: An Oral History of Russia's Cold War Generation* (New York: Oxford University Press, 2013); Kathleen E. Smith, *Moscow 1956: The Silenced Spring* (Cambridge, MA: Harvard University Press, 2017); Kozlov and Gilburd, *Thaw*; Gilburd, *To See Paris and Die*.
61. For examples of articles that discussed environmental problems, see Konstantin Paustovskii, "Za krasotu rodnoi zemli," *Literaturnaia gazeta*, July 7, 1955, 2; Leonid Leonov, "V zashchitu lesa," *Literaturnaia gazeta*, March 30, 1954, 2; Letters to the Editor, "Goniteli prirody," *Literaturnaia gazeta*, October 10, 1954, 2; A. Nesmeianov, "Sokhranim prirodnye bogatstva nashei rodiny," *Izvestiia*, January 25, 1959, 1; A. N. Akhunbaev, "Priroda i liudi," *Izvestiia*, June 30, 1957, 3; A. Girgor'ev, F. Nikol'skii, N. Kabanov, G. Dement'ev, and L. Shaposhnikov, "Bol'she vnimaniia okhrane prirody," *Pravda*, April 26, 1958, 2.
62. A. Nesmeianov, "Krepnut mezhdunarodnye sviazi uchenykh," *Izvestiia*, December 31, 1954, 3.
63. "Mezhdunarodnoe sotrudnichestvo uchenykh," *Pravda*, August 27, 1958, 1. For an article about the range of perceptions in the USSR about "peaceful coexistence," see Rosa Magnusdottir, "Be Careful in America Premier Khrushchev: Soviet Perceptions of Peaceful Coexistence with the United States in 1959," *Cahiers du Monde russe* 47, no. 1/2 (January–June 2006): 109–130.
64. RGAE, fond 544, opis' 1, delo 38, 1.
65. RGAE, fond 544, opis' 1, delo 51, 6. Participants were said to take particular interest in the efforts of the workers of the Pechoro-Ilychskii Zapovednik in training elk.
66. RGAE, fond 544, opis' 1, delo 38, 38.
67. Ibid.
68. Gilburd, *To See Paris and Die*, 39; RGAE, fond 544, opis' 1, delo 52, 5.
69. RGAE, fond 544, opis' 1, delo 38, 39. The commission regularly received issues of *National Parks Magazine* (USA), *Sveriges Nature* (Sweden), *Ciencia* (Mexico), *Wissen und Leben* (GDR), *Mens en Natur* (Netherlands), *Nature in Wales* (UK), *The Conservation of Nature* (Japan), *Pro Natura* (Italy), *Svensk Jakt* (Sweden), *Fur Unsere Freilebende Giezwelt* (West

Germany), *Viltrevy* (Sweden), *Naturschlutzparke* (West Germany), and *Natur en Landschap* (Netherlands).

70. RGAE, fond 544, opis' 1, delo 51, 9.
71. Robert D. English, *Russia and the Idea of the West: Gorbachev, Intellectuals, and the End of the Cold War* (New York: Columbia University Press, 2000), 66.
72. Denis Kozlov and Eleonory Gilburd, *The Thaw* 13; Gilburd, *To See Paris and Die*, 29.
73. Ibid.
74. RGAE, fond 544, opis' 1, delo 33, 10.
75. RGAE, fond 544, opis' 1, delo 149, 41–42.
76. Ibid.; IUCN, *Seventh General Assembly of the IUCN* (Brussels: IUCN, 1960), 97.
77. Weiner, *Little Corner of Freedom*, 295.
78. RGAE, fond 544, opis' 1, delo 82, 15. The growth of territory under *zapovednik* designation through the late 1950s was as follows: 1955: 1.466 million hectares in forty *zapovedniki*; 1957: 2.739 million hectares in sixty-one *zapovedniki*; 1958: 3.163 million hectares in sixty-nine *zapovedniki*; 1959: 5.305 million hectares in eighty-two *zapovedniki*.
79. Gilburd, *To See Paris and Die*, 26.
80. Bernhard Bissibl, Sabine Hohler, and Patrick Kupper, ed. *Civilizing Nature: National Parks in Global Historical Perspective* (New York: Berghahn, 2012), 9. For more on the international mission of the USNPS, see Terrance Young and Larry M. Dilsaver, "Collecting and Diffusing the World's 'Best Thought': International Cooperation by the National Park Service," *George Wright Forum* 28, no. 3 (2011): 269–278.
81. Roderick Nash, *Wilderness and the American Mind*, 4th ed. (New Haven, CT: Yale University Press, 2014), 364.
82. RGAE, fond 544, opis' 1, delo 81, 37.
83. RGAE, fond 544, opis' 1, delo 79, 71.
84. Ibid., 42.
85. Macekura, *Of Limits and Growth*, 60.
86. Ibid., 65; for more on the IUCN's efforts to promote national parks in Africa, see Nash, *Wilderness and the American Mind*, 364–374.
87. Adams, *First World Conference on National Parks*.
88. Ibid., 2.
89. Ibid., 161.
90. Ibid., 390.
91. Ibid., 15.
92. Weiner, *Little Corner of Freedom*, 297.
93. Ibid., 296.
94. Ibid., 297.
95. RGAE, fond 544, opis' 1, delo, 79.
96. Weiner, *Little Corner of Freedom*, 302. The total territory of *zapovedniki* decreased from 6,360,000 to 4,046,700 hectares.
97. RGAE, fond 544, opis' 1, delo 91, 11.
98. Ibid., 30.
99. RGAE, fond 544, opis' 1, delo 99, 39.
100. GARF, fond 9520, opis' 1, delo 447, 18; Vianor Pachuliia, "Muza stranstvii," *Literaturnaia gazeta*, October 10, 1966, 2; V. Tereshenkov, "Industriia turizma," *Literaturnaia gazeta*, July 9, 1966, 2; E. Busylev and A. Kraminov, "Marshrut poznaniia," *Izvestiia*, September 16, 1970, 5; B. Konovalov and A. Pushkar', "Zoloto Kamchatki: K probleme razvitiia turizma," *Izvestiia*, November 17, 1968. This article stated that tourism potentially had ten times greater value than gold on the Kamchatka peninsula. On the Kosygin reforms, see Evsei Liberman and Maurice Dobb, *Theory of Profit in Socialist Economy* (New Delhi: People's Publishing House, 1966), 8; Evsei Liberman, "Plan, Pribyl', Premiia," *Pravda*, September 9, 1962, 3; Evsei Liberman, "Are We Flirting with Capitalism? Profit and "Profits," *Soviet Life*, July 1965, 36–41. Liberman was on the cover of *Time* on February 12, 1965, in a story called "Borrowing from the Capitalists." Simon Huxtable, "In Search of the Soviet Reader: The Kosygin Reforms, Sociology, and Changing Concepts of Soviet Society, 1964–1970," *Cahiers du Monde russe* 54, no. ¾ (2013): 623–642.

101. Koenker, *Club Red,*, 223.
102. RGANTD, fond R-216, opis' 4–1, delo 140, 6.
103. GARF, fond 9520, opis' 1, delo 2524, 1.
104. V. V. Dvornichenko, *Turizm v sisteme mezhdunarodnykh kul'turnykh sviazei SSSR* (Moscow: Nauka, 1978), 54.
105. GARF, fond 9520, opis' 1, delo 1927, 1.
106. GARF, fond 9520, opis' 1, delo 2524, 1.
107. O. K. Gusev and S. K. Ustinov, *Po severnomu Baikalu i Pribaikal'iu* (Moscow: Fizkul'tura i sport, 1966); A. O. Kemmerikh, *Poliarnyi Ural* (Moscow: Fizkul'tura i sport, 1966); Iu. M. Kokorev, *Po rekam i ozeram Belorussii* (Moscow: Fizkul'tura i sport, 1966); E. N. Demin, *Na baidarkakh po Podmoskov'iu* (Moscow: Fizkul'tura i sport, 1967); A. Stepanov, *Turistskie marshruty Tuvy* (Moscow: Fizkul'tura i sport, 1967); Iu. A. Shtiumer, *Po Arkhangel'skoi oblasti* (Moscow: Fizkul'tura i sport, 1967); V. V. Arsenin, N. D. Bondarev, and E. D. Sergievskii, *Gornye puteshestviia po Zapadnomu Kavkazu* (Moscow: Fizkul'tura i sport, 1968); K. Ia. Vetra and P. A. Eglite, *Puteshestvie po Latviiskoi SSR* (Moscow: Fizkul'tura i sport, 1968); V. V. Lopatin, *Turistskie dorogi Severo-Zapada SSSR* (Moscow: Fizkul'tura i sport, 1968); V. I. Pagautstsi, *Fanskie gory i Iagnob* (Moscow: Fizkul'tura i sport, 1968); V. I. Rogal'skii, *Turistskie marshruty v Saianakh* (Moscow: Fizkul'tura i sport, 1968); N. N. Gorbunova, *Vodnye marshruty Ukrainy* (Moscow: Fizkul'tura i sport, 1968); A. O. Kemmerikh, *Severnyi Ural* (Moscow: Fizkul'tura i sport, 1969); O. K. Slavinskii and V. S. Tsarenkov, *Turistskie puteshestviia po Kol'skomu poluostrovu* (Moscow: Fizkul'tura i sport, 1969); Iu. Shtiumer, *Chara Udokan: Severnoe Zabaikal'e* (Moscow: Fizkul'tura i sport, 1969); A. O. Kemmerikh, *Pripoliarnyi Ural* (Moscow: Fizkul'tura i sport, 1970).
108. *Veter stranstvii* (Moscow: Fizkul'tura i sport, 1966).
109. For two recent histories of Soviet television, see Kristin Roth-Ey, *Moscow Prime Time: How the Soviet Union Built the Media Empire That Lost the Cultural Cold War* (Ithaca, NY: Cornell University Press, 2011) and Kristine Elaine Evans, *Between Truth and Time: A History of Soviet Central Television* (New Haven, CT: Yale University Press, 2016); GARF, fond 441, opis' 26, delo 603, 26; GARF, fond 441, opis' 26, delo 429, 265.
110. RGAE, fond 544, opis' 1, delo 172, 8.
111. GARF, fond 9520, opis' 1, delo 2524, 1.
112. Ibid., 203.
113. Iu. Efremov, "Krasa rodnogo kraia," *Pravda*, July 1, 1966, 4; D. L. Armand, "Priroda i turist," *Turist* 7 (July 1965): 21; G. P. Geptner, "Zapovednik: Slovo drevnee," *Znanie-Sila* 3 (March 1968): 44; David Armand, *Nam i vnukam* (Moscow: Mysl', 1964), 22; K. N. Blagosklonov and V. N. Tikhomirov, *Okhrana prirody* (Moscow: Vysshaia shkola, 1967). For literature on the environmental concerns raised by outdoor recreation in the United States at this time, see Silas Chamberlin, *On the Trail: A History of American Hiking* (New Haven, CT: Yale University Press, 2016), 180; James Morton Turner, "From Woodcraft to 'Leave No Trace': Woodcraft, Consumerism, and Environmentalism in Twentieth-Century America," *Environmental History* 7, no. 3 (July 2002): 462–484.
114. Armand, *Nam i vnukam*, 204.
115. V. Chizhova and E. Smirnova, *Slovo ob otdykhe* (Moscow: Znanie, 1976), 10.
116. Iu. Efremov, "Krasa rodnogo kraia," *Pravda*, July 1, 1966, 4; Chizhova and Smirnova, *Slovo ob otdykhe*, 14. According to some estimates, toward the end of the decade there were twenty-five metal cans, thirty-three pieces of paper, and 162 broken or whole glass bottles / cans for every one hundred meters.
117. V. Petrov, "Prishestvie iz goroda," *Izvestiia*, July 21, 1970, 6.
118. GAKK, fond 725, opis' 1, delo 22, 13–14; M. Smotryev, "Seliger v opasnosti," *Literaturnaia gazeta*, November 25, 1962, 2; V. Kozhemiako, "Vperedi—dolina geizerov," *Pravda*, July 3, 1967, 6; L. Iarkaia, "Zhiguli—tsentr turizma," *Volzhskii komsomolets*, December 5, 1969, 6; V. Sharov, "Trevoga v Bukhte Peschanoi," *Pravda*, August 2, 1967, 6; "Budut novye turbazy na Baikale," *Pravda*, September 28, 1967, 3; Zhemchuzhina russkoi prirody," *Pravda*, May 20, 1962, 6; V. Novgorodov, "Shchepotka zla," *Vostochno-Sibirskaia pravda*, July 31, 1968, 4. The author writes, "It is difficult to explain the reasons for the indifference and the harsh

relationship to nature that forced us to use these harsh words in the article's title." Also see Vladas Maltsiavichius et. al, "Kto za eto otvetit?" *Vostochno-Sibirskaia pravda*, August 15, 1968, 4, which predicted that the shoreline near Sand Bay would be completely denuded in five to ten years.

119. RGAE, fond 7486, opis' 33, delo 166, 71.
120. Ibid., 66. Also see Main Administration for Hunting and Zapovedniki, *Zapovedniki SSSR* (Moscow: Main Administration for Hunting and Zapovedniki, 1964), 6.
121. *Gosudarstvennyi zapovednik Stolby* (Krasnoyarsk: Krasnoyarskoe knizhnoe izdatel'stvo, 1960); A. G. Bannikov and Iu. P. Iazan, *Pechoro-Ilychskii zapovednik* (Moscow: Znanie, 1968), 39; Kim Aleksandrovich Andreev, *Zapovednik Kivach* (Petrozavodsk, 1963); M. E. Solov'eva, *Zapovednik na Pechore* (Komi knizhnoe izdatel'stvo, 1963), 111–115.
122. A. Chelebenko, "Vysoko v gorakh Tian Shana," *Pravda*, September 22, 1965, 6; N. Rozhdestvenskii, "U divnykh gor," *Pravda*, November 21, 1964, 4; V. Shepel', "Gornaia skazka," *Pravda*, October 16, 1967, 6.
123. RGAE, fond 7486, opis' 33 delo 166, 80.
124. Eva Mauer, "Al'pinizm as Mass Sport and Elite Recreation: Soviet Mountaineering Camps under Stalin," in *Turizm: The Russian and East European Tourist Under Capitalism and Socialism*, eds. Diane Koenker and Anne E. Gorsuch (Ithaca, NY: Cornell University Press, 2006), 141–162.
125. "Vremia letnikh otpuskov," *Izvestiia*, April 24, 1961, 6.
126. GARF, fond 404, opis' 1, delo 795, 13.
127. Ibid., 14.
128. Ibid., 17.
129. GARF, fond 358, opis' 3, delo 4729, 44.
130. Ibid., 48.
131. Nina Doronina, "Skonchalas' pervootkryvatel' doliny geizerov Tat'iana Ustinova," *Rossiiskaia gazeta*, July 9, 2009.
132. "Teplitsy na goriachikh kliuchakh Kamchatki," *Pravda*, April 4, 1946; "Dolina Geyzerov," Net-Film, https://www.net-film.ru/film-58873; "V Krayu Ognedyshashchikh Gor," Net-Film," https://www.net-film.ru/film-58875.
133. M. Nechaeva, "Khotim puteshestvovat'," *Sovetskaiia kul'tura*, July 12, 1957, 2.
134. Ibid.
135. RGAE, fond 7486, opis' 33, delo 165, 100.
136. B. Sobolev, B. Bandarchuk, M. Itsikson, A. Sviatlovskii, and V. Koptev-Dvornikov, "Sokhranit' volshebnye zamki," *Kamchatskaia pravda*, September 24, 1964, 2.
137. GAKK, fond 725, opis' 1, delo 22, 13–14; V. Kozhemiako, "Vperedi—dolina geizerov," *Pravda*, July 3, 1967, 6; B. Konovalov and A. Pushkar', "Zoloto Kamchatki: K probleme razvitiia turizma," *Izvestiia*, November 17, 1968.
138. Konovalov and Pushkar', "Zoloto Kamchatki."
139. GARF, fond 441, opis' 26, delo 740, 73.
140. I. Selivanova, "Ispytanie dolinoi geizerov," *Dalnii Vostok* 10 (October 1987): 126–135.
141. V. G. Geptner, "Zapovednik: Slovo drevnee," *Znanie-Sila* 3 (March 1968): 44; V. Kravchenko, "Proza doliny geizerov: O problemakh obsluzhivaniia turistov i okhrany prirody doliny geizerov i Kronotskogo Zapovednika," *Kamchatskaia pravda*, November 26, 1970, 2; V. Kravchenko, "Liudi i geizery," *Kamchatskii komsomolets*, November 2, 1971.
142. Konstantin Podyma, "Puteshestvie v dolinu geizerov," *Kamchatskii komsomolets*, October 13, 1973, 2; V. Kravchenko, Zemlia zapovednaia," *Kamchatskaia pravda*, September 8, 1973, 3; E. Lobkov, "Kronotskii zapovednik," *Okhota i okhotnich'e khoziaistvo* 1 (January 1980): 24–25.
143. V. Sabinov, "Zapovednik i turism," *Kamchatskaia Pravda*, February 3, 1974.
144. A. Bannikov, "Turizm, zapovedniki, okhota," *Okhota i okhotnich'e khoziaistvo* 1 (January 1965): 1; N. Gladkov, "Zapovedniki, dostoianie naroda," *Okhota i okhotnich'e khoziaistvo* 5 (May 1965): 13; E. Krutovskaia, "Organizovannyi turizm ne vrag zapovednikam," *Okhota i okhotnich'e khoziaistvo* 7 (July 1968): 16–17; O. Guzev, "Zapovedniki i turism," *Okhota i okhotnich'e khoziaistvo* 2 (February 1969): 2.

145. Among these institutions were the VOOP, the Central Laboratory of Nature Protection (formerly the Commission on Nature Protection), and the Main Administration for Hunting and Zapovedniki, and the Institute of Geography.
146. N. Filippovskii, *Natsional'nyi park: problema sozdoniia* (Moscow: Znanie, 1979), 4.
147. G. B. Kirillov ed, *Problemy okhrany prirody Sibiri i Dal'nego Vostoka* (Novosibirsk: Sibirskoe otdelenie AN SSSR, 1963); L. K. Shaposhnikov, ed., *6-oe Vsesoiuznoe soveshchanie po okhrane prirody* (Minsk: Nauka i tekhnika, 1965); L. K. Shaposhnikov, ed., *Piatoe Vsesoiuznoe soveshchanie po okhrane prirody* (Kishinev: Kartia Moldovenogo, 1963), 17; L. K Shaposhnikov, ed., *Tret'e Vsesoiuznoe soveshchanie po okhrane prirody* (Dushanbe: Kommisiia po okhrane prirody SSSR, 1961).
148. L. K. Shaposhnikov, *Piatoe Vsesoiuznoe soveshchanie po okhrane prioriy*, 17. In his opening speech at the 1962 conference, which focused extensively on national parks, Shaposhnikov stated, "For developing concrete proposals for the improvement of the planning of nature protection and the rational use of its resources in the USSR, the study and generalization of the experience of other countries, in particular, the United States, is very important."
149. For more on the disbanding of the Commission on Nature Protection, see Weiner, *Little Corner of Freedom*, 307–311.
150. RGAE, fond 544, opis' 1, delo 131, 74.
151. L. Shinkarev, "Baikala shchedryi dar," *Izvestiia*, September 24, 1965, 6; Ia. Grushko, "Krai tselebnykh istochnikov"; L. Shinkarev, "Vokrug Baikala," November 17, 1965, 6; "Russkii les," *Literaturnaia gazeta*, May 21, 1963, 2.
152. A book by the Main Administration for Hunting and Zapovedniki under the Ministry of Agriculture, *Zapovedniki Kazakhstana*, called for a park outside of Alma-Ata, about which the authors stated, "There is no doubt the national park will acquire quickly all-union significance and share the world recognition of the American National Park Yellowstone." *Zapovedniki Kazakhstana* (Alma-Ata: Kazakhskoe gosudarstvennoe izdatel'stvo, 1963), 129.
153. For more on the forest as the "quintessential" Russian landscape in the nineteenth century, see Christopher Ely, *This Meager Nature: Landscape and National Identity in Imperial Russia* (DeKalb: Northern Illinois University Press, 2009), and Jane T. Costlow, *Heart-Pine Russia: Walking and Writing in the Nineteenth-Century Forest* (Ithaca, NY: Cornell University Press, 2012).
154. Stephen Brain, *Song of the Forest: Russian Forestry and Stalinist Environmentalism, 1905–1953* (Pittsburgh: University of Pittsburgh Press, 2011), 5.
155. Ibid.
156. GARF, Fond 441 opis' 26, delo 742, 265; V. G. Nestorov, A. I. Popov, A. F. Mukin, and P. V. Vasil'iev were some of the other foresters involved. Leonid Leonov, *Russkii les* (Moscow: Molodaia Gvardiia, 1954).
157. GARF, fond 404, opis' 1, delo 680, 7.
158. Sergei L'vov, "*Russkii les*," *Izvestiia*, September 29, 1960, 3.
159. Ibid.
160. GARF, fond 404, opis' 1, delo 680, 15.
161. Sergei L'vov, "Russkii les," 3.
162. GARF, fond 404, opis' 1, delo 680, 19.
163. M. K. Bochkarev, "Budet li natsional'nyi park," *Pravda*, January 17, 1967, 4.
164. Ibid.; GARF, fond 404, opis' 1, delo 680, 3.
165. GARF, fond 441, opis' 26, delo 742, 272.
166. Interview with Julius Dobroshin, July 15, 2015, Moscow.
167. G. Kozhevnikov, "O neobkhodimosti ustroistva zapovednykh uchastkov dlia okhrany prirody," *Okhrana prirody i zapovednnoe delo SSSR* 1, no. 4 (April 1960): 93.
168. B. G. Barkov, "Losinyi Ostrov," in *Les i chelovek* (Moscow, 1982), 54–56.
169. S. V. D'iakov, "Losinyi ostrov," *Listki biostantsii iunykh naturalistov*, May 24, 1924; P. I. Sarsatskikh and V. D. Priakhin, "Sozdadim lesopark bliz Moskvy," *Stroitel'stvo Moskvy* (1934); N. V. Zabelina, B. L. Samoilov, and G. V. Morozova, *Natsional'nye parki i zakazniki* (Moscow: Mysl', 1996), 6.

170. Zabelina, Samoilov, and Morozova, *Natsional'nye parki i zakazniki*, 6; For more on discussion on environmental issues under Khrushchev, see Laurent Coumel, "A Failed Environmental Turn? Khrushchev's Thaw and Nature Protection in the Soviet Union," *The Soviet and Post-Soviet Review* 40 (2013): 167–189.
171. V. Kucherenko, "Nekotorye voprosy sovetskogo gradostroitel'stva," *Pravda*, June 1, 1960, 2.
172. RGAE, fond 544, opis' 1, delo 79, 57.
173. RGAE, fond 544, opis' 1, delo 81, 1.
174. B. Tobilevich, "Rasti, siiai, nasha Moskva!," *Izvestiia*, August 18, 1960, 4.
175. Anonymous, "Semiletka sozidaniia," *Izvestiia*, August 18, 1960, 4.
176. RGAE, fond 544, opis' 1, delo 80, 35.
177. Tobilevich, "Rasti, siiai, nasha Moskva!," 4; "Zelenoe ozherel'e stolitsy," *Izvestiia*, July 7, 1960, 4.
178. RGAE, fond 544, opis' 1, delo 81, 4, 15.
179. Ibid., 11.
180. GARF, fond 404, opis' 1, delo 740, 25.
181. Ibid., 5 and 72.
182. TsAGM, fond 779, opis' 1, delo 112, 1.
183. ARGO, fond 1-1967, opis' 1, delo 47, 42.
184. Ibid.
185. M. Smotriaev, "Seliger v opasnosti," *Literaturnaia gazeta*, November 25, 1962, 2.
186. R. A. Luiriia and M. S. Margulis, "Kurort Seliger," *Pravda*, July 23, 1937. Also see G. Korolev and A. Frantsev. "Zhemchuzhina russkoi prirody," *Pravda*, May 20, 1962, 6.
187. See Ia. Gorelik, "Na beregakh ozer i rek," *Literaturnaia gazeta*, August 24, 1954, 1; K. Kerchiner and I. Kondukov, "Priezzhaite otdykhat' na ozero Seliger," *Izvestiia*, June 17, 1956, 4; E. Simonov, "Pregrady na turistskoi trope," *Literaturnaia gazeta*, September 3, 1955, 2; "Turistskaiia baza uchenykh," *Sovetskaiia kul'tura*, September 16, 1954, 3; "Po turistskim tropam," *Literaturnaia gazeta*, June 26, 1958, 1; "V iiule na Seligere," *Pravda*, July 30, 1960, 6.
188. N. Grave and M. Seslavin, "Dary Valdaiia—velikim rekam," *Izvestiia*, September 11, 1960, 3.
189. M. Smotriaev, "Seliger v opasnosti," *Literaturnaia gazeta*, November 25, 1962, 2.
190. GARF, fond A-404, opis' 1, delo 734, 15.
191. M. P. Smotriaev and Yu. I Nikanorov, "Nastoiashchee i budushchee Seligera," *Priroda* 8 (August 1962): 85–95.
192. GARF, fond A-404, opis' 1, delo 734, 40.
193. GARF, fond 259, opis' 45, delo 6709, 7.
194. See A. Egorov, "Gotov'sya v dorogu turist," *Pravda*, April 27, 1972; O Matiatin and L. Pochivalov, "Seliger bez vostorgov," *Pravda*, March 16, 1973, 6; L. Pochivalov, "Tumany gorizonty Seligera," *Pravda*, August 28, 1979. 6; G. Zaitsev, "Ne povredit' by Seliger," *Pravda*, January 25, 1981.
195. V. Komarov, "Seliger, liubov' moia i trevoga," Net-Film, 1974, http://www.net-film.ru/film-7562/.
196. RGANTD, fond R-216, opis' 5–4, delo 258, 30; GARF, fond 259, opis' 46, delo 1897, 14.
197. GARF, fond A-404, opis' 1, delo 734, 14 and 20.
198. Correspondence with Iurii Vedenin, October 13, 2013.
199. RGAE, fond 544, opis' 1, delo 172, 65.
200. RGAE, fond 7486, opis' 33, delo 131, 21.
201. AVGO, 1-1967, 29.
202. Ibid., 30.
203. Ibid.
204. Oleg Volkov, "Uvazhenie k krasote," *Literaturnaia gazeta*, June 14, 1967, 12.
205. Ibid.
206. Ibid.
207. Krutovskaia, "Organizovannyi turizm ne vrag zapovednikam," 13; O. Gusev, "Zapovedniki i turizm," *Okhota i okhotnich'e khoziaistvo* 2 (February 1969): 12; Krutovskaia, "Organizovannyi turizm ne vrag zapovednikam," 16–17; I. Shmatok, "Natsional'nyi park

nuzhen," *Okhota i okhotnich'e khoziaistvo* 10 (October 1968): 13; N. Puzanov, "Nam nuzhny natsional'nye parki," *Okhota i okhotnich'e khoziaistvo* 2 (February 1968): 12–14.

208. Puzanov, "Nam nuzhny natsional'nye parki," 14.
209. RGAE, fond 7486, opis' 33, delo 166, 80.
210. Ibid., 136.
211. RGAE, fond 7486, opis' 33, delo 165, 138.
212. Ibid., 99.
213. O. K., Gusev, *Ot Barguzinzkogo zapovednika do Ushkan'ikh Ostrovov* (Irkutsk: Irkutskoe knizhnoe izdatel'stvo, 1960).
214. RGAE, fond 7486, opis' 33, delo 166, 79.
215. Ibid., 92.
216. RGAE, fond 7486, opis' 33, delo 165, 141.
217. Ibid., 140.
218. RGAE, fond 7486, opis' 33, delo 166, 33.
219. RGAE, fond 7486, opis' 33, delo 165, 148.
220. RGAE, fond 7486, opis' 33, delo 18, 41.
221. RGAE, fond 7486, opis' 33, delo 165, 148.
222. RGAE, fond 7486, opis' 33, delo 166, 76.
223. Ibid.
224. RGAE, fond 7486, opis' 33, delo 229, 34.
225. Adams, *First World Conference on National Parks*, xxxi.
226. *Tenth General Assembly of the IUCN* (Morges, Switzerland: IUCN, 1970), 156.
227. Denis Kozlov and Eleonory Gilburd, "The Thaw as an Event in Russian History," in Kozlov and Gilburd, *Thaw*, 53.
228. Nash, *Wilderness and the American Mind*, 347.

Chapter 3

1. Andrei Bannikov, "Garmoniia neprimirimogo," *Literaturnaia gazeta*, January 29, 1975, 13.
2. See S. Frederick Starr, "Soviet Union: A Civil Society," *Foreign Policy* 70 (Spring 1988): 26–41. S. Frederick Starr criticized Gorbachev for creating this misconception of Soviet society in the 1970s, which he believed to be a vibrant period. For an example of a portrayal of the stagnation era through this lens of decline, see Martin Malia, *The Soviet Tragedy: A History of Socialism in Russia, 1917–1991* (New York: Free Press, 1994), 351–401.
3. For recent works of the Brezhnev era that seek to move beyond the "stagnation" narrative, see Natalya Chernyshova, *Soviet Consumer Culture in the Brezhnev Era* (New York: Routledge, 2013); Neringa Klumbyte and Gulnaz Sharafutdinova, ed., *Soviet Society in the Era of Late Socialism: 1964–1985* (New York: Lexington, 2013); Dina Fainberg and Artemy M. Kalinovsky, ed., *Reconsidering Stagnation in the Brezhnev Era: Ideology and Exchange* (London: Lexington, 2016).
4. Arkady Ostrovsky, *The Invention of Russia: The Rise of Putin and the Age of Fake News* (New York: Viking, 2016), 49.
5. Christopher Ward, *Brezhnev's Folly* (Pittsburgh: University of Pittsburgh Press, 2009).
6. Alexei Yurchak, *Everything Was Forever Until It Was No More: The Last Soviet Generation* (Princeton, NJ: Princeton University Press, 2005).
7. For an example of this, see Matthew Jesse Jackson, *The Experimental Group: Ilya Kabakov, Moscow Conceptualism, Soviet Avant-Gardes* (Chicago: University of Chicago Press, 2010); Yurchak, *Everything Was Forever*, 128–131. Yurchak writes about the phenomenon of "*vne*" (out of) groups, which viewed themselves as outside of the Soviet system.
8. For English language works that showed some of the mounting environmental problems in the USSR under Brezhnev, see Phillip Pryde, *Conservation in the Soviet Union* (New York: Cambridge University Press, 1972); Marshall I. Goldman, *Environmental Pollution in the Soviet Union: The Spoils of Progress* (Cambridge, MA: MIT Press, 1972); Murray Feshbach, and Albert Friendly, *Ecocide in the USSR: Environment and Health under Siege* (New York: Basic Books, 1993).

9. For works on the Aral Sea, see Michael H. Glantz, ed. *Creeping Environmental Problems and Sustainable Development in the Aral Sea Basin* (Cambridge, MA: MIT Press, 1999); Philip Micklin, "Desiccation of the Aral Sea: A Water Management Disaster in the Soviet Union," *Science* 241 (September 1988): 1170; Phillip Micklin, *The Aral Sea: The Devastation and Partial Rehabilitation of a Great Lake* (Springer, 2013); I. Zonn, M. Glantz, Aleksei Kosarev, and Andrei Kostianoy, ed., *The Aral Sea Encyclopedia* (Berlin: Springer, 2010).
10. See Stanislav Gol'dfarb, ed., *Baikal'skii sindrom* (Irkutsk: Komsomol'skaia pravda—Baikal, 1996). This book is a collection of newspaper articles and reflections about the operation of the Baikalsk Cellulose and Paper Plant.
11. Paul Josephson et al., *An Environmental History of Russia* (Cambridge: Cambridge University Press, 2013), 186.
12. See Ward, *Brezhnev's Folly*, 19.
13. See Valentin Rasputin, *Farewell to Matyora*, trans. Antonina W. Bouis (Evanston, IL: Northwestern University Press, 1995).
14. Josephson et al., *Environmental History of Russia*, 188.
15. Boris Komarov, *The Destruction of Nature in the Soviet Union* (London: Pluto, 1980). Wolfson wrote under this pseudonym.
16. Stephen Brain, "The Appeal of Appearing Green: Soviet-American Ideological Competition and Cold War Environmental Diplomacy," *Cold War History* 16, no. 4 (October 2014): 1–19.
17. Kathleen Parthe, *Russian Village Prose: The Radiant Past* (Princeton, NJ: Princeton University Press, 1992).
18. Robert Poole, *Earthrise: How Man First Saw Earth* (New Haven, CT: Yale University Press, 2010).
19. Dina Fainberg and Artemy M. Kalinovsky, "Introduction: Stagnation and Its Discontents: The Creation of a Political and Historical Paradigm," in *Reconsidering Stagnation in the Brezhnev Era: Ideology and Exchange*, eds. Dina Fainberg and Artemy M. Kalinovsky (Lanham, MD: Lexington, 2016), vii.
20. Ostrovsky, *Invention of Russia*, 51.
21. I. P. Gerasimov, A. A. Mints, V. S. Preobrazhenskii, and N. P. Shelemov, "Estestvennye resursy. Okhrana i preobrazovanie prirody," *Izvestiia Akademii nauk SSSR: Seriia geograficheskaiia* 4 (1969): 47.
22. Ibid., 43.
23. For an article on Soviet exploration see N. G. Fradkin, "Geograficheskie otkrytiia sovetskogo perioda," *Izvestiia Akademii nauk SSSR: Seriia geograficheskaia* 3 (1967): 5–17.
24. John McCannon, *Red Arctic: Polar Exploration and the Myth of the North in the Soviet Union, 1932–1939* (New York: Oxford University Press, 1998).
25. David J. M. Hooson, "Some Recent Developments in the Content and Theory of Soviet Geography," *Annals of the Association of American Geographers* 49, no. 1 (March 1959): 75.
26. V. I. Anuchin, *Teoreticheskie voprosy v geografii* (Moscow, 1960); David J. M. Hooson, "Methodological Clashes in Moscow," *Annals of the Association of American Geographers* 52, no. 4 (December 1962): 469.
27. V. Anuchin, "Istoriia s geografei," *Literaturnaia gazeta*, February 18, 1965, 2.
28. Iu. Saushkin, "Sevodnia i zavtra geografii," *Literaturnaia gazeta*, June 17, 1965, 3.
29. V. M. Gokhman, M. B. Gornung, and V. P. Kovalevskii, "Mundira," *Literaturnaia gazeta*, May 20, 1965, 3–4.
30. D. L. Armand, "Ratsional'noe ispol'zovanie prirodnikh resursov i zadachi sovetskoi geografii," *Izvestiia Akademii nauk SSSR: Seriia geografiicheskaia* 5 (May 1961): 8.
31. K. C. McMurry, "The Use of Land for Recreation," *Annals of the Association of American Geographers* 20, no. 1 (Mar., 1930): 7–20. This article is widely considered to mark the beginning of recreational geography in the United States.
32. V. S. Preobrazhenskii, "Kratkii ocherk nauchnoi, nauchno-organizatsionnoi, pedagogicheskoi i obshchestvennoi deiatel'nosti," in *Innokentii Petrovich Gerasimov, 1905–1985*, ed. R. I. Kuz'menko (Moscow: Nauka, 1991), 6, 19; I. P. Gerasimov, "Okhrana prirody v natsionalnikh parkakh USA," *Izvestiia Akademii nauk SSSR: Seriia geograficheskaia* 4 (April 1962): 98–103.
33. ARAN, fond 1850, opis' 1, delo 24, 14.

34. I. Gerasimov, "Ischezla li geografiia," *Literaturnaia gazeta*, April 29, 1965, 2; D. Armand, "Davaite ne budem," *Literaturnaia gazeta*, March 25, 1965; Armand, "Ratsional'noe ispol'zovanie prirodnykh resursov," 56.
35. I. P. Gerasimov, "Konstruktivnaia geografiia; tseli, metody, rezul'taty," *Izvestiia vsesoiuznogo geograficheskogo obshchestva* 98, no. 5 (September-October 1966): 391–400.
36. Ibid., 391.
37. Ibid., 397. Gerasimov later listed the organization of recreational zones as one of the central tasks of constructive geography. See I. P. Gerasimov, "Chelovek i sreda: Sovremennye aspekty problem," *Izvestiia Akademii nauk SSSR: Seriia geograficheskaia* 1 (January 1971): 5–13.
38. V. M. Kotliakov, ed., *Vladimir Sergeevich Preobrazhenskii v vospominaniiakh i pis'makh* (Moscow: Institut geografii AN SSSR, 2005), 6.
39. V. Preobrazhenskii, "Dvizhenie po azimutu," *Na sushe i na more* 6 (June 1941): 12.
40. Ibid., 10.
41. Preobrazhenskii, "Kratkii ocherk nauchnoi," 77; I. P. Gerasimov, V. S. Preobrazhenskii, A. S. Abramov, D. L. Armand, S. V. Zon, I. V. Komar, G. M. Lappo, and N. F. Leont'ev, ed., *Teoreticheskie osnovy rekreatsionnoi geografii* (Moscow: Nauka, 1975), 9.
42. Preobrazhenskii, "Kratkii ocherk nauchnoi," 77.
43. V. S. Preobrazhenskii and N. P. Shelemov, "Problemy ispol'zovaniia estestvennykh resursov dlia otdykha i turizma," *Izvestiia Akademii nauk SSSR: Seriia geografiicheskaia* 5 (May 1967): 54–62.
44. Ibid.
45. AVGO, fond 1, opis' 1, delo 47, 36.
46. Simon Huxtable, "In Search of the Soviet Reader: The Kosygin reforms, sociology, and changing concepts of Soviet society, 1964–1970," *Cahiers du Monde russe* 54, no. 3/4 (2013): 623–642; Natalya Chernyshova, "Consumers as Citizens: Revisiting the Question of Public Disengagement in the Brezhnev Era," in *Reconsidering Stagnation in the Brezhnev Era: Ideology and Exchange*, eds. Dina Fainberg and Artemy M. Kalinovsky (London: Lexington, 2016), 7; Christine E. Evans, *Between Truth and Time: A History of Soviet Central Television* (New Haven, CT: Yale University Press, 2016), 58.
47. Robert English, *Russia and the Idea of the West: Gorbachev, Intellectuals, and the End of the Cold War* (New York: Columbia University Press, 2000), 109.
48. V. G. Baikova, A. S. Duchal, and A. A. Zemtsov, *Svobodnoe vremia i vsestoronee razvitie lichnosti* (Moscow: Mysl', 1965), 20.
49. Lappo and Leont'ev, *Teoreticheskie osnovy rekreatsionnoi geografii*, 5.
50. ARAN, fond 200, opis' 1, delo 31, 80.
51. Ibid., 83.
52. M. Cherkasova, "Turizm iavlenie planetarnoe," *Znanie-sila* 3 (March 1972): 38; N. S. Kazanskaia, "Izuchenie rekreatsionnoi digressii estestvennykh gruppirovok rastitel'nosti," *Izvestiia Akademii nauk SSSR: Seriia geograficheskaia*, no. 1, (1972): 52–60; N. S. Kazanskaia, "Opyt izmeneniia lesov pod vliianiem rekreatsionnogo ispol'zovaniia," *Izvestiia Akademii nauk: Seriia geografiicheskaia* 2 (1975): 60–68.
53. Kazanskaia, "Izuchenie rekreatsionnoi digressii estestvennykh gruppirovok rastitel'nosti." See also: V. P. Chizhova, *Rekreatsionnye nagruzki v zonakh otdykha* (Moscow: Lesnaia Promyschlennost', 1977), 33.
54. Cherkasova, "Turizm iavlenie planetarnoe," 12.
55. Lappo and Leont'ev, *Teoreticheskie osnovy rekreatsionnoi geografii*, 5.
56. V. S. Preobrazhenskii and Iu. A. Vedenin, *Geografiia i otdykh* (Moscow: Znanie, 1971), 32.
57. Lappo and Leont'ev, *Teoreticheskie osnovy rekreatsionnoi geografii*, 17.
58. Ibid.
59. Ibid.
60. V. P. Preobrazhenskii, I. V. Zorin, Yu. A. Vedinin, "Geograficheskie aspekty konstruktirovaniia novykh tipov rekreatsionnykh sistem," *Izestiia Akademii nauk SSSR: Seriia geograficheskaia* 1 (1972): 125–131.
61. Lappo and Leont'ev, *Teoreticheskie osnovy rekreatsionnoi geografii*, 33.
62. Ibid.
63. In addition to Kazanskaia, Chizhova worked on this question throughout the 1970s.

64. A. N. Tarasov, "Ob otsenke rekreatsionnoi funktsii lesa," *Lesnoe khoziaistvo* 3 (March 1976): 85–87; V. Taran, "O lesovodstvennykh aspektakh rekreatsionnoi deiatel'nosti v lesakh Zapadnoi Sibiri," *Lesnoe khoziaistvo* 5 (May 1979): 56–59; R. Khanvekov and S. Iu. Tsaregradskaia, "Klassifikatsiia i organizatsiia prigorodnykh lesov," *Lesnoe khoziaistvo* 5 (May 1979): 59–61.
65. V. S. Preobrazhenskii, I. V. Zorin, and Iu. A Vedenin, "Geograficheskie aspekty konstruktirovaniia novykh tipov rekreatsionnykh sistem," *Izvestiia Akademii nauk SSSR: Seriia geograficheskaia* 1 (January 1972): 36–41.
66. Richard West Sellars, *Preserving Nature in the National Parks: A History*. 2nd ed. (New Haven, CT: Yale University Press, 2009), 190. The Mission 66 program in the NPS dramatically increased infrastructure spending and resulted in significant increases in tourist traffic.
67. Lappo and Leont'ev, *Teoreticheskie osnovy rekreatsionnoi geografii*, 17.
68. N. Filippovskii, ed., *Chelovek i priroda* (Moscow: Znaniia, 1981).
69. Ibid., 18.
70. Oleg Ianitskii, "Urbanization in the USSR: Theory, Tendencies, and Policy," *International Journal of Urban and Regional Research* 10, no. 2 (June 1986): 265.
71. Interview with Nataliia Zabelina, October 15, 2013, Moscow.
72. N. M. Zabelina, *Opyt okhrany prirodnykh resursov v SShA* (Moscow: Ministerstvo sel'skogo khoziaistva SSSR, 1972).
73. RGAE, fond 544, opis' 1, delo 210, 199; Nataliia Zabelina, "Prirodnye landshafty SShA, ikh ispol'zovanie dlia turizma," PhD diss., (Moscow: Moscow State University, 1979).
74. RGAE, fond 544, opis' 1, delo 240, 114.
75. Ibid., 43.
76. RGAE, fond 544, opis' 1, delo 256, 39. V. D. Lebedev, the assistant chair of Gosplan. proposed the name "state parks" (*gosudarstvennye parki*); D. L. Armand proposed "people's parks" (*narodnye parki*); the All-Union Institute of Hunting proposed the name "reserve parks" (*zapovednye parki*); the Tbilisi Institute of the Forest recommended the name "regional parks" (*regional'nye parki*).
77. Ibid., 14.
78. Ibid., 27.
79. Ibid., 17.
80. Ibid., 41.
81. Robert W. Smurr, "Lahemaa: The Paradox of the Soviet Union's First National Park," *Nationalities Papers* 36, no. 3 (July 2008): 402; Paul Goriup, ed., "Protected Areas Program," *International Journal for Protected Area Managers* 14, no. 3. (2004): 6. See Paul Goriup, ed., *Protected Areas Program* (Newbury, UK: IUCN, 2004), 8.
82. RGAE, fond 544, opis' 1, delo 72, 2.
83. P. Bolin, "I avtomobili i sosny," *Literaturnaia gazeta*, August 12, 1970, 13. The Estonian Council of Ministers banned DDT in 1967, which was five years before the US banned it.
84. Smurr, "Lahemaa," 402.
85. State Archives of Latvia, fond, 270, opis' 3, delo, 5109, 260.
86. A. V. Kaazik, "Lakhemaaskii natsional'nyi park, ego uchrezhdenie i deiatel'nost'," *Lakhemaaskii natsional'nyi park: Nauchnye trudy po okhrane prirody* 5 (1982): 6.
87. RGANTD, fond R-216, opis' 4–1, delo 140, 30; RGAE, fond 544, opis' 1, delo 289, 20.
88. Smurr, "Lahemaa," 404.
89. "The Livonian Switzerland," http://www.latvians.com/index.php?en/CFBH/Livlandische Schweiz/schulz-001-intro.wiki. The Gauja River valley received this name from the photographer Carl Shulz, who produced a photo collection by this name.
90. Ionas Berkhol'tsas, *Natsional'nyi park Gauia* (Moscow: Lesnaia promyshlennost', 1982), 19.
91. State Archives of Latvia, fond 270, opis' 3, delo 5488, 51.
92. Aldis Lauzis, "Istochnik otdykha, vdokhnovleniia i znanii," *Nauka i tekhnika* 6 (June 1971): 31.
93. State Archives of Latvia fond 270, opis' 3, delo 5488, 2.
94. Ibid., 5.
95. Ibid., 78.
96. State Archives of Latvia, fond 270, opis' 3, delo 5109, 260.

97. Ibid., 258.
98. State Archives of Latvia, fond 270, opis' 3, delo, 5488, 189; State Archives of Latvia, fond 270, opis' 3, delo 5421, 155.
99. "Istochnik otdykha, vdokhnovleniia i znanii," 6.
100. Ibid.
101. "Dva rabochikh vykhodnykh," *Sovetskaia molodezh'*, July 2, 1975, 2.
102. Ibid.; N. Karpovskaia, "Leto nachinaetsia vesnoi," *Sovetskaia molodezh'*, April 9, 1977; A. Iurevits, "Nasha glavnaia zadacha—okhrana prirody," *Rigas Balss*, September 17, 1977, 6; G. Eberkhard, "Gde ostanovit'sia," *Rigas Balss*, October 19, 1978.
103. K. Smirnov, "Chtoby glubzhe dyshalos' planete," *Izvestiia*, June 7, 1977, 4.
104. K. P. Giniunas, "Opyt raboty natsional'nogo parka Litovskoi SSR," in *Organizatsiia natsional'nykh parkov SSSR*, ed. Iurii Petrovich Iazan (Vilnius: Mintis, 1982), 33.
105. Ibid., 32.
106. Lithuania Central State Historical Archives, fond R-754, opis' 1, delo 1137, 44–45.
107. See R Kaera, "Krai bukht," *Literaturnaia gazeta*, February 26, 1975, 11; RGANTD, fond R-216, opis' 4–1, delo 370, 48; RGAE, fond 544, opis' 1, delo 289, 22.
108. Berkhol'tsas, *Natsional'nyi park*, 4.
109. Ibid.
110. Ibid., 24.
111. L. A. Alibekov, "Narodnyi park Uzbekistana," *Priroda* 1 (January 1986): 41–52.
112. I. Vasil'ev, "Otkrytie," *Turist* 6 (June 1978): 20.
113. A. Bolokhnin and A. Kraminov, "Vse storony Sevana," *Izvestiia*, July 20, 1966, 3. Established in Georgia SSR in 1973, Tbilisi National Park was the first national park in the Caucasus region, but it received significantly less attention than Sevan.
114. A. A. Charogian, "Natsional'nyi park Sevan," in *Natsional'nye parki SSSR: Neobkhodimost' organizatsii, status, perspektivy*, 59.
115. Iu. Chernichenko, "Spasenie Sevana," *Pravda*, June 9, 1968.
116. Iu. Arakelian, "Sevanu zhit'," *Pravda*, January 12, 1978.
117. Charogian, "Natsional'nyi park Sevan."
118. Bolokhnin and Kraminov, "Vse storony Sevana," 3.
119. L. Rosenburg, "Arkhitektura landshafta," *Literaturnaia gazeta*, June 12, 1967, 12.
120. Chernichenko, "Spasenie Sevana," 2.
121. B. Mkrtchian, "Glubiny i meli Sevana," *Izvestiia*, February 4, 1974, 5.
122. Ibid.
123. G. Arekelian, "Sevan zovet," *Pravda*, July 10, 1972, 4; B. Mkrtchian, "Drevnie liki Sevana," *Izvestiia*, July 17, 1972, 5.
124. Arakelian, "Sevanu zhit'." For similar articles that suggest that the park would give Sevan new life, see S. Bablumian, "Zelenoe ozherel'e Sevana," *Izvestiia*, February 9, 1978, 2; S. Bablumian, "Vozrozhdenie Sevana," *Izvestiia*, March 21, 1981, 1; "Sevana," *Literaturnaia gazeta*, November 19, 1980, 11.
125. GARF, fond A-259, opis' 48, delo 6118, 25; Order no. 1443 from July 14, 1972 of the Moscow City Executive Committee ordered the Main Architectural Planning Administration of the city of Moscow to develop the technical-economic foundations for the establishment of a nature park "Losinyi Ostrov." Bureau Obkoma KPSS i Sovet Ministrov Komi ASSR, Postanovlenie 233, May 28, 1971, personal archive of Alexander Kokovkin, Syktyvkar, Russian Federation.
126. V. Gladkov, "Natsional'nyi park Komi ASSR," *Okhota i okhotnich'e khoziaistvo* 2 (February 1972): 18–19; I. V. Zaboeva, *Prirodnyi park Komi ASSR* (Syktyvkar: Komi knizhnoe izdatel'stvo, 1977); E. A. Kotliarov, *Geografiia otdykha i turizma* (Moscow: Mysl', 1978); O. Matiatin and L. Pochivalov, "O Seligere—bez vosorgov," *Pravda*, March 16, 6; I. Lagunov, "Kamchatke nuzhen natsional'nyi park?," *Kamchatskaia pravda*, March 6 and 10, 1977; G. Adamiants, "Berech' lesa Chernomor'ia," *Pravda*, April 5, 1978, 3; A. Bannikov, "Garmoniia neprimirimogo," *Literaturnaia gazeta*, January 29, 1975, 13; V. Vapderin, "Mariiskii natsional'nyi park," *Izvestiia*, April 13, 1972, 3; F. Shtil'mark, "Chto ishchet chelovek s riukzakom," *Literaturnaia gazeta*, October 30, 1974, 11; N. G. Salatova, "Razvitie seti zapovednikov i prirodnykh parkov kak osnova gornykh landshaftov

Sibiri," in *Okhrana gornykh landshaftov Sibiri*, ed. G. V. Krylov (Novosibirsk: Nauka, 1973); A. K. Skvortsov, "Reka Ugra—zhemchuzhina srednerusskoi prirody," *Priroda* 9 (September 1980): 14–24; B. N. Likhanov, "Problemy Sibirskikh Al'p," *Priroda* 4 (April 1970): 98–102; N. Novikov, "Posle pozhara," *Literaturnaia gazeta*, August 13, 1975, 11; M. Voinstenskii, "Sozdadim prirodnye parki," *Izvestiia*, March 25, 1969, 3; S. S. Shvartz, B. P. Kolesnikov, and B. C. Riabinin, *Dialog o prirode* (Sverdlovsk: Sredne-Ural'skoe knizhnoe izdatel'stvo, 1977); E. Kucherov, "Sozdat' prirodnye parki v Bashkirii," *Okhota i okhotnich'e khoziaistvo* 11 (November 1980): 19; I. I. Lagunov, "Sokhranit' prirodu Kamchatki," *Okhrana prirody* 12 (December 1976): 72–83; V. S. Preobrazhenskii, "Sozdanie zon rekreatsii," in *Resursy biosfery na territorii SSSR*, ed. I. P. Gerasimov (Moscow, Nauka, 1971): 264–273; Iurii Abdashev, "Zapovednik ili natsional'niy park?," *Don* 4 (April 1974): 156–158.

127. N. Filippovskii, *Natsional'nyi park: Problema sozdaniia* (Moscow: Znanie, 1979), 8.
128. For works by the Kiev Scientific Research Institute of Urban Design, see I. D. Rodichkin, *Chelovek, sreda, otdykh* (Kiev: Budyvel'nik, 1977); K. Grigor'ev and V. Khandros, "Shatskoe divo," *Literaturnaia gazeta*, February 26, 1975, 11.
129. Oleg Volkov, "Ditia podroslo—odezhda zhmet," *Pravda*, February 22, 1977, 6; Oleg Volkov, "Chur' zapovedano," *Nash sovremenik* 1 (January 1973): 60–76; Oleg Volkov, *Chur' zapovedano!* (Moscow: Sovetskaia Rossiia, 1976); Bannikov, "Garmoniia neprimirimogo"; V. N. Likhanov, "Konstruktivnaia geografiia i okhrana prirody," *Okhrana prirody* (Moscow: Moskovskii filial geograficheskogo obshchestva SSSR, 1977)
130. Abukov, "Strana massovogo turizma," *Turist* 6 (June 1979): 2–3.
131. L. B. Popchiikovskii, ed., *Istoriia Moskovskogo sportivnogo turizma v litsakh* (Moscow: Moskovskii gorodskoi turklub, 2000), 6.
132. Diane Koenker, *Club Red: Vacation Travel and the Soviet Dream* (Ithaca, NY: Cornell University Press, 2013), 268.
133. Ibid.
134. Koenker, *Club Red*, 186, 215.
135. Ibid., 260.
136. Aleksandr Georgievich Nikolaevskii, *Natsional'nye parki* (Moscow: Agropromizdat, 1985), 5.
137. Christian Noack, "Brezhnev's Little Freedoms: Tourism, Individuality, and Mobility in the Late Soviet Period," in *Reconsidering Stagnation in the Brezhnev Era: Ideology and Exchange*, eds. Dina Fainberg and Artemy M. Kalinovsky (Lanham, MD: Lexington, 2016), 66.
138. G. Sapozhnikov, "Kletki v tigrovoi balke," *Literaturnaia gazeta*, September 30, 1974, 2.
139. N. A. Shkliaev and L. N. Shkol'nikova, *Organizatsiia i razmeshchenie prirodnykh parkov na territorii SSSR* (Moscow: Gosstroi, 1974), 36.
140. R. Dormidontov, "Borzhomi nuzhen natsional'nyi park," *Okhota i okhotnich'e khoziaistvo* 3 (March 1973), 22–23.
141. RGANTD, fond R-216, opis' 4–1, delo 140, 34.
142. "Postanovlenie verkhovnogo soveta: O merakh po dal'neishemu uluchsheniiu okhrany prirody i ratsional'nomu ispol'zovaniu prorodnykh resursov," *Izvestiia*, September 21, 1972, 1.
143. RGANTD, fond R-216, opis' 4–1, delo 370, 13.
144. "Berech' i umnozhat' bogatstva strany," *Pravda*, September 21, 1972, 3.
145. GAMO, opis' 1, delo 45, 26.
146. V. P. Geptner, "Chelovek v puti: Ego prava i obiazannosti," *Turist* 9 (1970): 7; V. K. Lukanenkova, ed., *Turizm i okhrana prirody—eksperimental'naia programma* (Leningrad, 1972), 5; P. A. Aristov et al, *Sbornik informatsionnykh materialov* 10 (Moscow: *Turist*, 1973), 6; A. Grun, "Po kodeksu serdtsia," *Turist* 7 (July 1971): 12; R. A. D'iakova, *Vospitanie berezhnogo otnosheniia k prirode v ekskursiiakh (Metodicheskie rekomendatsii)* (Moscow, 1976), 3; G. Genzhentsev and I. Berman, "Kasaetsia vsekh," *Turist* 5 (May 1976): 8.
147. Vera Chizhova, "Muzei zhivoi prirody," in *Natsional'nyi park: Problema sozdaniia*, ed. N. Filippovskii, 26; A. Golovach, "Natsional'nye parki neobkhodimy," *Okhota i okhotnich'e*

khoziaistvo 12 (1975): 20–21; G. Galazii, "Ne nabliudatel', no borets," *Turist* 2 (February 1968): 20; M. Cherkasova, "Turizm: Iavlenie planetarnoe," *Znanie-sila* 3 (1972): 10–13.

148. Shvartz, Kolesnikov, and Riabinin, *Dialog o prirode*, 1978.

149. Victoria Donovan, "'How Well Do You Know Your *Krai*?' The *Kraevedenie* Revival and Patriotic Politics in Late Khrushchev-Era Russia," *Slavic Review* 74, no. 3 (September 2015): 464–483. For an example of voluntarism in nature protection activities during the 1970s, see Douglas Weiner, *A Little Corner of Freedom: Russian Nature Protection from Stalin to Gorbachev* (Berkeley: University of California Press, 1999), 404–414.

150. V. Gens "Dokhody turizma—pribyl'—zdorov'iu, *Turist* 6 (June 1970): 3; V. I. Azar, *Otdykh trudiashchikhsia SSSR* (Moscow: Statistika, 1972); P. Oldak and T. S. Dagbatsyrenov, "Turizm: Otsenki i suzhdeniia," *Literaturnaia gazeta*, October 20, 1971, 13; I. P. Gerasimov and V. S. Preobrazhenskii, "Terriotorial'nye aspekty organizatsii industrii otdykha i turizma," in *Problemy razvitiia industrii turizma*, ed. P. G. Oldak (Novosibirsk: Akademiia nauk SSSR, 1970).

151. P. Oldak, "Liudiam—radost', kazne—dokhod," *Literaturnaia gazeta*, June 2, 1971, 13.

152. N. Gladkov, "Usilit' okhrana prirody," *Okhota i okhotnich'e khozaistvo* 9 (September 1972): 12–14. For examples on the "economic turn" in environmental protection see Visvaldis Litsis, "Ekologiia i ekonomika," *Priroda* 9 (September 1972): 25–29; N. P. Fedorenko, V. Ia. Lemeshev, and N. F. Reimers, "Sotsial'no-ekonomicheskaia effektivnost' okhrany prirody," *Priroda* 10 (October 1980): 2–13.

153. Valentin Ivanov, "Zlataia tsep' vremen," *Smena* 1223 (May 1978): 22-23; http://smena-online.ru/stories/zlataya-tsep-vremen/page/6.

154. A. Nasimovich, "Natsional'nye parki Afriki," *Okhota i okhotnich'e khoziaistvo* 6 (June 1971): 43.

155. RGANTD, fond R-216, opis' 4–1, delo 140, 34–35.

156. Robert Poole, *Earthrise: How Man First Saw the Earth* (New Haven, CT: Yale University Press, 2008).

157. V. A. Chichvarin, *Okhrana prirody i mezhdunarodnye otnosheniia* (Moscow: Izdatel'stvo Mezhdunarodnye otnosheniia, 1970).

158. Ibid., 39.

159. Ibid., 62.

160. Ibid., 62.

161. Ibid., 32.

162. Ibid.

163. Ibid., 171.

164. Stephen J. Macekura, *Of Limits and Growth: The Rise of Global Sustainable Development in the Twentieth Century* (Cambridge: Cambridge University Press, 2015), 96.

165. Chichvarin, *Okhrana prirody i mezhdunarodnye otnosheniia*, 33.

166. Macekura, *Of Limits and Growth*, 96.

167. Chichvarin, *Okhrana prirody i mezhdunarodnye otnosheniia*, 63.

168. Ibid., 122.

169. D. Gvishiani and K. Ananichev, "Otvet prorokam 'Sudnogo dnia,'" *Literaturnaia gazeta*, September 13, 1972, 11; M. Podgoronikov, "Paradoks dlinoi v sto let," *Literaturnaia gazeta*, August 13, 1975.

170. Paul Ehrlich, *The Population Bomb* (New York: Ballantine, 1970).

171. National Archives (College Park), Record Group 59 (General Records of the Department of State: Subject Numeric Files, 1970–1973), box 2949.

172. L. Efremov, "Zdorov'e planety," *Izvestiia*, June 4, 1974, 5; Sergei Gerasimov, "Nashe obshchee delo," *Literaturnaia gazeta*, September 29, 1971, 1.

173. A. Zaitsev, "Zabota o prirode," *Izvestiia*, November 15, 1972, 5; See Josephson et al., *Environmental History of Russia*, 191; Jacob Feygin, "Reforming the Cold War State: Economic Thought, Internationalization, and the Politics of Soviet Reform, 1955–1985" (PhD diss., University of Pennsylvania, 2017), 291; English, *Russia and the Idea of the West*, 171.

174. Mark Fiege, Adrian Howkins, and Jared Orsi, "Beyond the Best Idea: A Look at Mount Rainer, Antarctica, and the Sonoran Desert," in *National Parks beyond the Nation: Global*

Perspectives on "America's Best Idea," eds. Adrian Howkins, Jared Orsi, and Mark Fiege (Norman: University of Oklahoma Press, 2016), 29–33; Roderick Nash, *Wilderness and the American Mind*, 4th ed. (New Haven, CT: Yale University Press, 2014), 376.

175. Alfred Runte, *National Parks; The American Experience*, 4th ed. (Lanham, MD: Taylor, 2010), 164; Hugh Elliott, ed., *Second World Conference on National Parks* (Morges, Switzerland: IUCN, 1974), 16.
176. V. V. Krinitskii, "Protected Areas in the World's Industrially Advanced Regions: Importance, Progress, and Problems," in *Second World Conference on National Parks*, ed. Hugh Elliott (Morges, Switzerland: IUCN, 1974), 74.
177. Elliott, *Second World Conference on National Parks.*
178. V. V. Krinitskii, "Problemy zapovednogo dela," *Okhota i okhotnich'e khoziaistvo* 3 (March 1973): 2.
179. Ibid.
180. National Archives (College Park): RG 59, box 2947.
181. See B. Borisov, "Pravo i okhrana prirody v SShA," *Okhota i okhotnich'e khoziaistvo* 3 (March 1974): 40–42. See "U.S. and U.S.S.R. Sign Environmental Cooperation Treaty," *EPA* https://archive.epa.gov/epa/aboutepa/us-and-ussr-sign-environmental-cooperation-treaty.html.
182. Josephson et al, *Environmental History of Russia*, 195.
183. A. G. Bannikov, "Mezhdunarodnoe sotrudnichestvo v dele okhrany prirody," *Priroda* 1 (January 1973): 78–79.
184. Russell Train, "My dovol'ny peregovorami v Moskve," *Literaturnaia gazeta*, September 27, 1972, 11.
185. RGAE, fond 7486, opis' 40, delo 2594, 8–14.
186. Russell Train Papers, box 23, folder 9.
187. RGAE, 7486, opis' 6, delo 6428, 8.
188. RGAE, fond 544, opis' 2, delo 18; RGAE, fond 7486, opis' 40, delo 5860, 29. In 1974, Krinitskii and Bannikov visited six Canadian national parks. For articles on visits to African national parks, see A. Bannikov, Iu. Kuptsov, and V. Flint "Natsional'nye parki Kenii," *Okhota i okhotnich'e khoziaistvo* 9 (1973): 40–43; O. Gusev et al., "Natsional'nye parki Ameriki," *Okhota i okhotnich'e khoziaistvo* 6 (June 1978): 42–44; Nasimovich, "Natsional'nye parki Afriki." For other relevant articles, see O. Gusev, M. Shvetsov, and S. Kryvda, "Natsional'nye parki Ameriki," *Okhota i okhotnich'e khoziaistvo* 8 (August 1978): 42–43; V. V. Krinitskii, "Problemy zapovednogo dela," *Okhota i okhotnich'e khoziaistvo* 3 (March 1973): 1; A. G. Bannikiov and A. A. Krishchinskii, "V natsional'nykh parkakh Kanady," *Priroda* 7 (July 1975): 46–57.
189. Garret Hardin, "The Tragedy of the Commons," *Science* 162, no. 13 (December 1968): 1243–1248.
190. Alfred Runte, *National Parks: The American Experience*, 4th ed. (Lanham, MD: Taylor, 2010), 177–184; Sellars, *Preserving Nature in the National Parks*, 214.
191. N. Zabelina, "V natsional'nykh parkakh SShA," *Okhota i okhotnich'e khoziaistvo* 3 (March 1972): 42.
192. Nasimovich, "V natsional'nykh parkakh Ameriki: Medvedi i liudi," *Okhota i okhotnich'e khoziaistvo* 5 (May 1973): 42.
193. RGAE, fond 7486, opis' 40, delo 2594, 7.
194. For examples of such characterizations, see S. N. Solomina, "Problemy ekologicheskie i sotsial'nye," *Priroda* 2 (February 1975): 121–123.
195. A. Bannikov and V. Krinitskii, 1–2.
196. See A. Bochkarev, "Kar'er v zapovednike," *Volzhskaia kommuna*, October 29, 1981, 2.
197. Oleg Volkov, "Ditia podroslo—odezhda zhmet," *Pravda*, February 22, 1977, 6.
198. For an example of the continued discussion over the terminological issues, see S. Knizhnik, "Garmoniia neprimirimogo," *Literaturnaia gazeta*, January 29, 1975, 11.
199. RGAE, fond 544, opis' 2, delo 18, 187; see R. Dormidontov, "Borzhomi nuzhen natsional'nyi park," *Okhota i okhotnich'e khoziaistvo* 3 (March 1973): 22–23.
200. GARF, fond 7486, opis' 52, delo 2455, 60.
201. Shvartz, Kolesnikov, and Riabinin, *Dialog o prirode*, 211.

202. K. Mitriushkin, "Okhrana prirody v SSSR," *Okhota i okhotnich'e khoziaistvo* 3 (March 1977): 3.
203. 1977 Soviet Constitution, *Sait Konstututsii Rossiiskoi Federatsii*, http://constitution.garant.ru/history/ussr-rsfsr/1977/.
204. GARF, fond, 5496, opis' 112, delo, 951, 23.
205. V. V. Krinitskii, "Natsional'nie parki Sovetskogo Soiuza," in *Organizatsyia natsional'nykh parkov SSSR*, ed. Iurii Porfir'evich Iazan (Vilnius: Mintis, 1982), 13.
206. Ibid., 6.
207. "Postanovlenie Gosplana SSSR i GKNT ot 27 aprelia 1981 g. N 77/106 'Ob utverzdenii tipovykh polozhenii o gosudarstvennykh zapovednikakh, pamiatnikakh prirody, botanicheskikh sadakh i dendrologicheskikh parkakh, zoologicheskikh parkakh, zakaznikakh i prirodnykh natsional'nykh parkakh," *Dokipedia*, http://dokipedia.ru/document/5168764?pid=107.
208. Ibid.
209. Ibid.
210. Ibid.
211. Krinitskii, "Natsional'nye parki Sovetskovgo Soiuza," 19.
212. Fainberg and Kalinovsky, "Introduction," x.
213. The passage of the "Model Regulation" supports Douglas Weiner's argument that environmentalists felt greater freedom to push for change than many other groups in Soviet society. See Weiner, *Little Corner of Freedom*.

Chapter 4

1. For works that show the shared environmental history of Russian and American sides of Beringia, see Bathsheba Demuth, "The Walrus and the Bureaucrat: Energy, Ecology, and Making the State in the Russian and American Arctic, 1870–1950," *American Historical Review* 124, no. 2 (April 2019): 483–510; Bathsheba Demuth, *Floating Coast: An Environmental History of the Bering Strait* (New York: W. W. Norton, 2019).
2. Interview with Nataliia Zabelina, July 16, 2015, Moscow.
3. Robert English, *Russia and the Idea of the West: Gorbachev, Intellectuals, and the End of the Cold War* (New York: Columbia University Press, 2000), 2.
4. GARF, fond 262, opis' 17, delo 2332, 19 and 28.
5. Ibid., 14.
6. Feliks Shtil'mark, *A History of the Russian Zapovedniks* (Edinburgh: Russian Nature Press, 2002), 193.
7. Iu. Aleksandrova, *Ekonomika i organizatsiia zapovednikov i natsional'nykh parkov* (Moscow: Gosudarstvennyi komitet SSR po okhrane prirody, 1991), 32.
8. For examples, see V. Petrov, "Prirodno-zapovednyi fond: Ob"ekt upravleniia i okhrany," *Okhota i okhotnich'e khoziaistvo* 4 (April 1983): 14; A. Shalybkov, "Sozdat' edinyi organ upravleniia," *Okhota i okhotnich'e khoziaistvo* 5 (May 1983): 20; Iu. Gorelov, "Ne zabyvat' o sevodniashnikh nuzhdakh," *Okhota i okhotnich'e khoziaistvo* 5 (May 1983): 21; B. Borisov, "Sistema okhraniaemykh territorii—edinoe rukovodstvo," *Okhota i okhotnich'e khoziaistvo* 11 (November 1983): 14; K. Storchevoi, "Natsional'nye parki: Kakim im byt'?" *Okhota i okhotnich'e khoziaistvo* 7 (July 1988): 17. Storechevoi argued that all national parks in the USSR needed to be under the State Committee of Nature Protection (Goskompriroda) USSR; K. Zykov, "Kto dolzhen soderzhat' natsional'nye parki?" *Okhota i okhotnich'e khoziaistvo* 3 (1988): 20; G. Sukhudian, "Byt' khoziaevami svoei territorii," *Okhota i okhotnich'e khoziaistvo* 5 (May 1988): 11–12; M. Pridnia and A. Kudaktin, "Sochinskii prirodnyi, natsional'nyi park: Proekt i real'nost'," *Okhota i okhotnich'e khoziaistvo* 11 (November 1988): 21.
9. For more on Rasputin's environmental protection advocacy see Valentin Rasputin, *Sibir', Sibir'* (Moscow: Molodaia gvardiia, 1991).
10. A. Bachnetsov, G. Vsdornov, V. Krupin, V. Rasputin, S Yamshikov, "Ne terpit otlagatel'stv: Sozdanie natsional'nogo parka 'Russkii Sever'," *Pravda*, September 13, 1990.
11. Arkady Ostrovsky, *The Invention of Russia: The Rise of Putin and the Age of Fake News* (New York: Viking, 2016), 93.

12. GAIO, R-3523, opis' 1, delo 44, 136.
13. GARF, A-259, opis' 48, delo 9334, 77.
14. V. Koveshnikov, "Kakoi byt' zavtra Mogutovoi Gore," *Volzhskaia kommuna*, February 28, 1988.
15. For more on the command economy's incentive system, see Marshall Goldman, *Environmental Pollution in the USSR: The Spoils of Progress* (Cambridge, MA: MIT Press, 1971).
16. V. V. Krinitskii, "Natsional'nye parki Sovetskogo Soiuza," in *Organizatsiia natsional'nykh parkov SSSR*, ed. Iurii Porfir'evich Iazan (Vilnius: Mintis, 1982), 19; Valerii Vokhmianin, "V raione Sochi," *Priroda i chelovek* 3 (March 1987): 40.
17. GARF, A-259, opis' 48, delo 9334, 81.
18. GARF, A-259, opis' 17, delo 4458, 215.
19. Ibid., 214.
20. P. Iakovlev, "Gostepriimnoe Priel'brus'e," *Pravda*, September 19, 1989, 6.
21. K. N. Blagosklonov and V. N. Tikhomirov, *Okhrana prirody* (Moscow, 1967). This was the first book published in the USSR that focused on the teaching of environmental protection. For articles that discuss the problems of urban forests and the nature protection brigades, see "Turizm: Iavlenie planetarnoe," *Znanie-Sila* 3 (March 1968): 42. For other examples of the problems of tourism in urban forests at the time, see R. Akchurin et al, "Kul'tura otdykha," *Pravda*, June 7, 1966, 4; Iu. Efremov, "Krasa rodnogo kraia," *Pravda*, July 1, 1966, 4; G. Galazii, "Ne Nabliudatel' no borets," *Turist* 2 (1968): 20; V. Petrov, "Prishestvie iz goroda," *Izvestiia*, July 21, 1970, 6; M. Cherkasova, "Turizm: Iavlenie planetarnoe," *Znanie-Sila* 3 (March 1972): 10–13. For more on Blagosklonov's role in the nature protection brigades, see Douglas Weiner, *A Little Corner of Freedom: Russian Nature Protection from Stalin to Gorbachev* (Berkeley: University of California Press, 1999), 406–414.
22. Interview with Boris Samoilov, September 16, 2014, Moscow.
23. GARF, A-259, opis' 48, delo 6118, 25.
24. IUCN, *IUCN Tenth General Assembly* (Morges, Switzerland: UNESCO, 1970), 156.
25. Interview with Boris Samoilov, September 16, 2014.
26. M. Chernolusskii and M. Belavin, "Trevoga nad ostrovom," *Literaturnaia gazeta*, March 29, 1978, 10.
27. Interview with Boris Samoilov, September 16, 2014.
28. B. L. Samoilov, "Kakim byt' natsional'nomu parku," *Priroda i chelovek* 5 (May 1988): 23.
29. National park supporters repeatedly argued that nature was an absolute necessity for urbanites. See Aleksandr Georgievich Nikolaevskii, *Natsional'nye parki* (Moscow: Agropromizdat, 1985), 5.
30. Samoilov, "Kakim byt' natsional'nomu parku," 23.
31. Ibid., 22.
32. GARF, A-259, opis' 48, delo 6118, 6.
33. V. Elufimov, "V lesu prigorodnom," *Sel'skaia zhizn'*, February 6, 1983.
34. GARF, A-259, opis' 48, delo 6118, 34.
35. Ibid., 34.
36. Ibid., 4.
37. V. Tsepliaev, "Kak berech' elku," *Izvestiia*, December 24, 1984, 6.
38. RGAE, fond 709, opis' 1, delo 310, 117. The park had only two ecological trails, no visitor center, and no land use plan by 1990. Also see TsGAM, fond 3200, opis' 1, delo 10, 18. In 1985, there were forty-one illegal cuts.
39. TsGAM, fond 3200, opis' 1, delo 10, 18; TsGAM, fond 3200, opis' 1, delo 26, 28.
40. V. Korneev, "Teni u losinogo ostrova," *Izvestiia*, September 21, 1987, 3; V. Korneev, "I na ostavshuiushchsia dich'," *Izvestiia*, September 12, 1987, 3; A. Ileesh and E. Shestiinskii, "Na okhotu v zapovednik," *Izvestiia*, August 30, 1987, 2.
41. A. Gorokhov, "Chelovek, zakon, i Losinyi Ostrov," *Izvestiia*, October 14, 1990, 44.
42. TsGAM, fond 3200, opis' 1, delo 41, 1.
43. V. Korneev, "Park pod vedomstvennym natiskom," *Izvestiia*, October 4, 1988, 3; A. Batygin and R. Fedorov, "Iauza bez lodochki," *Pravda*, December 24, 1988, 3.
44. G. Charodeev, "Pust' u nashei zemli budet svoi Losiniy Ostrov," *Izvestiia*, October 25, 1987, 1.

45. V. V. Dezhkin, ed., "Nelegkaia sud'ba Losinki," *V mire zapovednoi prirody* (Moscow: Sovetskaia Rossiia, 1989), 2.
46. Stephen Macekura, *Of Limits and Growth: The Rise of Global Sustainable Development in the Twentieth Century* (Cambridge: Cambridge University Press, 2015), 252.
47. B. L. Samoilov, "Kakim byt' natsional'nomu parku," 49.
48. B. L. Samoilov, N. M. Zabelina, and G. V. Morozova, "Natsional'nyi park," *Priroda i chelovek* 1 (January 1987): 46 and 48; GARF, A-262, opis' 17, delo 5373, 27.
49. GARF: A-262, opis' 17, delo 5373, 33.
50. GARF, fond 262, opis' 17, delo 6086, 138.
51. Ibid., 34.
52. GARF, fond 5446, opis' 150, delo 689, 10.
53. www.net-film.ru. "Kinozhurnal novosti dnia," Kinodokument no. 14651.
54. GARF, fond 5549, opis' 150, delo 687, 9.
55. "Kinozhurnal stroitel'stvo i arkhitektura" (8) 1989. www.net-film.ru, Kinodokument no. 49238.
56. TASS, "Pomoshch' Losinomu Ostrovu," *Pravda*, July 30, 1989, 2.
57. "Pomoshch' Losinomu Ostrovu," *Izvestiia*, September 14, 1989.
58. L. Sokol'chik and V. Shkatov, "Iz pochty AIF," *Argumenty i fakty*, February 17, 1990, 3.
59. R. Danilov, "Moskva na poroge energeticheskogo krizisa," *Izvestiia*, June 3, 1991, 3; Iu. Luzhkov, "Pochemu u nas v khoziaistvennykh delakh kak v futbole, razbiraiutsia vse," *Literaturnaia gazeta*, July 23, 1992, 11.
60. RGAE, fond 709, opis' 1, delo 310, 117. For similar comments, see "Losinyi Ostrov i ego zakhvatchiki," *Moskovskaia pravda*, October 18, 1990, 1.
61. RGAE, fond 709, opis' 1, delo 310, 119.
62. Iu. A. Shtiurmer, *Ekologicheskoe vospitanie turistov v turistkoi sektsii i klube* (Moscow: Turist, 1990), 24.
63. Nataliia Zabelina, *Natsional'nyi park* (Moscow: Mysl', 1987).
64. I. G. Ivanov, *Natsional'nye parki: Opyt SSSR i SShA—po materialism sovetsko-amerikanskogo seminara* (Moscow, 1990), 15.
65. Ibid., 54.
66. For a recent title on the economic reforms of the Gorbachev era, see Chris Miller, *The Struggle to Save the Soviet Economy: Mikhail Gorbachev and the Collapse of the USSR* (Chapel Hill: University of North Carolina Press, 2016).
67. See N. G. Salatova, "Razvitie seti zapovednikov i prirodnykh parkov kak osnova gornykh landshaftov Sibiri," in *Okhrana gornykh landshaftov Sibiri*, ed. G. V. Krylov (Novosibirsk: Nauka, 1973), 199. Also see RGAE, fond 544, opis' 1, delo 135, 51.
68. For examples of such propagandistic literature, see A. N. Akhutin, *Preobrazovanie rek SSSR* (Moscow: Voenizdat, 1950); I. M. Tsunts, *Velikie stroiki na rekakh Sibiri* (Moscow: Gospolitizdat, 1956); A. V. Markin, *Budushchee elektrifikatsii SSSR* (Moscow: Politicheskaia literatura, 1959); M. Davydov and T. Tsunts, *Ot Volkhova do Amura* (Moscow: Sovetskaia Rossiia, 1958), 325; M. Vasil'ev, *Voda rabotaet* (Moscow: Gostekhizdat, 1956); E. V. Boldakov, *Zhizn' rek* (Moscow: Gostekhizdat, 1953); S. F. Shershov, *Belyi ugol'* (Moscow: Gosenergoizdat, 1957).
69. Valentin Rasputin, *Farewell to Matyora*, trans. Antonina W. Bouis (Evanston, IL: Northwestern University Press, 1990).
70. Z. Aleksandrova, "U budushchei GESa," *Izvestiia*, June 27, 1981.
71. Z. Aleksandrova, "Pervaia stupen' kaskada," *Izvestiia*, October 8, 1983, 2; V. Sapov, "Dorogami Altaia," *Pravda*, March 10, 1982, 6; V. Sapov, "Katun bez legendy," *Pravda*, July 13, 1984, 6.
72. For more on the successful opposition to the river diversion project, see Robert S. Darst "Environmentalism in the USSR: The Opposition to the River Diversion Projects," *Soviet Economy* 4, no. 3 (March 1988): 223–252; Philip Micklin and Andrew Bond, "Reflections on Environmentalism and the River Diversions Projects," *Soviet Economy* 4, no. 3 (March 1988): 253–274; Philip M. Micklin, "The Fate of 'Sibaral': Soviet Water Projects in the Gorbachev Era," *Central Asia Review* 6, no. 2 (June 1987): 67–88; Philip M. Micklin, "The Status of the Soviet Union's Northern Water Transfer Projects before Their Abandonment in 1985–1986," *Soviet Geography* 27, no. 5 (May 1986): 287–329.

73. Iu. Vinokorov and N. Vitovtsev, "O deshevykh kilovattakh reki Katun," *Pravda*, December 1, 1986, 2.
74. "V tsentre vnimaniia—Katunskaia GES," *Zvezda Altaia*, November 17, 1989, 1; V. Elin, "Izuchit' i sokhranit'," *Zvezda Altaia*, January 19, 1989, 4; V. Kubarev, "Po sledam Sartakpaia," *Zvezda Altaia*, January 4, 1989, 4.
75. Valentin Rasputin, *Siberia, Siberia*, translated by Gerald Mickelson (Evanston, IL: Northwestern University Press, 1996), 207.
76. Ibid.
77. Open letter, "Trevozhnoe pis'mo," *Komsomolskaia pravda*, March 21, 1987, 2.
78. Ibid.
79. S. Brovashov, "U poslednei reki," *Komsomolskaia pravda*, March 21, 1987, 2.
80. Rasputin, *Siberia, Siberia*, 205.
81. Iu. Markov, "Vazhno izvlech' riad urokov," *Zvezda Altaia*, August 19, 1987.
82. "Chelovek i priroda," *Zvezda Altaia*, September 8, 1987; "Chelovek i priroda," *Zvezda Altaia*, September 10, 1987, 3; A. Surazakov, "Dve tochki zreniia," *Zvezda Altaia*, April 21, 1987, 3; "Dialog o katunskikh GES," *Zvezda Altaia*, May 12, 1987.
83. F. Shtilmark, "Trevozhnaia Sud'ba Katuni" *Turist* 11 (1987), 18.
84. V. Vostrepov, "Chtoby sokhranit' prirodu," *Zvezda Altaia*, July 18, 1989, 1; I. Sumachkov, "Nel'zia molchat'," *Zvezda Altaia*, July 21, 1989, 2; "Katunskaia GES: Kto za i kto protiv," *Zvezda Altaia*, September 19, 1989, 2; "Perekrestok mnenii," *Zvezda Altaia*, July 11, 1989, 2.
85. GARF, fond A-259, opis' 49, delo 2371, 13.
86. GARF, fond 10026, opis' 4, delo 1530, 53–54.
87. *Katunskii proekt: Problemy ekspertizy: Materialy k obshchestvenno-nauchnoi konferentsii, 13-15* April, 1990 (Novosibirsk: Akademiia Nauk SSSR), 95.
88. Ibid., 97–102; UNESCO Archives, box 135, File Plan SC/ECO/5865/8.51.534, UDC 502.7, A101, WHC (46)
89. GARF, fond 10026, opis' 4, delo 1530, 90.
90. GARF, fond 10026, opis' 4, delo 2545, 12–13, 16. For more on the Brundtland Commission, see Joachim Radkau, *The Age of Ecology: A Global History*, trans. Patrick Camiller (Cambridge, UK: Polity, 2014), 386–387.
91. V. Varvanets, "Parlamentskii komitet protiv GES na Katuni," *Zvezda Altaia*, September 5, 1990, 1.
92. GARF, fond 10026, opis' 4, delo 1530, 30.
93. Ibid., 9.
94. N. M. Zabelina, *Vspominaiu institut, kolleg, prirodu* (Moscow: Green Print, 2019), 246.
95. Ibid., 246.
96. I. Lagunov, "Kamchatke nuzhen natsional'nyi park?," *Kamchatskaia pravda*, March 6, 1977, 3.
97. GAKK, fond 587, opis' 1, delo 111, 27; O. Dziub, "Okhrannaia gramota," *Kamchatskaia pravda*, June 25, 1982, 3.
98. RGAE, fond 7486, opis' 52, delo 2455, 59.
99. A. G. Algarova, "Otdykh—na sluzhbu ekonomike: O probleme sozdaniia zony otdykha na Kamchatke," *Kamchatskii komsomolets*, December 24, 1981, 3; Pavel Torokhov, "Kamchatskimi marshrutami," *Kamchatskii komsomolets*, December 24, 1981; RGAE, fond 7486, opis' 52, delo 3375, 181. For an article about a later trip of the Central Scientific Institute for the Protection of Nature, see Iu. Shut, "Natsional'nyi park: Kakim emu byt'?," *Novaia zhizn'*, November 11, 1989, 2. For an account of one of Zabelina's trips to the Valley of Geysers, see N. Zabelina and N. Aralova, "Esli vstretish'." *Turist* 7 (July 1985): 22–23.
100. For examples of such films see A. Borontsov, *Zdes' sol'ntse rodiny vstaet*, 1983 (net-film.ru); V. Shorokhov, *Kroniki nashikh dnei*, 47 (1982). net-film.ru; I. Galin, *Za vzletom vzlet*, 1982; D. Mamedov and M. Mamedov, *Shestaia chast' sveta*, 1983.
101. N. M. Zabelina, *Vspominaiu institut, kolleg, prirodu* (Moscow, 2019), 154.
102. Vladislav Anikeev, "Kamchatskie geizery," *Priroda i chelovek* 6 (June 1982): 41; V. Vasil'ev, "Dolina dlia izbrannykh?," *Literaturnaia gazeta*, August 5, 1987, 11; V. Mertsalov, "Ni pora li otkryt' Kamchatku?," *Turist* 9 (September 1990): 6–7. He writes, "But the Ministry of the Maritime Fleet sends tourists to Iceland, New Zealand, and all corners of the world. Why is Kamchatka neglected, which has untouched, unique beauty more striking than anything I have ever seen?"

103. For some articles on the Valley of Geysers in the central press see "Kliuch ot Kamchatki," *Pravda*, May 24, 1990, 8; Valerii Bikasov, "Skol'ko stoit dolina geizerov," *Svet* 8 (August 1990): 39. Also see Vasil'ev, "Dolina dlia izbrannykh?," 11; L. Gromova, "Dolinu geizerov otkryvat' nado," *Leninskoe znamia*, September 22, 1990.
104. See A. Paperno, "Trolleibusom—v Dolinu geizerov," *Kamchatskii komsomolets*, May 6, 1989, 2; A. Papernko, "Nuzhen li Kamchatke valiutnyi turizm," *Kamchatskaia pravda*, December 23, 1989, 3; Maya Zalite and Lidiia Radinova, "Tam gde slyshno i vidno, kak dyshit zemlia," *Nauka i tekhnika* 8 (August 1989): 22–25.
105. A. Zhigulin, "Udivitel'noe riadom no ono zapreshcheno," *Kamchatskii komsomolets*, September 29, 1987.
106. Mertsalov, "Ni pora li otkryt' Kamchatku?," 22; Bikasov, "Skol'ko stoit dolina geizerov," 17; Paperno, "Trolleibusom—v Dolinu geizerov."
107. Zhigulin, "Udivitel'noe riadom no ono zapreshcheno." Zhigulin writes, "Unfortunately, today tourists from the mainland, yes, and Kamchatkans themselves, can only admire the beauty of the peninsula on the screen of the television."
108. Miller, *Struggle to Save the Soviet Economy*, 28.
109. A. Milovskii, "Ne zhdut na beregu turista," *Sovetskaia kul'tura*, December 25, 1986, 3.
110. I. Dvorov, "Kamchatskoe teplo," *Kamchatskii komsomolets*, April 8, 1986, 3.
111. I. Pavlikhin, "Prognoz podtverdilsia," *Pravda*, November 16, 1980; B. Kashintsev, "Resursy zemli Kamchatskoi," *Pravda*, December 16, 1981; A. Kurin, "Kamchatskii ugol'," *Kamchatskaia pravda*, June 15, 1982; R. Bakmukhamedov, "Kamchatskii gaz," *Izvestiia*, April 19, 1987.
112. Mertsalov, "Ni pora li otkryt' Kamchatku?," 23.
113. V. S. Kirpichnikov, "Sud'ba Kamchatki v nashikh rukakh!," *Priroda* 11 (November 1990): 40.
114. GAKK, fond 855, opis' 1, 4.
115. GAKK, fond 855, opis' 1, 5.
116. V. Semenov, *V kraiu zaoblachnykh vershin* (Petropavlovsk: Dal'nevostochnoe knizhnoe izdatel'stvo, 1970); V. Semenov, *V kraiu vulkanov i geizerov* (Moscow: Fizkul'tura i sport, 1973); V. I. Semenov, *Po vulkanam i goriachim istochnikam Kamchatki* (Petropavlovsk: Dal'n evostochnoe knizhnoe izdatel'stvo, 1983).
117. GAKK, fond 855, opis' 1, delo 90, 8.
118. Ibid.
119. GAKK, fond 855, opis' 1, delo 91, 19.
120. Ibid.
121. Interview with Men'shikov, April 20, 2015. Moscow, Russian Federation.
122. GAKK, fond 855, opis' 1, delo 90, 9.
123. Ibid., 6.
124. GAKK, fond 855, opis' 1, delo 91, 11.
125. Ibid., 13.
126. V. I. Semenov, *V kraiu goriachikh istochnikov* (Petropavlovsk: Dal'nevostochnoe knizhnoe izdatel'stvo, 1988), 140.
127. N. M. Zabelina, *Vspominaiu institut, kolleg, prirodu* (Moscow, 2019), 154–193.
128. Iu. Slezin, "Zachem Kamchatke flot," *Kamchatskaia pravda*, August 13, 1990.
129. See Michael S. Quinn, Len Broberg, and Wayne Freimund, ed., *Parks, Peace, and Partnership: Global Initiatives in Transboundary Conservation* (Calgary: University of Calgary Press, 2012).
130. Personal archive of Nataliia Zabelina.
131. Ibid.
132. RGAE fond 709, opis' 1, delo 310, 164.
133. Ibid.
134. International Park Program, *Beringia Heritage: A Reconnaissance Study of Sites and Recommendations* (Denver: National Park Service, 1989).
135. Frank Graham, Jr. "US and Soviet Environmentalists Join Forces across the Bering Strait," *Audubon*, July-August 1991, 53.
136. Paul Schurke, *Bering Bridge: The Soviet American Expedition from Siberia to Alaska* (Minneapolis: Pheifer-Hamilton, 1989), 9.

137. Patty A. Gray, *The Predicament of Chukotka's Indigenous Movement: Post Soviet Activism in the Russian Far North* (Cambridge: Cambridge University Press, 2005), 30.
138. Odd Arne Westad, *The Cold War: A Global History* (New York: Basic Books, 2016), 575.
139. See Yuri Slezkine, *Arctic Mirrors: Russia and the Small Peoples of the North* (Ithaca, NY: Cornell University Press, 1994), 133.
140. Ibid.
141. Schurke, *Bering Bridge*, front matter (n.p.).
142. Graham, "US and Soviet Environmentalists Join Forces across the Bering Strait," 53.
143. Hugh Elliott, ed., *Second World Conference on National Parks* (Morges, Switzerland: IUCN, 1974), 295.
144. National Archives (College Park) RG 59, box 2947.
145. "Beringiia," *Krainii sever*, July 6, 1995; Seventeenth Session of the General Assembly of IUCN and Seventeenth Technical Meeting, San Jose, Costa Rica, February 1–10, 1988, 142.
146. "SShA-SSSR, most vzaimodeistviia cherez Beringov proliv," *Izvestiia*, November 24, 1988.
147. *Beringian Heritage: A Reconnaissance Study of Sites and Recommendations.*
148. Ibid., 4.
149. Ibid.
150. Ibid., 2.
151. Frank Graham Jr., "US and Soviet Environmentalists Join Forces Across the Bering Straight," *Audubon* (July–August 1991), 45.
152. GARF, fond 10200, opis' 4, delo 4479, 127.
153. Ibid.
154. Ibid., 11.
155. GARF, fond, 10026, opis' 4, delo 892, 3.
156. Ibid.
157. Ibid.
158. Ibid., 66.

Chapter 5

1. Peter Mathiessen, *Baikal: Sacred Sea of Siberia* (San Francisco: Sierra Club Books, 1992), 3.
2. Bratsk was the classic case of such a city in Siberia. Located on the Angara River, which flows out of Baikal, the Bratsk dam was touted as the transformative project that would help make Siberia a center of Soviet industry.
3. L. Sheviakov, "Plodotvornaia rabota nauchnoi konferentsii," *Izvestiia*, August 12, 1947, 3. The plan was originally discussed conferences in 1931 and 1933. See I. G. Aleksandrov, *Problema Angary* (Moscow: Gosudarstvennoe sotsial'no-ekonomicheskoe izdatel'stvo, 1931); Gosplan SSSR, *Trudy pervoi Vsesoiuznoi konferentsii po razmeshcheniiu proizvoditel'nykh sil Soiuza SSR* 16, *Angaro-Eniseiskaia problema.* (Sovetskaia Aziia, 1932). See Boris Pomytkin, *Doch' Baikala* (Moscow: Gidrometeoizdat, 1961).
4. A. N. Akhutin, *Preobrazovanie rek SSSR* (Moscow: Voenizdat, 1950), 79–82; I. M. Tsunts, *Velikie stroiki na rekakh Sibiri* (Moscow: Gospolitizdat, 1956); A.V. Markin, *Budushchee elektrifikatsii SSSR* (Moscow: Politicheskaia literatura, 1959); M. Davydov and T. Tsunts, *Ot Volkhova do Amura* (Moscow: Sovetskaia Rossiia, 1958), 325; M. Vasil'ev, *Voda rabotaet* (Moscow: Gostekhizdat, 1956); E. V. Boldakov, *Zhizn' rek* (Moscow: Gostekhizdat, 1953); S. F. Shershov. *Belyi ugol'* (Moscow: Gosenergoizdat, 1957).
5. Nicholas Breyfogle, "At the Watershed: 1958 and the Beginnings of Lake Baikal Environmentalism," *East European Review* 93, no. 1 (January 2015): 147–180; Douglas Weiner, *A Little Corner of Freedom: Russian Nature Protection from Stalin to Gorbachev* (Berkeley: University of California Press, 1999), 357; Paul Josephson, *New Atlantis Revisited: Akademgorodok, the Soviet City of Science* (Princeton, NJ: Princeton University Press, 1997), 163–203; Thomas B. Rainey, "Siberian Writers and the Struggle to Save Lake Baikal," *Environmental History Review* 15, no. 1 (Spring 1991): 46–60.
6. Ia. M. Grushko, *Puteshestvie po Baikalu dlia otdykha i ukrepleniia zdorov'ia* (Irkutsk: Irkutskoe knizhnoe izdatel'stvo, 1956); V. N. Skalon, *Po Sibiri: V pomoshch' turistam* (Moscow: Izdatel'stvo VTsSPS, 1953).

7. For Skalon's efforts to address the pollution problem, see Breyfogle, "At the Watershed," 165; V. N. Skalon, "Pust' Baikal budet velichaishim iz velichaishikh zapovednikov mira," *Pravda Buryatii*, September 11, 1958, 2.
8. A. Bochkin et al., "V zashchitu Baikala," *Literaturnaia gazeta*, October 21, 1958, 2.
9. F. Taurin, "Baikal dolzhen byt' zapovednikom," *Literaturnaia gazeta*, February 10, 1959, 2.
10. G. I. Galazii, "Prirodnye bogatstva Sibiri nado ispol'zovat' v interesakh naroda," *Vostochno-Sibiriskaia pravda*, September 25, 1959, 3; O. Gusev, "Baikal pered nami: K voprosu o sozdanii zakaznika na Baikale," *Zvezda* 5 (1961): 173.
11. For tourist guidebooks on Baikal, see Oleg Volkov, *Puteshestvie po Baikalu* (Moscow: Sovetskaia Rossiia, 1958); Ia. M. Grushko, *Kurorty Vostochnoi Sibiri* (Irkutsk: Irkutskoe knizhnoe izdatel'stvo, 1961); B. R. Buiantev, *K narodnokhoziaistvennym problemam Baikala* (Ulan-Ude: Buriatskoe knizhnoe izdatel'stvo, 1960); B. V. Bashkuev and R. F. Tugutov, *Po Buryatii: Turistskie marshruty* (Ulan-Ude: Buriatskoe knizhnoe izdatel'stvo, 1961); V. V. Lamakin, *Po beregam i ostrovam Baikala* (Moscow: Nauka, 1965); L. L. Rossolimo, *Baikal* (Moscow: Nauka, 1966); O. K. Gusev, *Po severnomu Baikalu i Pribaikal'iu* (Moscow: Fizkul'tura i sport, 1966); O. K., Gusev, *Ot Barguzinzkogo zapovednika do Ushkan'ikh Ostrovov* (Irkutsk: Irkutskoe knizhnoe izdatel'stvo, 1960); V. V. Lamakin, *Po beregam i ostrovam Baikala* (Moscow: Nauka, 1965).
12. ANIIO, fond 2948, opis' 1, delo 5, 38.
13. ARAN, fond 1858, opis' 1, delo 24, 14.
14. P. K. Oldak, "Industriia turizma—odno iz vedushchikh napravlenii razvitiia sovremennoi ekonomiki," in *Problemy razvitiia industrii turizma*, ed. P. G. Oldak (Novosibirsk: AN SSSR:, 1970), 4.
15. L. Shinkarev, "Vokrug Baikala," *Izvestiia*, November 17, 1965, 6; A. Merkulov, "Trevoga o Baikale," *Pravda*, February 28, 1965, 1; B. Rubtsov, "Baikal nasha obshchaia zabota," *Literaturnaia gazeta*, December 13, 1967, 1; "Poezdka na Baikale," *Literaturnaia gazeta*, January 29, 1966, 2; Iakov Mikhailovich Grushko, "Krai tselebnykh istochnikov," *Izvestiia*, October 7, 1965, 6; L. Shinkarev, "Baikala shchedryi dar," *Izvestiia*, September 23, 1965, 6; I. P. Gerasimov, "Proekt baikalsko'go natsional'nogo parka," *Preobrazovanie prirody i razvitie geograficheskoi nauki v SSSR* (Moscow: Znanie, 1967), 60; Oleg Volkov, "Slavnoe more," *Literaturnaia gazeta*, October 6, 1966, 2; V. Timofeev, "Sviashchennyi Baikal: O stroitel'stve na Baikale natsional'nogo parka," *Sovetskaia molodezh'*, February 6, 1966, 2; O. Gusev and A. Nasimovich, "Barguzinskii zapovednik i natsional'nyi park," *Okhota i okhotnich'e khoziaistvo* 12 (December 1966): 1–3; Iu. A. D'iakonov, "Natsional'nyi park u ozera Baikal," *Stroitel'stvo i arkhitektura Leningrada* 1 (January 1966): 17; I. P. Gerasimov, *Preobrazovanie prirody i razvitie geograficheskoi nauki v SSSR* (Moscow: Znanie, 1967); I. P. Gerasimov and G. I. Galazii, *Goluboe serdtse Sibiri* (Moscow: Znanie, 1966), 15.
16. L. Shinkarev, "Baikala shchedryi dar," *Izvestiia*, September 24, 1965, 4.
17. Ibid. 95.
18. Ibid., 95.
19. Robert English, *Russia and the Idea of the West: Gorbachev, Intellectuals, and the End of the Cold War* (New York: Columbia University Press, 2000), 96.
20. V. I. Bologna, *Vnerabochee vremia i uroven'zhizni trudiashchikhsia* (Novosibirsk: Siberian Branch AN USSR, 1964), 19.
21. Ibid., 99.
22. Ibid.
23. Oldak, *Problemy razvitiia industrii turizma*, 12.
24. Ibid., 13.
25. Ibid., 8.
26. Ibid., 9.
27. Ibid., 22.
28. D. R. Darbanov, ed., *Voprosy razvitiia industrii turizma na Baikale* (Ulan-Ude: Buriatskoe knizhnoe izdatel'stvo, 1973), 65.
29. GAIO, fond R-2844, opis' 1, delo 34, 25–26; V. Sharov, "Trevoga v Bukhte Peschanoi," *Pravda*, August 2, 1967, 6; "Budut novye turbazy na Baikale," *Pravda*, September 28, 1967, 3; V. Novgorodov, Shchepotka zla," *Vostochno-Sibirskaia pravda*, July 31, 1968, 4; Oleg Volkov, "Slavnoe more," *Literaturnaia gazeta*, October 6, 1966, 2.

30. Iu. B. Khromov and V. A. Kliushin, *Organizatsiia zon otdykha i turizma na poberezh'e Baikala* (Moscow: Stroiizdat, 1976), 49; Iu. A. D'iakonov and I. A. Evlakhov, "Natsional'nyi park u ozera Baikal," *Stroitel'stvo i arkhitektura Leningrada* 1 (January 1966): 16–17.
31. GAIO, fond 2844, opis' 1, delo 34, 14.
32. Skalon did eventually receive fifteen thousand rubles for this work, but he does not indicate who provided the funds.
33. GAIO, R-2844, opis' 1, delo 90, 33.
34. Ibid., 34.
35. Ibid.
36. GAIO, R-2844, opis' 1, delo 142, 223.
37. GAIO, R-2844, opis' 1, delo 90, 34.
38. Ibid., 31.
39. Ibid.
40. Ibid., 40.
41. GAIO, R-2844, opis' 1, delo 90, 44.
42. Ibid., 56.
43. Ibid., 52.
44. I. P. Gerasimov, A. A. Mints, V. S. Preobrazhenskii, and N. P. Shelemov, "Estestvennye resursy. Okhrana i preobrazovanie prirody," *Izvestiia Akademii Nauk SSSR: Seriia geograficheskaiia* 4 (April 1969): 43; V. S. Preobrazhenskii and Iu. A. Vedenin, *Geografiia i otdykh* (Moscow: Znanie, 1971), 34; I. P. Gerasimov, V. S. Preobrazhenskii, A. S. Abramov, D. L. Armand, S. V. Zon, I. V. Komar, G. M. Lappo, N. F. Leontev, and Ia. G Mashbisch, *Teoreticheskie osnovy rekreatsionnoi geografii* (Moscow: Nauka, 1975), 17.
45. E. Erlomaev, "Zhivaia voda Baikala," *Pravda*, October 8, 1978, 3; O. Gusev, "Okaiannyi avtograf," *Literaturnaia gazeta*, November 22, 1978, 11; V. Khodin, "Baikalu—okhrannaia gramota," *Pravda*, November 20, 1974, 6.
46. RGAE, fond 7486, opis' 33, delo 22, 35; Oleg Gusev, "Baikal," *Smena* 13 (July 1977): 16–21; Oleg Gusev, "Sobolinyi krai," *Smena* 5 (March 1979): 16–17; A. Tivanenko, "Byt' natsional'nomu parku: Problema sozdaniia natsparka SSSR na beregu Baikala," *Vostochno-Sibirskaia pravda*, August 15, 1973; B. K. Moskalenko, *Baikal: Segodnia i v 2000 godu* (Irkutsk: Vostochno-Sibirskoe knizhnoe izdatel'stvo, 1978); V. Mikhailov, "Chivyrkuiskii zaliv. Proekt natsional'nogo parka v Buryatii," *Pravda Buryatii*, June 2, 1974; A. Shastin, "Maloe more—mir osobyi: O problemakh sozdaniia prirodnogo parka na poberezhe o. Ol'khon," *Sibir'* 6 (June 1975): 17–23.
47. Frants Taurin, "Zdravnitsa dukha," *Literaturnaia gazeta*, May 28, 1980, 11; N. Reimers, "Kakoi tropoi idti?" *Pravda*, September 8, 1980, 7.
48. O. K. Gusev, "O Baikale s nadezhdoi," *Vostochno-Sibirskaia pravda*, November 2, 1984, 2.
49. Ibid. See Oleg Gusev, "Sviashchennyi Baikal," *Sovetskaia Rossiia*, February 13, 1987, 1.
50. V. V. Vorob'ev, "Natsional'nyi park na Baikale," *Geografiia i prirodnye resursy* 4 (April 1986): 31. Unfortunately, these letters are located somewhere in a closed document collection in Russian State Archive of Modern History (RGANI).
51. GARF, fond A-259, opis' 48, delo 9334, 136; see V. Mazurov, "Parki na beregakh Baikala." *Lesnaia promyshlennost'*, November 4, 1986; S. Nazarenko and N. Mikhailovskaia, "Liubit'-znachit berech': O sozdanii na territoirii Irkutskoi oblasti Pribaikal'skogo natsional'nogo parka," *Sovetskaia molodezh'*, November 6, 1986, 2–3.
52. GARF, fond A-259, opis' 48, delo 9334, 33.
53. Ibid.
54. GARF, fond A-259, opis' 48, delo 9334, 105. For the next several years, writers from the Buryatia Republic emphasized that it would be more sensible to have one national park. See N. I. Rubtsov, "Slavnoe more ili zakhlamlennyi Baikal," *Molodezh' Buryatii*, September 12, 1987, 2.
55. M. Shagraev and F. Shtil'mark, "Natsional'nyi park—glazami ekologa: Sokhranit' Baikal nash sviashchennyi dolg," *Pravda Buryatii*, November 11, 1987, 2. The authors wrote, "With respect to its natural conditions, ZBNP is without doubt the most beautiful and scenic in the country."
56. GAIO, R-3523, opis' 1, delo 2, 2.

57. Among the organizations taking part in this study were the Institute of Geography SO AN SSSR, the Liminological Institute SO AN SSSR, the Institute of Soil Sciences and Agronomy, the Institute of Biology of the Buryatia Branch of the Academy of Sciences, and the administrations of several forestry districts.
58. Semen Klimovich Ustinov, "O Baikale s nadezhdoi," *Vostochno-Sibirskaia pravda*, December 12, 1986.
59. Z. Ibragimova, "Slavnoe more na vesakh chesti i ekonomiki," *Literaturnaia gazeta*, February 19, 1986, 11.
60. V. Molozhnikov, "V spasitel'nyi krug Baikala," *Vostochno-Sibirskaia pravda*, January 4, 1987, 4.
61. Ibid.
62. "Russian Federation, UNESCO," http://whc.unesco.org/en/statesparties/ru.
63. A. Sosunov, "Dvizhenie v zashchitu Baikala. Chto eto?," *Vostochno-Sibirskaia pravda*, November 19, 1988, 2. For another example of references to Baikal's "world significance," see "Iz pochty AIF," *Argumenty i fakty*, August 26, 1989, 3.
64. Charles P. Wallace, "Green Movement Flexes Muscle in Soviet Union," *Los Angeles Times*, October 27, 1991, OCA5.
65. Environmental historians have written extensively about the conflicts between national parks and populations who traditionally used the territory of the parks before their establishment. See Mark David Spence, *Dispossessing the Wilderness: Indian Removal and the Making of National Parks* (New York: Oxford University Press, 2000); Jim Igoe, *Conservation and Globalization: A Study of National Parks and Indigenous Communities from East Africa to South Dakota* (Belmont, CA: Wadsworth, 2006); Henry D. Delcore, "The Racial Distribution of Privilege in a Thai National Park," *Journal of Southeast Asian Studies* 38, no. 1 (February 2007): 83–105; David Aagesen, "Rights to Land and Resources in Argentina's Alerces National Park," *Bulletin of Latin American Research* 19 (2000): 547–569; Ananya Mukherjee, "Conflict and Coexestience in a National Park," *Economic and Political Weekly* 44, no. 23 (June 6–12, 2009): 52–59; Philip Burnham, *Indian Country, God's Country: Native Americans and the National Parks* (Washington, DC: Island, 2000); Kwokwo Barume, *Heading Towards Extinction? Indigenous Rights in Africa: The Case of the Twa and Kahuzi-Biega National Park, Democratic Republic of Congo* (Copenhagen: International Working Group for Indigenous Affairs, 2000); Karl Jacoby, *Crimes against Nature: Squatters, Poachers, Thieves, and the Hidden History of American Conservation* (Berkeley: University of California Press, 2014); Stan Stevens, ed., *Indigenous Peoples, National Parks, and Protected Areas: A New Paradigm Linking Conservation, Culture, and Rights* (Tucson: University of Arizona Press, 2014).
66. GAIO, fond R-3523, opis' 1, delo 17, 36.
67. V. Butygin, "Kakoi park nam nuzhen? O Pribaikal'skom natsional'nom parke," *Vostochno-Sibirskaia pravda*, July 7, 1988, 2. He blamed these problems on the mindset among the park's supporters that the national park must be "the best in the world."
68. GAIO, R-3523, opis' 1, delo 23, 1.
69. Ibid.
70. V. Kalinkin, "Valiutnaia okhota: O perspektivakh razvitiia Pribaikal'skogo prirodnogo natsional'nogo parka," *Lesnaia promyshlennost'*, April 26, 1990. Numerous groups in Siberia took advantage of the weakened state, which was unable to protect its natural resources. See Armin Rozencratz, "And Cutting Down Siberia: Like the Rainforest, the Vast Fragile Taiga Is Being Destroyed," *Washington Post*, August 18, 1991.
71. GANIIO, fond R-3018, opis' 1, delo 705, 5.
72. Ibid., 6.
73. GANIIO, fond 3018, opis' 1, delo 738, 4.
74. Ibid.
75. Z. Snimkina, "Bespravnyi park: O zadachakh, problemakh, perspektivakh razvitiia Pribaikal'skogo gosudarstvennogo prirodnogo parka," *Vostocnho-Sibirskaia pravda*, February 14, 1990.
76. GAIO, R-3523, opis' 1, delo 16, 183.
77. V. Kalinkin, "Den'gi dlia Baikala, 'O probleme Pribaikal'skogo gosudarstvennogo priordongo parka,'" *Lesnaia promyshlennost'*, June 5, 1990, 3.

78. N. Ugriumov, "Na beregu Chivyrkuiskogo zaliva," *Pravda Buryatiia*, August 31, 1988; V. S. Mel'nikov, Rubl' za vkhod," *Pravda Buryatiia*, August 3, 1990.
79. GAIO, fond R-3523, opis' 1, delo 17, 24.
80. Ibid., 192.
81. Ibid., 45.
82. Abramenok, "Den'gi za okhranu Baikala," *Voctochno-Sibirskaia pravda*, May 16, 1989; G. Mikheichik and Iu. Balykov, "Kakaia okhrana," *Vostochno-Sibirskaia pravda*, July 18, 1989, 3; Mel'nikov, "Rubl' za vkhod."
83. G. Mikheichik and Iu. Balykov, "Kakaia okhrana,", 3.
84. GAIO, R-3523, opis' 1, delo 44, 136.
85. GAIO, R-3523, opis' 1, delo 46, 103.
86. Ibid.
87. Ibid., 104.
88. Mikheichik and Balykov, "Kakaia okhrana," 3; Kalinkin, "Den'gi dlia Baikala," 3.
89. GAIO, R-3523, opis' 1, delo 46, 121.
90. Molozhnikov, "V spasitel'nyi krug Baikala."
91. Ibid., 105. In September of 1991, the Irkutsk Territorial Forestry Production Association ordered an illegal audit of the national park after the park's director, Peter Abramenok, published an article in *Vostochno-Sibirskaia pravda* accusing the director of the association of various forms of corruption. In turn, Abramenok wrote to the executive committee of the Irkutsk Oblast and the Ministry of Forestry RSFSR expressing "complete mistrust" in the association's director and requested that the national park be placed under the control of Goskompriroda.
92. GANIIO, fond 3018, opis' 1, delo 660, 15; Snimkina, "Bespravnyi park."
93. GAIO, R-3523, opis' 1, delo 33, 147–148.
94. Snimkina, "Bespravnyi park." For more on the fund of Lahemaa, see F. Nymmsaul, "Opyt Lakhemaaskogo parka," *Okhota i okhotnich'e khoziaistvo* 4 (April 1988): 13–14. Voluntary funds for national parks were more successful in the Baltic national parks than anywhere else in the USSR. The Latvian newspaper *Soviet Youth* called on its readers to help support the park. See N. Karpatskaia, "Leto nachinaetsia vesnoi," *Sovetskaia molodezh'*, April 9, 1977; E. Mazhan, "Dlia nas i potomkov: Pis'ma iz natsional'nogo parka Gauia Zhemchuzhina prirody," *Sovetskaia Latviia*, June 5, 1984, 4.
95. Michael Dobbs, "Russians Fight to Save Lake Baikal," *Washington Post*, October 11, 1990, A25. Also see Alexei Yablokov, "Russia: Gasping for Breath, Choking in Waste, Dying Young," *Washington Post*, August 18, 1991, C3. This article reveals the complete lack of faith of many of the most influential Russian environmentalists in the ability of the Soviet government to address the USSR's many environmental problems.
96. T. Vasil'eva, "Baikal pod okhranoi mirovogo soobshchestva," *Izvestiia*, February 19, 1989, 1.
97. UNESCO Archives, box 135, File Plan SC/ECO/5865/8.51.534, UDC 502.7, A101, WHC (470).
98. Eduard Shevardnadze, "Ekologiia i diplomatiia," *Literaturnaia gazeta*, November 22, 1989, 9.
99. Also see "US-Soviet Meeting," *New York Times*, August 2, 1990, A3; "Baker, Shevardnadze Discuss Arms, Summit," *Washington Post*, August 2, 1990, A22; Reuters, "Baker Nets New Friends but No Fish in Siberia," *Los Angeles Times*, August 1, 1990, VYP2; Jim Mann, "Baker, Shevardnadze OK Cooperation in Asia; No Afghan Breakthrough," *Los Angeles Times*, August 2, 1990, A8.
100. GAIO, R-3523, opis' 1, delo 44, 207.
101. UNESCO Archives, box 24, File Plan: WHC/74/534.2, UDC 502.7 (470) N.
102. GAIO, R-3523, opis' 1, delo 23, 145; GARF, fond A-259, opis' 49, delo 3400, 71.
103. GAIO, R-3525, opis' 1, delo 46, 71.
104. Personal archive of Julius Dobroshin (documents of Soiuzgiproleskhoz). During that time, they shot six video films that they would in turn send to different Soviet national parks to learn about the administration of national parks in the United States. GAIO, R-3525, opis' 1, delo 46, 69.
105. GAIO, R-3523, opis' 1, delo 46, 69. For more on David Brower, see Tom Turner, *David Brower: The Making of the Environmental Movement* (Berkeley: University of California Press, 2015).

106. GAIO, R-3523, opis' 1, delo 46, 69.
107. Jonathan Oldfield, "Russian Environmentalism," *Environmental Policy and Governance*, March 14, 2002.
108. Laura Henry, *Red to Green: Environmental Activism in Post-Soviet Russia* (Ithaca, NY: Cornell University Press, 2010), 42.
109. J. D. Oldfield and Denis Shaw, "Revisiting Sustainable Development: Russian Cultural and Scientific Traditions and the Concept of Sustainable Development" 34, no. 4 (December 2002): 391–400; Laura Henry, "Between Transnationalism and State Power: The Development of Russia's Post-Soviet Environmental Movement," *Environmental Politics* 19, no. 5 (2010): 761.
110. Henry, "Between Transnationalism and State Power," 761.
111. Oleg Ianitskii, "The Ecological Movement in Post-Totalitarian Russia: Some Conceptual Issues (1996)," in *Rossiia: Ekologicheskii vyzov*, ed. Oleg Ianitskii (Novosibirsk: Sibirskii khronograf, 2002), 139; David Ostergren and Peter Jacques, "A Political Economy of Russian Nature Conservation Policy," *Global Environmental Politics*, November 1, 2002, 103.
112. Mathiessen, *Baikal*, xii–xiii.
113. Ibid., xiv.
114. GAIO, R-3523, opis' 1, delo 75, 127.
115. For general comments on the problem of poaching throughout the Russian Federation see GARF, fond 10200, opis' 4, delo 4477, 19; personal archive of Julius Dobroshin (documents of Soiuzgiproleskhoz); I. Il'iashevich, "Pogranichnye kontory," *Sovetskaia molodezh'*, January 12, 1993, 2. According to this article, the park lacked the authority to fine poachers.
116. GAIO, R-3523, opis' 1, delo 62, 67. See A. Gorbunov, "Deviataia proverka," *Vostochno-Sibirskaia pravda*, September 10, 1992, 3. In this article, Gorbunov says that Abramenok said that he wanted to establish his own "village council" (sel'sovet) within the park's territory.
117. GAIO, R-3523, opis'1, delo 75, 56.
118. GAIO, R-3523, opis' 1, delo 44, 124; GAIO, R-3523, opis' 1, del 76, 10.
119. P. P. Abramenok, "V dvukh shagakh ot sine-zelenogo chuda," *Sovetskaia molodezh'*, June 6, 1992, 2.
120. Il'iashevich, "Pogranichnye kontory."
121. Ibid.
122. GAIO, R-3523, opis' 1, delo 63, 76.
123. P. Abramenok, "Shag nebol'shoi, no vse-taki vperod," *Sovetskaia molodezh'*, April 21, 1994.
124. GAIO, R-3523, opis' 1, delo 74, 69.
125. Personal archive of Julius Dobroshin (documents of Soiuzgiproleskhoz).
126. Ibid. Also see GARF, fond 10200, opis' 4, delo 4476, 87.
127. Personal archive of Julius Dobroshin (documents of Soiuzgiproleskhoz).
128. Ibid.
129. Ibid.
130. GAIO, R-3523, opis' 1, delo 76, 6. The decree of the Council of Ministers signed on August 10, 1993, established that the land of national parks was under federal jurisdiction.
131. Ministry of the Protection of the Environment and Natural Resources, *Problemy okhrany ozera Baikal i prirodopol'zovaniia v Baikal'skom regione* (Moscow, 1994), 89.
132. Henry, *Red to Green*, 3.
133. Steven Erlanger, "Sacred to Russians, not to US Budget Cutters," *New York Times*, September 3, 1995, 3. The United States Agency for International Development (USAID) gave $150,000 a year for four years to help Pribaikal'skii National Park develop recreational facilities on Olkhon Island.
134. Personal archive of Julius Dobroshin (documents of Soiuzgiproleskhoz).
135. S. Dombrovskii, "V parke dikoi prirody," *Pravda Buryatii*, December 28, 1993, 2. In Canada, the Society of Friends of Russia's National Parks was also established in 1993.
136. Dombrovskii, "V parke dikoi prirody," 2; Il'iashevich, "Pogranichnye kontory."
137. From May 11 to 17, 1994, the International Association for the Promotion of Cooperation with scientists from the Independent States of the former Soviet Union (INTAS) and the Siberian Branch of the Academy of Sciences sponsored a conference, Baikal as a Natural Laboratory of Global Change. From September 11 to 17, 1994, NATO's Scientific Affairs

Division and the Siberian Division of the Russian Academy of Sciences sponsored a conference, Sustainable Development of the Lake Baikal Region as a Model Territory for the World.

138. V. Ivanov, "Features of the Sustainable Development Model for Outlying Parts of Baikal Watershed," and Bernard Muller, "Sustainable Development and Tourism," in *Sustainable Development of the Lake Baikal Region as a Model Territory for the World* (Ulan-Ude: Siberian Branch of the Academy of Sciences, 1994).
139. Vladimir Krever et al. *Conserving Russia' Biodiversity: An Analytical Framework and Initial Investment Portfolio* (Washington D. C.: World Wildlife Fund, 1994), 107 and 113.
140. N. L. Dobretsov, "International Cooperation in Basic Research in Siberia: Major Results, Potentialities and Perspectives," in *International Conference: Baikal as a World Natural Heritage Site* (Ulan-Ude, : Commission of the Russian Federation for UNESCO, 1998), 30.
141. A. K. Tulokhonov, "Assessment of International Cooperation Effectiveness from the Position of the Baikal Region," in *International Conference: Baikal as a World Natural Heritage Site,* 71.
142. UNESCO Archives, Box 24, File Plan WHC/74/534.2, UDC 502.7 (470) N. In a letter from Jenny Sutton, the head of the NGO Baikal Wave, to the UNESCO World Heritage Committee about a UNESCO led workshop on Olkhon Island, Sutton described the "almost complete lack of presence of local inhabitants."
143. UNESCO Archives, box 24, File Plan WHC/74/534.2, UDC 502.7 (470) N.
144. Ibid.
145. P. Abramenok, "Sokhranit' v pervozdannosti," *Vostochno-Sibirskaia pravda,* April 13, 1996.
146. Valentin Rasputin, "Sibir': I khram, i masterskaia. Dialog o Sibiri," *Sibir'* 4 (1987): 3–13.
147. A. K. Tulokhonov, "Assessment of International Cooperation Effectiveness from the Position of the Baikal Region," in *International Conference: Baikal as a World Natural Heritage Site* (Ulan-Ude: Commission of the Russian Federation for UNESCO, 1998).

Chapter 6

1. T. Krainova, "Luchshe drugikh v Povolzh'e," *Samarskaia Luka* 4 (April 1992): 4; Aleksei Beliakov, "Krugosvetnoe puteshestvie," in *Legendy i byli Zhigulei* (Kuibyshev: Kuibyshevskoe knizhnoe izdatel'stvo, 1979), 106.
2. Krainova, "Luchshe drugikh v Povolzh'e." In a 1921 questionnaire of delegates to the Tenth Congress of the Russian Communist Party, to the question "What area of Russia do you like best?" Lenin answered, "The Volga is the best of all."
3. V. V. Chitova and S. V. Saksonov, *Samarskaia Luka: Zhemchuzhina Rossii* (Zhigulevsk, 2004), 6.
4. Ibid.
5. M. Mazenin, *Bol'shaia Volga* (Ivanovsk: Ivanovskoe knizhnoe izdatel'stvo, 1958).
6. K. Lapin, *Pokoriteli Volgi* (Kuibyshev: Kuibyshevskoe knizhnoe izdatel'stvo, 1956); L. Kovalev, *Shturm Volgi* (Kuibyshev: Kuibyshevskoe knizhnoe izdatel'stvo, 1956); *Volzhsko-Kamskii kaskad gidroelektrostantsii* (Moscow: Ministerstvo elektrostantsii, 1956); E. Riabchikov and V. Iachevich, "Piatyi shturm Volgi," *Pravda,* October 29, 1955, 2; S. Kuzmenko, "Volzhskaia nov'," *Pravda,* November 22, 1959, 6.
7. I Kozmin, "Vvesti v stroi Kuibyshevskuiu gidroeletrostantsiiu v 1955 godu," *Pravda,* August 21, 1955, 2; G. Krzhizhanovskii, "Dva giganta na Volge," *Izvestiia,* September 3, 1950, 2; Evgenii Kuzimov, "Zhigulevskaia letopis'," *Literaturnaia gazeta,* December 31, 1955, 2; See Paul Josephson, *Industrialized Nature* (Seattle: Island Press, 2002), 33.
8. A. N. Krizhanovskii, "Voploshchenie mechty," *Pravda,* August 10, 1958; Kuzmenko, "S beregov Volgi na Angaru," *Pravda,* August 21, 1961, 1; Koz'min, "Novyi industrial'nyi raion na Volge," *Pravda,* July 18, 1958, 2; Borisov, "Pered pavodkom na Volge," *Pravda,* March 26, 1953, 2; N. Koshelov, "Na Volge, u Zhigulei," *Izvestiia,* May 1, 1957, 4; Evgenii Kriger, "Nash svet," *Izvestiia,* January 1, 1956, 2.
9. Sharof Radishev, "Znamia druzhby," *Pravda,* September 16, 1952, 1; G. M. Malenkov, "Sovetskii Soiuz raspolagaet vsemi neobkhodimymi usloviiami chtoby v istoricheski korotkie sroki dognat' i peregnat' SShA po proizvodstvu eletroenergii," *Izvestiia,* February 19, 1956, 3.

10. Lewis Siegelbaum, "Modernity Unbound: The New Soviet City of the Sixties," in *The Socialist Sixties*: Crossing Borders in the Second World, eds. Anne Gorsuch and Diane Koenker (Bloomington: Indiana University Press, 2013), 69.
11. See S. Kuzmenko, "Novaia slava Zhigulei," *Pravda*, January 8, 1961, 3; S. Kuzmenko, "Volzhskie ogni," *Pravda*, April 18, 1965, 3; N. Koshelov, "Vesna v Zhiguliakh," *Izvestiia*, May 16, 1961, 1.
12. Viktor Vanynin, "Vsegda dumat' o cheloveke," *Literaturnaia gazeta*, December 3, 1959, 1.
13. Ibid.
14. G. Oreshko, "Vserossiiskii slet turistov," *Volzhskii komsomolets*, July 27, 1955, 1.
15. N. V. Zabelina, B. L. Samoilov, and G. V. Morozova, *Natsional'nye parki i zakazniki* (Moscow: Mysl', 1996); Iurii Roshchevskii, "Natsionalnyi prirodnyi park Samarskaia Luka," in *Zelenaia kniga Povolzh'ia* (Samara: Samarskoe knizhnoe izdatel'stvo, 1995), 335.
16. GARF, R-10010, opis' 5, delo 277, 53. The Kuibyshev Local History Museum began working with the VOOP on the question of reestablishing and expanding the *zapovednik* in 1965. See GARF, R-10100, opis' 5, delo 275, 66.
17. GARF, fond 404, opis' 1, delo 912, 195;Siegelbaum, "Modernity Unbound."
18. I. Egorov, "Byt' Volge bogache i krashe!," *Volzhskaia kommuna*, October 22, 1967, 3; A. Bochkarev, "Kar'er v zapovednik," *Sovetskaia Rossiia*, October 29, 1981, 2.
19. N. Koshelov, "Zhiguli zhdut," *Izvestiia*, August 29, 1968, 3.
20. Ibid.
21. RGAE, fond 544, opis' 1, delo 91, 30.
22. SGASPI, fond 616, opis' 1, delo 105, 94.
23. Egorov, "Byt' Volge bogache i krashe!," 3.
24. Christian Noack, "Songs from the Wood, Love from the Fields: The Soviet Tourist Song Movement," in *The Socialist Sixties: Crossing Borders in the Second World*, eds. Anne Gorsuch and Diane Koenker (Bloomington: Indiana University Press, 2013), 167–192. For a brief history of the festival and a description of the Grushin Festival, see "XV Festival'," *Volzhskaia zaria*, July 3, 1988, 15. For an article that discusses both the festival and the Zhigulevskaia krugosvetka, see M. Iur'ev, "Zacharovannaia Volga," *Volzhskii komsomolets*, June 13, 1969, 3; L. I. Krivolutskaia, *"Festival' na Volge," Samarskii kraeved* (Samara: Samarskoe knizhnoe izdatel'stvo, 1991).
25. SGASPI, fond 616, opis' 1, delo 128: 19; E. Manko, "Volzhskie zhemchuzhiny," *Pravda*, October 5, 1969, 3.
26. L. Iarkaia, "Zhiguli—tsentr turizma," *Volzhskii komsomolets*, December 5, 1969, 6.
27. Ibid.
28. GARF, R-10010, opis' 5, delo 275, 35.
29. GARF, R-10010, opis' 5, delo 295, 8.
30. GARF, R-10010, opis' 5, delo 278, 5 and 87.
31. L. V. Guseva, Iu. K. Roshchevskii, V. V. Erofeev, T. I. Marchenko, V. I. Khomianskaia, A. V. Vinogradov, and A. A. Ustinova, "Poteri nauki," *Samarskaia Luka: Problemy regional'noi i global'noi ekologii* 23, no. 1 (2014): 235.
32. SOGSPI, fond 656, opis' 197, delo 534, 22.
33. Ibid.
34. L. V. Guseva and V. N. Kolmianskaia, "Rol' Tat'iany Vladimirovny Tezikovoi v sozdanii Gosudarstvennogo prirodnogo natsional'nogo parka 'Samarskaia Luka'" *Samarskaia luka: Problemy regional'noi i global'noi ekologii* 4 (April 2014): 193–201. See L. B. Guseva and L. V. Stepchenko, "Nikakikh podvigov ia ne sovershala, Ocherk o zhizni i deiatel'nosti T. V. Tezikovoi," *Samarskaia Luka: Problemy regional'noi i global'noi ekologii 18*, no. 2 (2009): 13.
35. SGASPI, fond 616, opis' 1, delo 105, 140.
36. VOOP et al., *Problemy ratsional'nogo ispol'zovaniia i okhrany prirody Samarskoi Luki: Mezhvedomstvennyi sbornik* (Kuibyshev: VOOP, 1983), 4.
37. Ibid.
38. Guseva and Kolmianskaia, "Rol' Tat'iany Vladimirovny Tezikovoi," 197.
39. "Iz publikatsii i dokumentov," *Volzhskii komsomolets*, June 17, 1990; .
40. K. Iakovlev, "Volzhskie berega," *Trud*, February 24, 1974, 47.
41. Ibid.

42. ASLNP, delo 57: Biography of Victor Timofeev.
43. ASLNP: delo 57: Biography of Victor Timofeev; Valerii Erofeev, "Dvadtsat' let spustia," *Vremia* 10 (May 17, 1994): 2.
44. Interview with Iurii Roshchevskii, June, 15, 2013.
45. SGASPI, fond R-2305, opis' 3, delo 40, 5.
46. Ibid., 159.
47. Ibid.
48. Ibid., 4.
49. SGASPI, R-2305, opis' 3, delo 40, 194; see T. V. Tezikova, "Samarskaia Luka," *Kraevedcheskie zapiski* 3 (1975): 16–17.
50. T. V. Tezikova, "Samarskaia Luka," 16-17.
51. K. Iakovlev, "Volzhskie berega," *Trud*, February 24, 1974, 47.
52. Ibid.
53. Iakovlev, "Volzhskie berega," 47; Bochkarev, "Kar'er v zapovednik," 2.
54. Iakovlev, "Volzhskie berega," 47.
55. Iurii Roshchevskii, *Khronika obshchestvennoi okhrany Samarskoi Luki* (Tolyatti: Parkovei, 1998), 6.
56. Ibid.
57. T. Zapredel'naia, "Budet li spasen unikal'nyi zapovednik," *Volzhskii komsomolets'*, February 5, 1993.
58. SGASPI, fond 616, opis' 1, delo 353, 20.
59. N. Koshelov, "Prelestnye kartinki," *Izvestiia,* November 30, 1973, 3.
60. N. Mironov, "Logike vopreki," Pravda, December 29, 1976, 3.
61. Bochkarev, "Kar'er v zapovednik," 2.
62. Ibid., 2.
63. Interview with Iurii Roshchevskii, June, 15, 2013. Roshchevskii characterized the relationship of himself, Zakharov, and Tezikova as acrimonious and mutually suspicious.
64. SGASPI, fond R-2305, opis' 3, delo 40, 6.
65. "Byt' natsional'nomu parku!," *Volzhskaia zaria,* March 5, 1984, 2.
66. Personal Archive of Julius Dobroshin (documents of Soiuzgiproleskhoz)
67. SGASPI, fond 656, opis' 197, 534.
68. Ibid.
69. Ibid.
70. Interview with Iurii Roshchevskii, June 15, 2013.
71. Roshchevskii, *Khronika obshchestvennoi okhrany Samarskoi Luki,* 7.
72. ASLNP, delo 50.
73. Ibid.
74. Ibid.
75. See Lewis Siegelbaum, *Cars for Comrades* (Ithaca, NY: Cornell University Press, 2011).
76. ASLNP, delo 50.
77. Iu. Roshchevskii, "Nadobno speshit'," *Volzhskaia kommuna,* August 4, 1988, 4; Iurii Roshchevskii, "Kraevedy na Grushinskom," *Volzhskaia zaria,* July 13, 1987, 2.
78. Iu. Roshchevskii, "Kakoi byt' tebe Samarskaia Luka," *Volzhskaia zaria,* May 16, 1988, 4.
79. GARF, A-259, opis' 48, delo 6107, 3.
80. ASLNP, delo 54.
81. Iu. Roshchevskii, "Bushuiut strasti," *Stroitel'naia gazeta,* August 16, 1989, 3.
82. Personal archive of Valerii Erofeev, "Za pomoshch' Rossii," 1990 Letter to the Supreme Soviet of the USSR from Tezikova.
83. M. Lukin, "Park-natsional'nyi ili vedomstvennyi," *Volzhskaia zaria,* February 4, 1987, 3.
84. GARF, fond 262, opis' 17, delo 6086, 193.
85. ASLNP, delo 50.
86. ASLNP, delo 61; M. Lukin, "Park-natsional'nyi ili vedomstvennyi," 3; SGASPI, fond 656, opis' 197, delo 534, 173.
87. A. Fedorov, "Dacha v natsional'nom parke," *Volzhskaia zaria,* October 26, 1989, 4.
88. Ibid.

89. "Proekt est'. Chto dal'she? O nekotorykh problemakh sozdaniia prirodnogo parka Samarskaia Luka," *Volzhskaia kommuna*, October, 5, 1989, 4; Iurii Roshchevskii, "Bushuiut strasti," 3.
90. ASLNP, delo 50; V. Zhiliaeva, "Tupiki Samarskoi Luki: Pochemu parki v Rossii rastut tol'ko na bumage," *Sovetskaia Rossiia*, January 14, 1986, 2.
91. Marjorie Sun, "Environmental Awakening in the Soviet Union," *Science*, August 26, 1988, 1035.
92. A. Fedorov, "Prirodu—bul'dozerom," *Volzhskii komsomolets*, May 17, 1987; Iu. Roshchevskii, "Kakoi tebe byt' Samarskaia Luka?," *Volzhskaia zaria*, May 16, 1988, 4; V. Koveshnikov, Kakoi byt' zavtra Mogutovoi Gore," *Volzhskaia kommuna*, February 28, 1988; V. Erofeev, "O budushchem zadumait'sia seichas," *Volzhskii komsomolets*, June 5, 1987, 3.
93. Iu. Roshchevskii, "Nadobno speshit'," *Volzhskii kommunist*, August 4, 1988, 4.
94. A. Fedorov, "Prestuplenie protiv ekologii," *Volzhskii komsomolets*, June 17, 1989, 17.
95. SGASPI, fond 656, opis' 197, delo 534, 42.
96. Ibid., 173.
97. Roshchevskii, "Nadobno spezhit'," 4.
98. Fedorov, "Prestuplenie protiv ekologii," 17.
99. For more on the "imagined West," see Alexei Yurchak, *Everything Was Forever Until It Was No More* (Princeton, NJ: Princeton University Press, 2005); Juliane Furst, "Where Did All the Normal People Go? Another Look at the Soviet 70s," *Kritika: Exploration in Russian and Eurasian History 14*, no. 3 (Summer 2013): 631.
100. V. Koshevnikov, "Kakoi byt' zavtra Mogutovoi Gore," *Volzhskaia kommuna*, February 28, 1988.
101. "Khraniteli radugi protiv imperii kamnei," *Beringiia* 6 (1993): 8.
102. SGASPI, fond 656, opis' 197, delo 534, 50.
103. "Vovremia ostanovit'sia," *Volzhskaia kommuna*, March 31, 1988, 2; Otdel sovetskogo stroitel'stva, "Kakoi byt' zavtra Mogutovoi Gore," *Volzhskaia kommuna*, January 20, 1988.
104. Ivan Nikul'shin, "Kakoi byt' zavtra Mogutovoi Gore," *Volzhskaia kommuna*, May 26, 1988.
105. Ibid.
106. "Zashchitit' Samarskuiu Luku!," *Volzhskaia kommuna*, June 6, 1989, 3; also see E. Khrutina, "Sovmestit' nesovmestimoe?" *Volzhskii komsomolets*, January 24, 1987, 3.
107. For examples of such articles see Vladimir Emelianov, "Zhiguli dolzhny zhit'," *Volzhskaia zaria*, August 4, 1990; Vladimir Emelianov, "Politicheskie igry vokrug Zhigulei," *Samarskie izvestiia*, October 31, 1990, 4.
108. P. Zhigalov, "Po toske u kar'era," *Izvestiia*, July 12, 1990, 6.
109. Ibid.
110. GARF, A-259, opis' 48, delo 6107, 3.
111. Zhigalov, "Po toske u kar'era," 6.
112. T. Tezikova, "O natsional'noi gordosti," *Volzhskii komsomolets*, June 17, 1990, 17.
113. Zhigalov, "Po toske u kar'era," 6.
114. V. Komorovskii, *Argumenty i fakty*, June 3, 1989, 5; Alfred B. Evans, Jr., "Civil Society in the Soviet Union," in *Russian Civil Society: A Critical Assessment*, eds. Alfred B. Evans, Laura A. Henry, and Lisa McIntosh Sundstrom (Armonk, NY: M. E. Sharpe, 2006)46; RGAE, fond 709, opis' 1, delo 266, 170.
115. Vladimir Markov, "Demokratiia ili fraktsionnost'?," *Pravda*, April 18, 1990; Carole Sigman, "The End of Grassroots Ecology: Political Competition and the Fate of Ecology during Perestroika, 1988–1991," *Soviet and Post-Soviet Review 40* (2013): 190–213.
116. RGAE, fond 709, opis' 1, delo 266, 344.
117. O. N. Ianitskii, "Lager' protesta na Mogutovoi Gore," in *Rossiia: Ekologicheskii vyzov* (Novosibirsk: Sibirskii khronograf, 2002), 337.
118. Ibid.
119. Fomichev had close relationships with the Association of the Movement of Anarchists, the Initiative of Revolutionary Anarchists, and the Anarchist Shock Battalion.
120. Ianitskii, "Lager' protesta,", 283.
121. Ibid., 283.

122. See Anya Manner, "Rainbow Keepers—Who are They?," *Russian Conservation News* 5 (October 1995): 18.
123. Joshua Abrams and Matt Auer, "The Disappearance of Popular Environmental Activism in Post-Soviet Russia," in *Restoring the Cursed Earth: Appraising Environmental Policy Reforms in Eastern Europe and Russia*, ed. Matthew R. Auer (New York: Rowman & Littlefield, 2005).
124. Valerii Erofeev, "Iav' i mirazhi Zhigulei," *Svet* 12 (December 1993): 4.
125. Iu. Miganov, "Zhigulevskii sindrom: Problema sokhraneniia prirody Samarskoi Luki," *Volzhskaia kommuna*, November 9, 1994, 3.
126. Sbornik informatsii, "Grinpis zashchishchaet Samarsuiu Luku," *Delovoi mir*, September 15, 1993.
127. Zapredel'naia, "Budet li spasen unikal'nyi zapovednik."
128. In October 1990, the VOOP and the Zhiguli Zapovednik held a scientific-technical conference, "Samara Bend 90." This was when UNESCO designation was first discussed.
129. "Matrosy na Gore Mogutovoi," *Vremia*, August 1993.
130. "Srazhenie u Gory Mogutovoi," *Volzhskaia kommuna*, July 21, 1993.
131. Zapredel'naia, "Budet li spasen unikal'nyi zapovedniki."
132. Eduard Kondratov, "Konflikt v Zhiguliakh mozhet obernut'sia gibel'iu liudei," *Izvestiia*, July 22, 1993, 2.
133. "Lager' protesta na Mogutovoi Gore," 327.
134. Ibid., 329.
135. Ibid., 337.
136. Ibid., 331.
137. Ibid., 333.
138. "Stop, mashina," *Beringiia* 8 (August 1993).
139. Iurii Roshchevskii, "Zadachi menedzhmenta natsional'nogo parka 'Samarskaia Luka,'" *Samarskii krai v istorii Rossii: Materialy iubileinoi nauchnoi konferentsii, 6–7 fevralia 2001 g.* (Samara: DSM, 2001), 299. Roshchevskii said, "Unfortunately, the specific problems of managing the park were never considered important by the forest service."
140. Personal Archive of Julius Dobroshin (documents of Soiuzgiproleskhoz).
141. S. Saksonov, "Samarskaia luka stala zhertvoi bezzakoniia," *Zhigulevskii rabochii*, April 24, 1993; Iu. Miganov, "Zhigulevskii sindrom: Problema sokhraneniia prirody Samarskoi Luki," *Volzhskaia kommuna*, November 9, 1994, 3; Roshchevskii, "Zadachi menedzhmenta natsional'nogo parka 'Samarskaia Luka,'" 299.
142. Aleksandr Petrov, "Odni zashchishchaiut prirodu, drugie khotiat povesit' tekh, kto zashchishchaet," *Trud*, February 11, 1995.
143. Roshchevskii, *Khronika obshchestvennoi okhrany Samarskoi Luki*, 9.
144. Personal Archive of Julius Dobroshin (documents of Soiuzgiproleskhoz).
145. Ibid.
146. Jo Crotty, "Making a Difference? NGOs and Civil Society in Russia," *Europe-Asia Studies* 61, no. 1 (January 2009): 93.
147. Roshchevskii, "Zadachi menedzhmenta natsional'nogo parka Samarskaia Luka."
148. Interview with Iurii Roshchevskii, June, 15, 2013.
149. Juliane Furst and Stephen Bittner, "The Aging Pioneer: Late Soviet Socialist Society, Its Challenges and Challengers." in *The Cambridge History of Communism*, vol. 3, *Endgames? Late Communism in Global Perspective, 1968 to the Present*, eds. Julianne Furst, Silvio Pons, and Mark Seldon (Cambridge: Cambridge University Press, 2017), 283.
150. Valerii Erofeev, "Dvadtsat' let spustia," *Vremia* 10 (May 17, 1994).
151. Paul Josephson et al., *An Environmental History of Russia* (Cambridge: Cambridge University Press, 2013), 185.

Chapter 7

1. Alan Barenburg, *Gulag Town, Company Town: Forced Labor and its Legacy in Vorkuta* (New Haven, CT: Yale University Press, 2014); Miriam Dobson, Khrushchev's *Cold Summer: Gulag Returnees, Crime, and the Fate of Reform after Stalin* (Ithaca, NY: Cornell University Press, 2009).

2. NAKNTs UrO RAN, fond 1, opis' 15, delo 2, 40; N. A. Lazarev, "Ispol'zovanie i okhrana prirody Komi ASSR," *Okhrana prirody Komi ASSR* 1 (1961): 11.
3. F. F. Shillinger, "Zakliuchenie po proektu uchrezhdeniia natsional'nogo parka (zapovednika) v avtonomnoi oblasti Komi," *Okhrana prirody* 3 (March 1930): 66.
4. Ibid.
5. Ibid.
6. G. L. Sapukhanov, "Skhema perebroski stoka rek Pechory i Vychegdy v bassein r. Volgi," in *Problemy Kaspiiskogo moria*, eds. A. Apollova, K. K. Giul', and V. G. Zabrieva (Baku: AN USSR, 1963), 36.
7. See Paul R. Josephson, "'Projects of the Century' in Soviet History: Large-Scale Technologies from Lenin to Gorbachev," *Technology and Culture* 36, no. 3 (July 1995): 519–559. In terms of the size and scope, this project would have qualified as what Josephson refers to as "projects of the century."
8. L. N. Volkov, "Vliianie perebroski stoka rek Pechory i Vychegdy v basseine rek Kamy i Volgi na narodnoe khoziaistvo prikaspiiskikh raionov," in Apollova, Giul', and Zabrieva, *Problemy Kaspiiskogo moria*, 257; Dmitry Vorobyev, "Ruling Rivers: Discussions about the River Diversions Project in the Soviet Union," in *Understanding Russian Nature: Representations, Values, and Concepts*, eds. Arja Rosenholm and Sari-Autio Sarasmo (Helsinki: University of Helsinki, Aleksanteri Institute, 2005). For information on Soviet military spending at this time, see Timothy Sosnovy, "The Soviet Military Budget," *Foreign Affairs* 42, no. 3 (April 1964): 487–494.
9. Vladislav Larin et al., *Okhrana prirody Rossii: Ot Gorbacheva do Putina* (Moscow: KMK, 2003), 99.
10. Alan Barenburg, *Gulag Town, Company Town: Forced Labor and its Legacy in Vorkuta* (New Haven, CT: Yale University Press, 2014).
11. N. A. Morozov, *Osobye lageria MVD SSSR v Komi ASSR (1948–1954)* (Syktyvkar: Sytyvarskii Universitet, 1998).
12. E. Lopukhov, "Zhizn' trebuet," *Pravda*, August 1, 1958, 2; Laurent Coumel, "A Failed Environmental Turn? Khrushchev's Thaw and Nature Protection in Soviet Russia," *Soviet and Post-Soviet Review* 40 (2013), 167–189.
13. NAKNTs UrO RAN, fond 1, opis' 15, delo 2, 40.
14. G. Chernov, *Turistskie pokhody v pechorskie Al'py* (Syktyvkar: Komi knizhnoe izdatel'stvo, 1974).
15. From interview with Adolf Bratsev, July 28, 2012, Syktyvkar, Russian Federation. For more on the rivers diversion project see A. V. Samarin, "Proekty perebroski severnykh rek: uchenie Komi protiv sovetskoi gigantomanii," *Novyi istoricheskii vestnik* 4 (April 2009): 58–66.
16. For examples of this, see D. L. Armand, *Nam i vnukam* (Moscow, 1964). Also see I. P. Gerasimov, A. A. Mints, V. S. Preobrazhenskii, and N. P. Shelemov, "Estestvennye resursy: Okhrana i preobrazovanie prirody," *Izvestiia Akademii nauk SSSR: Seriia Geograficheskaia*, no. 4 (April 1969): 42.
17. Interview with Adolf Bratsev, July 28, 2012.
18. NAKNTs UrO RAN, fond 1, opis' 15, delo 16, 3; Alexander Borovinskikh et al., *Sokhranit' i* (Syktyvkar: Minprirodi Komi, 2008), 23
19. In addition to using the press, Bratsev and Gladkov also appeared on radio programs in the Komi Republic.
20. V. Gladkov, "Etalon severnoi prirody: Sozdadim Komi natsional'nyi park," *Krasnoe znamia*, August 8, 1970, 3.
21. Ibid.
22. "Bol'shinstvo-za! O Sozdanii natsional'nogo parka v Komi ASSR: Otkliki na stat'iu V. Gladkova 'Etalon severnoi prirody,'" *Krasnoe znamia*, October 1, 1970.
23. Ibid.
24. Vorobyev, "Ruling Rivers," 187.
25. Bureau Obkoma KPSS i Sovet Ministrov Komi ASSR, Postanovlenie 233, May 28, 1971, personal archive of Alexander Kokovkin, Syktyvkar, Russian Federation.
26. NAKNTs UrO RAN, fond 1, opis' 15, delo 18, 8. For more on recreational geography, see V. M. Kotliakov, ed., *Vladimir Sergeevich Preobrazhenskii v vospominaniiakh i pis'makh* (Moscow: Institut Geografii, 2005); I. P. Gerasimov, "Konstruktivnaia geografia: tseli,

metody, rezul'taty," *Izvestiia Vsesoiuznogo geograficheskogo obshchestva* 98, no. 5 (September-October 1966): 391–400; I. P. Gerasimov, V. S. Preobrazhenskii, et al., *Teoreticheskie osnovy rekreatsionnoi geografii* (Moscow: Nauka, 1975); V. S. Preobrazhenskii and N. P. Shelemov, "Problemy ispol'zovaniia estestvennykh resursov dlia otdykha i turizma," *Izvestiia Akademii nauk SSSR: Seriia Geograficheskaia* 5 (May 1967): 54–62
27. NAKNTs UrO RAN, fond 1, opis' 15, delo 18, 7–8.
28. Ibid., 7.
29. Ibid., 12.
30. NAKNTs UrO RAN, fond 1, opis' 1, delo 1029, 25.
31. Ibid., 93.
32. V. P. Gladkov, 1989 letter to Gosplan RSFSR, personal archive of Alexander Kokovkin. The supporters of the park frequently mentioned that they did not want to repeat the mistakes of US national parks where excessive infrastructural development caused environmental damage.
33. Yellowstone up Close and Personal, http://www.yellowstone.co/stats.htm.
34. "Prirodnyi park: o sozdanii Komi katsional'nogo parka," *Molodezh' Severa*, March 19, 1972, 19; G. Turev, "Park sozdan prirodoi: K sozdaniiu prirodnogo parka v Komi ASSR," *Krasnoe znamia*, September 2, 1976; "Prirodnyi park Komi ASSR," *Molodezh' Severa*, December 22, 1978; V. Gladkov, "V Alpakh nad Pechoroi," *Komsomol'skaia pravda*, July 30, 1971, 3; B. Vladimov, "Budet natsional'nyi park v Komi ASSR," *Krasnoe znamia*, April 15, 1973.
35. Zaboeva.
36. Ibid., 9. According to Gladkov, tourists had caused damage to the forests along the Kozhim River through cutting wood for their boats while destroying a large number of young salmon populations.
37. For more on environmental protection under Brezhnev, see Paul Josephson et al., *An Environmental History of Russia* (Cambridge: Cambridge University Press, 2013), 184–186.
38. V. P. Gladkov, *Lesnaia promyshlennost'*, March 29, 1979.
39. V. P. Gladkov, letter to the Komi ASSR Council of Ministers, "On the organization of a nature national park," October 3, 1982, personal archive of Aleksandr Kokovkin.
40. Gosplan, letter of August 4, 1983, personal archive of Aleksandr Kokovkin.
41. Iu. B. Khromov, *Organizatsiia sistem otdykha, turizma i okhranoi prirodnoi sredy na Severe* (Leningrad: Stroiizdat, 1981), 7.
42. Iu. S. Zakharov et al., *Natsional'nyi park v pripoliarnom Urale: argumenty i pretsedenty* (Moscow: Rossiiskoe NII kul'turnogo i prirodnogo naslediia, 1993) , 17.
43. Ibid., 8.
44. V. P. Gladkov, "Rol' obshchestvennosti v sozdanii sistemy okhraniaemykh prirodnykh territorii v Komi ASSR," in *Okhraniaemye prirodnye territorii Urala i prilegaiushchikh regionov* (Sverdlovsk: Akademiia nauk SSSR, 1989), 57. Also see N. V., Kovrizhnikh, "Natsional'nyi park Iugyd Va—nashe budushchee," *Siianie Severa*, June 21, 1994, 2.
45. This was a particular problem in the territory of the proposed Samara Bend National Park. See N. Koshelov, "Prelestnye kartinki," *Izvestiia*, November 30, 1973, 5.
46. V. Tretiakov, "Byt' natsional'nomu parku?" *Siianie Severa*, January 11, 1991, 3.
47. N. Melnikova and I. Burtsev, "Natsional'nyi park Iugyd Va: Ekonomika i ekologiia dolzhny idti vmeste," *Region* 8 (August 1998): 16.
48. GARKo, fond 2425, opis' 1, delo 8, 31
49. V. P. Gladkov, "Vliianie razrabotok rossypnykh mestorozhdenii na biologicheskii rezhim r. Kozhim," personal archive of Alexander Kokovkin.
50. For more on the environmental activism during perestroika see Marc Elie and Laurent Coumel, "A Belated and Tragic Ecological Revolution: Nature, Disasters, and Green Activists in the Soviet Union and the Post-Soviet States, 1960s–2010s," *Soviet and Post-Soviet Review* 40, no. 2 (2013): 157–165; Carole Sigman, "The End of Grassroots Ecology: Political Competition and the Fate of Ecology during Perestroika, 1988–1991," *Soviet and Post-Soviet Review* 40, no. 2 (2013): 190–213; Sonja D. Schmid, "Transformation Discourse: Nuclear Risk as a Strategic Tool in Late Soviet Politics of Expertise," *Science, Technology, and Human Values* 29, no. 3 (Summer, 2004): 353; Douglas Weiner, *Little Corner of Freedom*: Russian

Environmental Protection from Stalin to Gorbachev (Berkeley: University of California Press, 2002), 429–440; Josephson et al., *Environmental History of Russia*, 254–286.

51. GARKo, fond 2425, opis' 1, delo 39, 8.
52. Valentina Liakh, "Chtoby ne prishlo razocharovanie," *Siianie Severa*, August 17, 1995, 3.
53. S. Morokhin, "Perekhod granitsy," *Molodezh' Severa*, March 27, 1992.
54. George W. Breslauer, *Yeltsin and Gorbachev as Leaders* (Cambridge: Cambridge University Press, 2002), 124.
55. Melnikova and Burtsev, "Natsional'nyi park Iugyd Va," 16.
56. GARKo, fond 2425, opis' 1, delo 8, 143.
57. "Natsional'nyi park: Chto pokazala ekspertiza," *Respublika*, November 4, 1992.
58. GARKo, fond 2425, opis'1, delo 55, 5.
59. "Natsional'nyi park: chto pokazala ekspertiza."
60. GARKo fond 2425, opis'1, delo 55, 6.
61. Ibid., 8.
62. Ibid., 13–14.
63. Zakharov et al., *Natsional'nyi park v pripoliarnom Urale*, 6.
64. Ibid., 37.
65. "Ostrov nadezhdi," *Krasnoe znamia*, July 30, 1992.
66. Ibid.
67. "Tri vzgliadi na problemu Komi Natsional'nyi park," *Iskra*, January 23, 1993, available online at http://gsrk.ru/static/data/docs/0000/72.pdf.
68. Open Letter from the Young Ecologists and Teachers of the Republic Station of Naturalists, "Podarite nam park," *Siianie Severa*, March 18, 1993, 3.
69. GARKo fond 2425, opis' 1, delo 8, 57.
70. Ibid., 55.
71. Ibid., 54.
72. Ibid., 50.
73. Ibid., 40.
74. Federal'nyi zakon, "Ob osobookhraniaemykh territoriiakh," March 14, 1995, available online at http://base.garant.ru/10107990/.
75. UNESCO Archives, box 23, File Plan WHC/74/534, UDC 502.7 (469).
76. Ibid.
77. See Joachim Radkau, *The Age of Ecology: A Global History*, trans. Patrick Camiller (Cambridge, UK: Polity, 2014), 386.
78. Ministry of Natural Resources of Komi Republic, *Gosudarstvennyi doklad o sostoianii okruzhaiushchei prirodnoi sredy respubliki Komi v 1995 godu* (Syktyvkar: Ministry of Natural Resources of the Komi Republic, 1996).
79. Larin et al., 99.
80. Ibid., 185–187.
81. "Genprokuratura soglasilas' c Grinpis," *Greenpeace Russia*, September 25, 2012, http://www.greenpeace.org/russia/ru/news/2012/15-02-2012-komi-reshenie-prokuratury/.
82. UNESCO Archives, box 24, File Plan WHC/74/534.2, UDC 502.7 (470) N.
83. Melnikova and Burtsev, "Natsional'nyi park Iugyd Va," 18.
84. Ibid., 19.
85. Ibid., 19.
86. Interview with Adolf Petrovich Bratsev, July 22, 2012, Syktyvkar, Russian Federation. These were the words that Bratsev used when explaining his belief about the importance of having a strong economic rationale for nature protection projects.
87. Tatiana Fomicheva, "Budushchee parka nado reshat' za stolom peregovorov," *Respublika*, November 5, 2004, 5.
88. "Ocherednoe pokushenie na 'devstvennye lesa Komi," *Greenpeace Russia*, January 26, 2009, http://www.greenpeace.org/russia/ru/news/2951525/.
89. "Verkhovnyi sud RF vernul mestorozhdeniia zolota 'Chudnoe' v sostav natsparka 'Iugyd Va'," *BNK Informatsionnoe agenstvo*, March 10, 2014, https://www.bnkomi.ru/data/news/32342/.
90. "Genprokuratura soglasilas' c Grinpis," *Greenpeace Russia*, September 25, 2012.

91. Ibid.
92. Ofitsial'nyi sait mogo Inta, http://adminta.ru/index.php/news/9987-sss—l-r-s-s-sss-ss-2014-s.
93. Mikhail Kreindlin, "Mnenie eksperta," *Greenpeace Russia*, July 17, 2019, https://greenpeace.ru/expert-opinions/2019/07/17/zoloto-vmesto-prirody/.

Chapter 8

1. Maksim Gorky, ed., *Belomor: An Account of the Construction of the New Canal between the White Sea and the Baltic Sea*, trans. Amabel Williams-Ellis (New York: Harrison Smith & Robert Haas, 1935), 216.
2. GARF, fond A-259, opis' 49, delo 3399, 42.
3. Jane Costlow, "Imaginations of Destruction: The 'Forest Question' in Nineteenth-Century Russia," *Russian Review* 62, no. 1 (January 2003): 91–118.
4. Stephen Brain, *Song of the Forest: Russian Forestry and Stalinist Environmentalism, 1905–1953* (Pittsburgh: University of Pittsburgh Press, 2011).
5. Sari Autio-Sarasmo, "An Illusion of Endless Forests: Timber and Soviet Industrialization during the 1930s," in *Understanding Russian Nature: Representations, Values, and Concepts*, eds. Arja Rosenholm and Sari Autio-Sarasmo (Helsinki: University of Helsinki, Aleksanteri Institute, 2005), 125–145; Nick Baron, *Soviet Karelia: Politics, Planning and Terror in Stalin's Russia, 1920–1939* (London: Routledge, 2007), 177.
6. Leonid Leonov, *Russkii les* (Moscow: Molodaia gvardiia, 1954).
7. Leonid Leonov et al., "O nashem zelenom druge," *Literaturnaia gazeta*, May 7, 1957, 1; Gleb Goryshin and Evgenii Kutuzov, "Spor o Russkom lese," *Literaturnaia gazeta*, August 20, 1966, 2.
8. Interview with Oleg Cherviakov, June 20, 2015, Varishpel'da, Russian Federation.
9. Zemlia zapovednaia, "Kakoi ei byt'," *Literaturnaia gazeta*, November 30, 1974; B. Ermolin, "Kargopol'e, krai zapovednyi," *Severnyi komsomolets*, January 28, 1981; A. Davydov, "Razvedka Kenozera," *Pravda Severa*, May 8, 1982; V. Kustov, "Natsional'nyi park v Kenozere," *Stroitel' kommunizma*, August 28, 1982; V. Gromov, Byt' li natsional'nomu parku na Kargopol'e?," *Kommunist*, October 11, 1983; T. V. Pleshak, L. F. Ipatov, M. A. Danilov, ed., *Problemy organizatsii prirodno-istoricheskikh natsional'nykh parkov i razvitiia seti okhraniaemykh prirodnykh territorii na Russkom Severe* (Arkhangelsk, 1988), 3.
10. GARF, A-259, opis' 49, delo 3399, 42 and 53.
11. Pleshak et al., *Problemy organizatsii prirodno-istoricheskikh natsional'nykh parkov*, 29; NARK fond 689, opis' 1, delo 1461, 176.
12. AVNP, delo 2, 59.
13. Pleshak et al., *Problemy organizatsii prirodno-istoricheskikh natsional'nykh parkov*, 5.
14. AVNP delo 1, 2.
15. L. Peregud, "Doroga v nikuda," *Znamia truda*, May 18, 1988.
16. Nataliia Zabelina, *Natsional'nyi park* (Moscow: Mysl', 1987).
17. Mikhail Prishvin, *V kraiu nepuganykh ptits* (Moscow, 1906); Robert O. Crumney, *Old Believers and the World of the Ant-Christ: The Vyg Community & the Russian State, 1694–1855* (Madison: University of Wisconsin Press, 1970).
18. O. Cherviakov, "Pustynia ili natsional'nyi park," *Komsomolets*, November 10, 1988, 2.
19. Ibid.
20. Ibid.
21. Ibid.
22. Ibid.
23. L. Kitsa, "Bitva za Vodlozero," *Komsomolets*, February 21, 1989.
24. Interview with Oleg Cherviakov.
25. Jonathan Oldfield and Denis J. B. Shaw, "V. I. Vernadsky and the Noosphere Concept: Russian Understandings of Society-Nature Interaction," *Geoforum* 37 (2006): 145–154; V. I. Vernadsky, "The Biosphere and the Noosphere", *American Scientist* 33, no. 1 (January 1945): 1–12.

26. Paul Josephson et al., *An Environmental History of Russia* (Cambridge: Cambridge University Press, 2013), 243.
27. Vladimir Antipin, "Vodlozerskii natsional'nyi park," *Priroda glazami uchenykh*, no. 1 (Petrozavodsk: Vodlozerskii natsional'nyi park, 2007), 3; interview with S. N. Drozdov, May 15, 2013, Petrozavodsk, Russian Federation, 3; NARK, fond 6196, opis' 1, delo 5, 40.
28. A. Kurnosov, "Agrolesprom i ne natsional'nyi park," *Komsomolets*, May 4, 1989; A. Kiriasov, "Zamysly i real'nost: Natsional'nyi park v Vodlozero," *Leninskaia pravda*, December 20, 1989; Kitsa, "Bitva za Vodlozero"; NARK, fond R-690, opis' 7, delo 4926, 210.
29. V. P. Fokina, "Kogda molchat' nel'zia." *Komsomolets*, May 27, 1989.
30. Interview with Vladimir Antipin, May 20, 2013, Petrazavodsk, Russian Federation.
31. A. I. Pimenova, "Dumaiu, menia podderzhat mnogie," *Znamia truda*, May 27, 1989.
32. Ibid.
33. Oleg Cherviakov, "Sobytie obshcherossiiskovo masshtaba," *Lesnaia gazeta*, May 9, 1990; O. Cherviakov, "Eshcho ne pozdno," *Priroda i chelovek* 10 (October 1989): 10–12.
34. Cherviakov, "Eshcho ne pozdno," 10.
35. Ibid., 11.
36. L. Peregud, "Zemlia u okeana," *Znamia truda*, July 25, 1989, 3; Viktor Shevchenko, "Eshcho raz o natsional'nom parke," *Znamia truda*, May 27, 1989.
37. I. Selivanov, "O sozdanii Vodlozerskogo natsional'nogo parka," *Sel'skaia zhizn'*, January 10, 1990.
38. AVNP, delo 2, 206.
39. Ibid., 215.
40. Ibid., 216.
41. Ibid.
42. Ibid., 16.
43. Ibid., 282.
44. Ibid., 41.
45. Ibid., 39.
46. Ibid., 42.
47. Ibid., 252.
48. Ibid., 261.
49. For more on how "selling authenticity" often becomes an exercise in self-caricature, see Hal Rothman, *Devil's Bargains: Tourism in the Twentieth-Century American West* (Lawrence: University Press of Kansas, 1998).
50. AVNP, delo 2, 64.
51. Ibid., 41–42.
52. Ibid.
53. Stephen J. Macekura, *Of Limits and Growth: The Rise of Global Sustainable Development in the Twentieth Century* (Cambridge: Cambridge University Press, 2017), 219–260.
54. Interview with Nataliia Zabelina, July 21, 2015, Moscow, Russian Federation.
55. GARF, A-259, opis' 49, delo 3399, 57.
56. Ibid., 53.
57. Ibid., 90.
58. Interview with Cherviakov, June 20, 2015. Cherviakov explained these dynamics to me.
59. GARF, fond A-259, opis' 49 delo 3399, 5.
60. NARK, fond R-690, opis' 7, delo 5089.
61. GARF, A-259, opis' 49, delo 3399, 2.
62. Interview with Oleg Cherviakov.
63. N. N. Pervunskii, "Natsional'niy park ili eshcho odin kompleksnyi lespromkhoz?," *Pudozhskii vestnik*, March 19, 1992, 2.
64. V. Agarkov, "V natsional'nom parke," *Pudozhskii vestnik*, August 11, 1992, 2.
65. Interview with Oleg Cherviakov.
66. Interview with Vladimir Antipin.
67. A. Tamm and L. Peregud, "Legendy i byli Vodlozer'ia: v zalozhnikakh natsional'nogo parka," *Severnyi kur'er*, June 11, 1992. Also see E. V. Sidorova, "Po povodu sporov o natsional'nom

parke," *Pudozhskii vestnik*, April 28, 1992; I. Dobrynina, "V krivom zerkale Vodlozer'ia," *Severnyi kur'er*, December 9, 1994; V. Smirnov, "Komu nuzhny mal'chiki dlia bit'ia," *Pudozhskii vestnik*, December 23, 1994.

68. Vladimir Agarkov, "Ekodar na rasput'e," *Pudozhskii vestnik*, March 24, 1993.
69. Ibid.
70. Ibid.
71. N. Mikhailova, "Vokrug natsional'nogo parka Vodlozerskii," *Pudozhskii vestnik*, May 12, 1993.
72. Ibid.
73. Ibid.
74. Pavel Rusinov, "Lesom zhivi," *Pudozhskii vestnik*, July 13, 1993.
75. Tamm and Peregud, "Legendy i byli Vodlozer'ia."
76. Ibid.
77. Archive of Julius Dobroshin (documents of Soiuzgiproleskhoz).
78. Ibid.
79. Interview with Oleg Cherviakov.
80. Vladimir Agarkov, "Teper' vy nam park-pobratim," *Pudozhskii vestnik*, March 30, 1993.
81. Personal archive of Julius Dobroshin.
82. Ibid.; Interview with Oleg Cherviakov.
83. Interview with Oleg Cherviakov.
84. Ibid.
85. National'nyi park Vodlozerskii, http://vodlozero.ru.
86. http://karelinform.ru/?id=20335; National'nyi park Vodlozerskii, http://vodlozero.ru/ru/news/11058.html.
87. National'nyi park Vodlozerskii, http://vodlozero.ru/ru/news/11058.html.
88. Interview with Oleg Cherviakov.

Chapter 9

1. Victor Grebeshnikov, "Environmentalists Finally Find an Ear: Russia Expert Says Yeltsin Is Not Only Listening, He's Acting," *Los Angeles Times*, January 23, 1992.
2. Jerry A. McNeely, ed., *Parks for Life: Report of the IVth World Conference on National Parks and Protected Areas* (Gland, Switzerland: IUCN, 1993).
3. Ibid., 46.
4. Phillip Pryde, "Post-Soviet Development and Status of Russian Nature Reserves," *Post-Soviet Geography and Economics* 38, no. 2 (1997): 65; A. A. Nikol'skii, "Letopis' prirody obryvaetsia," *Spasenie* 13–14 (August 1995): 8.
5. Aleksandr Aleeksandrovich Kuchko, *Liubov' moia Paanajärvi* (Petrazavodsk: Institut lesa, 2002); P. Voutilainen, "Spasem i sokhranim: Sozdan ekologicheskii fond *Paanajärvi*," *Severnyi kur'er*, January 23, 1993, 4; V. Timofeev, "Ekologicheskie kirpichki: Pravitel'stvo Rossii reshilo byt' natsional'nomu parku *Paanajärvi*," *Severnyi kur'er*, May 27, 1992, 2; Iu. Systra, "Paanajärvi golubaia zhemchuzhina Severa," *Severnyi kur'er*, July 31, 1992, 2.
6. O. N. Ianitskii, "Lager' protesta na Mogutovoi Gore," in *Rossiia: ekologicheskii vyzov* (Novosibirsk: Sybirskii khronograf, 2002), 145; Laura A. Henry, "Russian Environmentalists and Civil Society," in Alfred B. Evans, Laura A. Henry, and Lisa McIntosh Sundstrom, *Russian Civil Society: A Critical Assessment* (New York: M. E. Sharpe, 2006), 212.
7. Feliks Shtil'mark, *A History of the Russian Zapovedniks*, translated by G. H. Harper (Edinburgh: Russian Nature, 2002), 193.
8. For an article that Paustovskii wrote about nature protection on the Oka River, see Konstantin Paustovskii, "Za krasotu rodnoi zemli!," *Literaturnaia gazeta*, July 12, 1955.
9. The first book oriented toward tourism in the region was published in 1966. See A. Popov, *Po Meshcherskomu kraiu* (Moscow: Profizdat, 1966).
10. V. P. Chizhova, *Rekreatsionnye nagruzki v zonakh otdykha* (Moscow: Lesnaia promyshlennost', 1977) 34.
11. N. V. Maksakovskii, Meshcherskii natsional'nyi park," *Riazanskii ekologicheskii vestnik* 1 (January 1993): 51.

12. Ibid., 52.
13. V. Pankratov, "Byt' Meshchere parkom," *Priokskaia pravda*, December 14, 1983, 4.
14. Douglas Weiner, *A Little Corner of Freedom: Russian Nature Protection from Stalin to Gorbachev* (Berkeley: University of California Press, 1999), 432.
15. Iu. Karelin, "Sokhranim Meshcheru," *Riazanskii komsomolets*, February 26, 1987, 3; V. Pankratov, "Natsional'nyi park v Meshchere," *Priokskaia pravda*, March 25, 1987, 4; Iu. Karelin, "Rytsar' prirody i literatury," *Riazanskii komsomolets*, March 12, 1988, 4; V. Pankratov, "Meshcherskii park. Vzgliad v budushchee," *Priokskaia pravda*, August 9, 1991, 3; T. Minakova, "Mesta zapovednye," *Priokskaia pravda*, May 17, 1990, 3.
16. L. Zhukova, "Za spasenie Meshchery," *Riazanskii komsomolets*, March 12, 1988, 4.
17. N. M. Zabelina, *Vspominaiu institut, kolleg, prirodu* (Moscow: Green Print, 2019), 252.
18. Ibid., 253.
19. Ibid., 254.
20. Personal archive of Julius Dobroshin (documents from Soiuzgiproleskhoz)
21. GARF, fond 10200, opis' 4, delo 2156, 36.
22. Ibid.
23. Ibid.
24. Ibid., 87.
25. Ibid.
26. Ibid., 92.
27. Ibid., 94.
28. Ibid., 98.
29. Personal archive of Julius Dobroshin (documents from Soiuzgiproleskhoz).
30. Zabelina, *Vspominaiu institut, kolleg, prirodu*, 266; Nadezhda Krasavina, "Natsional'nyi park 'Meshcherskii' prevratilsia v okotnich'e ugod'ia i rodovuiu usad'bu" *Insaider*, May 12, 2015 (http://in-sider.org/criminal/item/466-kriminal-uhodit-lesom.html).
31. GARF, fond 10200, opis' 4, delo 2151, 119.
32. GARF, fond 10200, opis' 4, delo 4479, 127.
33. Ibid., 120.
34. Patty A. Gray, *The Predicament of Chukotka's Indigenous Movement: Post-Soviet Activism in the Russian Far North* (Cambridge: Cambridge University Press, 2005).
35. "Russian-U.S. Park Plan in Bering Strait Becoming Fight to Develop or Protect," *Los Angeles Times*, March 6, 1992.
36. Gray, *Predicament of Chukotka's Indigenous Movement*, xii.
37. Ivan Konstantin, "Multiple Debates Arise over Plans for International Bering Strait Park," *WE/MbI*, March 1993, 1.
38. Ibid., 18.
39. Ibid., 25.
40. GARF, fond 10200, opis' 4, delo 4470, 127.
41. Gray, *Predicament of Chukotka's Indigenous Movement*, 1–2.
42. "Deklaratsiia svobodnogo razvitiia narodov Severa," *Sovetskaia Chukotka*, November 12, 1991.
43. GARF, fond 10200, opis' 4, delo 4479, 91.
44. Ibid.
45. Ibid., 92.
46. Ibid.
47. Ibid., 99.
48. See Mikhail Alexseev, *Center-Periphery Conflict in Post-Soviet Russia: A Federation Imperiled* (New York: St. Martin's, 1999).
49. Marjorie Mandelstam Balzer, "Dilemmas of Federalism in Siberia," in *Center-Periphery Conflict in Post-Soviet Russia: A Federation Imperiled*, ed. Mikhail Alexseev (New York: St. Martin's, 1999), 152.
50. GARF, fond 10200, opis' 4, delo 4479, 52.
51. Ibid., 53.
52. Gray, *Predicament of Chukotka's Indigenous Movement*, 191.

53. Ibid., 16 and 95.
54. Ibid., 13.
55. Ibid., 182.
56. Ibid.
57. GARF, fond 10200, opis' 4, delo 4479, 13.
58. Ibid.
59. Ibid., 51.
60. Ibid., 8.
61. "Russian-U.S. Park Plan in Bering Strait Becoming Fight to Develop or Protect."
62. Ibid., 51.
63. Vsevolod Stepanitskii, "Russia Adopts New Federal Law on Protected Territories," *Russian Conservation News*, May 1995, 4–5. The adoption of the law by the Soviet parliament was thwarted by the fall of the USSR. A second attempt failed in 1993 a few months before Yeltsin dissolved parliament.
64. "Beringiia," *Krainii Sever*, July 6, 1995.
65. Laura Henry, "Between Transnationalism and State Power: The Development of Russia's Post-Soviet Environmental Movement," *Environmental Politics* 19, no. 5 (May 2010): 763.
66. Ibid., 8.
67. Vladislav Larin et al., *Okhrana prirody Rossii: Ot Gorbacheva do Putina* (Moscow: KMK 2003), 188.
68. Nikol'skii, "Letopis' prirody obryvaetsia," 8.
69. Personal archive of Julius Dobrushin (documents of Soiuzgiproleskhoz).
70. Margaret Williams, "March for Parks—International Celebration of Natural Heritage," *Russian Conservation News*, May 1996, 18.
71. Pryde, "Post-Soviet Development and Status of Russian Nature Reserves," 68.
72. GARF, fond 10200, opis' 5, delo 2301, 2; GAIO, R-3523, opis' 1, delo 74, 69.
73. Larry Bowers, "Visitors Say Russian Parks Inaccessible but Improving," *Knoxville News Sentinel*, September 22, 1996, BC4.
74. Shtil'mark, *History of the Russian Zapovedniks*, 203.
75. Tatyana Pyatina, "Eco-Tourism Opportunities and Reality: Valdai National Park," *Russian Conservation News* 5 (October 1995): 7.
76. *Tol'ko vsem mirom*, Kinodokument 52098, www.net-film.ru.
77. Personal archive of Julius Dobroshin (documents of Soiuzgiproleskhoz).
78. GARF 10200, opis' 4, delo 2447, 6.
79. Personal archive of Julius Dobroshin (documents from Soiuzgiproleskhoz).
80. Ibid.
81. Andrei Baiduzhy, "Should We Forget about Ecology? Clean Air Is the Price of Economic Survival," *Current Digest of the Russian Press* 46, no. 11 (April 13, 1994). Originally in *Nezavisimaia gazeta*, 2. For more on the decline in environmental concern, see Joshua Abrams and Matt Auer, "The Disappearance of Popular Environmental Activism in Post-Soviet Russia," in *Restoring the Cursed Earth: Appraising Environmental Policy Reforms in Eastern Europe and Russia*, ed. Matthew R. Auer (New York: Rowman & Littlefield, 2005), 166.
82. Ranee K. L. Panjabi, *The Earth Summit at Rio* (Boston: Northeastern University Press, 1997), 1.
83. Larin et al., *Okhrana prirody Rossii*, 88.
84. Laura Henry, *Red to Green*: Environmental Activism in Post-Soviet Russia (Ithaca, NY: Cornell University Press, 2010), 58. Also see Larin et al., *Okhrana prirody Rossii*, 149.
85. Laura Williams, "WWF in Russia—Worldwide Fund For Nature," *Russian Conservation News*, January 1995, 24. V. Troianovskii, "Zhivet strana div," *Pozitsiia*. July 27, 1992. In 1993, they worked with the Socio-Ecological Union to compile an investment package on urgent measures for conserving Russia's biological diversity.
86. Vladimir Koshevoy, "Russia-USA: Ecology and Education, Five Years of Activity in Environmental Exchanges," *Russian Conservation News*, October 1995, 10.
87. GARF, fond 10200, opis' 4, delo 4478, 3.
88. Iurii Efremov, "Natsional'nye parki vopiiut o spasenii," *Okhota i okhotnich'e khoziaistvo* 4 (April 1994): 3.

89. GARF, fond 10200, opis' 4, delo 7726, 16.
90. Shtil'mark, *History of the Russian Zapovedniks*, 208–209.
91. Eugene Simonov and Vsevolod Stepanitskii, "Leaders of Russia's Protected Areas Take Desperate Measures in a Desperate Situation," *Russian Conservation News* 1 (January 1995): 3.
92. Ibid., 3.
93. Ibid., 3.
94. Ibid.
95. Ibid.
96. Simonov and Stepanitskii, "Leaders of Russia's Protected Areas Take Desperate Measures," 3.
97. Shtil'mark, *History of the Russian Zapovedniks*, 215.
98. RGAE, fond 709, opis' 1, delo 310, 122.
99. N. Ovsiannikov, "Kul'turnaia evoliutsiia v zapovednom dele," *Spasenie* 9 (1994): 5.
100. Shtil'mark, *History of the Russian Zapovedniks*, 217.
101. GARF, fond 10200, opis' 5, delo 2301, 9. This sentiment was commonly expressed. See N. Danilina, "Zapovedniki ne nuzhno reformirovat': Ikh nuzhno sokhranit'," *Zelenyi mir* 15 (1994): 11.
102. Henry, "Russian Environmentalists and Civil Society," 215.
103. Larin et al., *Okhrana prirody Rossii*, 244.
104. "Mezhdunarodnoe soveshchanie 'Na puti k ustoichivomu razvitiiu Rossii': Ekologicheskaia politika," *Zapovedniki i natsional'nye parki* 27 (1999): 4.
105. UNESCO Archives, box 23, File Plan WHC/74/534, UDC 502.7 (469).
106. Ibid.
107. Celestine Bohlen, "Petropavlovsk-Kamchatsky Journal; Russia Permits Just a Peek at Nature in the Raw," *New York Times*, October 28, 1992.
108. Interview with Vitalii Men'shikov, April 18, 2015, St. Petersburg.
109. G. Sheveleva, "Neklasicheskaia nauka i problemy unikal'nykh regionov," *Znanie-sila* 4 (April 1993): 68.
110. Ibid., 78.
111. Interview with Vitalii Men'shikov.
112. Ibid.
113. Ibid.
114. UNESCO Archives, box 24, File Plan: WHC/74/534.2, UDC 502.7 (470) N.
115. Interview with Vitalii Men'shikov.
116. Ibid.
117. Ibid.
118. Ibid.
119. Ibid.
120. Larin et al., *Okhrana prirody Rossii*, 128.
121. Ibid., 128.
122. Alfred B. Evans, Jr., "Civil Society in the Soviet Union?" in *Russian Civil Society: A Critical Assessment*, eds. Alfred B. Evans, Laura A. Henry, and Lisa McIntosh Sundstrom (Armonk, NY: M. E. Sharpe, 2006).
123. Larin et al., *Okhrana prirody Rossii*, 191.
124. G. Nadareishvili, "Luchshe raz uvidet'," *Lesnaia gazeta*, September 10, 1999, 3.
125. Larin et al., *Okhrana prirody Rossii*, 190.
126. UNESCO Archives, box 24, File Plan WHC/74/534.2, UDC 502.7 (470) N.
127. Personal archive of Julius Dobroshin (documents of Soiuzgiproleskhoz).
128. A. M. Volkov, "K kontseptsii osobo okhraniaemykh prirodnykh territorii Rossii," *Zapovedniki i natsional'nye parki mira* 28 (1999): 36.
129. Ibid.

Conclusion

1. G.A. Yavlinsky and A.V. Yablokov, "Ob ekologicheskoi politike nakanune ocherednogo 'Goda ekologii'," *Iabloko*, December 26, 2016, https://www.yabloko.ru/news/2016/12/27.
2. Ibid.

3. V.B. Stepantskii, “Pochemu ia pokinul Minprirody Rossii,” *Live Journal*, April 10, 2017, http://shpilenok.livejournal.com/297030.html.
4. Ibid.
5. V. B. Stepanitskii and M. L. Kreidlin, *Gosudarstvennyie prirodnye zapovedniki i natsional'nye parki: Ugrozy, neudachi, upushchennye vozmozhnosti* (Moscow: Greenpeace Russia, 2004), 33; O. Skosyrskaia, “Ostrovki prirody,” *Barguzinskaia pravda*, January 22, 2004.
6. Stepanitskii and M. L. Kreidlin, *Gosudarstvennyie prirodnye zapovedniki i natsional'nye parki*, 41.
7. For more on the “Foreign Agent” law, see Kate Pride-Brown, *Saving the Sacred Sea: The Power of Civil Society in an Age of Authoritarianism and Globalization* (New York: Oxford University Press, 2018), 169–189.
8. Press Center, “Grinpis i WWF Rossii ne khotiat byt' ‘inoagentami,” *Interfaks*, June 5, 2013, http://www.interfax.ru/presscenter/310813.
9. “Den' ekologa v god okhrany okruzhaiushchei sredy,” *Greenpeace Russia*, June 5, 2013, http://m.greenpeace.org/russia/ru/high/news/2013/05-06-eko-nko/.
10. Sabrina Tavernise, “MacArthur Foundation to Close Offices in Russia,” *New York Times*, July 22, 2015, https://www.nytimes.com/2015/07/23/world/europe/macarthur-foundation-to-close-offices-in-russia.html.
11. Amur Tiger Center website, http://amur-tiger.ru/en/.
12. GARF, fond 10200, opis' 5, delo 7360, 26; “Far Eastern Nature Park and Amur Tiger Museum at Russky Island in Vladivostok,” Amur Tiger Center, June 29, 2018, http://amur-tiger.ru/en/press_center/news/1110/.
13. “Putin poprivetstvoval uchastnikov festivalia ‘Den' tigra' vo Vladivostoke,” *RIA Novosti*, September 29, 2018, https://ria.ru/20180929/1529615027.html.
14. For more on using “showcase” projects to impress foreigners, see Michael David-Fox, *Showcasing the Great Experiment: Cultural Diplomacy and Western Visitors to the Soviet Union, 1921–1941* (New York: Oxford University Press, 2011).
15. A. Yablokov, “Ob ekologicheskoi politike nakanune ocherednogo ‘Goda ekologii,” *Iabloko*, December 26, 2016.
16. Suren Gazarian, “Sochi-2014: kak Olimpiada pomogla ukrast' zemli natsional'nogo parka,” *Radio Ekho Moskvy*, January 23, 2014, https://echo.msk.ru/blog/suren_gazaryan/1243836-echo/.
17. Roman Korolev, “Okhrana bez granits,” *Moskovskaia pravda*, September 17, 2015.
18. Aleksandra Mertsalova and Khalil' Aminov, “Voennye zeseliat Veshnie vody,” *Kommersant Daily*, August 21, 2017, 7; “V pravitel'stve predlozhili provesti zheleznuiu dorogu cherez ‘Losinyi ostrov'. Chast' parka i tak planuruiut vyrubit' dlia stroitel'stva shosse,” *Novaia gazeta*, July 13, 2019, https://www.novayagazeta.ru/news/2019/05/30/152114-v-pravitelstve-predlozhili-provesti-zheleznuyu-dorogu-cherez-losinyy-ostrov-chast-parka-i-tak-planiruyut-vyrubit-dlya-stroitelstva-shosse.
19. Michael B. Mascia and Sharon Pailler, “Protected Area Downgrading, Downsizing, and Degazettement (PADDD) and Its Conservation Implications,” *Conservation Letters* 4 (2011): 9–20.
20. Joe Fox, Lauren Tierney, Seth Blanchard, and Gabriel Florit, “What Remains of Bears Ears,” *Washington Post*, April 12, 2019, https://www.washingtonpost.com/graphics/2019/national/bears-ears/?utm_term=.13cfc83df809; Brian Maffly, “Trump's Team Offers a New Vision for Utah's former Grand Staircase: Nearly 700,000 Acres Would Be Open to Mining or Drilling,” *Salt Lake Tribune*, August 15, 2018, https://www.sltrib.com/news/environment/2018/08/15/feds-release-management/.
21. Steven Mufson, “Trump Administration Takes Another Step toward Oil Drilling in Arctic National Wildlife Refuge,” *Washington Post*, December 20, 2018, https://www.washingtonpost.com/national/health-science/trump-administration-takes-another-step-toward-oil-drilling-in-arctic-national-wildlife-refuge/2018/12/20/5fb93f40-0469-11e9-b5df-5d3874f1ac36_story.html?utm_term=.776fb2fe854f.
22. Alfred Runte, *National Parks: The American Experience*, 4th ed. (New York: Taylor, 2010).
23. Warwick Frost and C. Michael Hall, “American Invention to International Concept,” in *Tourism and National Parks: International Perspectives on Development, Histories and Change*, eds. Warwick Frost and C. Michael Hall (London: Routledge, 2015), 30. Although not

focused on Russia, the authors write, "If national parks arose from uniquely American factors, how could the concept spread to other countries where these conditions were not present and, in some cases, arguably even antithetical?"

24. Donald Worster, "Epilogue: Nature, Liberty, and Equality," in *American Wilderness: A New History*, ed. Michael Lewis (New York: Oxford University Press, 2007), 264.
25. Diane Koenker, *Club Red: Vacation Travel and the Soviet Dream* (Ithaca, NY: Cornell University Press, 2013).
26. Martin Mowforth and Ian Munt, *Tourism and Sustainability: Development, Globalisation, and New Tourism in the Third World* (London: Routledge, 2016), 19.
27. World Bank, "International Tourism, Receipts (current US$)—Russian Federation," https://data.worldbank.org/indicator/ST.INT.RCPT.CD?locations=RU.
28. Ibid.
29. World Travel and Tourism Council, *Travel and Tourism Economic Impact 2018: Russian Federation* (London: World Travel and Tourism Council, 2018), 8.
30. Roberto Crotti and Tiffany Misrahi, eds., *The Travel and Competitiveness Report* (Geneva: World Economic Forum, 2017), 287.
31. Martin Müller, "From Sacred Cow to Cash Cow: The Shifting Political Ecology of Protected Territories in Russia," *Zeitschrift für Wirtschaftgeografie* 58 (2014) 138.
32. Ibid., 139.
33. Alexandra Odynova, "Tourism Brings Revenue and Conflict to Russia's Park System," *Moscow Times*, June 6, 2012, https://www.themoscowtimes.com/2012/06/06/tourism-brings-revenue-and-conflict-to-russias-park-system-a15289; Müller, "From Sacred Cows to Cash Cow," 139.
34. Odynova, "Tourism Brings Revenue."
35. "Putin poruchil podderzhat razvitie ekoturizma," *Ekonomicheskie novosti*, September 21, 2017.
36. http://turstat.com/ecotourismrussia2016; Jim Robbins, "How a Surge in Visitors is Overwhelming America's National Parks," *Yale Environment360*, July 31, 2017, https://e360.yale.edu/features/greenlock-a-visitor-crush-is-overwhelming-americas-national-parks; https://irma.nps.gov/Stats/Reports/National.
37. Vsevolod Stepanitskii, "Gosudarstvom zapovedano," *Rossiiskaia gazeta*, May 22, 2018.
38. Ibid.
39. "O territorii Pribaikal'skogo natsional'nogo parka ubrali 25 tonn musora," *Sibirskie novosti*, April 24, 2019, http://snews.ru/news/s-territorii-pribaykalskogo-nacionalnogo-parka-ubrali-25-tonn-musora.
40. Natsional'nyi park pod Samaroi prevratili v svalku," *Vesti. Nedvizhimost'*, https://realty.vesti.ru/gorod/nacionalnyy-park-pod-samaroy-prevratili-v-svalku; "Natsional'nyi park 'Samarskaia luka' prevratilsia v svalku—video," 5-tv, April 17, https://www.5-tv.ru/news/247628/nacionalnyj-park-samarskaa-luka-prevratilsa-vsvalku-video/.
41. Andrey Korolev, "Sochi. Natsional'nyi park prevrashchaiut v svalku," *Radio Svobody*, October 1, 2013, https://www.svoboda.org/a/25123528.html.
42. "Sobravshim musor posetiteliam parka v Sochi vozvrashchaiut den'gi za bilet," *TVU*, November 5, 2017, https://www.tvc.ru/news/show/id/126910; on entry fees, see Müller, "From Sacred Cow to Cash Cow," 138; Tatiana Smol'iakova, "Muzei pod otkrytom nebom," *Rossiiskaia gazeta*, September 4, 2014, 17.
43. David Louter, *Windshield Wilderness: Cars, Roads, and Nature in Washington's National Parks* (Seattle: University of Washington Press, 2010); Marguerite Shaffer, *See America First: Tourism and National Identity, 1880–1940* (Washington DC: Smithsonian Books, 2001).
44. Paul Sutter, "Putting Wilderness in Context: The Interwar Origins of the Modern Wilderness Idea," in *American Wilderness: A New History*, ed. Michael Lewis. (New York: Oxford University Press, 2007), 168.
45. Paul Sutter, *Driven Wild: How the Fight against Automobiles Launched the Modern Wilderness Movement* (Seattle: University of Washington Press, 2001).
46. Robert Marshall, "The Problem of the Wilderness," *Scientific Monthly* 30, no. 2 (February 1930): 141–148.
47. Mark Harvey, "Loving the Wild in Postwar America," in *American Wilderness: A New History*, ed. Michael Lewis (New York: Oxford University Press, 2007), 190.

48. Runte, *National Parks*, 157.
49. Jerry Frank, *Making Rocky Mountain National Park: The Environmental History of an American Treasure* (Lawrence: University Press of Kansas, 2013), 41; Richard West Sellars, *Preserving Nature in the National Parks: A History* (New Haven, CT: Yale University Press, 1997), 149–180; Bernard De Voto, "Let's Close the National Parks," *Harper's Magazine* (October 1953): 49–52.
50. William Cronon, ed., *Uncommon Ground: Rethinking the Human Place in Nature* (New York: W. W. Norton, 1996); J. Baird Callicott and Michael P. Nelson, *The Great New Wilderness Debate* (Athens, GA: University of Georgia Press, 1998); Michael P. Nelson and J. Baird Callicott eds., *The Wilderness Debate Rages On: Continuing on the Great New Wilderness Debate* (Athens, GA: University of Georgia Press, 2008); Lewis, *American Wilderness.*
51. In Nelson and Callicott's *The Wilderness Debate Rages On*, Russia does not even appear in the index.
52. Roderick Nash, *Wilderness and the American Mind*, 4th ed. (New Haven, CT: Yale University Press, 2014); Runte, *National Parks.*
53. Mark David Spence, *Dispossessing the Wilderness: Indian Removal and the Making of National Parks* (New York: Oxford University Press, 2000).
54. Ramachandra Guha, "Radical American Environmentalism and Wilderness Preservation: A Third World Critique," *Environmental Ethics* 11 (1989): 71–83; Roderick P. Neumann, *Imposing Wilderness* (Berkeley: University of California Press, 2002); Christopher Conte, "The Internationalization of the American Wilderness Concept," in *American Wilderness: A New History*, ed. Michael Lewis, 223–241.
55. William Cronon, "The Problem of Wilderness; or, Getting Back to the Wrong Nature," in *Uncommon Ground: Rethinking the Human Place in Nature.*
56. James Morton Turner "From Woodcraft to 'Leave No Trace': Wilderness, Consumerism, and Environmentalism in Twentieth Century America," *Environmental History* 7, no. 3 (July 2002): 462–484; James Morton Turner, *The Promise of Wilderness: American Environmental Politics since 1964* (Seattle: University of Washington Press, 2012); Silas Chamberlain, *Ramble On: A History of American Hiking* (New Haven, CT: Yale University Press, 2016)
57. Hal Rothman, "Shedding Skin and Shifting Shape: Tourism in the Modern West," in *Seeing and Being Seen: Tourism in the American West*, eds. David M. Wrobel and Patrick T. Long (Lawrence: University Press of Kansas, 2001), 105.
58. Cronon, "The Problem of Wilderness," 81.
59. William Cronon, "The Trouble with Wilderness: A Response," *Environmental History* 1, no. 1 (January 1996): 44–55.
60. Cronon, "The Problem of Wilderness."
61. For a recent essay emphasizing the importance of ideas in shaping motivations to spend time in nature, see Michael P. Nelson and J. Baird Callicott, eds., *The Wilderness Debate Rages On: Continuing the Great New Wilderness Debate* (Athens, GA: University of Georgia Press, 2008), 2–4.
62. For an example of this in Japan, see Carolin Funck and Malcolm Cooper, *Japanese Tourism: Spaces, Places, and Structures* (New York: Berghahn, 2013).
63. Christopher Ely, *This Meager Nature: Landscape and National Identity in Imperial Russia* (DeKalb: Northern Illinois University Press, 2002), 216–222.
64. Ibid., 225.
65. Lauren Leighton, "The Great Soviet Debate over Romanticism, 1957–1964," *Studies in Romanticism* 22, no. 1 (Spring 1983): 41–64.
66. J. Baird Callicott, "Contemporary Criticisms," in *The Wilderness Debate Rages On: Continuing the Great New Wilderness Debate*, 357.
67. William Cronon, "The Trouble with Wilderness: A Response," *Environmental History* 1, no. 1 (January 1996): 49.
68. Jennifer Price, *Flight Maps: Adventures with Nature in Modern America* (New York: Basic Books, 1999), xx. Price argues that seeing nature as "out there" was a particularly American understanding.

69. For more on the importance of *istina* in the late Soviet Union, see Alexei Yurchak, *Everything Was Forever Until It was no More* (Princeton, NJ: Princeton University Press, 2005).
70. For more about infrastructure development in the national parks, see Neil H. Maher, *Nature's New Deal: The Civilian Conservation Corps and the Roots of the American Environmental Movement* (New York: Oxford University Press, 2008).
71. GAIO, R-2844, opis' 1, delo 90, 33.

BIBLIOGRAPHY

Archives

Archive of the Komi Scientific Center (AKNTsUrORAN)
Archive of the Russian Academy of Sciences (ARAN)
Archive of the Russian Geographical Society (ARGO)
Central Archives of the City of Moscow (TsAGM)
Lithuanian Central State Archives (LCSA)
National Archives, College Park, MD
National Archive of the Republic of Karelia (NARK)
National Archive of Latvia (NAM)
Russell Train Papers, Library of Congress
Russian State Archive of the Economy (RGAE)
Russian State Archive of Scientific Technical Documentation (RGANTD), Samara Branch
Samara State Archive of Social and Political History (SGASPI)
State Archive of Contemporary History of the Irkutsk Oblast (GANIIO)
State Archive of the Russian Federation (GARF)
State Archive of the Irkutsk Oblast (GAIO)
State Archive of the Kamchatka Krai (GAKK)
State Archive of the Komi Republic (GARKo)
State Archive of the Moscow Oblast (GAMO)
UNESCO Archives

Personal Documents

Archive of Samara Bend National Park (ASLNP). Zhigulevsk.
Archive of Vodlozerskii National Park (AVGNP). Petrozavodsk.
Personal Archive of Aleksandr Kokovkin. Syktyvkar.
Personal Archive of Julius Dobroshin. Moscow.
Personal Archive of Nataliia Zabelina. Moscow.
Personal Archive of Valerii Erofeev. Samara.

Interviews

Antipin, Vladimir. May 20, 2013, Petrozavodsk.
Bratsev, Adolf Petrovich. July 22, 2012, Syktyvkar.
Cherviakov, Oleg. June 20, 2015, Varishpel'da.

Dobroshin, Julius. July 15, 2015, Moscow.
Men'shikov, Vitalii. April 20, 2015, St. Petersburg.
Roshchevskii, Iurii. June 15, 2013, Zhigulevsk.
Samoilov, Boris. September 16, 2014, Moscow.
Zabelina, Nataliia. October 15, 2013, and July 20, 2015, Moscow.

Periodicals Consulted

Argumenty i Fakty
Audubon
Barguzinskaia Pravda
Beringiia
Biulleten' Moskovskogo obshchestva ispytatelei prirody
Chicago Tribune
Current Digest of the Russian Press
Dal'nii Vostok
Delovoi mir
Don
Ekonomicheskie novosti
Foreign Policy
Geografiia i prirodnye resursy
Geographical Journal
Imperatorskoe Russkoe geograficheskoe obshchestvo: Postoiannaia prirodookhranitel'naia komissiia
Iskra
Izvestiia Akademii nauk
Izvestiia Akademii nauk SSSR: Seriia geografiicheskaia
Izvestiia Komi filiala geograficheskgogo obshchestva
Izvestiia vsesoiuznogo geograficheskogo obshchestva
Izvestia
John Muir Newsletter
Kamchatskaia pravda
Kamchatskii komsomolets
Knoxville News Sentinel
Kommersant
Kommersant Daily
Kraevedcheskie zapiski
Krainii Sever
Krasnoe znamia
Leninskaia pravda
Lesnaia gazeta
Lesnaia promyshlennost'
Lesnoe khoziaistvo
Listki biostantsii iunykh naturalistov
Literaturnaia gazeta
Los Angeles Times
Mir puteshestvii
Molodaia gvardiia
Molodezh' Buriatii
Molodezh' Severa
Molodoi kommunist
Moscow Times
Moskovskaia pravda
Nasha okhota

Na sushe i na more
Nauchnoe slovo
Nauka i tekhnika
New York Times
Novaia zhizn'
Novgorodoskaia pravda
Ogonek
Okhota i okhotnich'e khoziaistvo
Okhrana prirody i zapovednogo dela SSSR
Ornitologicheskii vestnik
Pozitsiia
Pravda
Pravda Severa
Priokskaia gazeta
Priokskaia pravda
Priroda
Priroda i chelovek
Pudozhskii vestnik
Region
Regional Review
Respublika
Riazanskii ekologicheskii vestnik
Riazanskii komsomolets
Rigas Balss
Rossiskaia gazeta
Russian Conservation News
Samarskaia luka: Problemy regional'noi i global'noi ekologii
Science
Sel'skaia zhizn'
Severnyi komsomolets
Sibir'
Siianie Severa
Smena
Sovetskaia Chukotka
Sovetskaia kul'tura
Sovetskaia Latviia
Soviet Life
Sovetskaia molodezh'
Sovetskaia Rossiia
Spasenie
Stroitel' kommunizma
Stroitel'naia gazeta
Stroitel'stvo i arkhitektura Leningrada
Stroitel'stvo Moskvy
Svet
Trud
Turist
Turistskie tropy
Ural'skii sledopyt
Veter stranstvii
Volzhskaia kommuna
Volzhskaia zaria
Volzhskii kommunist

Volzhskii komsomolets
Voprosy geografii
Vostochno-Sibirskaia pravda
Vostok Rossii
Vremia
Vremia X
Vsemirnyi turist
Washington Post
Zapovedniki i natsional'nye parki mira
Zelenyi mir
Zemlia novgorodskaia
Zhigulevskii rabochii
Znamia truda
Znanie-sila
Zvezda
Zvezda Altaia

Conference Proceedings

Adams, Alexander, ed. *First World Conference on National Parks*. Washington: US Department of the Interior, 1962.

Commission of the Russian Federation for UNESCO. *International Conference: Baikal as a World Natural Heritage Site*. Ulan-Ude, September 9–12, 1998.

Denver Service Center, National Park Service. *Beringian Heritage: A Reconnaissance Study of Sites and Recommendations*. Denver: NPS, 1989.

Elliot, Hugh, ed. *Second World Conference on National Parks*. Morges, Switzerland, 1974.

Gosplan SSSR. *Angaro-Eniseiskaia problema*. Moscow: Sovetskaia Aziia, 1932.

International Conference: Baikal as a World Natural Heritage Site. Ulan-Ude: Commission of the Russian Federation for UNESCO, 1998.

International Park Program. *Beringia Heritage: A Reconnaissance Study of Sites and Recommendations*. Denver: National Park Service, 1989.

IUCN. *Seventh General Assembly of the IUCN*. Brussels: IUCN, 1960.

Katunskii proekt: Problemy ekspertizy: Materialy k obshchestvenno-nauchnoi konferentsii, April 13–15, 1990. Novosibirsk: Akademiia nauk SSSR.

Makarov, V. N., and A. G. Giller, eds. *Vsesoiuznyi s"ezd po okhrane prirody v SSSR*. Moscow: Vlast' Sovetov, 1935.

Material from the Third Congress of the Geographical Society of the USSR, 1959.

McNeely, Jerry A., ed. *Parks for Life: Report of the IV World Conference on National Parks and Protected Areas*. Gland, Switzerland: IUCN, 1993.

Ministry of Natural Resources, Komi SSR. *Gosudarstvennyi doklad o sostoianii okruzhaiushchei prirodnoi sredy respubliki Komi v 1995 godu*. Syktyvkar, 1996.

Ministry of the Protection of the Environment and Natural Resources. *Problemy okhrany ozera Baikal i prirodopol'zovaniia v Baikal'skom regione*. Moscow, 1994.

Secretariat of IUPN, ed. *International Technical Conference on the Protection of Nature: Proceedings and Papers*. Paris: IUPN, 1949.

17th Session of the General Assembly of IUCN and 17th Technical Meeting. San Jose Costa Rica, 1–10 February, 1988, 142.

Shaposhnikov, L. K., ed. *Piatoe Vsesoiuznoe soveshchanie po okhrane prirody*. Kishinev: Kartia Moldoveniaske, 1963.

Shaposhnikov, L. K., ed. *6-oe Vsesoiuznoe soveshchanie po okhrane prirody*. Minsk: Nauka i tekhnika, 1965.

Shaposhnikov, L. K., ed. *Tret'e Vsesoiuznoe soveshchanie po okhrane prirody*. Dushanbe: Kommisiia po okhrane prirody USSR, 1961.

Tenth General Assembly of the IUCN. Morges: IUCN, 1970.

PRIMARY PUBLISHED SOURCES

Akhutin, A. N. *Preobrazovanie rek SSSR*. Moscow: Voenizdat, 1950.

Akselrod, M. A., et al. *Tebe turist Urala*. Sverdlovsk: Sverdlovskoe knizhnoe izdatel'stvo, 1961.

Aleksandrov, G. *Problema Angary*. Moscow: Gosudarstvennoe sotsial'no-ekonomicheskoe izdatel'stvo, 1931.

Aleksandrova, Iu. *Ekonomika i organizatsiia zapovednikov i natsionalnykh parkov*. Moscow: Gosudarstvennyi komitet SSSR po okhrane prirody, 1991.

Andreev, Kim Aleksandrovich. *Zapovednik Kivach*. Petrozavodsk: Karel'skoe knizhnoe izdatel'stvo, 1963.

Anuchin, V. I. *Teoreticheskie problemy geografii*. Moscow: Geografgiz, 1960.

Apollova, B. A., K. K. Giul', and V. G. Zabrieva. *Problemy Kaspiiskogo moria*. Baku: Izdatel'stvo Akademii nauk Azerbaidzhanskoi SSR, 1963.

Aristov, P. A., et al. *Sbornik informatsionnykh materialov: Turist, vypusk 14*. Moscow: Turist, 1973.

Arkhangel'skaia, O. A. *Rabota iacheiki OPET po samodeiatel'nomu turizmu*. Moscow: Izdanie OPTE, 1935.

Armand, D. L. *Nam i vnukam*. Moscow: Mysl', 1964.

Arsenin, V. V., N. D. Bondarev, and E. D. Sergievskii. *Gornye puteshestviia po Zapadnomu Kavkazu*. Moscow: Fizkul'tura i sport, 1968.

Azar, V. I. *Otdykh trudiashchikhsia SSSR*. Moscow: Statistika, 1972.

Azarkh, M. *Turistskie znachki rasskazyvaiut*. Sverdlovsk: Sredne-Ural'skoe knizhnoeizdatel'stvo, 1966.

Baikova, V. G., A. S. Duchal, and A. A. Zemtsov. *Svobodnoe vremia i vsestoronee razvitie Lichnosti*. Moscow: Mysl', 1965.

Bannikov, A. G., and Iu. P. Iazan. *Pechoro-Ilychskii zapovednik*. Moscow: Znanie, 1968.

Bashkuev, B. V., and R. F. Tugutov. *Po Buriatii: Turistskie marshruty*. Ulan-Ude: Buriatskoe knizhnoe izdatel'stvo, 1961.

Beliakov, Aleksei. *Legendy i byli Zhigulei*. Kuibyshev: Kuibyshevskoe knizhnoe izdatel'stvo, 1979.

Berkhol'tsas, Ionas. *Natsional'nyi park Gauia*. Moscow: Lesnaia promyshlennost', 1982.

Blagosklonov, K. N., and V. N. Tikhomirov. *Okhrana prirody*. Moscow: Vysshaia shkola, 1967.

Boldakov, E. V. *Zhizn' rek*. Moscow: Gostekhizdat, 1953.

Bologna, V. I. *Vnerabochee vremia i uroven' zhizni trudiashchikhsia*. Novosibirsk: Akademiia nauk SSSR, 1964.

Borodin, I. P. "Okhrana pamiatnikov prirody," *Imperatorskoe Russkoe geograficheskoe obshchestvo: Postoiannaia prirodookhranitel'naia komissiia* 1 (1914): 6–31.

Buiantev, B. R. *K narodnokhoziaistvennym problemam Baikala*. Ulan-Ude: Buriatskoe knizhnoe izdatel'stvo, 1960.

Cammerer, Arno, "National Parks and New World Idealism" *The Regional Review*, vol. 4-6 (June 1940), 6.

Chernov, G. *Turistskie pokhody v "Pechorskie Alpy."* Syktyvkar: Komi knizhnoe izdatel'stvo, 1974.

Chichvarin, V. A. *Okhrana prirody i mezhdunarodnye otnosheniia*. Moscow: Izdatel'stvo "Mezhdunarodnye otnosheniia," 1970.

Chizhova, V. P. *Rekreatsionnye nagruzki v zonakh otdykha*. Moscow: Lesnaia promyshlennost', 1977.

Chizhova, V., and E. Smirnova. *Slovo ob otdykhe*. Moscow: Znanie, 1976.

Crotti, Roberto, and Tiffany Misrahi, eds. *The Travel and Competitiveness Report*. Geneva: World Economic Forum, 2017.

Darbanov, D. R., ed. *Voprosy razvitiia industrii turizma na Baikale*. Ulan-Ude: Buriatskoe knizhnoe izdatel'stvo, 1973.

Davydov, M., and T. Tsunts. *Ot Volkhova do Amura*. Moscow: Sovetskaia Rossiia, 1958.

Demin, E. N. *Na baidarkakh po Podmoskov'iu*. Moscow: Fizkul'tura i sport, 1967.

De Voto, Bernard. "Let's Close the National Parks." *Harper's Magazine*, October 1953, 49–52.

Dezhkin, V. V., ed. "Nelegkaia sud'ba 'Losinki.'" In *V mire zapovednoi prirody*. Moscow: Sovetskaia Rossiia, 1989, 1–3.

D'iakova, R. A. *Vospitanie berezhnogo otnosheniia k prirode v ekskursiiakh (Metodicheskie rekomendatsii)*. Moscow: VTsSPS, 1976.

Dormidotnov, R. "Natsional'nye parki: Problemy vybora territorii i organizatsiia." In *Zemlia i liudi*. Edited by V. A. Bashanov. Moscow: Mysl', 1975.

Dubianskii, V. A., ed. *Mirovaia okhrana prirody*. Petrograd: Imperatorskoe Russkoe geograficheskoe obshchestvo, 1915.

Dunham, Vera. *In Stalin's Time*. Cambridge: Cambridge University Press, 1976.

Ehrlich, Paul. *The Population Bomb*. New York: Ballantine, 1970.

Filippovskii, N., ed. *Chelovek i priroda*. Moscow: Znanie, 1981.

Filippovskii, N. *Natsional'nyi park: Problema sozdaniia*. Moscow: Znanie, 1979.

Gerasimov, I. P. *Preobrazovanie prirody i razvitie geograficheskoi nauki v SSSR*. Moscow: Znanie, 1967.

Gerasimov, I. P. *Teoreticheskie osnovy rekreatsionnoi geografii*. Moscow: Nauka, 1975.

Gerasimov, I. P., and G. I. Galazii. *Goluboe serdtse Sibiri*. Moscow: Znanie, 1966.

Gorbunova, N. N. *Vodnye marshruty Ukrainy*. Moscow: Fizkul'tura i sport, 1968.

Goriup, Paul, ed. *Protected Areas Program*. Newbury, UK: IUCN, 2004.

Gorky, Maksim, ed. *Belomor: An Account of the Construction of the New Canal between the White Sea and the Baltic Sea*. Translated by Amabel Williams-Ellis. New York: Harrison Smith & Robert Haas, 1935.

Grubich, L. *Sotsialisticheskoe stroitel'stvo i proletarskii turizm*. Moscow: OGIZ-Fizkul'tura i turizm, 1931.

Grushko, Ia. M. *Kurorty Vostchnoi Sibiri*. Irkutsk: Irkutskoe knizhnoe izdatel'stvo, 1961.

Grushko, Ia. M. *Puteshestvie po Baikalu dlia otdykha i ukrepleniia zdorov'ia*. Irkutsk: Irkutskoe knizhnoe izdatel'stvo, 1956.

Gukov, V. I. *V kraiu netronutykh sokrovishch*. Moscow: Fizkul'tura i sport, 1959.

Gusev, Oleg. *Ot Barguzinzkogo zapovednika do Ushkan'ikh Ostrovov*. Irkutsk: Irkutskoe knizhnoe izdatel'stvo, 1960.

Gusev, Oleg, and S. K. Ustinov. *Po severnomu Baikalu i Pribaikal'iu*. Moscow: Fizkul'tura i sport, 1966.

Hackers, Henry. "The Albert National Park." *Geographical Journal* 4 (1937): 269–286.

Hardin, Garret. "The Tragedy of the Commons." *Science* 162, no. 13 (December 1968): 1243–1248.

Huxley, Julian. *Africa View*. New York: Harper & Brothers, 1931.

Ianitskii, O. N. *Rossiia: Ekologicheskii vyzov*. Novosibirsk: Sibirskii khronograf, 2002.

Iazan, Iurii Petrovich, ed. *Organizatsiia natsional'nykh parkov SSSR*. Vilnius: Mintis, 1982.

Ivanov, I. G. *Natsional'nye parki: Opyt SSSR i SShA—po materialism sovetsko-amerikanskogo seminara*. Moscow, 1990.

Kaazik, A. V. "Lakhemaaskii natsional'nyi park, ego uchrezhdenie i deiatel'nost'." *Lakhemaaskii natsional'nyi park: Nauchnye trudy po okhrane prirody*. Tartu, 1982, 6–30.

Kemmerikh, A. O *Poliarnyi Ural*. Moscow: Fizkul'tura i sport, 1966.

Kemmerikh, A. O. *Pripoliarnyi Ural*. Moscow: Fizkul'tura i sport, 1970.

Kemmerikh, Aleksandr. *Puteshestvie tseloi zhizni*. Moscow: Moskovskie uchebniki i Kartolitografiia, 2004.

Kemmerikh, A. O. *Severnyi Ural*. Moscow: Fizkul'tura i sport, 1969.

Kirillov, G. B., ed. *Problemy okhrany prirody Sibiri i Dal'nego Vostoka*. Novosibirsk: AN SSSR, 1963.

Kirillov, I. A. *Tainy Krasnykh peshcher*. Moscow: Fizkul'tura i sport, 1959.

Khromov, I. B. *Organizatsiia system otdykha, turizma i okhranoi prirodnoi sredy na Severe*. Leningrad: Stroiizdat, 1981.

Khromov, Iu. B., and V. A. Kliushin. *Organizatsiia zon otdykha i turizma na poberezh'e Baikala*. Moscow: Stroiizdat, 1976.

Kokorev, Iu. M. *Po rekam i ozeram Belorussii*. Moscow: Fizkul'tura i sport, 1966.

Komarov, Boris. *The Destruction of Nature in the Soviet Union*. *TRANS*. New York: M. E. Sharpe, 1980.

Kotliarov, E. A. *Geografiia otdykha i turizma*. Moscow: Mysl', 1978.

Kovalev, L. *Shturm Volgi*. Kuibyshev: Kuibyshevskoe knizhnoe izdatel'stvo, 1956.

Kovda, V. A. *Velikie stroiki kommunizma i preobrazovanie prirody*. Moscow: Pravda, 1951.

Krever, Vladimir, et al. *Conserving Russia's Biodiversity: An Analytical Framework and Initial Investment Portfolio*. Washington D. C.: World Wildlife Fund, 1994.

Krylov, G. V., ed. *Okhrana gornykh landshaftov Sibiri*. Novosibirsk: Nauka, 1973.

Lamakin, V. V. *Po beregam i ostrovam Baikala*. Moscow: Nauka, 1965.

Lapin, K. *Pokoriteli Volgi*. Kuibyshev: Kuibyshevskoe knizhnoe izdatel'stvo, 1956.

Lazarev, N. A. "Ispol'sovanie i okhrana prirody Komi ASSR." *Okhrana prirody Komi ASSR* 1 (1961): 11.

Leonov, Leonid. *Russkii les*. Moscow: Molodaia gvardiia, 1954.

Liberman, Evsei, and Maurice Dobb. *Theory of Profit in Socialist Economy: A Discussion in the Recent Economic Reforms in the USSR*. New Delhi: People's Publishing House, 1966.

Lopatin, V. V. *Turistskie dorogi Severo-Zapada SSSR*. Moscow: Fizkul'tura i sport, 1968.

Lukanenkova, V. K., ed. *Turizm i okhrana prirody—eksperimental'naia programma*. Leningrad, 1972.

Luknitskii, P. *Tadzhikistan*. Moscow: Molodaiia gvardiia, 1951.

Makarov, V. N. *Okhrana prirody v SSSR*. Moscow: Voenizdat, 1949.

Makarov, V. N. *Zapovedniki SSSR*. Moscow: Sel'khozgiz, 1940.

Markin, A. V. *Budushchee elektrifikatsii SSSR*. Moscow: Politicheskaia literatura, 1959.

Marshall, Robert. "The Problem of the Wilderness." *Scientific Monthly* 30, no. 2 (February 1930): 141–148.

Mathiessen, Peter. *Baikal: Sacred Sea of Siberia*. San Francisco: Sierra Club, 1992.

Mazenin, M. *Bol'shaia Volga*. Ivanovsk: Ivanovskoe knizhnoe izdatel'stvo, 1958.

McMurry, K. C. "The Use of Land for Recreation." *Annals of the Association of American Geographers* 20, no. 1 (March, 1930): 7–20.

Morrison, Millicent. *Wild Life and Rare in National Parks and Paradises Round the World*. London: Green Cross Society, 1938.

Moskalenko, B. K. *Baikal: Segodnia i v 2000 godu*. Irkutsk: Vostochno-Sibirskoe knizhnoe izdatel'stvo, 1978.

Muir, John. *Our National Parks*. Madison: University of Wisconsin Press, 1981.

Mullo, I. M. *Po rodnomu kraiu*. Petrozavodsk, Gosizdat KFSSR, 1955.

Nikolaevskii, Aleksandr Georgievich. *Natsional'nye parki*. Moscow: Agropromizdat, 1985.

Oldak, P. G. *Problemy razvitiia industrii turizma*. Novosibirsk: AN SSSR, 1970.

Pagautstsi, V. I. *Fanskie gory i Iagnob*. Moscow: Fizkul'tura i sport, 1968.

Pleshak, T. V., L. F. Ipatov, and M. A. Danilov, eds. *Problemy organizatsii prirodno-istoricheskikh natsional'nykh parkov i razvitiia seti okhraniaemykh prirodnykh territorii na Russkom Severe*. Arkhangelsk: VOOP, 1988.

Pomtkin, Boris. *Doch' Baikala*. Moscow: Gidrometeoizdat, 1961.

Predybailo, A. T. *Krai ozer, lesov i rek*. Moscow: Fizkul'tura i sport, 1960.

Predybailo, A. T. *Po znoinoi Srednei Azii*. Moscow: Fizkul'tura i sport, 1959.

Preobrazhenskii, V. S., and Iu. A. Vedenin. *Geografiia i otdykh*. Moscow: Znanie, 1971.

Prishvin, Mikhail. *V kraiu nepuganykh ptits*. Moscow, 1906.

Pritvits, N. *Saianskii dnevnik*. Moscow: Fizkul'tura i sport, 1959.

Problemy ratsional'nogo ispol'zovaniia i okhrany prirody Samarskoi Luki: Mezhvedomstvennyi sbornik. Kuibyshev, 1983.

Promptov, Iu. G. *Po nebesnym goram*. Moscow: Fizkul'tura i sport, 1959.

Promptov, Iu. G. *V gorakh i dolinakh: Zapiski turista peshekhoda*. Moscow: Fizkul'tura i sport, 1954.

Rasputin, Valentin. *Farewell to Matyora*. Translated by Antonina W. Bouis. Evanston, IL: Northwestern University Press, 1995.

Rasputin, Valentin. *Sibir', Sibir'*. Moscow: Molodaia gvardiia, 1991.

Reimers, Nikolai Fedorovich, and F. R. Shtil'mark. *Osobo okhraniaemye prirodnye territorii*. Moscow: Mysl', 1978.

Rodichkin, L. D. *Chelovek, sreda, otdykh*. Kiev: Budyvel'nik, 1977.

Rogal'skii, V. I. *Turistskie marshruty v Saianakh*. Moscow: Fizkul'tura i sport, 1968.

Roshchevskii, Iurii. "Natsionalnyi prirodnyi park Samarskaia Luka." In *Zelenaia kniga Povolzh'ia*, Roshchevski, Iurii ed. Samara: Samarskoe knizhnoe izdatel'stvo, 1995, 335–345.

Rossolimo, L. L. *Baikal.* Moscow: Nauka, 1966.
Rubel' Raisa. *Turisty Sverdlovska.* Moscow: Fizkul'tura i sport, 1957.
Rubel', B. *Po Uralu.* Moscow: Profizdat, 1953.
Schvarts, S. S., B. P. Kolesnikov, and B. C. Riabinin. *Dialog o prirode.* Sverdlovsk: Sredne-Ural'skoe knizhnoe izdatel'stvo, 1978.
Schurke, Paul. *Bering Bridge: The Soviet American Expedition from Siberia to Alaska.* Minneapolis: Pheifer-Hamilton, 1989.
Semenov, V. I. *Po vulkanam i goriachim istochnikam Kamchatki.* Petropavlovsk: Dal'nevostochnoe knizhnoe izdatel'stvo, 1983.
Semenov, V. I. *V kraiu goriachikh istochnikov.* Petropavlovsk: Dal'nevostochnoe knizhnoe izdatel'stvo, 1988.
Semenov, V. I. *V kraiu vulkanov i geizerov.* Moscow: Fizkul'tura i sport, 1973.
Semenov, V. I. *V kraiu zaoblachnykh vershin.* Petropavlovsk: Dal'nevostochnoe knizhnoe izdatel'stvo, 1970.
Semenov-Tian-Shanskii, Andrei. *Nasha blizhaishaiia zadacha na Dal'nem Vostoke.* St. Petersburg, 1908.
Shcherbakov, Dmitrii. *Po goram Kryma, Kavkaza i Srednei Azii.* Moscow: Geografgiz, 1954.
Shershov. S. F. *Belyi ugol'.* Moscow: Gosenergoizdat, 1957.
Shkliaev, N. A., and L. N. Shkol'nikova. *Organizatsiia i razmeshchenie prirodnykh parkov na territorii SSSR.* Moscow: Gosstroi, 1974.
Shtiurmer, Iu. A. *Ekologicheskoe vospitanie turistov v turistkoi sektsii i klube.* Moscow: Turist, 1990.
Shtiurmer, Iu. A. *Kodar, Chara Udokan: Severnoe Zabaikal'e.* Moscow: Fizkul'tura i sport, 1969.
Shtiurmer, Iu. A. *Obshchestvenno-poleznaia rabota samodeiatel'nykh turistov.* Moscow, 1990.
Shtiurmer, Iu. A. *Po Arkhangel'skoi oblasti.* Moscow: Fizkul'tura i sport, 1967.
Skalon, V. N. *Po Baikalu.* Moscow: Profizdat, 1956.
Skalon, V. N. *Po Sibiri: V pomoshch' turistam.* Moscow: Izdatel'stvo VTsSPS, 1953.
Skalon, V. N. *Rechnye bobry Severnoi Azii.* Moscow: Izdatel'stvo Moskovskogo obshchestva ispytatelei prirody, 1951.
Skalon, V. N. *Russkie zemleprokhodtsy XVII veka v Sibiri.* Novosibirsk: Dom Sovy, 1956.
Slavinskii, O. K., and V. S. Tsarenkov, *Turistskie puteshestviia po Kol'skomu poluostrovu.* Moscow: Fizkul'tura i sport, 1969.
Solov'eva, M. E. *Zapovednik na Pechore.* Syktyvkar: Komi knizhnoe izdatel'stvo, 1963.
Stepanov, A. *Turistskie marshruty Tuvy.* Moscow: Fizkul'tura i sport, 1967.
Snytko, M. K. *Turistskie marshruty po Tambovskoi oblasti.* Tambov: Tambovskoe knizhnoe izdatel'stvo, 1961.
Tsunts, I. M. *Velikie stroiki na rekakh Sibiri.* Moscow: Gospolitizdat, 1956.
Turner, Samuel. *In Siberia: A Record of Travel and Exploration.* London, 1905.
Vasil'ev, M. *Voda rabotaet.* Moscow: Gostekhizdat, 1956.
Vernadsky, V. I. "The Biosphere and the Noosphere." *American Scientist* 33, no. 1 (January 1945): 1–12.
Vetlina, Vera. *Krymskie puteshestviia.* Moscow: Molodaiia gvardiia, 1955.
Vetra, K. Ia., P. A. Eglite. *Puteshestvie po Latviiskoi SSR.* Moscow: Fizkul'tura i sport, 1968.
Vinokurov, P. *Po Iuzhnomu Sakhalinu.* Moscow: Ministerstvo Prosveshcheniia, 1950.
Vitkovich, Viktor. *Puteshestvie po sovetskomu Uzbekistanu.* Moscow: Molodaia gvardiia, 1951.
Volkov, Oleg. *Chur, zapovedano*! Moscow: Sovetskaia Rossiia, 1976.
Volkov, Oleg. *Puteshestvie po Baikalu.* Moscow: Sovetskaia Rossiia, 1958.
Vonzblein, Iu. *Otdykhaite v lesu!* Leningrad: Leningradskaia pravda, 1929.
World Travel and Tourism Council. *Travel and Tourism Economic Impact 2018: Russian Federation.* London: World Travel and Tourism Council, 2018.
Zabelina, Nataliia. *Natsional'nyi park.* Moscow: Mysl', 1987.
Zabelina, N. M. *Opyt okhrany prirodnykh resursov v SShA.* Moscow: Ministerstvo sel'skogo khoziaistva SSSR, 1972.
Zabelina, N. M. *Puteshestvie v natsional'nom parke.* Moscow: Fizkul'tura i sport, 1990.

Zabelina, N. M. *Vspominaiu institut, kolleg, prirodu*. Moscow: Grin Print, 2019.
Zaboeva, I. V. *Prirodnyi park Komi ASSR*. Syktyvkar: Komi knizhnoe izdatel'stvo, 1977.
Zakharov, Iu. S. et al. *Natsional'nyi park v pripoliarnom Urale: Argumenty i pretsedenty*. Moscow, 1993.
Zelenko, Grigorii Andreevich. *Gde iskat' zhemchuzhinu Altaiia*. Moscow: Fizkul'tura i sport, 1957.
Zlatova, E., and V. Kotel'nikov. *Puteshestvie po Moldavii*. Moscow: Molodaiia gvardiia, 1957.

Secondary Books, Articles, and Websites

Aagesen, David. "Rights to Land and Resources in Argentina's Alerces National Park." *Bulletin of Latin American Research* 19 (2000): 547–569.
Abrams, Joshua, and Matt Auer. "The Disappearance of Popular Environmental Activism in Post-Soviet Russia." In *Restoring Cursed Earth: Appraising Environmental Policy Reforms in Eastern*, edited by Matthew R. Auer, 145–174. Rowman & Littlefield, 2005.
Alexeyeva, Liudmilla, and Paul Goldberg. *The Thaw Generation: Coming of Age in the Post-Stalin Era*. Pittsburgh: University of Pittsburgh Press, 1990.
Alexseev, Mikhail *Center-Periphery Conflict in Post-Soviet Russia: A Federation Imperiled*. New York: St. Martin's, 1999.
Anisimov, Evgeny, V. *The Reforms of Peter the Great: Progress through Violence in Russia*. London: Routledge, 1993.
Anisimov, Evgeny, et al. "Books that Link Worlds: Travel Guides, the Development of Transportation Infrastructure, and the Emergence of the Tourism Industry in Imperial Russia, Nineteenth–Early Twentieth Centuries." *Journal of Tourism History* 8, no. 12 (2016): 184–204.
Antipin, Vladimir. "Vodlozerskii natsional'nyi park." In *Priroda glazami uchenykh*. Petrozavodsk: Vodlozerskii natsional'nyi park 2007, 3.
Babiracki, Patty, and Kenyon Zimmer, eds. *Cold War Crossings: International Travel across the Soviet Bloc, 1940s–1960s*. College Station: Texas A&M University Press, 2014.
Balzer, Harley D., ed. *Russia's Missing Middle Class: The Professions in Russian History*. London: Routledge, 1996.
Balzer, Marjorie Mandelstam: "Dilemmas of Federalism in Siberia." In *Center-Periphery Conflict in Post-Soviet Russia: A Federation Imperiled*, edited by Mikhail Alexseev. New York: St. Martin's Press, 1999.
Baron, Nick. *Soviet Karelia: Politics, Planning and Terror in Stalin's Russia, 1920–1939*. London: Routledge, 2007.
Barume, Kwokwo. *Heading Towards Extinction? Indigenous Rights in Africa: The Case of the Twa and Kahuzi-Biega National Park, Democratic Republic of Congo*. Copenhagen: International Working Group for Indigenous Affairs, 2000.
Bassin, Mark. *Imperial Visions: Nationalist Imagination and Geographical Expansion in the Russian Far East, 1840–1865*. Cambridge: Cambridge University Press, 2006.
Bassin, Mark. "The Russian Geographical Society, the 'Amur Epoch,' and the Great Siberian Expedition, 1855–1863." *Annals of the Association of American Geographers* 73, no. 2 (June 1983): 240–256.
Bissibl, Bernhard, Sabine Hohler, and Patrick Kupper, ed. *Civilizing Nature: National Parks in Global Historical Perspective*. New York: Berghahn, 2012.
Black, George. *Empire of Shadows: The Epic Story of Yellowstone*. New York: St. Martin's Griffin, 2013.
Bonhomme, Brian. *Forests, Peasants, and Revolutionaries: Forest Conservation and Organization in Soviet Russia*. Boulder, CO: East European Monographs, 2005.
Boreiko, V. E. *Doroga k zapovednomu: Priorodookhrannaia propaganda i ekoprosveshchenie v zapovednykh ob"ektakh*. Moscow: WWF, 1996.
Boreiko, V. E. *Istoriia okhrany prirody v Ukraine: X-vek-1980 g*. Kiev: Kievskii ekologo-kul'turnyi tsentr, 1995.
Boreiko, V. E. *Ocherki o pionerakh okhrany prirody*. Kiev: Kievskii ekologo-kul'turnyi tsentr, 1996.
Borovinskikh, Alexander, et al. *Sokhranit' i priumnozhit'*. Syktyvkar: Minprirody Komi, 2008.

Bostrum, Kenneth. *Avvakum: The Life Written by Himself.* Ann Arbor: Michigan Slavic Publications, 1979.

Brain, Stephen. "The Appeal of Appearing Green: Soviet-American Ideological Competition and Cold War Environmental Diplomacy." *Cold War History* 16 (October 2014): 1–19.

Brain, Stephen. "The Great Stalin Plan for the Transformation of Nature." *Environmental History* 15, no. 4 (January 2010): 670–700.

Brain, Stephen. *Song of the Forest: Russian Forestry and Stalinist Environmentalism, 1905–1953.* Pittsburgh: Pittsburgh University Press, 2011.

Brain, Stephen. "Stalin's Environmentalism." *Russian Review* 61, no. 1 (January 2010): 93–118.

Brennan, William H. "John Muir in Russia, 1903: Part 2." *John Muir Newsletter* 4, no. 1 (Winter 1993–1994).

Brennan, William H. "John Muir in Russia, 1903: Part 3." *John Muir Newsletter* 4, no. 3 (Summer 1994).

Breslauer, George W. *Yeltsin and Gorbachev as Leaders.* Cambridge: Cambridge University Press, 2002.

Breyfogle, Nicholas. "At the Watershed: 1958 and the Beginnings of Lake Baikal Environmentalism." *Russian and East European Review* 93, no. 1 (January 2015): 147–180.

Breyfogle, Nicholas, ed. *Eurasian Environments: Nature and Ecology in Imperial Russian and Soviet History.* Pittsburgh: University of Pittsburgh Press, 2018.

Brooks, Jeffrey. "The Press and its Message." In *Russia in the Era of NEP,* edited by Sheila Fitzpatrick, Alexander Rabinowitch, and Richard Stites, 231–253. Bloomington: Indiana University Press, 1991.

Brower, David. *For the Earth's Sake: The Life and Times of David Brower.* Salt Lake City: Peregrine Smith, 1990.

Bruno, Andy. *The Nature of Soviet Power: An Arctic Environmental History.* Cambridge: Cambridge University Press, 2016.

Bruno, Andy. "What does it mean to liberate the land? Towards an Environmental History of the Russian Revolution." In *Russia's Home Front in War and Revolution. Book 3: National Disintegration and Reintegration,* edited by Christopher Read et al., 257–277. Bloomington: Indiana University Press, 2018.

Burnham, Philip. *Indian Country, God's Country: Native Americans and the National Parks.* Washington, DC: Island, 2000.

Callicott, J. Baird. "Contemporary Criticisms." In *The Wilderness Debate Rages On: Continuing the Great New Wilderness Debate,* edited by Michael P. Nelson and J. Baird Callicott, 355–377. Athens, GA: University of Georgia Press, 2008.

Callicott, J. Baird, and Michael P. Nelson. *The Great New Wilderness Debate.* Athens, GA: University of Georgia Press, 1998.

Cameron, Sarah. *The Hungry Steppe: Famine, Violence, and the Making of Soviet Kazakhstan.* Ithaca, NY: Cornell University Press, 2018.

Carruthers, Jane *National Park Science: A Century of Research in South Africa.* Cambridge: Cambridge University Press, 2017.

Carson, Rachel. *Silent Spring.* New York: Crest, 1964.

Chamberlain, Silas. *Ramble On: A History of American Hiking.* New Haven, CT: Yale University Press, 2016.

Chernyshova, Natalya. *Soviet Consumer Culture in the Brezhnev Era.* New York: Routledge, 2013.

Clowes, Edith, Samuel Kassow, and James West, eds. *Between Tsar and People: Educated Society and the Quest for Public Identity in Educated Russia.* Princeton, NJ: Princeton University Press, 1991.

Conte, Christopher. "The Internationalization of the American Wilderness Concept." In *American Wilderness: A New History,* edited by Michael Lewis, 223–242. New York: Oxford University Press, 2007.

Conterio, Johanna. "Inventing the Subtropics: An Environmental History of Sochi, 1929–1936." *Kritika: Explorations in Russian and Eurasian History* 16, no. 1 (Winter 2015): 91–120.

Costlow, Jane. *Heart-Pine Russia: Walking and Writing in the Nineteenth-Century Forest*. Ithaca, NY: Cornell University Press, 2012.

Coumel, Laurent. "Building a Soviet Eco-Power while Looking at the Capitalist World: The Rise of Technocratic Environmentalism in Russian Water Controversies, 1957–1989." In *Nature and the Iron Curtain: Environmental Policy and Social Movements in Communist and Capitalist Countries, 1945–1990*, edited by Astrid Mignon Kirchhof and J. R. McNeill, 17–35. Pittsburgh: University of Pittsburgh Press, 2019.

Coumel, Laurent, and Marc Elie. "A Belated and Tragic Ecological Revolution: Nature, Disasters, and Green Activists in the Soviet Union and Post-Soviet States, 1960s–2010s." *Soviet and Post-Soviet Review* 40 (2013): 157–165.

Cronon, William. "The Trouble with Wilderness: A Response." *Environmental History* 1, no. 1 (January 1996): 47–55

Cronon, William. "The Trouble with Wilderness; or, Getting Back to the Wrong Nature." In *Uncommon Ground: Toward Reinventing Nature*, edited by William Cronon, 69–90. New York: W. W. Norton, 1994.

Cronon, William, ed. *Uncommon Ground: Rethinking the Human Place in Nature*. New York: W. W. Norton, 1996.

Crotty, Jo. "Making a Difference? NGOs and Civil Society in Russia." *Europe-Asia Studies* 61, no. 1, January 2009): 85–108.

Cybrisky, Roman A. *Along Ukraine's River: A Social and Environmental History of the Dnipro*. Budapest: Central European University Press, 2018.

Darst, Robert S. "Environmentalism in the USSR: The Opposition to the River Diversion Projects." *Soviet Economy* 4, no. 3 (March 1988): 223–252.

David-Fox, Michael. *Crossing Borders: Modernity, Ideology, and Culture in Russia and the Soviet Union*. Pittsburgh: University of Pittsburgh Press, 2015.

David-Fox, Michael. *Showcasing the Great Experiment: Cultural Diplomacy and Western Visitors to the Soviet Union, 1921–1941*. New York: Oxford University Press, 2011.

Dawson, Jane I. *Eco-Nationalism: Anti-Nuclear Activism and National Identity in Russia, Lithuania, and Ukraine*. Durham, NC: Duke University Press, 1996.

Demuth, Bathsheba. *Floating Coast: An Environmental History of the Bering Strait*. New York: W. W. Norton, 2019.

Demuth, Bathsheba. "The Walrus and the Bureaucrat: Energy, Ecology, and Making the State in the Russian and American Arctic." *American Historical Review* 124, no. 2 (April 2019): 483–510.

Delcore, Henry D. "The Racial Distribution of Privilege in a Thai National Park." *Journal of Southeast Asian Studies* 38, no. 1 (February 2007): 83–105.

Denning, Andrew. *Skiing into Modernity: A Cultural and Environmental History*. Berkeley: University of California Press, 2014.

Dobson, Miriam. *Khrushchev's Cold Summer: Gulag Returnees, Crime, and the Fate of Reform After Stalin*. Ithaca, NY: Cornell University Press, 2011.

Donovan, Victoria. "'How Well Do You Know Your *Krai?*' The *Kraevedenie* Revival and Patriotic Politics in Late Khrushchev-Era Russia." *Slavic Review* 74, no. 3 (September 2015): 464–483.

Dowie, Marc. *Conservation Refugees: The Hundred Year Conflict Between Conservation and Native Peoples* Cambridge, MA: MIT Press, 2011.

Dvornichenko, V. V. *Razvitie turizma v SSSR 1917–1983*. Moscow: Tsentral'noe reklamnoe-informatsionnoe biuro "Turist," 1985.

Dvornichenko, V. V. *Turizm v sisteme mezhdunarodnykh kul'turnykh sviazei SSSR*. Moscow: Nauka, 1978.

Elie, Mark. "Formulating the Environment: Soviet Soil Scientists and the International Desertification Discussion, 1968–1991." *Slavonic and East European Review* 93, no. 1 (January 2015): 181–204.

Ely, Christopher. "The Origins of Russian Scenery: Volga River Tourism and Russian Landscape Aesthetics." *Slavic Review* 62, no. 4 (Winter 2003): 666–682.

Ely, Christopher. *This Meager Nature: Landscape and National Identity in Imperial Russia.* DeKalb: Northern Illinois University Press, 2009.

English, Robert. *Russia and the Idea of the West: Gorbachev, Intellectuals, and the End of the Cold War.* New York: Columbia University Press, 2000.

Evans, Kristine Elaine. *Between Truth and Time: A History of Soviet Central Television.* New Haven, CT: Yale University Press, 2011.

Evtuhov, Catherine. "Voices from the Regions: Kraevedenie Meets the Grand Narrative." *Kritika: Explorations in Russian and Eurasian History* 13, no. 4 (2012): 877–887.

Engelstein, Laura. *Slavophile Empire: Imperial Russia's Illiberal Path.* Ithaca, NY: Cornell University Press, 2009.

Engelstein, Laura. *Russia in Flames: War, Revolution, Civil War, 1914–1921.* New York: Oxford University Press, 2017.

Evans, Alfred B., Laura A. Henry, and Lisa McIntosh Sundstrom. *Russian Civil Society: A Critical Assessment.* Armonk, NY: M. E. Sharpe, 2006.

Fainberg, Dina, and Artemy M. Kalinovsky, eds. *Reconsidering Stagnation in the Brezhnev Era: Ideology and Exchange.* London: Lexington, 2016.

Feshbach, Murray, and Albert Friendly. *Ecocide in the USSR: Environment and Health under Siege.* New York: Basic Books, 1993.

Fiege, Mark, Adrian Howkins, and Jared Orsi, eds. *National Parks beyond the Nation: Global Perspectives on "America's Best Idea."* Norman: University of Oklahoma Press, 2016.

Fradkin, N. G. "Geograficheskie otkrytiia sovetskogo perioda." *Izvestiia Akademii nauk SSSR: Seriia geograficheskaia* 3 (1967): 5–17.

Frank, Jerry. *Making Rocky Mountain National Park: The Environmental History of an American Treasure.* Lawrence: University Press of Kansas, 2013.

Frost, Warwick, and C. Michael Hall. "American Invention to International Concept." In *Tourism and National Parks: International Perspectives on Development, Histories and Change,* edited by Warwick Frost and C. Michael Hall, 30–44. London: Routledge, 2015.

Frost, Warwick, and C. Michael Hall, eds. *Tourism and National Parks: International Perspectives on Development, Histories and Change.* London: Routledge, 2015.

Funck, Carolin, and Malcolm Cooper eds. *Japanese Tourism: Spaces, Places, and Structures.* New York: Berghahn, 2013.

Furst, Juliane. *Stalin's Last Generation: Soviet Post-War Youth and the Emergence of Mature Socialism.* Oxford: Oxford University Press, 2010.

Furst, Juliane. "Where Did All the Normal People Go? Another Look at the Soviet 1970s." *Kritika: Exploration in Russian and Eurasian History* 14, no. 3 (Summer 2013): 621–640.

Furst, Julianne, Silvio Pons, and Mark Seldon, eds. *The Cambridge History of Communism.* Vol. 3. *Endgames? Late Communism in Global Perspective, 1968 to the Present.* Cambridge: Cambridge University Press, 2017.

Gilburd, Eleonory. *To See Paris and Die: The Soviet Lives of Western Culture.* Cambridge, MA: Belknap Press of Harvard University Press, 2018.

Glantz, Michael H., ed. *Creeping Environmental Problems and Sustainable Development in the Aral Sea Basin.* Cambridge, MA: MIT Press, 1999.

Gol'dfarb, Stanislav, ed. *Baikal'skii sindrom.* Irkutsk: Komsomol'skaia pravda, 1996.

Goldman, Marshall I. *Environmental Pollution in the Soviet Union: The Spoils of Progress.* Cambridge, MA: MIT Press, 1972.

Gorsuch, Anne. *All This is Your World: Soviet Tourism at Home and Abroad after Stalin.* Oxford: Oxford University Press, 2011.

Gorsuch, Anne. "'There's No Place Like Home': Soviet Tourism in Late Socialism." *Slavic Review* 62, no. 4 (Winter 2003): 760–785.

Graham, Loren. *Science in Russia and the Soviet Union: A Short History.* Cambridge: Cambridge University Press, 1993.

Gray, Patty A. *The Predicament of Chukotka's Indigenous Movement: Post Soviet Activism in the Russian Far North.* Cambridge: Cambridge University Press, 2005.

Guha, Ramachandra. "Radical American Environmentalism and Wilderness Preservation: A Third World Critique." *Environmental Ethics* 11 (1989): 71–83.

Harris, Stephen E. *Communism on Tomorrow Street: Mass Housing and Everyday Life after Stalin.* Baltimore: Johns Hopkins University Press, 2013.

Harvey, Mark. "Loving the Wild in Postwar America." In *American Wilderness: A New History,* edited by Michael Lewis, 187–204. New York: Oxford University Press, 2007.

Henry, Laura. "Between Transnationalism and State Power: The Development of Russia's post-Soviet Environmental Movement." *Environmental Politics* 19, no. 5 (May 2010): 756–781.

Henry, Laura. *Red to Green: Environmental Activism in Post-Soviet Russia.* Ithaca, NY: Cornell University Press, 2010.

Hirsch, Francine. *Empire of Nations: Ethnographic Knowledge and the Making of the Soviet Union.* Ithaca, NY: Cornell University Press, 2005.

Holdgate, Martin. *The Green Web: A Union for World Conservation.* London: Earthscan, 1999.

Husband, William. "Correcting Nature's Mistakes: Transforming the Environment in Soviet Children's Literature, 1928–1941." *Environmental History* 11, no. 2 (April 2006): 300–318.

Huxtable, Simon. "In Search of the Soviet Reader: The Kosygin reforms, Sociology, and Changing Concepts of Soviet Society, 1964–1970." *Cahiers du Monde russe* 54, no. 3–4 (2013): 623–642.

Ianitskii, Oleg. "Urbanization in the USSR: Theory, Tendencies, and Policy." *International Journal of Urban and Regional Research* 10, no. 2 (June 1986): 265–287.

Igoe, Jim. *Conservation and Globalization: A Study of National Parks and Indigenous Communities from East Africa to South Dakota.* Belmont, CA: Wadsworth, 2006.

Jackson, Mathew Jesse. *The Experimental Group: Ilya Kabakov, Moscow Conceptualism, Soviet Avant-Gardes.* Chicago: University of Chicago Press, 2010.

Jacoby, Karl. *Crimes against Nature: Squatters, Poachers, Thieves, and the Hidden History of American Conservation.* Berkeley: University of California Press, 2014.

Jones, Ryan Tucker. *Empire of Extinction: Russians and the North Pacific's Strange Beasts of the Sea.* New York: Oxford University Press, 2014.

Jones, Ryan Tucker. "A Havock Made among Them: Animals, Empire, and Extinction in the Russia North Pacific." *Environmental History* 16, no. 4 (October 2011): 585–609.

Josephson, Paul. *The Conquest of the Russian Arctic.* Cambridge, MA: Harvard University Press, 2014.

Josephson, Paul. *Industrialized Nature: Brute Force Technology and the Transformation of the Natural World.* Washington, DC: Island, 2002.

Josephson, Paul. *New Atlantis Revisited: Akademgorodok, the Soviet City of Science.* Princeton, NJ: Princeton University Press, 1997.

Josephson, Paul R. "'Projects of the Century' in Soviet History: Large-Scale Technologies from Lenin to Gorbachev." *Technology and Culture* 36, no. 3 (July 1995): 519–559.

Josephson, Paul, et al. *An Environmental History of Russia.* Cambridge: Cambridge University Press, 2013.

Keller, Tait. *Apostles of the Alps: Mountaineering and Nation-Building and Germany and Austria, 1860–1939.* Chapel Hill: University of North Carolina Press, 2015.

Kirchhof, Astrid Mignon, and J. R. McNeill. "Environmentalism, Environmental Policy, Capitalism, and Communism." In *Nature and the Iron Curtain: Environmental Policy and Social Movements in Communist and Capitalist Countries, 1945–1990,* edited by Astrid Mignon Kirchhof and J. R. McNeill, 3–14. Pittsburgh: University of Pittsburgh Press, 2019.

Kirchhof, Astrid Mignon, and J. R. McNeill, eds. *Nature and the Iron Curtain: Environmental Policy and Social Movements in Communist and Capitalist Countries, 1945–1990.* Pittsburgh: University of Pittsburgh Press, 2019.

Khlevinuk, Oleg. *Stalin: New Biography of a Dictator.* Translated by Nora Seligman Favorov. New Haven, CT: Yale University Press, 2016.

Klumbyte, Nearing, and Gulnaz Sharafutdinova, eds. *Soviet Society in the Era of Late Socialism, 1964–1985.* New York: Lexington, 2013.

Koenker, Diane. *Club Red: Vacation Travel and the Soviet Dream.* Ithaca, NY: Cornell University Press, 2013.

Koenker, Diane, and Anne Gorsuch, eds. *The Socialist Sixties: Crossing Borders in the Second World.* Bloomington: Indiana University Press, 2013.

Koenker, Diane, and Anne E. Gorsuch. *Turizm: The Russian and East European Tourist under Capitalism and Socialism.* Ithaca, NY: Cornell University Press, 2006.

Kozlov, Denis, and Eleonory Gilburd, eds. *The Thaw: Soviet Society and Culture During the 1950s and 1960s.* Toronto: University of Toronto Press, 2013.

Kotkin, Stephen. *Stalin: Waiting for Hitler, 1929–1941.* New York: Penguin, 2017.

Kotliakov, V. M., ed. *Vladimir Sergeevich Preobrazhenskii v vospominaniiakh i pis'makh.* Moscow: Institut geografii AN SSSR, 2005.

Krivolutskaia, L. I. "Festival' na Volge." In *Samarskii kraeved.* Samara: Samarskoe knizhnoe izdatel'stvo, 1991.

Kuchko, A. A. *Liubov' moia—Paanajärvi.* Petrazavodsk: Institut lesa, 2003.

Kupper, Patrick *Creating Wilderness: A Transnational History of the Swiss National Park.* New York: Berghahn, 2014.

Kupper, Patrick. "Science and the National Parks: A Transatlantic Perspective on the Interwar Years." *Environmental History* 14, no. 1 (January 2009): 58–81.

Kuz'menko, R. I., ed. *Innokentii Petrovich Gerasimov, 1905–1985.* Moscow: Nauka, 1991.

Larin, Vladislav, et al. *Okhrana prirody Rossii: Ot Gorbacheva do Putina.* Moscow: KMK, 2003.

Lebedev, A. B. *Istoriia i organizatsiia samodeiatel'nogo turizma.* Leningrad: Gosudarstvennyi institut fizkul'tury, 1988.

Leighton, Lauren. "The Great Soviet Debate over Romanticism, 1957–1964." *Studies in Romanticism* 22, no. 1 (Spring 1983): 41–64.

Lekan, Thomas. *Imagining the Nation in Nature: Landscape Preservation and German Identity, 1885–1945.* Cambridge, MA: Harvard University Press, 2005.

Louter, David. *Windshield Wilderness: Cars, Roads, and Nature in Washington's National Parks.* Seattle: University of Washington Press, 2010.

Magnusdottir, Rosa. "Be Careful in America, Premier Khrushchev: Soviet Perceptions of Peaceful Coexistence with the United States in 1959." *Cahiers du Monde russe* 47, no. 1/2 (January–June 2006): 109–130.

Malia, Martin. *Alexander Herzen and the Birth of Russian Socialism.* Cambridge, MA: Harvard University Press, 1961.

Malia, Martin. *Russia Under Western Eyes: From the Bronze Horseman to the Lenin Mausoleum.* Cambridge, MA: Belknap Press of Harvard University Press, 2000.

Malia, Martin. *The Soviet Tragedy: A History of Socialism in Russia, 1917–1991.* New York: Free Press, 1994.

Martin, Terry. *The Affirmative Action Empire: Nations and Nationalism in the Soviet Union, 1923–1939.* Ithaca, NY: Cornell University Press, 2001.

Mascia, Michael B., and Sharon Pailler. "Protected Area Downgrading, Downsizing, and Degazettement (PADDD) and Its Conservation Implications." *Conservation Letters* 4 (2011): 9–20.

Maher, Neil H. *Nature's New Deal: The Civilian Conservation Corps and the Roots of the American Environmental Movement.* New York: Oxford University Press, 2008.

McCannon, John. *Red Arctic: Polar Exploration and the Myth of the North in the Soviet Union, 1932–1939.* New York: Oxford University Press, 1998.

McReynolds, Louise. "The Pre-Revolutionary Russian Tourist." In *Turizm: The Russian and East European Tourist under Capitalism and Socialism,* edited by Dianne Koenker and Anne Gorsuch, 17–42. Ithaca, NY: Cornell University Press, 2006.

McReynolds, Louise. *Russia at Play: Leisure Activities at the End of the Tsarist Era.* Ithaca, NY: Cornell University Press, 2002.

Meskell, Lynn. *A Future in Ruins: UNESCO, World Heritage, and the Dream of Peace.* Oxford: Oxford University Press, 2018.

Micklin, Philip. *The Aral Sea: The Devastation and Partial Rehabilitation of a Great Lake*. New York: Springer, 2013.

Micklin, Philip M. "The Fate of 'Sibaral': Soviet Water Projects in the Gorbachev Era." *Central Asia Review* 6, no. 2 (June 1987): 67–88.

Micklin, Philip M. "The Status of the Soviet Union's Northern Water Transfer Projects Before their Abandonment in 1985–1986." *Soviet Geography* 27, no. 5 (May 1986): 287–329.

Micklin, Philip, and Andrew Bond. "Reflections on Environmentalism and the River Diversions Projects." *Soviet Economy* 4 (March 1988): 253–274.

Miller, Chris. *The Struggle to Save the Soviet Economy: Mikhail Gorbachev and the Collapse of the USSR*. Chapel Hill: University of North Carolina Press, 2016.

Moon, David. *The Plough That Broke the Steppes*. Oxford: Oxford University Press, 2014.

Moranda, Scott. *The People's Own Landscape: Nature, Tourism, and Dictatorship in East Germany*. Ann Arbor: University of Michigan Press, 2014.

Mowforth, Martin, and Ian Munt. *Tourism and Sustainability: Development, Globalisation, and New Tourism in the Third World*. London: Routledge, 2016.

Mukherjee, Ananya. "Conflict and Coexistence in a National Park." *Economic and Political Weekly* 44, no. 23 (June 6–12, 2009): 52–59.

Müller, Martin. "From Sacred Cow to Cash Cow: The Shifting Political Ecology of Protected Territories in Russia." *Zeitschrift für Wirtschaftgeografie* 58 (2014): 127–143.

Nash, Roderick. *Wilderness and the American Mind*. 4th edition. New Haven, CT: Yale University Press, 2014.

Nathans, Benjamin, and Kevin Platt. "Socialist in Form, Indeterminate in Content: The Ins and Outs of Late Soviet Culture." *Ab Imperio* 2 (2011): 301–324.

Nelson, Michael T., and J. Baird Callicott, eds. *The Wilderness Debate Rages On: Continuing the Great New Wilderness Debate*. Athens, GA: University of Georgia Press, 2008.

Neuman, Roderick R. *Imposing Wilderness: Struggles over Livelihood and Nature Preservation in Africa*. Berkeley: University of California Press, 1998.

Nicholson, Marjorie Hope. *Mountain Gloom, Mountain Glory: The Development of the Aesthetics of the Infinite*. Reprint edition. Seattle: University of Washington Press, 1997.

Noack, Christian. "Brezhnev's Little Freedoms: Tourism, Individuality, and Mobility in the Late Soviet Period." In *Reconsidering Stagnation in the Brezhnev Era: Ideology and Exchange*, edited by Dina Fainberg and Artemy M. Kalinovsky, 59–76. Lanham, MD: Lexington, 2016.

Noack, Christian. "Songs from the Wood, Love from the Fields: The Soviet Tourist Song Movement." In *The Socialist Sixties: Crossing Borders in the Second World*, edited by Anne Gorsuch and Diane Koenker, 167–192. Bloomington: Indiana University Press, 2013.

Oldfield, Jonathan. "Russian Environmentalism." *Environmental Policy and Governance*, March 14, 2002.

Oldfield, Jonathan, and Denis Shaw. *The Development of Russian Environmental Thought*. London: Routledge, 2015.

Oldfield, Jonathan, and Denis J. B. Shaw. "V. I. Vernadsky and the Noosphere Concept: Russian Understandings of Society-Nature Interaction." *Geoforum* 37 (2006): 145–154.

Orlov, Igor', and Elena Iurchikova. *Massovyi turizm v stalinskoi povsedevnosti*. Moscow: ROSSPEN, 2010.

Ostergren, David, and Peter Jacques. "A Political Economy of Russian Nature Conservation Policy." *Global Environmental Politics*, November 1, 2002.

Ostrovsky, Arkady. *The Invention of Russia: The Rise of Putin and the Age of Fake News*. New York: Viking, 2016.

Panjabi, Ranee, K. L. *The Earth Summit at Rio: Politics, Economics, and Environment*. Boston: Northeastern University Press, 1997.

Parthe, Kathleen. *Russian Village Prose: The Radiant Past*. Princeton, NJ: Princeton University Press, 1992.

Permiakova, L. G. "Iz istorii razvitiia vzaimootnoshchenii Rossii i UNESCO v sovetskii period." *Vestnik Tomskogo gosudarstvennogo universiteta* 2, no. 18 (2012): 129–132.

Philpott, William. *Vacationland: Tourism and the Environment in the Colorado High Country.* Seattle: University of Washington Press, 2014.

Pipes, Richard. *Russia under the Old Regime.* New York: Penguin, 1995.

Pollack, Ethan. *Stalin and the Soviet Science Wars.* Princeton, NJ: Princeton University Press, 2008.

Poole, Robert. *Earthrise: How Man First Saw the Earth.* New Haven, CT: Yale University Press, 2008.

Popov, A. *Po Meshcherskomu kraiu.* Moscow: Profizdat, 1966.

Pravilova, Ekaterina. *A Public Empire: Property and the Quest for the Common Good in Imperial Russia.* Princeton, NJ: Princeton University Press, 2014.

Price, Jennifer. *Flight Maps: Adventures with Nature in Modern America.* New York: Basic Books, 1999.

Pride-Brown, Kate. *Saving the Sacred Sea.* New York: Oxford University Press, 2018.

Pryde, Phillip. *Conservation in the Soviet Union.* New York: Cambridge University Press, 1972.

Quinn, Michael S., Len Broberg, and Wayne Freimund, eds. *Parks, Peace, and Partnership: Global Initiatives in Transboundary Conservation.* Calgary: University of Calgary Press, 2012.

Radkau, Joachim. *The Age of Ecology: A Global History.* Translated by Patrick Camiller. Cambridge, UK: Polity, 2014.

Rainey, Thomas B. "Siberian Writers and the Struggle to Save Lake Baikal." *Environmental History Review* 15, no. 1 (Spring 1991): 46–60.

Raleigh, Donald J. *Soviet Baby Boomers: An Oral History of Russia's Cold War Generation.* New York: Oxford University Press, 2013.

Reid, Susan. "Cold War in the Kitchen: Gender and the De-Stalinization of Consumer Taste in the Soviet Union." *Slavic Review* 61, no. 2 (Summer 2002): 211–252.

Reid, Susan. "Who Will Beat Whom? Soviet Popular Reception of the American National Exhibition in Moscow, 1959." *Kritika: Explorations in Russian and Eurasian History* 9, no. 4 (Fall 2008): 855–904.

Righter, Robert. *The Battle over Hetch Hetchy: America's Most Controversial Dam and the Birth of Modern Environmentalism.* New York: Oxford University Press, 2006.

Rosenholm, Arja, and Sari-Autio Sarasmo, eds. *Understanding Russian Nature: Representations, Values, and Concepts.* Helsinki: University of Helsinki, Aleksanteri Institute, 2005.

Roshchevskii, Iu. "Khronika obshchestvennoi okhrany Samarskoi Luki." Tolyatti: Parkovei, 1998: 9.

Roshchevskii, Iu. "Zadachi menedzhmenta natsional'nogo parka 'Samarskaia Luka." In *Samarskii krai v istorii Rossii: Materialy iubileinoi nauchnoi konferentsii, 6–7 fevralia 2001 g. 2001.* Samara: DSM, 2001.

Roth-Ey, Kate. *Moscow Primetime: How the Soviet Union Built the Media Empire that Lost the Cultural Cold War.* Ithaca, NY: Cornell University Press, 2014.

Rothman, Hal. *Devil's Bargains: Tourism in the Twentieth-Century American West.* Lawrence: University Press of Kansas, 1998.

Rothman, Hal. "Shedding Skin and Shifting Shape: Tourism in the Modern West." In *Seeing and Being Seen: Tourism in the American West,* edited by David M. Wrobel and Patrick T. Long, 100–119. Lawrence: University Press of Kansas, 2001.

Runte, Alfred. *The National Parks: The American Experience.* 4th ed. New York: Taylor, 2010.

Runte, Alfred. *Trains of Discovery: Railroads and the Legacy of Our National Parks.* 5th ed. Lanham, MD: Roberts & Rinehart, 2011.

Samarin, A. V. "Proekty perebroski severnykh rek: Uchenye Komi protiv sovetskoi gigantomanii." *Novyi istoricheskyi vestnik* 4 (2009): 58–66.

Schenk, Frithjof Benjamin. "This New Means of Transportation Will Make Unstable People Even More Unstable: Railways and Geographical Mobility in Tsarist Russia." In *Russia in Motion: Cultures of Human Mobility since 1850,* edited by John Randolph and Eugene M. Avrutin, 218–234. Urbana: University of Illinois Press, 2012.

Schmid, Sonja D. "Transformation Discourse: Nuclear Risk as a Strategic Tool in Late Soviet Politics of Expertise." *Science, Technology, & Human Values* 29, no. 3 (Summer 2004): 353–376.

Schmidt, Peter. *Back to Nature: The Arcadian Myth in Urban America*. 2nd ed. Baltimore: Johns Hopkins University Press, 1990.

Sellars, Richard West. *Preserving Nature in the National Parks: A History*. 2nd ed. New Haven, CT: Yale University Press, 2009.

Shaeffer, Marguerite. *See America First: Tourism and National Identity, 1880–1940*. Washington DC: Smithsonian Books, 2001.

Shaw, Denis J. B. "Mastering Nature through Science: Soviet Geographers and the Great Stalin Plan for the Transformation of Nature, 1948–1953." *Slavonic and East European Review* 93, no. 1 (January 2015): 120–146.

Sheail, John. *Nature's Spectacle: The World's First National Parks and Protected Places*. London: Routledge, 2010.

Shtil'mark, Feliks. *History of the Russian Zapovedniks, 1895–1995*. Translated by G. H. Harper. Edinburgh: Russian Nature, 2003.

Shtil'mark, F. R. *Zapovednoe delo Rossii: Teoriia, praktika, istoriia*. Moscow: Lagota, 2014.

Shtil'mark, F. R., and G. S. Avakov. "Pervyi proekt geograficheskoi seti zapovednikov dlia territorii SSSR." *Biulleten' Moskovskogo obshchestva ispytatelei prirody: Otdel biologicheskii* 2 (1977).

Siegelbaum, Lewis, *Cars for Comrades*. Ithaca, NY: Cornell University Press, 2011.

Siegelbaum, Lewis. "Modernity Unbound: The New Soviet City of the Sixties." In *The Socialist Sixties: Crossing Borders in the Second World*, edited by Anne Gorsuch and Diane Koenker, 66–83. Bloomington: Indiana University Press, 2013.

Sigman, Carole. "The End of Grassroots Ecology: Political Competition and the Fate of Ecology during Perestroika, 1988–1991." *Soviet and Post-Soviet Review* 40 (2013): 190–213.

Slezkine, Yuri. *Arctic Mirrors: Russia and the Small Peoples of the North*. Ithaca, NY: Cornell University Press, 1994.

Slezkine, Yuri. *The House of the Government: A Saga of the Russian Revolution*. Princeton, NJ: Princeton University Press, 2017.

Smith, Kathleen E. *Moscow 1956: The Silenced Spring*. Cambridge, MA: Harvard University Press, 2017.

Smurr, Robert W. "Lahemaa: The Paradox of the Soviet Union's First National Park." *Nationalities Papers* 36, no. 3 (July 2008): 6–30.

Sosnovy, Timothy. "The Soviet Military Budget." *Foreign Affairs* 42, no. 3 (April 1964): 487–494.

Spence, Mark David. *Dispossessing the Wilderness: Indian Removal and the Making of National Parks*. New York: Oxford University Press, 2000.

Stepanitskii, V. P., and M. L. Kreidlin. *Gosudarstvennyie prirodnye zapovedniki i natsional'nye parki: Ugrozi, neudachi, upushchennie vozmozhnosti*. Moscow: Greenpeace Russia, 2004.

Stevens, Stan, ed. *Indigenous Peoples, National Parks, and Protected Areas: A New Paradigm Linking Conservation, Culture, and Rights*. Tucson: University of Arizona Press, 2014.

Stites, Richard. *Revolutionary Dreams: Utopian Vision and Experimental Life in the Russian Revolution*. New York: Oxford University Press, 1989.

Suny, Ronald Grigor, and Terry Martin, eds. *A State of Nations: Empire and Nation-Making in the Age of Lenin and Stalin*. New York: Oxford University Press, 2001.

Sutter, Paul. *Driven Wild: How the Fight against Automobiles Launched the Modern Wilderness Movement*. Seattle: University of Washington Press, 2002.

Sutter, Paul. "Putting Wilderness in Context: The Interwar Origins of the Modern Wilderness Idea." In *American Wilderness: A New History*, edited by Michael Lewis, 167–186. New York: Oxford University Press, 2007.

Tezikova, T. V. "Samarskaia Luka." *Kraevedcheskie zapiski* (3) *Samarskaia Luka v drevnosti*. Kuibyshevskoe knizhnoe izdatel'stvo, 1975.

Tissot, Laurent. "From Alpine Tourism to the 'Alpinization' of Tourism." In *Touring Beyond the Nation: A Transnational Approach to European Tourism History*, edited by Eric Zuelow, 59–78. Burlington, VT: Ashgate, 2011.

Tocqueville, Alexis de. *Democracy in America*. Chicago: University of Chicago Press, 2000.

Tuan, Yi Fu. *Topophilia: A Study of Environmental Perception, Attitudes, and Values.* New York: Columbia University Press, 1990.

Turner, James Morton. "From Woodcraft to 'Leave no Trace': Woodcraft, Consumerism, and Environmentalism in Twentieth-Century America." *Environmental History* 7, no. 3 (July 2002): 462–484.

Turner, James Morton. *The Promise of Wilderness: American Environmental Politics since 1964.* Seattle: University of Washington Press, 2012.

Turner, Tom. *David Brower: The Making of the Environmental Movement.* Berkeley: University of California Press, 2015.

Tyrell, Ian. "America's National Parks: The Transnational Creation of National Space in the Progressive Era." *Journal of American Studies* 46 (2012): 1–21.

Usyskin, Grigorii. *Ocherki istorii rossiiskogo turizma.* Moscow: Gerda, 2000.

Vihavainen, Timo, and Elena Bogdanova. *Communism and Consumerism: The Soviet Affluent Society.* Leiden: Brill, 2015.

Wakild, Emily. *Revolutionary Parks: Conservation, Social Justice, and Mexico's National Parks, 1910–1940.* Tucson: University of Arizona Press, 2010.

Ward, Christopher. *Brezhnev's Folly.* Pittsburgh: University of Pittsburgh Press, 2009.

Weiner, Douglas. *A Little Corner of Freedom: Russian Environmental Protection from Stalin to Gorbachev.* Berkeley: University of California Press, 1999.

Weiner, Douglas. *Models of Nature.* 2nd edition. Pittsburgh: University of Pittsburgh Press, 2000.

Weiner, Douglas. "The Predatory Tribute-Taking State." In *Global Environmental History: An Introductory Reader,* edited by J. R. McNeill and Alan Roe, 283–319. London: Routledge, 2013.

Westad, Odd Arne. *The Cold War.* New York: Basic Books, 2016.

Worster, Donald. "Epilogue: Nature, Liberty, and Equality." In *American Wilderness: A New History,* edited by Michael Lewis, 263–272. New York: Oxford University Press, 2007.

Worster, Donald. *A Passion for Nature: The Life of John Muir.* New York: Oxford University Press, 2009.

Young, Terrance, and Larry M. Dilsaver. "Collecting and Diffusing the World's 'Best Thought': International Cooperation by the National Park Service." *George Wright Forum* 28, no. 3 (2011): 269–278.

Yurchak, Alexei. *Everything Was Forever Until It Was No More: The Last Soviet Generation.* Princeton, NJ: Princeton University Press, 2005.

Zabelina, N. M., B. L. Samoilov, and G. V. Morozova. *Natsional'nye parki i zakazniki.* Moscow: Mysl', 1996.

Zonn, I., M. Glantz, Aleksey Kosarev, and Andrey Kostianoy, eds. *The Aral Sea Encyclopedia.* New York: Springer, 2010.

Zubkova, Elena. *Russia after the War: Hopes, Illusions, Disappointments, 1945–1957.* Armonk, NY: M. E. Sharpe, 1998.

Zubok, Vladimir. *Zhivago's Children.* Cambridge, MA: Harvard University Press, 2011.

Zuelow, Eric, *A History of Modern Tourism.* New York: Palgrave, 2015.

Zuzanek, Jiri. *Work and Leisure in the Soviet Union: A Time-Budget Analysis.* New York: Praeger, 1980.

Dissertations

Conterio, Johanna. "The Soviet Sanatorium: Medicine, Nature and Mass Culture in Sochi, 1917–1991." Doctoral Dissertation: Harvard University, 2014.

Feygin, Jacob, Reforming the Cold War State: Economic Thought, Internationalization, and the Politics of Soviet Reform, 1955–1985." Ph.D. Dissertation University of Pennsylvania, 2017.

Zabelina, Nataliia. "Prirodnye landshafty SShA, ikh ispol'zovanie dlia turizma." Kandidatskaia dissertatsiia. Moscow, 1979.

INDEX

For the benefit of digital users, indexed terms that span two pages (e.g., 52–53) may, on occasion, appear on only one of those pages.